Shards of Light

SEATTLE'S
JEWISH FAMILY SERVICE
1892 TO 2012

BY
CAROLEE DANZ

WITH
DAVID WILMA

Book Publishers Network
P.O. Box 2256
Bothell • WA • 98041
PH • 425-483-3040
www.bookpublishersnetwork.com

10 9 8 7 6 5 4 3 2 1
Printed in the United States of America

LCCN 2015936646
ISBN 978-1-940598-67-3

Editor: Julie Scandora
Cover designer: Laura Zugzda
Layout: Melissa Vail Coffman
Indexer: Carolyn Acheson

In memory of my two grandmothers,
Jessie Mohr Danz and
Minnie Cohn Goldstein Bernhard.

Contents

Community and Staff Members   vii

Foreword   ix

Acknowledgements   xiii

Introduction   xvii

    Chapter 1 – 1892: Beginnings   1

    Chapter 2 – Emergency Services   25

    Chapter 3 – 1900: Helping the Poor   49

    Chapter 4 – Aging & Adult Programs   67

    Chapter 5 – 1926–1939: From Relief to Rehabilitation   87

    Chapter 6 – Counseling Services   103

    Chapter 7 – Fund Development and Marketing   127

    Chapter 8 – 1939–1947: War and Transformation   145

    Chapter 9 – 1945: Repairing the Wounds of War—
          A Community Working Together   163

    Chapter 10 – 1951-1967: Window into the Past, Guide and
          Inspiration for the Future   189

    Chapter 11 – 1965-1975: Keeping the Lights On   211

Chapter 12 – 1967–1992: Resettlement of
            Russian Immigrants   227
Chapter 13 – 1974–1984: Evolution and Expansion   253
Chapter 14 – Family Life Education   279
Chapter 15 – 1984–1994: New Directions   297
Chapter 16 – Seattle Association for Jews with Disabilities 321
Chapter 17 – Project DVORA   349
Chapter 18 – Alternatives to Addition   363
Chapter 19 – 1995–2005: Continued Growth   381
Chapter 20 – Immigration in the 21st Century   409
Chapter 21 – 2006 - 2012: A Plan for the Future   423
Chapter 22 – Volunteers: The Heart and Soul of JFS   437
Afterword – Looking Forward   455
Appendix 1: Presidents   456
Appendix 2: Executive Directors   458
Appendix 3: Members of the Board of Directors, 1892-2012   459
Appendix 4: Names and Addresses of JFS   472
Appendix 5: Partners and Coalitions 2012   473
Appendix 6: Annual Meeting Awards   483
Selected Bibliography   491
Index   493

Community Members and Present and Former Staff who generously shared their JFS memories and experiences.

Contributing Community Members

Emily Alhadeff	Janet Lackman
Kenny Alhadeff	Dianne Loeb
Jerry Anches	Steve Loeb
Joe Barer	Bob Low
Howard Behar	Jeanette Lowen
Donna Benaroya	Sandy Melzer
Joyce & Ray Benezra	Rabbi James Mirel
Kathy Berman	Judy Neuman
Larry Broder	John E. Phillips
Jeannie Butler	Lucy & Herb Pruzan
Olga Butler	Merrill Ringold
Harold "Buzz" Coe	Joani Diskin Saran
Eleanor Cohon	Julie Schoenfeld
Ted Daniels	Cantor David Serkin-Poole
Carolyn Danz	Peter Shapiro
Jon Fine	Shelly Shapiro
Abby Franklin	Rabbi Beth Singer
Josh Gortler	Rabbi Jonathan Singer
Joe Greengard	Irene Steinberg
Michele Hasson	Henry Stevens
Renee Herst	Isabel & Herb Stusser
Lauren Jassny	Laura Stusser-McNeil
Irv Karl	Barbara Sulman
Carolyn Kessler	Dennis Warshal
Nancy Koppel	Anthony Wartnik

Contributing Staff

Don Armstrong
Sarah Barash
Claudia Berman
Diane Burnett
Thelma Coney
Deb Crespin
Jane Deer-Hileman
Bill Drummund
Davis Fox
Jeff Gold
Lisa Schultz Golden
Margaret Hinson
Laura Kramer
Rachel Kwong
Michelle Lifton
Jeanette Lozovsky
Ed Meyer
Lesley Mills

Steve Morris
Robin Moss
Carol Mullin
Joel Neier
Marie North
Julie Olson
Patsy Policar
Jane Relin
Merrill Ringold
Natalie Merkur Rose
Salie Rossen
Richard Rosenwald
Eve Ruff
Ruth Saks
Marjorie Schnyder
Cliff Warner
Ken Weinberg

Foreword

Our story is our compass. Without it, we are in the wilderness, directionless and confused. This sense of wandering eats at our souls. Floating without connection to our collective past, we become untethered and aimless. We are lost. The origin story of the Jewish people is that of wanderers, of the exodus, but ultimately one of redemption, of coming home.

When we hear the story of the cultures we know are foreign to us, we become adventurers. We visit them as tourists, anthropologists, citizens of the world. We are pleased with ourselves when we share them with our children and celebrate how our journeys have enriched us. We are proud of our open-mindedness. After all, our travels confirm that we are cosmopolitan, curious, engaged citizens of the world.

How much harder it is then for us to have some vague notion of our own story, familiar enough to be recognizable, but only vaguely so. We can neither narrate the journey for our children nor bask in the glow of intellectual and cultural adventurism. Our own story is as alien to us as that of an Amazonian tribe.

Without our touchstones—our history, our narrative, and the values that reflect the marriage of the two—we wander. The reflection we see is no longer that of the curious intellectual but is now instead the confused illiterate. The seduction of something alien becomes the despair of alienation.

Shards of Light reflects a 120-year history of Jewish Family Service; but even more, it is a compass, the invaluable tool we need to map our future. The story of JFS is the story of the Jewish community in Western Washington. It reminds us that we were *all* once strangers here, making our way to this westernmost and most beautiful corner of the nation to make good lives—lives of safety, opportunity, and the freedom to believe (or not) as we choose.

The Ladies' Hebrew Benevolent Society was differently named but not so differently aimed than the JFS of today. Jewish refugees from all across Europe fled religious persecution, conscription, and lack of economic opportunity. The ladies understood that success depended upon the outstretched, helping hand of those who already had the good fortune to be settled here. They built the model that we still use in refugee resettlement today—financial aid bolstered by support for housing, learning, food, job training, and acculturation.

The 19th and early 20th century waves from Russia and Rhodes became the mid-century survivors—those who escaped Europe early or miraculously survived the horrors and found their ways here and, then again, those who came en masse from the former Soviet Union, bringing the last century to an unexpected close. At each point in our Jewish story, this community extended the ladder to those who needed just to get their feet upon the first rung to make their ways.

We reflect that same value now, welcoming men, women, and children from all corners of the globe. They speak dozens of languages we may not know, eat foods we have not encountered, and practice religions distant (and sometimes near) to our own. But we *know* them because of our story and from our history. Our value is and must always be to welcome the stranger because we were once strangers. The ladder does not belong to us—it was simply extended for our use when we needed it, and now it is our responsibility to extend it so that others can plant their feet on that first rung and use their own strength and determination, just as we did, to climb up and contribute.

In each core service area at JFS—feeding the hungry, welcoming the stranger, honoring our parents, lending safe harbor to children made "fatherless" because of domestic violence, or removing the stumbling blocks so that those with cognitive disabilities or mental illness can live with dignity and independence—we amalgamate our experience and translate it to action.

And in our story, the actions are not options from which we can pick and choose. Whomever we are serving and however we are helping, our work is always in response to the imperative, "If I am not for myself, who is for me? If I am not for others, what am I? If not now, when?" With each offering and every service, in our legislative agenda and across our partnerships, we strive to fulfill this greatest of challenges by providing those who are most vulnerable the tools that all human beings deserve in this world in order to live with dignity.

Our story is both our inheritance and our legacy. It demands action and involvement in every generation. When we engage with it, telling it to our children in words and demonstrating it through our deeds, we can find our way back—to our place, our purpose and ourselves.

—Will Berkovitz

Acknowledgements

Sometimes you step into a new endeavor with an idea of what the journey will entail and along the way discover an entirely different reality. That's what happened on the expedition to discover the detailed history of Seattle's Jewish Family Service.

Both of my grandmothers had been involved with the agency beginning in the 1920s when it was the Hebrew Benevolent Society and continued as it was renamed Jewish Child and Family Service before it was JFS. They shared with me and my sisters and cousins their experiences of meeting refugees from the Holocaust at the Seattle docks. My stepmother, Carolyn Danz, served on the board of directors, as did my brother-in-law, Ted Daniels, and I served on the board myself for more than a dozen years. I thought I knew quite a bit about this remarkable organization and its history, but I was wrong. I was very wrong. I knew the current agency, and a bit about the founding of the organization and a tiny fraction of the work of the agency during the 1930's and 40's, but I knew very little about the other 80 years.

My journey began with more than a year of research in the University of Washington Libraries Special Collections. There, with the assistance of the librarians and staff, I explored the history of the Seattle Jewish Community, including that of JFS, and the Washington State Jewish Historical Society. Many thanks to Lizabeth (Betsy)

Wilson, Vice Provost for Digital Initiatives and Dean of University Libraries for permitting the use of some of the photographs I found stored in those archives. Leonard Garfield, Executive Director of the Museum of History and Industry in Seattle not only granted me the use of a few photographs from the MOHAI collection, he also provided high definition copies.

I was helped along on my journey of discovery by a great many people. Almost 100 members of the Jewish Community, including every former JFS board president who was able, participated willingly in a recorded interview. Many current and former JFS staff members, and several members of the general Jewish community shared their experiences, memories and insights, which informed and enhanced the broader historical context. (See the list of Contributing Community Members). Ken Weinberg, who worked at JFS for 38 years (almost one-third of the entire history of the organization), and served as Executive Director from 1984 to 2012, has an incredible memory for detail and a delightful storytelling style.

Executive Assistant Julie Olson has been at JFS even longer than Weinberg, having started as assistant to Executive Director Irv Goldberg, continuing as assistant to Weinberg for his entire JFS career and then staying to help Will Berkovitz as he stepped in to the Executive Director position. Julie was a constant advisor, fact searcher, detail confirming participant on this book project.

I owe a great debt to my family and friends who put up with the constant presence of my computer during my visits, and the continuous, probably monotonous detailing of my discoveries.

The book would not exist at all without the participation and collaboration of my co-writer and editor, David Wilma. David not only provided the broad historical context for the story, but he was always available to coach, support, suggest, and elucidate.

My publisher, Sheryn Hara at Book Publishers Network kept an eye on the process and shepherded the book through the writing, editing, design, indexing and printing processes.

The editing process was endless, with reviews, input and guidance from several senior staff members, particularly Claudia Berman and Lisa Schultz Golden. One difficult concern was making the story come alive by including many client experiences while still maintaining confidentiality. Board President Gail Mautner spent a significant amount of her time, energy and expertise to guarantee compliance with various regulations and legal concerns.

JFS Executive Director Will Berkovitz came on the scene during the editing process and jumped in with both feet to help create what is hoped to be a valuable asset for the JFS community, as well as for the broader Seattle Jewish Community.

Deb Frockt took responsibility for managing the agency side of the project. Megan Pahl solicited, gathered, edited and managed the photos. Finally we were able to put it all together with the help of designer Melissa Coffman. To each of you, a huge thank you for helping make this five year project a reality.

My heartfelt thanks goes out to all who participated, shared, edited, and in many other ways supported my efforts to bring to fruition this history of the Jewish Family Service of Seattle.

—Carolee Danz

Introduction

There were 42,387 people living in Seattle in 1890. More than a third of the residents were immigrants. Many did not know English and were poor and jobless. Some of these recent arrivals were Jewish. In recognition of their needs, Esther Levy, herself an immigrant from Prague, led 37 Jewish women in establishing the Ladies' Hebrew Benevolent Society (LHBS). Their mission was "for benevolent and charitable purposes among worthy persons of the Hebrew Nationality who may be in indigent circumstances, and generally to distribute alms and to care for such persons." *Shards of Light* tells the remarkable journey of the organization they formed and which readers know as Seattle's Jewish Family Service (JFS).

In their first year, the ladies made a combined contribution of $294.50 and distributed $164.25. In 1896, they raised $360.35 and spent $318.15. By 1902, the society had 100 members. Over the next 120 years, the name of the agency changed four times. The budget grew from $14,075 in 1945 to $433,771 in 1980 to $8,600,000 in 2012. In 1980, JFS had a staff of 11. Today it has over 100 employees. However, with all its changes and enormous growth, the core mission of JFS remained the same: "We deliver essential human services to alleviate suffering, sustain healthy relationships, and support people in times of need."

Throughout Seattle's history, JFS has worked to meet the needs of the greater Seattle community, Jewish and non-Jewish. In the early 1900s, the Ladies' Hebrew Benevolent Society provided loans and emergency services to help arrivals from Europe and Mediterranean countries. In the 1970s, '80s and '90s, JFS helped resettle Jews from Russia and refugees from the war in Southeast Asia. Services gradually increased to include family counseling, family life education, and programs for our youth and elderly. JFS was instrumental in forming and providing the organizational umbrella for Jews with disabilities. The agency has continued to recognize and address the needs of our community with emergency services, including the food bank and support for victims of domestic violence.

Shards of Light is not only the history of the Jewish Family Service but also a history of the Jewish community of Seattle. To make the history come alive, the author has personalized it with stories of key community members, board members, and past and present staff. It is great storytelling, lovingly written by Carolee Danz, whose family has been closely tied to the agency for four generations.

—Peter Shapiro

Shards of Light

Ancient rabbis believed when God was creating the universe,
he placed his divine light into special celestial containers ...
The vessels were broken, and the universe became filled
with the sparks of divine light and shards of broken vessels.
The rabbis believed the task of creation wouldn't be complete
until those sparks were gathered together.

We call it *tikkun olam*, or repairing the world.
All who work for the [benefit of the] community,
let them work for the sake of Heaven [i.e., sincerely], ...
and their righteousness endures forever.

—Mishnah, AVOTH, II, 2

Chapter 1

1892: Beginnings

"Suddenly there came a shrill scream from the street—the frightful, awful scream of a woman in terror. Then came the sharp cry of a child. A moment later, there came to us the wild roaring of a mob in rage, the sound of heavy footsteps in the streets, and the cry of a neighbor calling upon the mob we could not see to spare her daughter. A shouting, raging mob whirled madly in the street, clustering about some object lying at their feet. I could see arms upraised, and could see blows being struck at something lying on the ground. Then the mob parted for a moment, and I saw lying there a girl who lived across the street. She was trying to shelter her aged mother from the blows which were being rained upon her."
—Jacob Freedman, 1903, *Sunday Seattle Times,*
May 17, 1903

"The very same evening the massacre of Armenians began without the least provocation. It was a veritable butchery. I saw with my own eyes some groups of Armenians put to death with terrible tortures. Turks first cut off their noses, then their ears and their hands. Even women and children were not spared."

—Robert Nader, 1922, *New York Times,*
September 19, 1922

"Then there was a knock at the door and before we could even respond, the door fell in and about four or so people came in and dragged my father out by his legs. That was the last we saw of him. One of them said: "Let's make sure that he is dead with this." I didn't move an inch, nor did I make any noise. They must have thought that I was dead."

—Hamis Kamuhanda, 11 years old in 1994,
"Rwanda: Eyewitness to Genocide,"

These stories from 1903, 1922, and 1994 were repeated in 1914, 1943, and countless times in-between and after. Refugees came to Seattle from civil wars in Africa, ethnic cleansing in the Balkans, "transfers of population" in Anatolia, Ukraine, and Bohemia, Soviet oppression and deportations, the Holocaust, and czarist pogroms. They were almost all penniless and confused but grateful to be safe from the killers. In every instance, Seattle's Jewish community came together in the spirit of *tikkun olam* (repairing the world) to help those in need. For more than 120 years, whether as the Ladies' Hebrew Benevolent Society, the Hebrew Benevolent Association, Jewish Welfare Society, Jewish Family & Child Service, or Jewish Family Service, the agency's staff and volunteers have reached out to the hungry, the destitute, the disabled, and the homeless to improve lives and to contribute to the well-being of fellow Jews and of the wider community. Throughout those years, the agency was joined in its work by several other Jewish charitable organizations, including the Montefiore Society, the Hebrew Ladies Free Loan Society, and the Jewish Federation of Greater Seattle.

By the winter of 1892, Seattle had come a long way in a very short time. Just two and one-half years before, 32 blocks of downtown and four wharves along Elliott Bay went up in flames in a single afternoon. This was not an unusual occurrence as most growing cities of the West burned down at some point. In the summer of 1889, flames destroyed Spokane Falls, Cheney, and Republic just as Washington was poised for statehood. Several other booming towns of the West also burned. These conflagrations usually proved both traumatic and serendipitous, and so they were to Seattle. The shock and loss gave way to a boundless expression of energy and optimism. Residents who stayed to recover were joined by the constant flow of newcomers who set to work rebuilding in masonry and stone while living under canvas. City planners jumped on the opportunity to realign the streets that didn't quite meet along Yesler Way, a legacy of two pioneers (Arthur A. Denny and Doc Maynard) with different visions for the new metropolis. Not satisfied with just rebuilding, the city council doubled the size of Seattle by annexing Magnolia, Green Lake, Wallingford, Fremont, and Brooklyn.

Tall sailing barques and schooners, steamships, local steamboats from the mosquito fleet, and even Indian canoes pushed into wharves from all over the region and the world to feed the appetites of industry, farm, and home and to deliver immigrants hopeful for new lives. Coal, wheat, fish, and lumber filled holds and railcars for markets over the horizon, and Seattle readied itself for a place on the world stage. The newly completed Great Northern, Northern Pacific, and Seattle, Lake Shore, and Eastern railroads stoked the growing economy of the region like fuel lines firing a boiler and steam lines coursing out. Even though Tacoma was the designated terminus of the Northern Pacific, the first transcontinental railroad to reach Puget Sound, Seattle had the traffic. The NP was forced to adjust its schedules and trackage accordingly.

Entrepreneurs, opportunists, homesteaders, mill workers, migrants following crops and rumor of opportunity, loggers, fishermen, and penniless refugees all crowded into Pullman cars, boxcars, mosquito fleet steamers, and tall ships bound for the city that sprawled from Elliott Bay. They found a city that had grown up and across hills so steep that visionary city engineer Reginald Heber Thomson laid ambitious plans to cut down the hills and dump the spoils into the tide flats for yet more development. Thomson didn't stop with moving mountains. He designed a system to bring fresh water into the city and to ship sewage out. What would become Seattle University and Seattle Pacific University started in 1891. The University of Washington moved from its crumbling, columned birthplace downtown to a new campus overlooking Portage Bay, still home to a bear or two.

Newcomers to Seattle ballooned the population by a factor of 13 between 1880 and 1890, 3,533 to 42,837 in just ten years. More than a third of the residents at the end of the decade were immigrants. In this melting pot, Jews, both native and foreign born, began to coalesce into a distinct community. Most of the families of the first Jews who came to the New World had first fled the Spanish Inquisition to other Southern European countries as refugees. They began to migrate to New Amsterdam in the early 1600s.

By 1820, Jews nationally numbered only about 3,000 with just 650 in New York City, 550 in Philadelphia, and the largest Jewish community in Charleston, South Carolina. In the following decades, these numbers expanded far beyond the rate of growth for the nation as a whole.

Under the short rule of Napoleon Bonaparte, Jews in Europe experienced a relaxation of the restrictions imposed upon them over the centuries. Then, after the Peace of Vienna in 1815, many of the old measures confining Jews to ghettos, excluding Jews from higher education, and placing limits on how they could work were restored. The New World offered opportunity and freedom, and "German" Jews from France, Germany, and the Austrian Empire made their way across the Atlantic. These German Jews established thriving communities in the eastern United States and made their way west, particularly after gold was discovered in California in 1848. More Jews fled the failed revolutions in Europe in 1848.

This wave of immigrants generally fit well into a society with no limit to ambition and its eyes on the occupation of an entire continent. In the 1850s, when American nativist groups like the No Nothings railed against immigrants in general and Catholics in particular, Jews were regarded as good immigrants, known for their respect for the law, education, and industry. Marriage outside the faith became more common, and some worried about the survival of the Jewish culture.

In 1849, when news of gold in California electrified the United States and the world, Jewish men and women also joined the Gold Rush. Aaron Levy, born in Poland, and his wife Esther, born in Prague, were two such migrants. They met and married in San Francisco in 1859 and moved to French Gulch near Mount Shasta where Aaron owned a gold mine and a general store. From French Gulch, they ran businesses in San Francisco, Sitka, Alaska, and Genesee, Idaho. Years later, Esther described her life in the West to a reporter. It could have been the story of any other entrepreneurial Jewish family in the West.

"My husband made a great deal of money in California during the Gold Rush and I helped him to save it. I was content to live without luxury when money was scarce. Then he lost all that he had and we went to Alaska in the gold rush. It was the same in the North. We saved money and later lost it. He made a third fortune in Idaho."[1]

Aaron sold out in Genesee and moved to Seattle with Esther and their three sons. They checked into the Bellevue Hotel, about a mile north of what was then downtown. It was from the Bellevue that, just six weeks after they arrived, they watched the Great Fire of June 6, 1889. As the ashes cooled, Seattle launched into a fury of construction while conducting business out of tents. Aaron Levy seized the opportunity and did his part by buying a vacant lot on the northeast corner of Fifth Avenue and Pike Street. There he constructed the two-story Idaho Block. Aaron, Esther, and sons Aubrey, Eugene, and Louis took up residence in an apartment on the second floor.[2]

By 1890, Jews in the United States numbered about 450,000, a 30-fold increase over 50 years against three and one-half times for the whole population. The Levys joined a small but growing Jewish community in Seattle. One Jewish pioneer was banker and businessman Jacob Furth who came to Seattle in 1882 to organize the Puget Sound National Bank. The following year, he helped organize the B'nai B'rith, Chapter 343, but the group was too small yet even to arrange a burial ground for Jews, one of the first efforts of any Jewish community. The population continued to increase, and in 1884, Seattle's Jews managed to celebrate the 100th anniversary of the birth of Sir Moses Montefiore, the English Jew prominent in business and philanthropy (he was still living). One hundred couples attended a ball held in Montefiore's honor.

Beginning in 1881, earlier waves of Jewish immigration were dwarfed by the refugees from czarist pogroms. Czar Alexander III blamed Jews for the murder of his father and instituted sweeping repressions upon Russia's Jews. Hundreds of thousands were forcibly relocated out of cities to the Pale of Settlement where Jews fell victim to discriminatory laws and, worst of all, pogroms—organized, state-approved violence involving beatings, destruction of property, rape, and murder. Thousands of Jewish immigrants to the United States became tens of thousands, hundreds of thousands, and over the next 40 years, three and a half million.

Most of these Jews remained in the east, but many made their way west on newly completed transcontinental railroads to find something, anything better than the Old World. Men and families frequently followed friends and relatives who wrote glowing accounts of life on Puget Sound and a place where Jews were left in peace and even included in the wider community. But what they found in Seattle still felt strange. The Jews already here looked and talked like Americans. They didn't even speak Yiddish. And the Reform brand of Judaism conflicted with Orthodox practices.

Reform Judaism was an outgrowth of the Jewish experience in Germany that moved to America with the immigration of its proponents. Under the influence of American Protestantism,

Reform Judaism incorporated many new practices, which differed from more orthodox practices. Services used the Minhag America prayer book, both English and Hebrew, and mixed-sex seating. Congregants often chose not to dress in traditional clothing, and many families, perhaps most, did not keep kosher homes.

As in the rest of America in the 1890s, growth and success did not extend to all in Seattle. The social safety net of unemployment compensation, workers' compensation, free medical care for the poor, shelters for the homeless, and other human services programs lay decades in the future. Widows, orphans, the unemployed, the unemployable, and the disabled shifted for themselves, struggling on their own and drifting into the netherworld of pain, homelessness, desperate poverty, crime, and vice. The lucky ones managed a few handouts from family, kindly individuals, churches, religious orders, and other charitable groups. In the 19th century, it fell generally to women to organize and provide help to the needy.

The Sisters of Providence began operating a home for the poor in 1877. Seattle's first charity was the Ladies Relief Society (later the Seattle Children's Home), formed by 15 women in 1884 to care for six orphans. Local women gathered for social, charitable, and even political purposes forming the Women's Suffrage Association, the Seattle Library Association, and The Century Club. The women's groups often corresponded to so-called secret or fraternal societies for men—the Grand Army of the Republic, Odd Fellows, Eagles, Knights of Pythias, Masons, and Elks—which initially served the needs of their members with life and burial insurance, as well as social and political missions. African American women organized the Ladies Colored Social Circle in 1889.

The prosperity of the early 1890s allowed middle-class women the time and resources to devote themselves to building a genteel society in the Far West where social standing was measured by one's visibility in the women's pages of local newspapers. The society notes attracted women readers by featuring accounts of weddings, teas, balls, parties, vacation travel, and community service.

In July 1889, just a month after the Great Fire, a group of Jews, committed to the principles of liberal Judaism, organized Congregation Ohaveth Shalom ("lovers of peace"), the first Jewish congregation in Seattle. The believers, comprised mostly of German and Polish immigrants, adopted the Reform prayer book, used both English and Hebrew during their services, and seated men and women together.

Aaron Levy served as treasurer and as a trustee of the new congregation. About 100 Jews regularly attended services in space rented in hotels or public halls. That same year, the trustees purchased a corner of the Mount Pleasant Cemetery on Queen Anne Hill and set it aside for burials as the Hills of Eternity.[3]

In November 1891, Orthodox Jews incorporated Chevra Bikur Cholim (Society for Visiting the Sick) to provide for care of the sick and their proper burial. A few months later in 1892, enough Jews lived in Seattle, not only for the formation of a second and more traditional congregation called Temple Emanuel but also for each to build its own synagogue. Temple Emanuel followed the Orthodox branch of Judaism. That same year, Congregation Ohaveth Shalom built a permanent temple at Eighth Avenue and Seneca Street, where the Exeter Hotel was eventually built. In a 1956 *Seattle Times* interview, Eugene Levy remembered how difficult it was to get 10 men together for a *minyan* (the quorum required for Jewish communal worship), so his dad would say, "Aubrey, you run and get So-and-so, and Eugene, you get So-and-so and So-and-so."[4] He went on to comment that Ohaveth Shalom lived and languished and came to live again as Temple de Hirsch.

It was this critical mass of community and prosperity that enabled Esther Levy to call together other Jewish women to form a charitable organization. Thirty-seven women gathered at Chisholm Hall, one of the rented spaces used for services, and Levy presented to them the idea of forming a relief organization to help those in the community who were struggling to survive. The urgent needs of the immigrant newcomers and the Talmudic precept that exhorts

Ohaveth Shalom
(Cooper and Levy Families
Photograph Collection,
University of Washington
Libraries.)

Esther Levy
(JFS photo collection.)

man to help his fellow man to help himself inspired Levy and her neighbors.

Dated March 7, 1892, the proposed articles of incorporation of the Ladies' Hebrew Benevolent Society (LHBS) were presented. Eva Aronson was chosen secretary pro tem and wrote down the names of those present who wished to become members of the society. Forty-one charter members founded the society. Esther Levy was elected president and continued in that role until 1912. Other officers were selected, an advisory committee appointed, and dues were set at one dollar per quarter.

No original list of founding members has been discovered, and several different versions have been passed down over the years. The following list appears in an unpublished 75-year history written by Mrs. Harry Buttnick, Mrs. John Danz, Mrs. Elias Lescher and Mrs. Meyer Newberger.

A. Aronson (Eva, wife of Sigismund, treasurer, Schwabacher Brothers)
Frank Aronson (wife of travel agent)
J. Berkman (Mina, wife of Jacob)
F. Brown (wife of Rev Aaron Brown, Ohaveth Shalom)
A. L. Cohn (Marietta, wife of Aaron, merchant tailor)
H. Cohn
J. J. Cole (Sophie, wife of Jacob, manager, S. Cohn & Co.)
I. Cooper (Lizzie, wife of Isaac, Cooper & Levy Hardware)
Mrs. Simon Davis (Jetta wife of owner of Men's Furnishing Goods)
H. Elster (wife of Harry Elster, general merchandise)
A. Fortlouis (Carrie, wife of Albert, Wholesale Liquors and Cigars)
C. Friend (Carrie, widow of Edward B. Friend; proprietor with Nathan Degginger, Friend-Degginger Importing Co., wholesale and retail wines and liquors; proprietor of The Slaughter Malt and Brewing Co., Slaughter,* Washington)
E. Goodman (Jane, wife of Emmanuel, boots and shoes)

---

* Auburn

K. Gottstein (Rebecca, wife of Kassel, M&K Gottstein, liquor merchant)

M. Gottstein (Rosa, wife of Meyer, liquor merchant)

M. A. Gottstein (Rosa, wife of "Mike" Gottstein, M&K Gottstein, liquor merchant)

J. L. Jaffe (Johanna, wife of J. Louis, L. Jaffe & Co., liquors and cigars wholesale and retail, wine merchant)

L. Kaufman (Emma, wife of Louis)

A. Kline (wife of Abraham, J&A Kline Clothing)

Mrs. S. Kohn (wife of Leo Kohn)

I. Korn (Carrie, wife of Isaac, proprietor, Korn Block)

M. Korn (Barbara, wife of Moses, proprietor, Korn Block)

Malvina Kurski (wife of William)

Mrs. Henry Lapworth (Emma, clairvoyant and wife of Henry, real estate agent)

J. Lesser (Julia, wife of Jacob, owner of San Francisco Shoe Co.)

Mrs. Aaron Levy (Esther, wife of Aaron Levy, developer, store owner)

B. C. Levy (Lina, wife of Benjamin, clerk, King County Treasurer)

L. Mandelbaum

E. Morgenstern (Minnie, wife of Elkan, bookkeeper and notary public)

E. Rosenberg (Henrietta, wife of Emmanuel)

Mrs. Samuel Rosenberg (wife of owner of Klein and Rosenberg Clothing)

B. Rosenthal

R. Rosenthal

L. Schoenfeld (Hannah, wife of Louis)

P. Singerman (Jennie, wife of Paul, Toklas, Singerman & Co., clothing and men's furnishing goods)

A. Wilzinski (Gertrude, wife of Albert)

G. Winehill (Henrietta, wife of Gustav, real estate and financial broker)

S. Wolff (Louisa, wife of August, bottler, soda manufacturer)

At the second meeting, the women were ready to accept a constitution and bylaws for their new organization (which was originally incorporated for a period of 50 years). It began:

Know all men by these Presents [*sic*]: that, we, the undersigned, have this day voluntarily associated ourselves together for the purpose of forming a corporation under the laws of the State of Washington.

The name of said corporation is the Ladies' Hebrew Benevolent Society
14th Day of March, A.D. 1892

The object of said corporation is for benevolent and charitable purposes among worthy persons of the Hebrew Nationality who may be in indigent circumstances, and generally to distribute alms and to care for such persons as in the judgment of the corporation, or the Trustees thereof, may be thought worthy.

The third meeting convened at Hinkley Hall, which had been rented for a fee of one dollar. More women joined, bringing the number of original members to 86.

Thus began the saga. A line in King Solomon's poem, "A Woman of Valor," aptly describes the Jewish woman in Seattle at the turn of the century, "Her hands stretched forth to the needy." The focus of the organization was providing relief to those in need, and the group did not seem to have considered using social events to advance their efforts until 1898 when the record shows that coffee and cake were served at the meeting to induce more sociability among the members. Each woman was asked to contribute a nickel to pay the janitor's wife for serving, while members donated the cakes, coffee, cream, and sugar.

At the end of three months, $200 had been collected, and three families benefited from relief. The society welcomed all Jewish women as members, but women from the Reform congregation predominated. Many Orthodox women spoke only Yiddish and did not find much in common with their English-speaking counterparts. These American Jews, even though born outside the United States, often did not speak or even understand the Yiddish of their parents. Later, the Ladino-speaking Sephardic women also had difficulty feeling comfortable with the existing Jewish community, and the doctrinal differences between Reform and Orthodox, and Ashkenazi and Sephardic traditions presented other barriers.

Jews in the larger US cities, like New York, Chicago, and St. Louis, organized programs and agencies to help immigrants settle in the new country. One attempt in New York folded after a few years but reemerged in 1892 as the Hebrew Immigrant Aid Society (HIAS). Some agencies even attempted agricultural colonies in the open lands of the Far West, but with limited success. In Seattle, there was no corresponding organization, but the city was just 40 years old and still rebuilding after the fire. Everyone was an immigrant of some kind. The needs of the refugees from the pogroms went beyond warm clothing and a basket of food. The new arrivals needed to learn a new language, find employment, figure out how to enter a strange society, and how to negotiate the process of becoming citizens. The best that the ladies of the society could do at first was help by providing clothes, food, and a little cash.

The society did not get off to an encouraging start. The first applicant for help, a young man who wanted to go to Portland, was turned down after an investigation showed him to be an impostor. He had been in Seattle a week and had obtained money from several different people, telling each a different story.

The second case, which met more of the expectations of the organizers, was a needy family. Esther Levy and Eva Aronson visited the family and gave them $11. The record does not show whether the need was for food, clothing, medical care, or other necessity.

Work was found for a third applicant, and relief given to two more, for a total expenditure of $32.

So began the work of the Ladies' Hebrew Benevolent Society (LHBS). How people heard about the program was not found in the records, but most likely, news spread by word of mouth and at the synagogues. However those in great need discovered a possible answer to their difficulties, many a night the officers of the society left their supper tables for a knock on the door from a supplicant.

Among the society's first clients were Russian Jews fleeing the czarist pogroms. Tens of thousands fled Russia to resettle in the other empires of Europe or to find a way to the New World. The refugees arrived penniless, unable to speak English, completely unfamiliar with the new country and the idea of urban living. The vast majority were unsophisticated farmers, peasants really, who never knew plumbing, electricity, paved streets, or the demands of life in America's cities. This left them subject to exploitation and continuing poverty. Their only friends were other Jews who established immigrant agencies and charities.

That first year, the work of the society seems modest by modern standards. The ladies distributed just $164.25 (against $294.50 in revenues), collected from among themselves. If we remember that in 1892 a working man might earn two or three dollars a day—when he worked—from which he paid rent and fed and clothed his family, we see that a few dollars in the hands of a desperate family or an ambitious entrepreneur made the difference between success and failure, life and death. The society's dues were augmented by the members with luncheon fundraisers, card parties, entertainments, and balls. In addition to their work to help members of the Seattle Jewish community, the organization put on an entertainment specifically for the benefit of the survivors of a mine explosion in Roslyn, Washington. They raised $167.25 and contributed it to the miners' families to add to the other relief provided by citizens of Seattle.

All the work of the society was done by the members as volunteers, and there was no office and no employees. Monthly meetings, held in the homes of the officers, usually the president, and later in the temple meeting room, were announced in the society pages of the *Seattle Post-Intelligencer* and the *Seattle Times*. The organizational year began every year in March when the ladies elected new officers and tallied up their work. (This practice continued until 2008, the 116th year of the organization, when both the fiscal year and the board year commenced in July.)

In early 1892, the matter of charity also came to the attention of Seattle community leaders who organized the Bureau of Associated Charities (later called Wellspring Charities) to consolidate giving to the needy and dispensing of benefits. Applicants for aid had to present themselves to an office to be qualified by a bureau official, and if the official deemed the applicant able to work or, as was the case with some women, considered to be of "low moral character," they were refused aid.

The Ladies' Hebrew Benevolent Society came into being just a year before the most severe economic downturn the nation had ever experienced, the Panic of 1893. Tens of thousands of people lost their jobs in an era when there was no social safety net, such as unemployment insurance or Social Security. The country wallowed in a depression that continued for more than five years. The work of the society was sorely strained as previously self-sufficient families became destitute and new immigrants continued to arrive. The members of the society also felt the pinch of the hard times, but they kept giving, although several members were lost when they followed their husbands as they left Seattle for better economic opportunities.

Another entertainment event held in March of 1893 raised $451.35, out of which expenses of $105.70 were paid. Three years later, the annual report for 1896 gives the total of funds raised at $360.35 with $318.15 paid out.

The report continues:

What the Society has thus accomplished within the short period of four years existence and may be expected to accomplish in the future, becomes palpably manifest to anyone who may be permitted to glance over its records that bear silent yet eloquent testimony to the noble work performed.[5]

The ladies of the society actively sought out clients and did their best to overcome linguistic and cultural barriers to deliver aid, often a basket of food or a bag of clothing. One segment of needy Jews remained a bit outside the reach of the ladies: single men. Thousands of men labored in unspeakable conditions at logging camps, in canneries, aboard fishing boats, and on farms, only to be paid off and turned out until the next season. Every winter, Seattle filled with these unattached men who found shelter in flophouses south of Yesler Way, the "Deadline," the acknowledged and somewhat porous border between the area set aside for vice and the more genteel part of Seattle. To meet this need, the ladies' husbands formed the Seattle Hebrew Benevolent Society to "minister to the needs of newcomers who arrived penniless and without possessions."[6]

The founders of this new organization were Gustave Winehill, Leo Kohn, Paul Singerman, Morris L. Grunebaum, Elkan Morgenstern, Emanuel Rosenberg, and Jacob J. Cole, many of whose wives founded the ladies' society. The men's group expanded upon the work of the women by including burial services for needy Jews.

In the course of relief work, the members frequently discovered clients in need of medical attention. Two Seattle doctors from the community, Dr. Emil Bories and Dr. Witherspoon, volunteered their time and expertise and, for several years, regularly treated the sick without charge.

In 1895, another Jewish charitable group appeared, this one designed by Goldie Shucklin and composed of women of the Orthodox Jewish faith. Shucklin was born in Lithuania in 1851 and arrived in Seattle in 1892. She chose to call the organization The Ladies Montefiore Aid Society, in memory of Sir Moses Montefiore. These women, or often Shucklin acting alone, were able to bridge the cultural gulf between Americanized "German" Jews and Yiddish-speaking immigrants to reach Orthodox Jews in need. Shucklin was noted as very open with her giving and did not question the requests for assistance.

The first Montefiore officers were Shucklin, president; Mrs. David Taylor, recording secretary; Mrs. J. S. Kane, financial secretary; and Mrs. Isaac Lurie, treasurer. Mrs. Jacob Freidman and Mrs. Harry Ross were also involved in the first efforts and worked faithfully and diligently for many years.

The Montefiore Society furnished food, fuel, clothing, and funds to needy families, almost all new arrivals in the United States. The Montefiore ladies went to the coal yards and the wood yards to solicit contributions of fuel and made deals with some real estate firms to give a needy family a little free rent for cleaning up a house. They also set up a system for collecting and distributing good used clothing.

With dues of 35 cents a month, or three dollars a year, Montefiore Society's principal fundraiser was a grand Purim Ball held in Morris Hall at Broadway and Yesler. The Montefiore ladies also received generous donations from Donald E. Frederick (founder of Frederick and Nelson Department Store), Fraser Patterson, McDougall Southwick, Louis Schwabacher, Julius Lang, Jacob Furth, and many others.

By 1898, the Ladies' Hebrew Benevolent Society had distributed funds totaling close to $1,700—almost $40,000 in 2012 dollars. From the annual report of 1900:

> On our records can be found the sum of money expended during these years, but these are utterly inadequate to carry to those unacquainted with our work, how much has really been done. Our officers braved many a stormy day to visit the poor. Many a special meeting of our advisory council board had been called to decide upon a case. Admitting no delay, many a delicacy has been carried to the sick, and many a child has been provided with warm and comfortable clothing without drawing on the funds of the Society.

Esther Levy's daughter, Lizzie, married storeowner Isaac Cooper in Genesee, Idaho, in 1886, and the couple followed her parents to Seattle in 1891. Despite the economic downturn, Isaac partnered with his father-in-law, Aaron Levy, and his brother-in-law, Louis Levy, forming Cooper and Levy, selling hardware, clothing, and wood products. Cooper and Levy were able to tap into the torrent of gold seekers that began filling every steamship berth bound for Alaska. This grew into the Klondike Gold Rush. The beginning of the gold rush is often marked as 1897 when the SS *Portland* and its "ton of gold" docked in Seattle. In fact, prospectors had been heading north for at least three years, and Cooper and Levy was right there on Front Street (now First Avenue) to help them get a solid start. Cooper and Levy became one of the major (if not the primary) providers of equipment to the thousands of men heading for the gold fields. A photograph of the Cooper and Levy store with supplies stacked in front speaks clearly of the furious drive to get rich quick and the resulting economic blessing to Seattle. Cooper, Levy, and other Seattle merchants did not even have to leave the waterfront to strike it rich. Cooper and Levy joined names like Schwabacher, Furth, Gatzert, and Schoenfeld among the leading

Cooper & Levy Store ca. 1897.
(Photo by Asahel Curtis, Cooper and Levy Families Photograph Collection, University of Washington Libraries.)

lights of the Seattle business community. In 1903, Cooper and Levy sold out to The Bon Marche and retired, occupying themselves with a variety of investments.

Lizzie Cooper added her energy and her family's prosperity to her mother's in the work of the benevolent society. All across the country, Jewish women were coming together for the betterment of themselves and their communities. At the 1893 World's Fair: Colombian Exposition in Chicago, the Jewish Women's Congress met as part of the World's Parliament of Religions. They formed the National Council of Jewish Women to "further the best and highest interests of Judaism and humanity."[7] Lizzie also helped organize the Seattle section of the National Council of Jewish Women in 1900. She remained a major force in relief and philanthropy until her sudden death in 1915.

The Jewish Women's Congress emerged at a time when Seattle, like all the country, was absorbing the influx of European and Russian Jews making their way to the New World in the miserable holds of many ships. The new agency faced many challenges in helping to settle the newly arrived families. There was even a regular feature in a popular New York City newspaper, the *Jewish Daily Forward*, called the "Bintel Brief" (bundle of letters), best described as a Jewish advice column. The letters paint a vivid and poignant picture of immigrant Jews as they struggled to acclimate to this new environment. Their problems are the stuff of the immigrant experience—adjusting to life in a country with unfamiliar social and religious customs, the economic exploitation of the immigrant, the despicable employment conditions, lost contact with loved ones, and later, the agonies of two world wars and the debate over women's rights.

The Ladies' Hebrew Benevolent Society could have published a similar column from the letters regularly received by Esther Levy. Mrs. A. wrote in 1893:

Dear Mrs. Levy:

We are a small family who recently came to the "Golden Land." My husband became a peddler. The "pleasure" of knocking on doors and ringing bells cannot be known by anyone but a peddler. If anybody does buy anything "on time," a lot of the money is lost, because there are some people who never intend to pay. In addition, my husband has trouble because he has a beard, and because of the beard he gets beaten up by the hoodlums.

Also, we have problems with our boy, who throws money around. He works every day till late at night in a grocery for three dollars a week. I watch over him and give him the best because I am sorry he has to work so hard. But he costs me plenty and he borrows money from everybody. He has many friends and owes them all money. I get more and more worried as he takes here and borrows there. All my talking does not help. I am afraid to chase him away from home because he might get worse among strangers. I want to point out that he is well versed in Russian and Hebrew and he is not a child anymore, but his behavior is not that of an intelligent adult.

I don't know what to do. My husband argues that he does not want to continue peddling. He doesn't want to shave off his beard, and it's not fitting for such a man to do so. What can we do? We want to move to your community where friends of ours settled last year. Will you help us?

Esther Levy replied:

Dear Mrs. A.,

On behalf of our Society, I wish to extend my sympathy for your troubles and tell you that we will help you as best we can to settle in our community. We have some funds for relief and good people like Mrs. Fortlouis on Madison Street can offer you temporary shelter until we find a little house for your family and work for your husband. There is a possible job in my husband's general store, Cooper and Levy. It is our purpose to help immigrants and we will welcome you to our growing community. Please let us know when you will expect to be here, and what household belongings you will be bringing, and how much savings you have to start with.[8]

As the 20th century opened, there came to the attention of the officers the case of a young man who wished to go to Portland. He had been given five dollars for this journey, and the matter provoked a great deal of discussion. The members decided that money would not be given to people to enable them to travel from one city to another, except perhaps in extraordinary circumstances, and each request would need to be investigated before funds were expended. A new committee was formed and charged with investigating cases as appropriate.

By 1902, there were 100 members of the society. Members of the Hospital Committee visited hospitals daily, and by 1905, meetings had been moved to Broadway Hall.

Esther Levy stepped down from the presidency of the organization in 1912,

Lizzie Cooper ca. 1900.
(JFS photo collection.)

and her daughter, Lizzie Cooper, became the second president of the LHBS .

⁕

Gmilith Khesed is Hebrew for the bestowing of loving kindness, or true charity. In Jewish communities of Eastern Europe, *shtetl* organizations bore this name. (A *shtetl* is a small town with a large Jewish population; they existed in Central and Eastern Europe before the Holocaust.) Rabbis regarded this bestowal as a divine commandment to help one's fellow man in whatever way possible, including a short-term loan. These loans were looked upon as a *mitzvah*, a good deed, and lending money without profit— with no interest—was termed by the Talmud "loving kindness." The repayment of a loan was considered not a part of a business transaction, but rather a moral obligation.

In 1909, a group of women from the Orthodox Congregation Bikur Cholim organized a whist and sewing club, with dues of 25 cents a month. When they found they had accumulated $64 in their treasury, they offered to buy something for the synagogue. The rabbi refused their gift on the grounds that it was gambling money. Jennie Friedman, the club president, suggested this money could be used to give free loans to needy Jews, thereby allowing them to repay and to keep their dignity. Thus, with an initial capitalization of $64, the Gmilith Khesed, or what became known as the Hebrew Ladies' Free Loan Society of Seattle, was born. At first, only small loans were made, and these could be repaid at the rate of 25 cents a month. For larger loans, such as $15, the ladies would take from their own pockets and wait to be reimbursed when the loan was repaid.

In 1916, the rules were changed to allow a maximum loan of $50 to any one Jewish person. No interest was expected, but two endorsers residing in Seattle were required to guarantee the loan. Dora Zeeve, who was financial secretary from 1916 to 1952 (36 years!), collected the dues, made the loans, kept the records, and gave the reports. In the beginning, she said, the loans were for such things as clothes and food for the holidays. People also needed money for rent, for food, and for clothes for the children. As the program continued, loans were made for a greater variety of purposes: to help finance cars, pay tuition fees, reunite families, and pay for citizenship preparation, births, weddings, divorces, and funerals, and to help young people start in business. The Hebrew Ladies' Free Loan Society helped send children to camp, assisted a school, a synagogue, and a yeshiva, and in one unusual case, loaned money to make repairs on a hearse.

Times changed, and the growing need was recognized so that by 1948 the maximum loan became $100 for individuals with a special fund set aside to assist displaced persons who had no connections in the community. These loans required no endorsers if recommendation had been made by Jewish Family & Child Service (JFCS) (the name of Jewish Family Service between 1947 and 1978) or by the Jewish Welfare Board. During this period, loans were made for such things as refrigerators, rent payments, dental help, and workmen's tools. In 1957, the Free Loan Society bylaws were revised again raising the loan maximum to $1,000 and requiring four endorsers. In addition, for the first time, loans were made available to Jewish organizations in Seattle with a maximum set at $3,000 and a requirement of 12 local endorsers. All loans were always confidential, protecting the borrowers' dignity.

In 1964, JFCS decided to establish a revolving loan fund in Israel, starting with $1,000. Throughout its history, the fee for membership in the society remained at only one dollar a year.

1. "Gadding Wives Are Blamed for Misery and Divorce," *Seattle Post-Intelligencer*, October 6, 1919.
2. The Coliseum Theater would be built on the site in 1914.
3. Temple de Hirsch purchased this site in 1910, and it remains the primary burial site for members of that temple.
4. *The Seattle Times,* January 4, 1956.
5. Paper, Jewish Family Service, University of Washington Special Collections, Seattle.

6. Molly Cone, Howard Droker, and Jacqueline Williams, *Family of Strangers: Building a Jewish Community in Washington State* (Seattle: Washington State Jewish Historical Society, 2003), 83.

7. "Council of Jewish Women," *American Jewish Year-Book*, 5661. (http://jewishencyclopedia.com, accessed November 23, 2011).

8. Paper, Jewish Family Service, University of Washington Special Collections, Seattle.

Chapter 2

Emergency Services

It often began with a knock on the door, sometimes in the late evening hours. The caller might declare "Our baby is sick, and I have no money for medicine. Can you help?" "I have no work and cannot feed my family." Or perhaps, "I can't pay the rent for our room, and the landlord is going to kick us out. Can you help me?" Sometimes a message was left by a rabbi or a local merchant reporting the distressed condition of a family made known to them. "There is a family with four children; they have no food and no warm coats," or "The family of one of my warehouse workers needs help."

For 30 years, the Ladies' Hebrew Benevolent Society had no formal office location, so the knock on the door would often be at the home of one of the members of the society. In a city that was still small and with the Jewish population located downtown or in what today we call First Hill and the Central Area, it was not difficult for these desperate people to find their way to a friendly door, which might show a familiar *mezuzah* (the small case containing a scroll of verses from the Torah marking a Jewish home).

From its inception, the primary work of the agency was to provide these most basic types of relief to desperate immigrant Jews from Europe, Russia, and the Ottoman Empire. The volunteers from the Ladies' Hebrew Benevolent Society hiked up and down the hills and rickety staircases of Seattle carrying baskets of food and bundles of clothing to hungry families and provided much-needed warm clothing and succor to confused, shivering children, frightened mothers, and men struggling to support their suffering families.

In later years, as the work of the organization began to focus more on helping families discover and solve fundamental family issues, relief work remained an important part of the effort, what JFS today calls Emergency Services (ES), providing food, housing, financial assistance, and case management.

Carol Mullin has worked with the Emergency Services program of JFS for 25 years. She grew up in Detroit in a Reform Jewish family with a grandfather who was a key figure in that Reform community. Later, as she became more familiar with the Seattle Jewish community, she related it to her family history in Michigan. She fell in love with the Northwest when she moved to Seattle after college, first working on research projects at the University of Washington and then moving to the University of Washington in-patient psychiatric services where she spent 12 years.

In the spring of 1988, having recently given birth to her daughter, Mullin responded to an ad in the *Seattle Weekly* for a half-time social service professional at Jewish Family Service. (The name had changed again in 1978.) She interviewed with then assistant director Cliff Warner at the Boylston office and immediately started as the caseworker in the Emergency Services program, working with director Miriam Myerson. A year later, Myerson left, and Mullin became the director of the Emergency Services program.

In 1989, the Emergency Services program primarily served Jewish clients. Mullin's role was much the same as it is now. She was in charge of the food bank (a 10-foot-by-4-foot closet, called the Kosher Food Bank), she interviewed and provided financial assistance to clients, and in those early days, she directed the Volunteer program and managed summer camp scholarships. After a few years, she also took on the management of the Big Pals program.

The mission of Emergency Services is similar to that of JFS as a whole: "to deliver essential human services to alleviate suffering,

sustain healthy relationships, and support people in times of need."
The values of both include:

- being guided by the Jewish tradition of *tikkun olam*—repairing the world
- being committed to treating people with dignity and compassion
- providing culturally relevant services
- helping people help themselves
- reflecting the changing face of the community
- collaborating with others to broaden their reach.

Over the last 25 years, Emergency Services has not changed significantly, although the clientele has grown considerably in size and includes non-Jews. The program still focuses on basic services providing immediate relief to families in crisis. Professional social work principles have always been employed, and case-management services provided when needed. The major changes have been in the size of the program in terms of the amount of money spent and the number of people served. Many clients have a onetime need, some require ongoing assistance over several weeks, and a few are people with long-term needs. This last group includes people who have chronic medical problems or mental illness and people living on small fixed incomes. The most acute needs usually require just a single visit.

A major part of Mullin's work still involves interviewing and compiling a brief assessment with the client, determining what funds are available, and then processing and keeping track of the disbursements.

Food

In the beginning, the work of the Ladies' Hebrew Benevolent Society meant a volunteer would carry a basket of food on her arm to a family in need. Once the first real office was established on Second

Avenue in the 1920s, a few emergency rations were kept on hand. This became a shelf of kosher food in a closet in the Jackson Street offices of the 1950s, kept primarily to assist elderly clients. Thelma Coney, who came to JFS as a counselor in 1966 and worked in that capacity for 12 years, remembers a volunteer named Estelle Broder who took charge of the early food drives. (Broder later became the agency bookkeeper, a position she held for many years.) Counselors would provide a small bag of food for a client when the cupboard at home had been emptied.

In the offices on Harvard Avenue in the 1970s and on Boylston in the 1980s, the shelf became an entire closet and then a food pantry about the size of a small private office. When the pharmacy on the street level at 1214 Boylston Avenue vacated in 1992, JFS took over the space, and a true food bank opened its doors.

This food bank employed a customer service model with a service station in the front and shelves of food in back. Clients received a list of the items that were available that week—canned goods, dried goods, personal needs—like a menu, with additional specials posted on a bulletin board. The clients checked off what they wanted—perhaps peas, carrots, pasta, and rice. Some clients checked everything, and some checked just a few items. A volunteer then took the list and collected the items requested. In 1989, there were 1,338 households served in a total of 3,238 visits. Of those total households, 89 percent were Jewish with only a few non-Jewish households served.

For many years, the agency has worked as a contributing member of the community food coalition, and JFS staff has continuously played a leadership role in the coalition. Being a member of the coalition allows JFS to receive a large quantity of free food from Food Lifeline and Northwest Harvest, the region's food bank distribution centers. Of the 348,000 pounds of food distributed in 2012, almost one-third (approximately 110,000 pounds), came from those two providers. The Fall Food Drive brought in another 35,000 pounds of food. An additional 30,000 of supplies, like pet food, local coffee, bread from local businesses, etc., was contributed by various donors. Twenty-five thousand pounds came from the city of Seattle through the bulk-buy program. The remaining148,000 pounds of food was purchased by JFS in 2012 (compared to 50,000 pounds of food purchased in 2003).

Even when the food bank was only a little shelf of food, JFS served both Jews and non-Jews. Once the project became a formal food bank, an agreement was reached with the local food coalition (the Seattle Food Committee) that the JFS food bank would provide service to three zip codes: 98101 (downtown Seattle from the waterfront to Melrose and from Virginia to Spring), 98121 (a triangle from Denny and Harrison down Denny to the waterfront and Virginia to the waterfront), and 98122 (basically the Central District from Lake Washington to Broadway and from Denny to Yesler). Zip Code 98122 proved to be too big for the tiny enterprise to maintain and had to be dropped from the agency's responsibilities. However, after the move in 1995 to the Jessie Danz Building at 1601 16th Avenue (the current campus), service to 98122 resumed, and the number of clients served increased dramatically. Today about 44 percent of walk-in clients at the Polack Food Bank live in that zip code. Zip code 98112 (from Lake Washington to 13th and from the Ship Canal to Denny) was also added, but there is very little activity from that area.

When JFS purchased the Jessie Danz Building in 1995, the new Polack Food Bank opened on the ground floor with separate access for its clients. (The food bank was renamed following a generous Polack family contribution to the Jessie Danz Building Capital Campaign.) An optical center occupied most of the ground floor leaving only a small space in the back available for the food bank, but it was still a huge improvement. When the optical center left, the food bank moved into the vacated street-front space.

The expanded space made serving clients easier, but the three residential refrigerators and two residential freezers still severely limited the amount of fresh or frozen food that could be stored. Then in 2007, former board member Larry Hamlin, who was in the restaurant business, approached JFS to explore a personal project he wanted to pursue. He raised more than $10,000 to provide the first walk-in cooler that enabled the Polack Food Bank to receive, keep, and distribute significantly more perishable food.

A couple of expansions and remodels later, the most significant changes occurred with a major makeover made possible with federal stimulus funds in 2008.

JFS was very fortunate to have an attractive shovel-ready project already in the works, plus the support of the city of Seattle and of long-time JFS supporters Kathy and Steve Berman. The Polack Food Bank was expanded and, with the use of moveable tables, counters, and other specialized equipment, was able to shift its service model to one of self-serve consumer choice. Clients shop for the items they want and need from the selection of foods and non-food items that are available on that day.

The remodel also added a large delivery door that allows food to be delivered directly into the storage area. The service space was expanded significantly, and the moveable tables allow for maximum flexibility, enabling work parties and classes to be held in the space during non-food distribution times. The new walk-in freezer enables the program to accept five times the amount of frozen food they had been able to store previously. Locked storage rooms provide space for bulky items, such as diapers, bales of grocery bags, and canned and packaged non-perishables. In 2012, there were 23,000 visits to the Polack Food Bank by 4,200 households, compared to 1,338 households in 1989. Some clients use the food bank 10 to 12 times a year, and some might come just twice a year.

There is an assumption made by people involved in food-bank management that these increased numbers, which are reported to United Way, show the impact of more people in the community receiving more and healthier food. During 2013, with the use of a VISTA (Volunteers in Service to America) volunteer, the food bank collected information about the ways clients prepare more nutritious food because they have better access to fresh produce.

As the economy recovered from the 2007–2012 downturn, visits to the Polack Food Bank by clients declined because more

ES clients were holding down jobs, were eligible for state funds, or were not living on fixed incomes. Some still turned to JFS for assistance with a mortgage or rent payment or a large utility bill. The drop in food bank usage by ES clients might also be due to shifts in population density as the community has spread out.

In earlier years, it was unusual to have an ES client who lived even as far away as Bellevue. Now clients are often located in Kent, Federal Way, Renton, or Tukwila, making it too difficult and too long a journey, especially by bus. Consequently, those Jewish clients who live in South King County may not make the trip to Seattle to use the JFS food bank. There are a few, however, who have cars and do make the trip, and some will make specific appointments if they cannot meet the regular hours of service.

Since 2010, JFS has offered a monthly food bank specifically for individuals and families who keep a kosher home. During the first few months, representatives from the Vaad (Council of Rabbis) worked with the JFS food bank manager to make the appropriate food selections. Participants RSVP for this event, which is held at a different day and time from the regular food bank shift. Kosher food and quantities of produce are purchased to meet the needs of those 50 to 60 individuals/families served.

Only 20 percent of ES clients now also use the Polack Food Bank, while the majority of food bank clients do not use other emergency services.

◦◦◦◦◦

Adding more fresh produce was intentional. A few years ago, the food bank staff developed a gleaning relationship with the Broadway Farmers Market. A volunteer went to the market at the end of the day and collected leftover produce from various vendors. After the second year, VISTA volunteer Emma Kent joined the team. She prepared a beautiful guide, called "A Glimpse of Gleaning at Seattle Farmers Markets," which was made available to other food banks. Kent was able to devote two Sundays a month organizing volunteers to do the gleaning and filling in when necessary. In 2012, gleaning produced just under 5,000 pounds of wonderful, fresh produce. (After Kent completed her year of VISTA service, she was hired by the JFS marketing department.)

Kent was succeeded by fellow VISTA volunteer Anna Goren, whose assignment was to increase the amount of fresh produce people received. She took over the farmers' market gleaning project and then found new opportunities to double the amount of fresh produce. She researched a little farm in the Central Area called Alley Cat Acres, as well as a project that helps glean from neighborhood backyard farmers. She also posted notices asking, "Are you a backyard farmer?" and she started seedling projects by providing the materials and showing Polack Food Bank clients how to start seedling vegetables so they could grow some of their own fresh food. In addition, children in the Jewish Community Center's summer camp planted and sprouted seedlings that they then donated to the food bank project.

The next part of Goren's assignment was helping clients improve their nutrition. Within six weeks, she had located a partnership with a program of the anti-poverty agency Solid Ground, called Cooking Matters. Cooking Matters visits schools, clinics, and food banks and produces cooking classes that teach people how to better use fresh produce. They created a class setting in the Polack Food Bank and invited clients to sign up and to make a commitment to participate in at least six of the eight sessions. The classes focused on recipes using what was available in the food bank, perhaps grains, carrots, onions, or potatoes. During a class shopping trip, participants learned how to read grocery store labels and to identify the better buy for their money. One series of classes was made available for people who keep a kosher kitchen by carefully conforming to the laws of Kashrut, purchasing new utensils and sets of bowls, and adapting the recipes for people who keep kosher.

In year three, VISTA volunteer, Amelia Righi worked on a two-pronged joint project between JFS Volunteer Services and Emergency Services to build a stronger program with students in the Seattle University and Seattle Community College neighborhoods.

The goals included recruiting more students for community service and helping build a stronger social service infrastructure. She helped develop policies and procedures, orientation manuals and other materials, and then participated in the recruiting efforts.

In the late1980s early1990s, when Russians from the former Soviet Union arrived, many settled in the Crossroads neighborhood on the east side of Lake Washington. It was unlikely that those who were over age 60 were going to find viable work in the United States because they had neither the language nor the necessary skills. Many received Food Stamps and Supplemental Security Income for individuals over age 65 who are unable to work because of disabilities or other allowed circumstances. They needed the JFS food bank, but they had to take at least two buses to get to Seattle.

The director of the Jewish Day School was looking for a volunteer opportunity for his students at the same time as the Jewish Federation of Greater Seattle was offering a start-up grant for a new project. JFS and the Jewish Day School received funding for a shed, and after transferring food every week from the Seattle campus to Bellevue, they were finally able to arrange for deliveries from the food sources directly to the shed.

The Day School* program began with an after-school project for the middle school students. Eight to 15 students participated in pre-packing bags for up to 100 clients twice a month, the usual schedule for food banks. The numbers soon rose to 125 and stayed steady at that level. When twice-a-month service became too burdensome, distributions changed to once a month, increasing the

---

* JFS purchases the majority of the food distributed. This is a Jewish community food bank and not open to the general public. Clients are expected to pre-enroll and to demonstrate some connection to JFS, either because they were resettled or they are family members or loved ones of people who were resettled by JFS originally. (The relationship with Food Lifeline and Northwest Harvest is based on the membership in the Seattle Food Committee, and that food is intended to serve people who live in Seattle.)

amount of food provided. The recipients arrived after school was dismissed for the day and received a large, prefilled bag that held the equivalent of two regular bags.

The program operated that way until 1997 when the school asked for a change. Teachers wanted to incorporate the project as part of their curriculum. Staff started working with students during the last half hour of the school day to fill the 100 bags; then after school, parents and students handled distribution. Eventually, erring on the side of safety, direct student contact with clients was discontinued in favor of simply providing the students the opportunity to fill the bags as their *tzedakah* (charity) project.

Many of the Russian immigrants who arrived in Seattle in their 50s and 60s still receive food from the Eastside facility with perhaps 60 to 70 percent of current recipients part of the original group who used that food bank. The rest are the families or children of those early participants, and others who live in the same apartment complexes.

Three times, the JFS food bank program has won awards from Food Lifeline for best practices. In 2007, the program received the first place award for Excellence in Collaboration, which provided a monetary prize, and another for the Fall Food Drive. In 2011, the Polack Food Bank received the top award for excellent practices for development of a project called Resource Access Project (RAP).

When Mullin became aware that many potential food bank clients in Seattle were not able to participate in the program for a variety of physical or psychological reasons, including being unable to walk there and carry filled bags home, she started a delivery program, recruiting a handful of volunteers to serve the homebound. Originally, 20 volunteers came every month, each with a list of clients to visit. The program grew over the years until 2006, when Steve and Kathy Berman provided funds for a van and Jack Wagstaff, the food bank manager, secured city of Seattle funds intended to assist organizations in providing home delivery. With the use of the van, the Polack Food Bank developed a second very vibrant home-delivery program that cast JFS into the broad community while

Ready for delivery. (JFS photo collection.)

creating a strong partnership with the city of Seattle. A $60,000 annual grant supports an extra staff person and the purchase of the additional food needed every Monday for home delivery to several hundred people living in various apartment buildings throughout the city. The combined home-delivery program now serves more than 400 people every month, approximately one-third of the 23,000 food bank visits and deliveries each year.

Some recipients are eligible solely because they live in a particular building where the city has asked JFS to provide service. Most of those buildings are part of the community's low-income housing group, either Seattle Housing Authority buildings or other not-for-profit low-income housing buildings, such as the YWCA's Opportunity Place. Each week, the bags are all the same with an effort made to vary the contents from week to week. Because delivery is on Monday, there is wonderful fresh produce added during the farmers' market season. The rest of the year, there are usually potatoes, carrots, onions, and hard fruit, like apples and oranges.

The program is also making an effort to meet more of the cultural food needs, particularly for one building in which the residents are primarily Asian. Food bags delivered to this building might contain rice, soy sauce, ginger, noodles, tofu, and fresh produce like bok choy and other greens from an International District Asian grocery store, as well as other staple food items.

During training for volunteers, a very clear procedure is presented instructing, "If at any time when you are delivering to someone, you have any concerns about that person's well-being, remember that you might be the only person who will have contact with that elderly or infirm person that week." There have been occasions when a volunteer will call and say, "I was just at Mrs. X's apartment, and she seemed to be confused" or "Mr. Y seemed different" or "I knocked on the door, and nobody answered." The information is then reported to the building manager, a caseworker, or whoever else in the community has that responsibility.

The Polack Food Bank is one of the most popular programs with JFS donors. In 2012, of the 864 restricted gifts to the agency, which totaled almost $800,000, 428 were directed specifically for use by the food bank.

Financial Assistance

One of the most common ways non-Jewish people first reach JFS is through the Call 211 program. People in need of assistance dial 211, which feeds into the King County Community Information line. The most frequent portals for Jewish clients are other clients or somebody connected in the Jewish community, perhaps a friend, rabbi, or teacher. Often clients who come to ES for help have been provided service by another JFS program.

Harking back to the first services provided by the Ladies' Hebrew Benevolent Society, JFS Emergency Services now provides financial assistance to more than 450 local households each year. In 2012, the program distributed almost $150,000 for a variety of needs, including avoiding evictions, first and last month's rent for previously homeless families, shelter for single homeless adults, avoiding utility shutoffs, and back-to-school supplies for children in need. One of Emergency Services' early cases involved a woman who was well groomed, articulate, and intelligent but who also had a variety of serious problems. She refused to engage the medical or mental health system. She did use the JFS counseling program for a short time and the Polack Food Bank on a long-term basis. ES could help her once or twice a year with small amounts of financial assistance for utilities and the like. Sadly, as her health deteriorated, she continued to refuse to seek mainstream medical care. When she died, the JFS staff member who had been her case manager was one of only two people at the funeral.

Another case involved a couple with a child who had a chronic illness. They had health insurance coverage, but it didn't pay 100 percent of the child's care. They were just barely making ends meet, but as the economy worsened, so did the child's health. One parent's employment was drastically reduced, bills mounted, they weren't poor enough to qualify for Medicaid, and the financial difficulties soon brought them to ES for help. Because the situation was related to a child's emergency need, extraordinary steps were taken to meet the need. Fortunately—or unfortunately—the family's financial situation dropped to the level of need qualifying them for more assistance from other sources.

The JFS 2006 Strategic Plan (see Chapter 21, "A Plan for the Future") struggled with the issue of ES helping either more people with less or fewer people with more. After much back-and-forth questioning, Mullin concluded that it need not be one or the other but could actually go both ways. Many clients can be helped through a crisis with a $200 grant for something like a utility payment, while adequate assistance for other clients requires taking a deeper look at the situation and trying to make appropriate decisions that will really help over the long run. ES staff will, of course, always look for red flags: Is there something else going on? Are we missing something? Is the money going in one door and out another bad door?

With each new client, ES begins by developing a profile of the situation. "Why are you turning to us?" "What is the nature of your problem?" Assuming the client has some source of income (many have very little coming in; often they live on inadequate fixed incomes, State Temporary Assistance for Needy Families, or perhaps Social Security or disability income), the caseworker looks at their rent—usually the largest single expense—and then at other expenses, including food, utilities, out-of-pocket medical, transportation costs, and then at what remains. Usually what is left is nothing, and any extra expense, like a high winter utility bill or having to move, could push the family into crisis. During the 2007–2012 economy shift, people often lost their homes or had to move with no choice when the home they were renting was foreclosed on. They were often evicted through no fault of their own.

ES then looks at what they can offer. Currently the program receives funding from the Consolidated Homeless Grant through King County. Some years, there is a small amount of federal money available also from the Emergency Food and Shelter program (formerly funded through the Federal Emergency Management Agency and the program that began as McKinney Funds for families who have previously been homeless).

One of the larger funding sources for JFS Emergency Service comes from Temple Beth Am's Homeless to Renter program (H2R). Temple Beth Am developed it specifically to help previously homeless families with children move into stable housing, which is the primary unmet need for homeless families. Since 2006, the ES program has administered these funds. In 2012, the contribution reached $32,000, double that of the previous year. H2R is one excellent example of funds raised in the Jewish community and given to JFS to administer with no expectation or intention that the funds will primarily serve Jewish families.

The guidelines for H2R are very specific. JFS is expected to help move families with children from homelessness to being housed by granting them up to $1,000 to cover the cost of first and last months' rent plus a security deposit. Families must live in King County and have the ability then to maintain their rent.

Before H2R, the average grant for housing was between $400 and $500. Suddenly being able to give out $1,000 was a significant improvement in helping families. It was also the beginning of seeing a change in the face of clients being served. The Beth Am contribution is 25 to 30 percent of total funds ES has available for rent assistance. It is available for anyone, Jewish or not. Several other funders also expect the agency to serve the broader community. In 2013, of a $175,000 ES budget (not including the Polack Food Bank), close to $100,000 was used for rent support. At least $25,000 of that came from the Beth Am H2R program to move people from homelessness to being housed. The majority of these clients were not Jewish.

The H2R program follows families for one year, finding that 80 percent remain housed. The other 20 percent may come back and try again, with decisions made on a case-by-case basis. Generally, if people receiving housing assistance have not kept JFS informed of their situation, they will not be assisted again. However, those who have lost their housing and kept the program informed will most likely be helped again. The issues in these cases are accountability, responsibility, and dependability.

The rest of the ES program is funded with money the JFS Development Department raises through grants, foundations, or private donors. Few donors have specific restrictions, although occasionally someone will request that their contribution be used for families with children, to help children go to camp, to assist the elderly, or for some other specific service.

Although not an everyday occurrence, there are families that JFS Emergency Services has assisted over generations as they strive in many different ways to achieve financial stability. Things may be fine for a few years running and then, all of a sudden, a job is lost, a child is in crisis, a parent is facing a life threatening health issue. The extended family does its best to meet the escalating financial and emotional needs, but stability is often tenuous. That is when they turn to JFS for assistance with a utility bill, rent, food, even the Chanukah Tzedakah program for the children (a JFS holiday-season gift-collection program in which many Jewish community families and individuals participate).

Another family, for example, lived month-to-month on one parent's income while the other was the primary caregiver for both an aging and an ill relative. When an emergency required them to forego a month's income, the financial challenges mounted. The family turned to a variety of local social service agencies without any luck—until they knocked on the door of JFS, which assisted them with the rent. Many organizations require a three-day-or-vacate notice in-hand before they are able to act. However, ES has flexible funding that sidesteps that requirement and avoids the red-tape roadblock.

Having flexible funding is a tremendous resource for community members with special needs. Today they are finding fewer and fewer places with the ability to help "in the moment." Not so at JFS. Just recently, the ES flexible funding assisted an elderly client on a fixed income who was in need of medical care that the insurance company would not cover. Another example is helping the neediest families purchase back-to-school supplies for their children who otherwise would go without.

Sometimes the necessity is for eyeglasses or hearing aid repair. A note was received recently saying, "Now I can hear again, thank you." The cost was $250.

From her 25 years of experience, Mullin recognizes that these families could be any one of us or one of our children.

ES works in collaboration with a number of other community programs, including Chaplain Gary Freedman and the Jewish Prisoner Services International, an organization that can help people getting out of prison find work and housing. Unfortunately, they often have nothing except the clothes they entered prison with and no money to pay for transportation. With flexible funding, ES is able to use a gift card to help with clothing and can provide a limited number of bus tickets.

For the past several decades, the Alpha Omega Dental Fraternity (the oldest international dental organization) has been involved with the ES program. Many members provide a consultation or professional dental services pro bono. Low-cost dental clinics are available in the community but often have lengthy waiting lists. This type of professional service is greatly appreciated by clients and JFS alike.

People's lives are changed every day with a simple "yes we can help." That "yes we can" is part of the legacy of the organization. There are very few times that somebody is turned away, although repeat customers may be refused after several visits. An applicant will also be turned away if the caseworker thinks the client could be doing more for himself or herself or didn't follow through with earlier recommendations. Occasionally, there may be a suspicion that money is going to something that is not healthy or appropriate. However, in general, if someone has a need, ES staff will try to find a way to help. It might not be with money; instead, they might say, "Come use our food bank" or "Come sit down with our caseworker," and ES will spend time one on one.

For 2012, the direct assistance budget for ES was over four times more than in 1990 when the program gave out $45,000. There are also six times as many clients. The average grant in those days was under $200 a person and now is closer to $400 a person.

ES surveys clients each year to determine the effectiveness of the program in providing housing stability. In 2012, 99 percent of the clients reported that the assistance added to their housing stability, although 66 percent had needed additional funds in order to have fully paid their rent and had to approach other agencies and funding sources. Many of the respondents commented that the assistance they received from JFS got them through a rough period and kept them housed. Almost everyone was still in the housing for which they had received the assistance. They commented, "[The help] you gave me added a positive outlook on humanity," "I was able to stay put and just got a job—this would not have been possible before as things were in chaos," and "The help stopped me from being homeless."

Loan Program

During Mullin's early years, JFS provided grants, short-term loans, and longer-term interest-free loans. A loan through the Hebrew Ladies' Free Loan Society (HLFLS) was an endorsed (guaranteed by the persons cosigning) loan. Grants were given only to people who needed emergency financial assistance and would not be able to pay it back. Short-term loans were used for emergency financial assistance of a short-term nature for people who could most likely pay it back, like a person who had lost his or her job but was starting working again. A third type of loan was meant for an emergency on a larger scale where people had a cosigner who would guarantee the loan in case of default.

The original philosophy behind the HLFLS was that the community was connected in many different ways and members of the community knew and supported each other. If someone took out a loan and a friend from their congregation was willing to be a cosigner, those people were probably acquainted. The client would first talk to their friend about being a cosigner. Then JFS approached him or her saying, "Your acquaintance, Mrs. X, needs an emergency loan, and we want to know if you are willing to be the cosigner for her." They would usually agree and were reminded that if the person did not pay the loan back, JFS would turn to them to pay it off.

It was a wonderful concept adapted from the old country, and many communities used a similar free-loan program. There were clearly defined guidelines and bylaws for those cosigned loans, which JFS monitored and for which it issued invoices and billings. In the early years, the return rate was higher, possibly due to the more stable economy but also because both the agency and people in the community knew each other, both knew their cosigners, and the cosigners knew them. The return rate eventually changed significantly when borrowers defaulted on some of the loans that were not cosigned and then spread to cosigned loans. The burden in staff time and effort was soon greater than the collected benefits.

The loans stopped entirely in 2005. It was apparent that many of those people who needed money did not have the means to pay it back. During the 2006 strategic planning process, it was agreed that ES would do its best not only to help more people with grants but also devote more money that would truly assist people achieve stability. (Providing $100 or $200 grants was not helping achieve stability when clients needed $800 or $1,000 for a medical emergency or for first and last months' rent, plus a security deposit.)

A number of other programs work with Emergency Services to assist clients in other ways. The community-wide Fall Food Drive to support the Polack Food Bank is a wonderful ambassadorship program operated in coordination with JFS Volunteer Services. It not only generates a significant amount of food, but also provides a wonderful way to reach out to people as volunteers and gets classrooms, youth groups, and entire congregations involved. In recent years, the one-day Food Sort event has hosted more than 250 volunteers each year to sort over 10 tons of food.

Volunteer Services also manages a Holiday Gift Basket project four times a year that is focused on food with a Jewish and holiday content. Delivery of those baskets to elderly and homebound clients is done with the help of volunteers for Rosh Hashanah, Purim, Pesach (Passover), and Chanukah.

In 2009, ES applied for United Way funds to pursue a new program that came out of asking, "What could we do if we had the money for an additional staff person?" The idea was to give people standing in line at the JFS food bank access to a counselor who could assist with other pressing issues. Wouldn't it be nice to sit down with a caseworker to iron out a problem by asking a few questions in a confidential setting? Once this Resource Access Project (RAP) was fully implemented, clients were offered the opportunity to step out of the line and meet with a staff person. In being approached, a client might say, "I need help with transportation," and then be able to meet with a caseworker for 10 or 15 minutes. Perhaps the caseworker would discover the client had disabilities and could be using a reduced-fare transit pass or the MetroAccess paratransit program. The client would be given the information needed and a bus ticket to go to the METRO (the King County Public Transit Authority) office for the pass. Everybody who reported during the first year of the program said the resource was useful.

The idea of a live person to sit down with and receive an immediate reply with appropriate resources was a unique concept that has since won several awards. People immediately receive printed instructions, directions, and if needed, bus tickets to get there—everything they need to follow through.

Chanukah Tzedakah

In the late 1980s, two JFS volunteers, Jennifer Malakoff and Laura Karl, had an idea for a program during the winter holiday season of providing Chanukah *Tzedakah* (charity) to clients of the agency. They started with a small group of friends contributing a few thousand dollars while Mullin contacted some needy families to inquire about what they wanted as a special gift. In the early years, there were 30 or 40 recipients primarily receiving gift cards, so they could do a little shopping. Most of the families were trying to provide gifts and a few holiday goodies for their children. One family desperately needed tires for their car. Over the years, other special needs that gift cards have been able to provide have included a used dryer, a vacuum, ballet shoes, payment of utility bills, special Judaica items, and a blender for someone who was not able to swallow solids.

The current Chanukah Tzedakah Program was created because more donors wanted to shop for their gift recipients themselves. There are now more than 150 donors who are matched with specific clients, an equal number of donors who give money, and more than 360 recipients. Recipients are asked for a list of wishes, and the donors are provided with that information. Some give money or a gift card, and others go shopping. There has never been a single year when a need went unmet, whether for newborns or 95-year-olds, and there has never been a time that a family came in, even if it was the very last night of Chanukah, that the program did not meet the need. Seniors and adults with disabilities are also recipients, a part of the program that has been enormously gratifying for both the recipients and the donors. Often a gift is being given to someone who might not receive a gift from any other source.

Over time, the Chanukah Tzedakah Program expanded to include gift donation programs hosted by the Jennifer Rosen Mead Preschool, Stroum Jewish Community Center, Herzl-Ner Tamid Religious School, and classrooms at Temple de Hirsch. Classrooms get involved by taking a family or two for whom the class jointly provides holiday gifts and food.

Camperships

For many years, JFS has provided funds to help Jewish children attend Jewish overnight and day camps. At one time, there was also a program through United Way to offer children the opportunity to attend secular camps, such as the Girl Scout or the YMCA camp, but other agencies handle those camps now.

The Samis Foundation has continuously supported the summer camp program for many years, and several private donors have joined the effort. One donor family asked that their contribution be used to provide special items like sunglasses, sunscreen, or new socks and underwear. That same donor also wanted to help children who were not Jewish go to camp, so JFS invited other organizations—primarily church groups—to select children. Another donor stepped in to send non-Jewish children to camp as well, and then a local family, as a Chanukah gift to their own children, specifically donated funds to provide a church camp family weekend for 75 children a year. While JFS staff do not spend a significant amount of time on these projects, they do get the pleasure of providing the funding so that outside agencies can provide these opportunities to their clients.

Emergency Shelter

For years, the Emergency Services program provided funds to pay for shelter-bed nights for men and women who were homeless. The city of Seattle has since changed the way shelters are operated, and women no longer must pay for a shelter bed. At a walk-in center in downtown Seattle, women can now sign up for a bed and receive a ticket for the night. If the primary shelters are full, there are overflow shelters. During the years that women had to pay for a night in a shelter, they often turned to social service agencies for the fee.

There is more strategizing about homelessness these days with regions all over the country creating 10-year plans. In King County, which is more than halfway through its Commission to End Homelessness 10-year plan, solving the housing problems has been extremely difficult as there are different points of view about the best way to proceed. Many professionals who work with the homeless population agree that the need for transitional housing leading to permanent housing is the highest priority and that shelter beds are just a bandage to stop the bleeding.

JFS remains committed to helping homeless people with the cost of nightly shelters, although this is done on a small scale. Ten to 12 individuals are helped each month at a cost of approximately $2,500 a year.

People who are homeless may not have easy access to a phone. JFS provides a dedicated housing line for those clients with a designated day and time to call to reach a live person. Clients can leave a detailed message to get a callback or can call during the specific time the housing specialist is available. The housing specialist can screen for rent assistance eligibility and can offer a shelter voucher.

There is agreement among members of the JFS board of directors and staff that the emergency shelter program must move towards housing stability. The year before the new initiative was put in place, rent was given out 29 times at a cost of $7,000. The year following, rent was given out 193 times at a cost of $117,000.

While the average rent has doubled, ES is now helping more people meet a greater portion of their rent burden. Mullin gives credit and accolades to the JFS Development Department for its increased fundraising and grant-writing results.

As a quarterly follow-up, clients who have received money for rent are asked questions like, "Are you still stable in your housing? If not, how much would have made the difference? Did you need more money? Did you have to turn to other social service agencies?" The data collected indicates that the average rent grant of just over $600 is very close to what is actually needed.

Rarely has someone who received one of these grants sent money back. Mullin remembers one time when someone sent $1,000 with a note saying "25 years ago you helped me and my family, so I'm going to send this back to you."

Many of the same issues that confronted Esther Levy and Lizzie Cooper in the 1890s persist in the 21st century. JFS staff still work hard to move clients to stability and self-sufficiency.

Chapter 3

1900: Helping the Poor

"As a philanthropist she is unsurpassed. No man has excelled the philanthropic virtue of Miriam, Dorcas, Florence Nightingale, or Helen Gould. When the history of practical philanthropy has been written, its most illustrious pages will contain the names of the world's peerless heroines in the field of charity."

—Reverend Mark A. Mathews
To the Ladies' Hebrew Benevolent Society, 1903

"Let people who criticize our work visit the poor and see for themselves; let them visit the aged mother whose son was cared for during illness until death ended his sufferings; let them visit the widow with four children whose husband committed suicide months before the last child was born; let them visit many others and they will not hinder but help our work."

—Lizzie Cooper
To the Ladies' Hebrew Benevolent Society, 1912

One of the major themes running throughout the 120-year history of JFS has been the need to raise money to support its work. From the start, income was primarily raised through efforts to attract and recruit new members whose annual dues, combined with fees charged for member teas, luncheons, and other social events, provided the funds used to help the poor and indigent clients of the agency.

The ladies soon began expanding their fundraising outreach. In 1901, they reached out to members of the business community by offering a series of merchant lunches. According to the *Seattle Daily Times,* one of the lunches was held in an upstairs room at Germania Hall, located at Second Avenue and Seneca Street, for three days from 11:00 a.m. to 2:00 p.m. with the menu changing daily. Attendance was expected to be large as the town was experiencing growth and prosperity and the ladies were known to be good cooks. On December 4, 1901, they served smoked salmon, bouillon, queen olives, celery, pickles, hot roast beef with mashed potatoes, cold turkey and cranberry sauce, sugar corn, potato salad, lettuce salad, fancy cakes, assorted fruits, cheese, salter wafers, and coffee.

An early effort to involve the broader Jewish community was a charity ball held in January of 1905 that grossed $569.67. The event was repeated the following year netting $739.40. Another 100 years would pass before the primary fundraising efforts were no longer based on recruiting new members and holding various entertainments.

In spite of the pressure to raise and distribute funds for the needy, the society regularly supported other worthy causes. For example, in October 1905, $10 was contributed to the Florence Crittendon Home for unwed mothers. (Opened in 1899, this was the only secular facility for unwed mothers in Seattle and continued to operate at its original site on Renton Avenue South until 1973.)

At a meeting on December 13, 1905, Rabbi Samuel Koch of Pensacola, Florida, was introduced to the membership, giving an interesting address on charity. Rabbi Koch, who became the senior rabbi of Temple de Hirsh in 1906 and continued in that role until

1942, became a major force in the development and strengthening of the Reform Jewish community in Seattle. He was a consistent advisor and supporter of the work of the Ladies' Hebrew Benevolent Society and later helped create the Seattle Community Fund (now United Way).

Caroline Kline Galland Home for the Aged

Caroline Kline Galland was another member of the community who devoted considerable energy and wealth to serving the poor of Seattle. Born Caroline Rosenberg in Germany, she was an early resident of Seattle. She married Lazarus "Louis" Kline of Kline and Rosenberg Clothing and the Kline and Rosenberg Building at First and Cherry. When he died in 1892, she inherited a real estate empire. Her second marriage to Bonham Galland took place in 1903. It was said she never turned down a request for help, and when she died in 1907, she left significant funds to several worthy causes including a bequest to build a home for the aged. Her will directed:

> It is my desire that the Caroline Kline Galland Home for the Aged be so constructed and managed that it may bring to the lives of the aged men and women who shall be domiciled therein the greatest degree of contentment and happiness in their declining years ... There shall be admitted all aged and feeble Jewish men and women and also members of the Universal Religion.

Litigation generated by Kline Galland's other heirs tied the will up in court for years, and then it took more time to liquidate the extensive real estate holdings that made up the bulk of the estate. The trustees found an existing home on 10 acres near the Wildwood Station on the Renton Interurban line at 7500 Wilson Avenue in Seward Park and bought it for $23,000.* The old, private home,

---

* Later Seward Park Avenue.

Dutton home, the original Kline Galland Home. (Kline Galland Center Photograph Collection. University of Washington.)

which had many rooms, became the Caroline Kline Galland Home for the Aged and Feeble Poor .

Although the *Seattle Times* described it in 1916 as a "big, roomy, modern residence," in an interview in 1979 Bernice Degginger Greengard remembered the original home (the Dutton home) as an old, dilapidated wooden building that was a firetrap and that some of the neighbors complained bitterly about it.[1] There was room for seven residents with one woman and five men being the first occupants, and a waiting list before it was even opened. When it opened, the trustees planned a new home costing $150,000, but that was never built.* Over the years, there were several additions, including an expansion project in 1930, but the original house remained with upgrades and frequent small fixes until, in 1967, the fire marshal threatened to close the building down. Despite the tentative condition of the house itself, the location proved quite prescient. Today, the modern Caroline Kline Galland Home, built on the expansive property and beautiful setting, is a valued community asset.

Caroline Kline Galland's last will and testament directed that the oversight of the operation would be the responsibility of a four-

---

* $2.5 million in 2011 dollars (www.measuringworth.com).

person advisory board, made up of the president and secretary of Temple de Hirsch and the president and secretary of the Ladies' Hebrew Benevolent Society, likely also to be members of Temple de Hirsch. Voting power was vested in these four members, and structurally the board could not be enlarged without an order from a court. Later, one additional, non-voting person from each of the two organizations was added to the advisory board. Kline Galland's directive also provided that, if accumulation from the income of her estate was in excess of the amount provided for the home, "the LHBS should be allocated $5,000 to be used to alleviate poverty but not to encourage mendacity."

The four-member advisory board investigated and approved all applications for residence in the home until 1937. At that time, Mae Goldsmith, executive secretary of the former LHBS, began processing the applications. (The LHBS had been renamed the Jewish Welfare Society in 1929.) Goldsmith became the Kline Galland Home's fieldworker and was formally invited to attend board meetings.

In 1967, the officers of the advisory board were still those six appointees. Then, when the organization was about to launch a campaign to build a new Caroline Kline Galland building, one non-voting representative was added to the advisory board from each of four other synagogues—Herzl, Bikur Cholim, Beth Am, and Sephardic Bikur Holim. Governance was still in the hands of Seattle Trust and Savings Bank, which meant that when Kline Galland advisory board member Sol Esfeld took on the responsibility of raising funds to build the new home, the checks were payable to the bank, not to the home. Years later, land-use attorney John Phillips recalled his battles with the neighbors each time the Kline Galland began a new expansion.

Josh Gortler, executive director of the Caroline Kline Galland Home from 1969 to 2006, explained, "Until 1975, Kline Galland was an appendix of a bank, Seattle Trust." It wasn't until 1967, by superior court decision, that the board was enlarged from four to 15.

On the volunteer side, the ladies of the Jewish Welfare Society (JWS) began making monthly visits to the home, during which they would often take the residents for rides around the area.

Some of the original rules for the home might seem harsh by today's standards. These rules included:

Applicants for admission to the Home or to receive its benefits must be worthy or infirm men or women, over fifty five years of age. In extreme and meritorious cases, infirm and poor persons under the age of fifty may, in the discretion of the Board, be admitted to the Home.

Applicants shall be of good character, and shall furnish such references and such information with respect to themselves ...

...residents from King county receiving first consideration.

Applicants for admission to the Home shall be free from mental or contagious disease.

Persons blind or physically helpless are not eligible for admission.

If at any time the mental condition of the guests becomes such that in the opinion of a physician acceptable to the Advisory Board, he or she is no longer a proper person to be retained in the Home, ... such person must be removed therefrom by the party seeking his or her admission.

Guests of the Caroline Kline Galland Home ... shall sign [and] ... agree to ... convey and transfer ... any and all money and property of value ..., life insurance policies or endowments or lodge benefits....

Guests had to apply to the superintendent for permission to go out, and male and female guests could not visit in each other's rooms. Visitors were welcome on Wednesdays, Saturdays, and Sundays from two to five p.m. and were expected to call upon the superintendent to obtain permission to visit the rooms of guests.

As far as celebrations in the facility:

> It shall be the duty of the Board to observe annually the natal anniversary (December 8th) and the Yarzheit, February 13th) of Caroline Kline Galland. The natal anniversary to be in the nature of a community reception and entertainment and the Yarzheit in the nature of a memorial.

From time to time, a guest who had been admitted to the home would experience a "failure to make an adjustment" and would be asked to leave. It wasn't until 1948 that the home adopted a more lenient policy under which the social workers of Jewish Family & Child Service (JFCS) studied each situation to see if there were alternatives before a decision was made to ask the guest to leave.

Society caseworkers and member volunteers continued to provide social work services to Kline Galland residents up to three days a week. In September 1959, a full-time caseworker was hired by the home, but even then, all potential residents were first screened by the JFCS social workers who presented their findings to the Admissions Committee. Each applicant's situation was described in detail, and it was then the committee's decision whether to accept the person. At that time, Kline Galland served only 75 people, and there was a long waiting list. JFCS workers continued to help the workers prioritize who would best benefit from services at the facility until 1966 when the home began conducting its own admissions studies.

As this era ended, Sol Frankel, the executive director of the Caroline Kline Galland Home wrote in The *Jewish Transcript*:

> The JF&CS has provided excellent service for many years to applicants to the Home and their families. The warmth, skill and sensitivity exercised by the staff has greatly facilitated the adjustment of residents to the Home.

⌒∞⌒

Over the decades, the name of what began as the Ladies' Hebrew Benevolent Society changed several times. The first name change came on May 2, 1917, when the men's group, Seattle Hebrew Benevolent Society (founded in September 1895), merged with the LHBS and six of the men formed an advisory committee intended to assist with legal, financial, and funding decisions. The new organization became the Hebrew Benevolent Society (HBS) and operated under that name from 1917 to 1929. In addition to consolidating the raising of money and the delivery of services, this change was probably motivated by the recent entry of the United States into the Great War—World War I. The mission changed to "minister the needs of newcomers who arrive penniless and without possessions."

For 25 years, all the work of the society was accomplished primarily by board members with the occasional participation of member volunteers. Mae Goldsmith later recalled:

> Those in need called at the homes of either the president or members of the board, and then the family was assigned to one of the visitors who would carry a basket of food, clothing, or if needed, cash. Remember, there were few street cars and this meant climbing the hills to make the visits.

In 1917, another significant development occurred when Florine Coblentz became the first paid clerical worker. She performed her tasks from the home of Ida Cohen, the president of the board from 1917 to 1920 (then served again for the 1921-1922 term). In 1920, Coblentz was given a salary of $75, and an office was established with the provision of a desk at the Young Men's Hebrew Association (YMHA) at 1403 17th Avenue. Gertrude Pearl offered her services as a volunteer to write letters and perform stenographic work, joining Coblentz at the YMHA. This arrangement continued until 1922 when the first HBS office was established in suite 611 of the Pacific Block, later known as the Smith Tower Annex. The offices of the society remained in that location until 1947.

As the 1920s roared in, HBS was able to extend its ability to provide medical assistance to needy clients with the volunteer work of Dr. A. J. Davidson and Dr. Irvin Weichbrodt. Later, Dr. Harry Friedman joined the ranks of the physicians offering their services. Louis Rubenstein provided medicines, and other physicians became involved with the work of the society, including Dr. Trudeau, Dr. Henry Bories, Dr. Philip Schoenwald, Dr. Frederick Falk, and Dr. S. Maimon Samuels.

The board welcomed attorney Melvin Monheimer, who began providing legal services to the society. He continued in that role for decades and would be succeeded by his son Melville, who joined the board in 1949 and continued to serve as legal advisor throughout his active career.

Bernice Degginger (later Greengard), the first paid professional worker, tells of a professional caseworker from New York named Miss Berman who reported for work at HBS September 15, 1922. However, she did not find the situation to be to her liking and soon returned to New York. Degginger replaced this woman and became the executive secretary. Before there were professional caseworkers, several members of the board would each accept three or four families to care for. With a basket of food on their arm, they would visit families and work to discover what was needed and what help could be provided and then report to the appropriate committee. Degginger would remember later that these women were wonderfully committed to providing assistance but were not always terribly realistic, as they sometimes complained if a family did not keep house as well as their own homes were kept (which Degginger recognized would have been impossible for them to do).

In the 1979 interview with Bernice Degginger Greengard conducted by Meta Buttnick for the Jewish Historical Society, we learn that the executive secretary was responsible for the casework. Most of her work was with Russian Ashkenazi and Sephardic immigrants whose primary problems were economic, and they needed help adjusting to the new society so that they could find employment.

As she began her new role, Degginger's goal was first to provide for the most basic needs of food, shelter, and clothing and to help the immigrants start learning a Western (American) way of living. There was always the recognition that a person needs basic survival first, and then assistance could be given in job finding and other concerns. She met regularly with the Sephardic and Russian groups that had formed to help take care of their own people, particularly assisting with the language problems.

During the 1992 celebration of the 100th anniversary of the agency, Degginger Greengard was quoted in the *Mishpacha* (the agency newsletter) saying, "The aim was social service first. They got what they needed most. After all, you can't teach a person traditions or anything else when their tummies are empty. They had to have jobs and they had to have money first."

After the most basic needs were met, other issues, like juvenile delinquency and marital or family discord, could be addressed. Greengard gave advice, although she remarked, "Who was I to give counseling?" She recalls that the juvenile court would provide someone to go to a home with her to help with difficult issues concerning recalcitrant youth. One case involved a girl who was determined to become the madam of the most expensive "house" in town, and there was no talking her out of it.

Degginger also recalled one especially difficult case in which a man was a compulsive gambler. He made a decent wage, but if he received his check, it would be gone before he got home, so she would personally collect the check from the employer each week and take it to the wife.

Some of Degginger's work involved the many single transient men who were housed primarily at the Hebrew Immigrant Aid Society (HIAS) Settlement House, at 17th and Jefferson where they slept and were provided with three meals a day. The men who were escaping from service in the Red Army and coming to Seattle through Harbin and Shanghai in China, seemed to her more stable and responsible, trying to make new lives for themselves in a new country. But many others were more like tramps moving from city to city. "They would take everything they could for three days and then they'd go on," she said.

A few years later, she wrote in her annual report:

> The progress made in the efficiency of this organization since I started as secretary for the first time in 1921 is astounding. At this time one volunteer secretary kept and filed all case records, attended to all correspondence and recorded all the minutes, her office being her home. As you know, the work is now being handled in a downtown office with far greater efficiency, by an executive secretary and a professional stenographer. The office of corresponding secretary has also been created.

The society was also trying to increase the professionalism of the casework. The annual report in 1927 states:

> One of our hardest problems is dealing with transient men. We have established a check system with all coast agencies, including Portland, San Francisco, Los Angeles, Oakland and Duluth, Minneapolis and St. Paul, whereby we mail out each day a description of those who come

into our office for aid and these agencies mail to us their like reports. In that way we can check and know what help had been given to these transients. In the last year we secured 44 jobs for 44 men.

Many of these transients have deserted their families and are living from day to day with the help of agencies. Some are vagrants. Our organization does not condemn them without investigation and during the period of investigation immediate emergency relief is given. Help was given in accordance with the rules of the National Conference of Social Service of which we are a member.

Members of the society were instructed not to distribute help from individual business offices. Supplicants were to be directed to the HBS.

Degginger gave out tickets for board and lodging at the Puget Sound Hotel and referred people to the Hebrew Free Loan Society if she felt they would be able to establish a small business with a bit of help. Dora Zeeve, who managed the loans for many years, once told Degginger that she had promised the founder, Jennie Friedman, on her deathbed that she would carry on the work of the Free Loan Society.

In 1921, what we know today as United Way was organized as the Seattle Community Fund, later called the Community Chest. This was different from the 1892 Bureau of Associated Charities, which attempted to deliver relief directly to recipients. The Community Chest combined the fundraising of 43 separate charitable health and welfare agencies. The Hebrew Benevolent Society, which was one of the first organizations to join, received $550.83 in the first monthly allotment from the community campaign.

The committed women who took on responsibilities as officers of the organization did an astounding amount of work. Viola Silver served as secretary in 1921 reporting the following year that between March 1921 and March 1922 she had attended 43 regular board meetings, four special board meetings, nine regular monthly membership meetings, and five luncheon meetings, for a total of 61 meetings, recording complete minutes of each. In addition, her office as secretary of the HBS meant that she also served as secretary of the Caroline Kline Galland Home board. It was during this year that the Kline Galland board began plans for the first wing of what at the time was considered a modern brick home.

In her description of the work of the Hebrew Benevolent Society, Silver reported, "During this time 260 old cases and 97 new ones were handled, making a total of 357 cases," and one part of her duties was to record the discussions and history relative to each case. She also sent thank-you letters for every donation, cards of condolence, letters of acceptance to each new member, plus miscellaneous business correspondence, making a total of 518 letters, and 39 telegrams.

During the year ending March 1921, membership in the HBS reached 401 members (280 women, 72 men, and 49 junior members). One year later, membership had increased to 512.

Viola Silver closed her report with an acknowledgement of the progress made with the establishment of an office and the assistance of Mrs. Coblenz from nine to noon, her afternoons being devoted to fieldwork. Silver's final message was a hope that within the next few years a professional director and more office staff would be added. Board president Henrietta Schneider reported in 1923 that 69 transient men had been assisted in the previous four months at an average cost of $1.78 per man, with employment having been found for 11 of these men. She also reported that an average of 62 families were assisted each month at a cost of $7.58 per individual per month, and that a number of children had been provided clothing in time for the start of the school year.

Having developed their own support systems, the members of the Sephardic community did not usually become members of the Hebrew Benevolent Society. However, they did participate in the charitable work. One valuable contribution was made through a sewing club, which provided clothing and sleeping garments for the children for many years. The relationship was reflected in a 1925 report stating:

> We still continue a close cooperation with the Sephardic Jews meeting with heads of various congregations and clubs as the occasion demands. We are compelled to segregate this group and make note of it, particularly, as they do not assimilate the language or the notions of our community as the Russian or German Jews.

Becoming a member of the board was no small commitment, and the 22 women who served kept very busy. During the 19 months from March 1924 to October 1925, there were 36 regular board meetings, seven special board meetings, 15 meetings with the Sephardic Committee, and 1,089 visits to various families.

As the culture of the agency turned towards more professional services, it continued to provide for the most basic needs of clients. Food baskets still were provided, and immigrants were met at the boat and the train, but the work became more professional, and family casework became an integral part of the agency. This change was reflected in the president's report of 1925: "Our first duty is to meet promptly the immediate needs and sympathetically find the cause and remove it."

The work with families fell into three main groups, generally represented by the widow with young children unable to leave her home to go out to work, the aged couple unable to maintain themselves independently, and the foreign father with a large family of small children who was incapable of earning a sufficient amount to meet his family's needs. With the first group, the Hebrew Benevolent Society created a budget of the family's requirements, assisted in obtaining a mother's pension if she was eligible, and the woman who was handling the case as a "friendly visitor" visited the family at least twice a month.

Widows also received regular visits, and efforts were made to help them get connected to other women and to social support through their synagogues. Visitors also coached immigrant women on American ways of raising children and learning to live in their new country.

The large families living on too small an income were assisted with budgeting and provided with clothing and shoes for the children and a bit of extra assistance for food and for heat in the winter.

The visitors paid close attention to all the needs of each client, including the progress of the children in school and the health and dental needs of all, helping them acquire eyeglasses or dentures or other important items in addition to food and appropriate clothing. A team of volunteer doctors, dentists, and lawyers donated their time to help, and a large cupboard of clothes in every size and description was kept in the office.

A 1925 report, possibly given by president Gertrude Shopera, (president 1923-1925, 1926-1929, and 1932-1933) told of cold, hungry, ill, and unemployed migratory or transient men who would also apply for assistance. They would be given meal tickets, a night's lodging, and warm clothing. They were allowed assistance for only three days. After that, they either found work or left the city. If they were ill, they were taken care of until able to work again.

Shopera continued, "Sometimes a young man of 18 or 19, just starting on his hobo life comes to the office for aid. He has left his home to see the world or because of family disagreements." The society would try to find work for the young man but would also try to help re-establish the connection to the family. One young boy was sent to Canada from England by his father "to make good." He tried working as a prizefighter but did not succeed and began selling his clothes to survive, finally drifting to Seattle. He was discovered in Chinatown, completely destitute. The father was notified, and within two weeks, the boy was on his way to New York to meet his father and go home. The young man wrote, thanking the society for its assistance and assuring them that he had learned his lesson and was happily at work with his father.

Another type of work was correspondence cases. Letters would be received from organizations in other cities requesting intervention on behalf of a relative, help locating a missing son or daughter, or assistance finding a home for an orphaned child or aged relative. One letter was from a widowed mother in London in search of her son. She knew he had been in Seattle and was a member of a union there. With this slight clue, the society was able to locate the young man, who then wrote a letter to his mother explaining that he had been ashamed to write to her because he was unable to enclose the check he usually sent to her.

In one month in 1925, 23 single men were given food, lodging, and other assistance at a cost of $124.54, plus 46 articles of clothing. During the same period, 87 families (comprised of 321 individuals) were helped, including the provision of 967 quarts of milk.

One effort was begun at this time that would appear again later in the century as the Big Pals program. In the 1920s, it was found to be beneficial for young boys whose fathers were not active in their lives to be paired with a "big brother." Social-minded young men were asked to volunteer to be an occasional companion to a fatherless boy, and they usually found that this work gave them as much pleasure as was received by the child.

In another 1925 report, the president, Shopera, discussed the finances of the organization, reporting that disbursements regularly exceeded income by $200 to $300 each month and that while they were very pleased to have been informed by the Community Chest that the allocation would increase in the coming year by $100 a month, she urged "Ways and Means Committee [to] meet at once to try to find ways and means" to cover the deficit. Those Community Chest allocations continued to grow over the next year or two becoming $12,000 and then $14,000 a year.

The 35th Annual Luncheon was held February 16, 1927. The program included sketches about the organization and a complete history of the agency, written by Jessie Danz and read by Minnie Goldstein. They were assisted by Louise Stern and Rachel Silverstone. Members Carrie Bories and Edna Nagler were elected to the board.

Members kept busy working on a variety of committees. In 1927, Rose Lurie was chair of a successful Sewing Committee,

Libby Goldsby was chair of the Membership Committee, Dora Kane headed the Old Clothes Committee, and Mina Eckstein, the New Garment Guild. Mrs. Klineberg (first name unknown) led the Ways and Means Committee, and Minnie Freidberg was chair of the Telephone Committee.

1. "Galland Home Opens for Aged Poor, Open to Sufferers," *Seattle Daily Times*, August 7, 1916, 11.

Chapter 4

Aging & Adult Programs

Aging & Adult Programs represents one of the earliest programs of Jewish Family Service. Needy elderly immigrants, often unable to communicate their needs in English, were grateful for the assistance received from the ladies of the 1890s and 1900s who visited with baskets on their arms, bringing a little food, a warm blanket, a kind word, and a gentle smile.

Today the majority of services the agency offers are provided to individuals over the age of 60 through three distinct programs designed specifically to address the needs of older people: Aging & Adult Programs, Endless Opportunities, and HomeCare Associates.

For many years, what is now called Aging & Adult Programs was called Senior Services until senior clients decided they did not want to be called senior. From its earliest days, the society had been one of the primary resources for older Jewish adults needing help with housing, food, family issues, financial emergencies, and the myriad of other issues the older generation often faces. The original kosher food shelf, perhaps dating from as early as 1922 when the first office was established, was kept primarily for these clients. In addition, a committee of the society's directors reviewed all applications to the Caroline Kline Galland Home, and another helped manage the operations of the Home.

One of the early mentions of programming specifically for the aged (besides the Caroline Kline Galland Home) was documented in board minutes in 1953 after then executive director Albert S. White returned from participating in the National Conference of Jewish Communal Service in Atlantic City. He noted that agencies across the country were experiencing increased requests for services for older people. Jewish family agencies were defining as their responsibility the job of helping older people who were not chronically ill to maintain independent living arrangements through homemaker services, casework help, and employment opportunities. Some organizations were even setting up housing facilities suitable for older people.

Board discussions on the topic were held sporadically over the next decade, and many references to specific programming coincide with the period of time during which Jerry Grossfeld was executive director (1965–1974). An experimental project for providing casework services specifically for senior citizens was proposed in 1966 to address a problem long recognized throughout the Jewish community.

This problem often started with the change that occurred as a person moved from an economically productive position in society to (often unwanted) retirement. Seniors not only faced loss of status but also frequently dealt with illness or death of a spouse and friends, medical problems of their own, and fear of their own death or senility. The golden years were often filled with loneliness and feelings of uselessness and hopelessness.

At the time, the Jewish Community Center of Seattle (JCCS), in a co-sponsored program with the National Council of Jewish Women, Jewish Family & Child Service (JFCS, as the agency was once again renamed in 1947), and the Caroline Kline Galland Home, provided services to the aged Jewish population. Kline Galland services were restricted to residents of the home and their families. JCCS reached as many as 400 seniors through the classes and discussion groups they offered.

Jerry Grossfeld recruited Thelma Coney in 1966 immediately after she received her master's degree from the University of

Washington School of Social Work. Coney remembers Grossfeld as a wonderful person, supportive of the staff, and willing to be flexible so that requests like adjusting a schedule to accommodate the need to be home when children returned from school were easily accepted. Coney's caseload dealt with a variety of clients, including elderly people (whom she always enjoyed working with), couples, children, and a number of adoptions.

The staff was very upset when Grossfeld left to take a new position in Denver, Colorado. Supported by Grossfeld's recommendation to the board, Coney took on the responsibilities of acting director for about 18 months. Overall, she spent what she remembers as 12 wonderful years at JFCS. The services she provided to her older clients usually involved many of the same case-management services that are provided today: making sure that medical appointments are made and kept; appropriate meals, housekeeping, and homecare are accomplished as necessary; at least a minimum amount of social contact is provided when possible; and generally overseeing the health and welfare of the client.

In those earlier days, if an elderly client reached the point where staying home was no longer feasible, and if he or she was willing to go to the Caroline Kline Galland Home, the social worker at JFCS would write a report that went to the board of JFCS and to Kline Galland. The applicant's name would be put on a waiting list for a placement, and when the individual's name came up, the social worker would review the case before the Kline Galland Admissions Committee (which was a co-JFCS committee). Coney remembers the process as slightly nerve-racking because placements in the Kline Galland were scarce and the social worker was trying to persuade the committee that this person needed to leave his or her private home and move to the home. Coney's respect for Kline Galland has never wavered. She describes it as an excellent institution with exceptional care for people and always open to any kind of suggestion from JFCS staff members.

When working with the elderly, a staff member was expected to remain professional but also would often become a friend. Some of the elderly clients lived in the National Council of Jewish Women's Council House, which Coney remembers as "a very nice place." One of her clients always had cookies and tea waiting for her. Another was an Egyptian woman who was a "colorful, lovely person." She didn't have much contact with family, so Coney keeping in touch by phone and visiting frequently was important to her life.

During the late 1960s and '70s, JFCS instituted new services to provide more support for elderly clients. One of these services, developed by a couple of board members, became what today is called Friendly Visitors. This service arranges for volunteers to visit specific elderly clients and create one-on-one relationships with them. Before that program was developed, social workers had acted in this capacity, occasionally making recommendations for changes in the way various clients were living. In addition, in November of 1970, following a successful one-year demonstration program, JFCS also launched a homecare program for the elderly.

When Coney left Jewish Family & Child Service in 1978, she missed her work with those elderly clients and discussed with program director Debby Baskin the need for guardianship services for some of them. Coney was then able to reconnect with JFCS and Kline Galland as she developed a guardianship program, which she continued to provide for Jewish and non-Jewish clients from the 1970s until 2005, when her "last client left this world."

Sarah Barash was the director of services for the elderly for 17 years. Her parents had immigrated to the United States as children—her father from Poland, her mother from Russia. Her father worked as a junk peddler during 1930s and into the 1940s when precious metals were needed for the war effort. After the war, he opened a plumbing supply store.

Barash was born and raised in Denver, Colorado. After two years at the University of Denver, she transferred to Stern College for Women in New York, the sister college for Yeshiva University. There she met Josh Gortler, who was studying for his master's in social work at Yeshiva. They first met on a double date to the Yiddish theater, and soon after she graduated, they married.

When Josh Gortler accepted the position of director of the Caroline Kline Galland Home in Seattle, sight unseen, Barash was happy to be moving back to the mountains and water. She taught school for several years, until after her children reached junior high school. She then returned to school to earn a master's in counseling at Seattle University.

She joined the staff of the JFS Senior Services program in February of 1985, just before director Debby Baskin left the agency. Barash became the program director, finding the position to be quite varied in its responsibilities. Case management was a significant portion of the work as she spent most of her time seeing clients at the office, at Council House, and at the Caroline Kline Galland Home. This is when she started using her maiden name at work because her married name of Gortler was so associated with her husband's work at the Caroline Kline Galland Home that clients would often be afraid that she was going to recommend they be moved from their private homes to the Kline Galland facility.

Another of her responsibilities was managing what had become a larger and still growing Friendly Visitors service. At the time, many women were homemakers and more willing to do volunteer work. Barash says that it has been harder to recruit Friendly Visitors in recent years as many women remain in the workforce after marriage.

The large caseload of approximately 125 senior services clients received various services. Some participated in the Friendly Visitors program, many received case management, some received food from the food pantry, and some received kosher food vouchers for the purchase of meat at Varon's Kosher Meats. There was also a service in which seniors would be telephoned by a telephone-reassurance volunteer on a regular basis, and the volunteer would have an opportunity to ask if there was anything the senior clients needed and make sure they were doing all right. These regular contacts enabled staff members to be kept up-to-date and respond to whatever issues might arise. In addition to managing the program for seniors, during the time the office was on Boylston and the food bank was a little shelf in the closet, counselors came to Barash's office needing food for their clients who were waiting in the counselor's office. She was also responsible for the emergency financial assistance program until Carol Mullin joined the staff in 1988.

Taking care of a typical case-management client began with a visit to see the person and performing an assessment to determine what was needed. Sometimes the follow-up required filling out applications for Medicaid and in-home health care through the Washington State Community Options Program Entry System (COPES) for people who qualify for a nursing home but wish to stay in their homes. COPES also paid for care in adult family homes, adult residential care facilities, and assisted living facilities. Without COPES, more people would need to be in nursing homes. The state provided the aging program's clients with a specified number of hours of in-home care, and the counselor would arrange for a health care agency to provide companion care, which might include assistance with such things as bathing, cooking, shopping, hygiene, and medication monitoring.

Soon the agency contracted with the Catholic Community Services homecare program. Catholic Community Services would place an employee in the home to provide personal care service to the JFCS client, with JFCS staff providing case management, intervening if the client was not receiving the expected care or if the caretaker needed more instruction about the medical needs of the client. Sometimes caregivers needed more information about specific Jewish issues of their clients, which might include dietary restrictions and Sabbath observances.

Barash still provided the assessment, filled out the forms confirming financial eligibility, and interfaced with the Department of Social and Health Services. She continued to see her frail, elderly clients, monitoring their medical appointments and in-home care and any financial assistance they received from JFCS. Barash feels that the agency remains the Cadillac of services for seniors. Many other services open a case, provide whatever service is required, and then close the case. JFS continues contact with clients, recognizing that very often, as people age, they will need continuous casework. With this continuity, the clients learn to interface and trust the staff as they interact with them over time. Staff also works with clients' adult children, advising them about the changing needs of their parents.

As Barash became more familiar with the situation of each of her clients, she was able to whittle down her caseload from 125 clients to 65 or 70. Over time, additional resources were added until there were four part-time staff members sharing the workload. During 2012, three staff members managed the older adult programs. Barash stepped down from her position as director in 2004 but remained on the staff working three days a week. In 2012 the program was providing service to about 80 clients, although there was quite a surge in requests for assistance as the baby boomers began to call for support.

The question of how the needs of the baby boomers will be met with the same level and quality of service is being considered across the country and is a significant concern. The service is very expensive in terms of staff time, with many clients requiring a great deal. Several years ago, the agency held focus groups with people who were of retirement age, asking them if JFS should charge for services. They all said yes, so JFS created a fee scale and was planning to charge for services. However, in practice, it became obvious that people were not willing to pay. The number of clients who elected to use JFS services when a fee was mentioned was initially zero. (The name of the agency was changed in 1978.)

At the present time, the fee scale is still in place. However, older adults often have limited resources, and while children or grandchildren might pay for an assessment, they are often unwilling to pay for additional services. For some, services are paid for by insurance, and when older adults have used up their resources, they might be eligible for Medicaid. A few clients pay as little as five dollars. Unfortunately, two or three hours of filling out forms for COPES (or for other services) is costly. Barash expects that at some point appropriate fees will have to be charged.

Very often people who live in Seattle bring their parents from other places, perhaps the East Coast or California. Having family close can provide emotional, financial, and physical support for senior parents, and the adult children care about and want to be supportive of their parents. This means they are often putting themselves into the awkward role of being the sandwich generation (needing to provide assistance to their parents on one side and to their children on the other). The availability of retirement and assisted living homes and apartments greatly increased in recent years, and once a parent goes into assisted living or a nursing home, some of the pressure is often taken off the adult children. The advent of those facilities proved to be an attractive option for many people who had been staying in their own homes.

Somewhere in the range of 80 percent of the baby boomer generation say they want to stay in their own homes, and many will need a variety of services. The expectation is that there will be a significant increase in the number of senior clients for whom the Aging & Adult Program will be asked to provide services.

At one time, the agency petitioned the court for guardianship on behalf of clients unable to manage their own affairs, paying the court fee and interfacing with the guardian ad litem appointed to represent the client, but the agency stopped the practice after several incidents made it clear that such arrangements often were extremely difficult and complex and took an enormous commitment of time and effort. They also put the agency at risk of legal entanglements.

In one case the client suffered from dementia. JFS received a call from her bank. The bank was concerned because the woman had befriended a street person, brought the person into the bank, and wrote out a check of considerable value. It was quite apparent that the woman was unable to manage her finances. In fact, she was not capable of handling many of her daily affairs. Working hand in hand with Adult Protective Services, JFS caseworkers petitioned the court as she was in dire need of a guardian to manage and protect her finances. The judge agreed. Thelma Coney, who had previously worked at JFS, was appointed as the client's guardian. They met weekly making sure she was eating and that her bills were paid. The woman who had been in the bank with the client had not only fleeced her of funds, but committed financial fraud and elder abuse as well. Legal action was initiated.

In the late 1980s, JFS received a $5,000 grant from the Conference on Jewish Material Claims Against Germany (also called the Claims Conference) to be used solely for Holocaust survivors to provide case management and financial assistance for emergency bills, dental bills, electricity, doctors, glasses, dentures, and other needs.* Over the years, money has also been set aside for HomeCare Associates (HCA) to provide in-home care at no charge for Holocaust survivors who qualify financially. (HCA is a JFS program that provides personal care and homemaker services to people requiring assistance while living in their own homes.)

Two of the grants from the Claims Conference—the Harry and Jeanette Weinberg Foundation and the Holocaust Survivors Emergency Assistance Program (HSEAP)—may be used for medical bills, dental bills (which is the biggest need), rent, food and other essential needs. For example, the agency once paid for new carpeting for a man who had severe allergies caused by mold in his carpeting.

Generally, the maximum given to each Holocaust survivor is $2,500. For some clients, this amount is insufficient to meet their unique needs. Another client, for example, resides in a retirement facility. She lives with a disabling disease that requires her to use various costly supplies and medications but is running out of money. JFS pays her co-insurance and the bills for some of her equipment.

JFS also receives funding for case management services for Holocaust survivors. The agency has a number of clients who qualify, and there are lengthy forms the staff completes on their behalf. When the survivors receive the grants, they contract with the JFS HomeCare Associates program for a homecare assistant.

---

* The Claims Conference was established in 1952 between Jewish organizations and the Federal Republic of Germany to compensate Holocaust victims.

In 2010, some of the Claims Conference workers were found to have defrauded the system of $60 million or more by faking paperwork in the names of people who were not Holocaust survivors. After this, the rules changed so that much more paperwork is now required, making the work more arduous and time consuming for agency staff. Survivors now have to prove that they are survivors, which is often difficult since the Nazis did not issue discharge certificates from the concentration camps. Those who escaped persecution by hiding or adopting non-Jewish identities have no proof either.

Applications were prepared for an 87-year-old survivor who never married, has no immediate family, and receives homecare from JFS. The application process was very complicated as the client's dementia precluded providing the required information. This resulted in more paperwork. A neighbor has since agreed to assume the durable power of attorney on the survivor's behalf.

Don Armstrong, director of the JFS HomeCare Associates program, has secured a grant for family caregiver support under which the Older Adult staff provides six sessions of counseling on how to care for an older person.

The older adult program charges fees for various services, although the fees are on a very liberal sliding scale. However, Holocaust survivors are not asked to pay directly because their fees are collected through the Claims Conference.

During the 1990s, the program (then called Senior Services) operated a homemakers referral service but found that clients were not satisfied with many of the homecare workers that were being provided. In addition, staff was spending a great amount of time trying to be the go-between for people who wanted to provide homecare and the clients who needed the service. At the same time, it was thought that expanding the service into a licensed homecare program might provide a steady source of revenue to help support the work of the agency. After thorough discussion and investigation by the board, JFS began the process of developing its own in-house service, now called HomeCare Associates.

The Friendly Visitors service, still in place from the 1890s, is now primarily used to visit senior clients. Friendly Visitor volunteers are expected to visit their senior "friend" weekly, document each visit, and make a commitment for at least six months.

For Barash, one of the biggest challenges is finding the time to take care of her continuing clients as she takes on new ones. It is also difficult to balance the services needed with the services for which a client is able and willing to pay. Barash calls her clients frequently, making sure everything is okay.

Her counseling clients are also careful about the expense involved and may agree to participate in a counseling session only every three to four weeks.

Barash thinks that, as the baby boomers reach their senior years, JFS will have to more carefully control the care-management services it provides. The issue will be exasperated because the following generation will not be large enough to pay for the baby boomers' needs, and the cost of care will skyrocket. Older adults will be afraid of depleting their life savings,

When Sarah Barash stepped down as director of Senior Services, Jane Relin assumed the responsibility.

Relin loves working with the elderly. "The problems they face are very complex and very difficult," she says. "You don't solve them; you just help people cope with things. But the elderly are also very grateful. They appreciate what you do and are grateful for your help, and that's very nice."

Jane Relin, whose parents' families were from the same town in Ukraine, was born and raised in Rochester, New York. She received her bachelor's degree in chemistry from Barnard, taught for a few years, and then raised her family. After moving to Seattle, she earned a master's in social work at the University of Washington.

Relin has worked in social services for almost 30 years. She served as clinical director in a mental health center and was executive of another. She also taught geriatric mental health at the University of Washington.

When she joined JFS in 2006, the agency had just completed the strategic planning process and had decided to expand services for older adults. The agency needed a program director who had experience in geriatrics and administration. Relin had both and was the first person hired under the new strategic plan expansion.

She works with a team of geriatric care managers. Relin explains that care management and case management are different. Case management follows individual clients confirming that their medical and other appointments, care givers and financial arrangements are all in place and functioning properly. Care management focuses on health and support, helping people live long term but also helping people understand what their illnesses are, the complications of the illness, the medications that they use, and how they affect their life and mental health.

Three years after Relin became the director of what at the time was called Services for Older Adults, the director of Counseling Services position came open, and Relin agreed to take on that role too. By moving some of her responsibilities to others, she was able to manage the two departments as director of both of these very core pieces of the agency's mission.

In the Aging & Adult Program, there are three geriatric care managers; in the counseling program, three counselors. The two programs share an intake assistant specialist. A clinical supervisor added to assist Relin works with the counselors one day a week on the clinical issues, which helps increase their expertise and skill.

Externs will be added to the counseling program and possibly interns from the University of Washington School of Social Work. (An extern is somebody who has already graduated from a master's program and must acquire two years of supervised practice before being licensed; an intern is a student placement.)

The Aging & Adult Programs frequently receives phone calls from people who say something like, "I'm going to move my mother here from New York. We are wondering if there is a retirement community that provides a Jewish environment. How will she do?" These callers are told that the Summit at First Hill (a housing facility offering independent and assisted living) operated by Kline Galland and the Caroline Kline Galland Home are the only Jewish facilities, although there are other senior residences that are very Jewish friendly. The Kline Galland and Summit are both kosher and have religious observances.

When Relin first took over Aging & Adult Programs, she reorganized the department so that everybody would take a turn responding to information and assistance calls and each person does counseling and care management. Caseloads have remained constant at about 40 per counselor, a combination of care and case management and counseling. There is always an emotional component when making care arrangements or when working with families that are in distress enough to come for help. Each of the counselors is a geriatric care manager, which is a new profession that has developed around the country. They have to be educated not only in physical health problems and resources but also in emotional aspects, as many of the decisions that have to be made as people age are emotion related.

Relin teaches a "Caring for Your Aging Parent" series through the JFS Family Life Education (FLE) program where she looks at issues like long-distance care giving. A great many of the calls that ensue are from adult children who are caring for an aging parent and are concerned for the parent's safety. Seattle has a large number of people who have moved away from their families and whose parents have aged, live in the East, and are not doing well. The children want their parents to be safe, and the parents want their children to leave them alone. The series discusses dignity versus safety, or dignity of risk, and addresses this dichotomy, helping children understand how to help their parents without taking away their freedom or their dignity because no one wants his or her children telling him or her what to do.

The case managers often work with families where the older adult does not want the care the children think he or she should have to remain safe. Sometimes all the children can do is wait for an emergency that puts the parents in a different situation where they need to accept the help.

In 2012, the geriatric care managers for Aging & Adult Programs assisted 211 clients. Information on dementia and on various resources in the community are offered, and in 2013, a program called "When to Worry" was offered for families seeking information on caring for their elderly parents/grandparents. The program provided information on how one can know when parents need help and how adult children can talk to their parents about it.

One lecture presented for the baby boomers was on the subject of "How to Sign Up for Social Security and Medicare," presented by Eva Genauer, a professional who is very knowledgeable and helpful with these complex topics. One of the pieces of information that Genauer told the group is that only about 10 percent of people are reviewing their plans every year, but the insurance companies are changing every year, and their formulas, deals, and products change. She reminded those attending that it is important to look at that every year.

Congregation Kol HaNeshamah originated a "Death and Dying" series because they have a young congregation and people did not know how to respond when there was a death in the community. The series is always presented by a rabbi with Relin or other staff person presenting the social service aspects—topics like "Getting Your Affairs in Order." Attorneys discuss the legal issues, and someone from the Jewish Chapel talks about Jewish burial rituals, so people can feel more comfortable in those situations.

Caseloads over the years have remained comparatively stable. One of the goals of the 2006 Strategic Plan was to make a stronger effort to reach out to people who have the wherewithal to pay. The program has always had a philosophy that people who are either unable or unwilling to pay will not be charged. Some clients who have significant means are being seen for free because they do not want to pay a social worker but want to have the service. Relin thinks part of that is generational from thinking that donations to the agency entitle donors to free social services. However, she speaks to many major donors who are dealing with aging parents or with their own aging issues who say specifically, "Be sure you send me a bill." Most loyal donors greatly appreciate what JFS does and the expenses that are involved in providing those services.

⟨∞⟩

JFS, through Aging & Adult Programs, is the Washington State representative to the Claims Conference and currently serves 40 to 50 Holocaust survivors. The service rarely closes the case of a Holocaust survivor, even when the person does not want any services. About 10 percent die every year, and one would expect that the caseload would go down. That is not the case as new people are added regularly. People who never needed help before, but are now getting into their 80s and 90s find they can use assistance. JFS provides homecare and care management to those clients and can offer emergency financial assistance for things like dentures or hearing aids and medical bills. The staff feels that it is both a privilege and a very important function that JFS provides.

Relin spearheaded the creation of a portrait gallery that was placed in the upstairs hallway in the new JFS building in 2012. She had attended a Claims Conference training in Los Angeles several years before where a representative from Santa Barbara talked about their free-standing museum to the Holocaust where Holocaust survivors volunteer as docents. Santa Barbara JFS has a display that is open to the public with portraits of Holocaust survivors and some of their artifacts. They also bring street kids through to see the exhibit and work with them to help understand that they are not the only ones who have suffered. Relin thought that was a lovely idea, and the staff tried to interview all the people on their caseloads as well as those who are on the Holocaust Survivors Advisory Committee. Holocaust survivors can be very emotional, and when JFS put together the portrait gallery and interviewed the survivors, some of the people cried through the entire interview.

The Holocaust Survivors Advisory Committee members were originally all survivors, but some have died and others are now getting frail. Current committee members are either survivors or the children of survivors.

At this time, there are 35 to 40 active survivor clients. Most of these clients are in the King County area, although JFS does occasionally send money on behalf of the Claims Conference to people who live in other parts of the state.

The job of the advisory committee is to oversee the distribution of emergency assistance funds and care management services to Holocaust survivors. The committee members don't see the individual clients but hear about how many people are served and what kinds of services they received. The minutes of the meetings show the number and amounts of the grants for the quarter.

The Claims Conference continues to advocate for additional funds. One program called ZRBG, the German acronym for the Ghetto Pension Law concerning pensions for former workers in the ghettos, was expanded. ZRBG paid a stipend for people who did voluntary or wage labor in the ghettos, although who knows how voluntary that work was? Germans were not in the ghettos, and the "volunteers" were being directed by other Jews, so the work was considered voluntary. People are able to get a stipend, but applying to the German government is so complicated that it almost takes a lawyer to fill out the information. For a time, with the lead of Bet Tzedak, a legal representation clinic in Los Angeles that deals with a large number of Holocaust survivors, JFS Seattle was working with three different law firms in Seattle. A system was set up in which people would call JFS if they thought they might qualify for that claim, and then JFS referred them to the law firms. One lawyer distributed the cases amongst the firms, which then helped people fill in the applications and get them filed correctly. It was a terrifically successful program on all sides, as the lawyers enjoy working with and providing their required pro bono work to the Holocaust survivors.

The Claims Conference keeps pursuing the German government, and recently they received a ruling that changed who qualifies as a Holocaust survivor to include people who were in the Siege of Moscow and of Leningrad (St. Petersburg). Several countries have also been added where people were under Nazi occupation. Algeria was never on the earlier list, although Jews and others were imprisoned and deported by the Vichy government and never received any recognition as survivors of the Holocaust.

Some will assert they are not a survivor because they were never in a camp. However, under the Claims Conference guidelines, a Jewish person only has to have been in an occupied country when the Germans controlled that country. These victims lost a tremendous amount, and they are considered survivors.

Sarah Barash is working with a non-Jewish client who is a Holocaust survivor who does not qualify for any of these programs but experienced all the same horrors. The client's father was a political target of the Nazis and was sent to a camp, and her family was destroyed.

Some Holocaust survivor clients receive both case management and counseling. Many were very young, and some still teenagers in 1938 when they were taken into the camps after Kristallnacht. A few escaped or survived through the kindness of friends or strangers, lived in hiding in attics or in the woods or survived through other means. Many eventually came to Seattle.

For various reasons, some of these survivors became estranged from other family who had survived. It was not unusual for them to be unable to trust other people, and often they were unable to form friendships. Occasionally JFS would get involved when one of these now elderly survivors was unable to maintain their living space and/or their personal hygiene adequately. Some were on the verge of being evicted by the time the agency got involved. Once contacted to provide case management for these Holocaust survivors, JFS is often able to provide free chore services using a grant from the Claims Conference. It sometimes takes quite a bit of time to get a survivor to accept a chore worker but once they do the worker might go once a week to do laundry, clean a little, and help with various other needs.

JFS staff will continue to provide case management services to these clients, even helping them get admitted to a hospital when necessary. Privacy fears might make it difficult for a survivor to even give necessary information to the doctors. When independent living is no longer safe, or possible for other reasons, the agency will help the client gain admittance to the Caroline Kline Galland Home or other appropriate facility, and continue to follow and assist as necessary.

Often, because some of these clients don't want what they perceive as people invading their privacy, they hide things, and when they can't find them, accuse others of stealing from them. Of course, often things disappear because they forget where it was hidden.

With one client, when JFS staff was asked to help with his finances and went through his bank accounts, it turned out that he had a considerable amount. That was the account that held all of his reparations from Germany; he never touched it. He was asked what he wanted to do with the funds, and his banker suggested he write a will. Not having family or friends, he decided to split his money between Kline Galland and JFS.

It is also not unusual when the folks at Kline Galland are cleaning out a deceased resident's room that they discover photo albums of his or her family. Sometimes the photos show very nice surroundings, and they look as if the family had a comfortable life before the war. Even after working with a client for many years, the case manager might have had no idea that the client had the kind of history that came out of those photo albums. Usually, if there is no family, those albums are donated to the Holocaust Education Center or the Washington State Jewish Historical Society.

Relin knows that it is those people who are psychologically isolated who need JFS services the most.

In addition to the Holocaust survivors and other local seniors, the Aging & Adult Program works with many Russian seniors who were resettled in the Seattle area during the 1980s and into the 21st century. Relin arranged to have a group of these seniors participate at the annual Shoah (destruction) commemoration at the Jewish Community Center.

The Russian Jews started telling Relin that they would be interested in more Jewish education but that it is not very accessible. The only Russian language services are those provided by Chabad, and since for the most part these people have always been secular Jews, Chabad is not always a comfortable environment for them. Relin asked JFS development director Lisa Schultz Golden to help find funds. Marina Belenky, then cantor at Temple de Hirsch, who speaks Russian, and Wendy Marcus at Temple Beth Am helped create an annual Seder for the Russian Community. Rabbi Jonathan Singer was able to get a Russian Language Haggadah, which is the same Union for Reform Judaism Haggadah that many people use, but all in Russian. The Russians were delighted, not only because they could go to a Seder and understand what was going on but also because they just loved the music. The band Marianna, with two accompanists, add their music to the event, including for dancing after the Seder.

Elderly Russians who do not speak English sometimes attend some of the Endless Opportunities events, often when they are centered on music. There is also a full-time Russian information systems specialist who helps this population figure out how to negotiate the systems here. Relin feels that JFS and the Jewish community need to do more to help integrate them into the community.

Relin thinks that in her 28 years of being a social worker, JFS is clearly the most mission-driven organization she has worked with. She also thinks that Ken Weinberg (JFS executive director from 1984 to 2013) was able to keep the mission in view all the time and, although difficult financial decisions had to be made, the bottom line remained the mission.

Chapter 5

1926-1939: From Relief to Rehabilitation

In 1926, a Hebrew Benevolent Society (HBS) caseworker reported, "Relief itself is the problem. The problem of rehabilitation is won by work that is outstanding."

The work of the society was primarily carried out by the volunteer board members, and they strived to make the transition from relief to more complete rehabilitation. They studied the newest findings in social science literature to learn how better to serve those who sought their help.

In order to continue to be a beneficiary of the new Seattle Community Fund, the Hebrew Benevolent Society was required to hire an experienced social service worker, so when Bernice Degginger Greengard resigned as executive secretary in 1927 to welcome the arrival of her first child, she was replaced by Mae B. Goldsmith, with Sylvia Weil serving as office secretary.

Goldsmith was from Portland, Oregon, where her father served as mayor. She attended college in the East and returned to Portland in the 1890s to volunteer as a social worker. When she moved to Seattle, she volunteered for the Ladies Relief Society (Seattle Children's Home) and the Social Welfare League (Family Society). Her first paid job was as a "visitor" for the Social Welfare League doing fieldwork for 11 years with needy clients. She was also assigned case investigations for the Caroline Kline Galland Home, which is how the officers of the HBS became well acquainted with her and her work.

Mae Goldsmith was described as a benevolent person who was committed to helping others. Throughout her life, she was interested in social science. She kept abreast of the advances in social service by auditing social science classes at the University of Washington. With her professional approach and ongoing study, she was able to guide the HBS and the members from the basket-on-the-arm, volunteer callers in the home era, when all they could give was a little charity and sympathetic understanding, to a more professional approach, providing increasingly more skilled counseling and guidance. She was the first to hire graduate social workers and to refer clients to psychoanalysts and psychologists for treatment.

As a high school student in the early 1930s, Jeanette Millstein (later Jeanette Lowen) volunteered at the office in the Smith Tower Annex typing case records. She remembers Mae Goldsmith "as a very petite woman, less than five feet tall. But when she opened up that voice and gave those guys hell, and she didn't hesitate to give them hell" about finding a job, not abusing their wives or children, or reducing their use of alcohol. "She gave it to them straight off the cuff, and I could see those guys quivering inside," recalls Lowen.[1]

Goldsmith provided financial assistance to families and individuals in distress and did case work studies for the society and for the Caroline Kline Galland Home. She also organized English language classes for Sephardic immigrants, aided Skid Road transients, and helped out with Jewish delinquents in juvenile court.

In the 1930s, Goldsmith was well-known and well-liked by the Orthodox ladies of the Montefiore Aid Society. They trusted her and accepted her advice on their cases, taking advantage of the advances in social science when a needy family on their rolls needed therapy or rehabilitation.

JFS (the Ladies' Hebrew Benevolent Society at the time), the Seattle Hebrew Benevolent Society, and the Montefiore Aid Society worked together for the common good and developed an excellent working relationship over the years.

The Montefiore board of 18 directors met monthly at the Congregation Bikur Cholim, employing Mrs. P. Tovin as a part-time secretary. Its work included providing guaranteed loans and extending other financial and medical assistance to Jewish families, most long known to the members. Its focus changed in 1933 when the decision was made to restrict work to rendering "friendly service" to new applicants while referring all new relief problems to the Jewish Welfare Society.

Their recommendation was:

That the cases being aided by the Ladies Montefiore Aid Society be provided for by a small Community Fund allotment to that Society, to be administered as a special fund at the Ladies' Hebrew Benevolent Society office.

That a list of the active cases be submitted to the Community Fund office, and that no new cases be accepted by the LMAS thereafter.

After founder Goldie Shucklin's death in 1936, the Montefiore Society went inactive, and its remaining cases were adopted by JFS (renamed the Jewish Welfare Society in 1929). The night before her death at 95, Shucklin was on the phone trying to get a load of coal for a poor family. Indeed, as the *Jewish Transcript* noted, "Her tired hands have borne the burden of a lifetime's work for Judaism."

In 1928 and 1929, Goldsmith attended the Pacific Conference for Social Workers in Yosemite Valley with expenses paid by the society, the state conference in Yakima, and the National Conference of Social Work in San Francisco. Through her efforts and guidance, the type of work the organization concentrated on gradually changed. One report to the organization related:

The emphasis is more on rehabilitation than on relief all over the country. The major aim is to restore the family to society. How does the social worker proceed? He takes interviews, talks to the mother of the family, draws story from mother …

The worker also sees the husband as head of the family, relatives, former employees, rabbis, doctors, and teachers. After making the diagnosis from all the material, the worker makes plans for the family. The plans are often changed and finalized after weeks or months. The worker does not dictate but wants to be leader.

The report of board secretary Viola Silver at an open meeting in March of 1929 told of the constant cry for coal and wood during the winter and for food for cold, hungry bodies. She reported that, since November, board members and officers had made 406 visits to needy families. The demand was so high and funds reached such a minimum amount that the men on the advisory board were asked for assistance, agreeing to raise $1,000, a task Otto Guthman undertook. In only a few days, he had raised $1,235 from just a handful of men in the community.

The following June, Libby Goldsby, chairman and sole member of the Delegate Fund, reported that a variety of small afternoon and evening entertainments raised the funds needed for Goldsmith to attend the National Conference of Social Work in San Francisco. These events, with the addition of checks sent by those unable to participate, successfully raised $248.10.

In the fall, Thanksgiving baskets were donated and distributed and an agreement made with the Educational Center calling for all collections of old clothing to be sent to the center with the society having access to their store to clothe the needy families being served.

A special meeting of the Hebrew Benevolent Society was held Wednesday, November 20, 1929, at the Temple Center at which time the name of the organization was changed by unanimous vote to the Jewish Welfare Society (JWS). Its goal restated:

To furnish relief to the poor and needy, to ameliorate distress, to dispense charity and to furnish a means for educating the poor and needy, and to engage generally in social service work upon the broadest principles of humanity.

The board consisted of 24 women directors, elected annually for a term of one year. There was also an advisory board of nine men who were ready to give help on legal matters or investment counsel. From a report of *Social Work in Seattle* magazine:

All sorts of problems involving Jewish individuals are dealt with, special emphasis being placed on the family disturbances caused by changing standards of observances represented in the older foreign-born generation and their American-born children. Seattle, Los Angeles and New York are the three cities where are found large congregations of Sephardic Jews from the old world Turkish and Spanish cities of the Mediterranean. The women of these families live a secluded life, observe a strictly orthodox regime, speak little or no English, and are completely out of touch with the American unorthodox ideas of their adolescent children. The girls particularly are prone to develop problem relationships to older members of the family group, since they are kept more or less restricted at home while the boys have the benefits of higher education and Hebrew school.

In the summer of 1930, the Great Depression arrived in Seattle in full force after a decade of unprecedented building and economic growth. New tariffs and drops in imports left sailors, longshoremen, teamsters, and anyone who depended on a paycheck almost totally out of work. Construction stopped, stock values tanked, credit dried up, banks failed, taxes went unpaid, and every sector of the economy joined in the worst economic catastrophe in US history. Addressing the problems created by the Depression became the chief activity of the JWS. When, in 1933, the JWS became a zone of the Washington Emergency Relief Administration (WERA), vouchers were available for food and clothing, but for medical appliances, housing for older people who were not citizens, and some rent payments, the society had to rely on its own resources. The state paid the salary of a caseworker and part of the salary of a secretary and provided two extra clerks.

The office dealt with both residents and transients, and the staff found that they were keeping, on an average, a monthly active caseload of 183, requiring three separate kinds of case records and statistical reporting to two national offices, to the Seattle Community Fund monthly, and to WERA weekly.

To manage the enormous workload a number of changes were recommended:

> That the Society transfer the bulk of its relief cases to the State Department of Public Welfare and carry on its special racial and nationality services on its Community Fund budget.

> That it sever its financial connection with the State Department of Public Welfare before September 1935.

> That it set aside as a special fund for the Ladies Montefiore Aid Society's cases now active, such appropriation as the Community Fund is able to allot to the Ladies Montefiore Aid Society.

Jessie Danz was elected president for the 1929-30 term and would continue to serve in that capacity, off and on, for a total of 11 years. In her 1930 President's Report, she discussed the country's financial situation and the effect on JWS, telling the membership, "Today we have very little time for Social Service. One can say that families now applying are asking for relief. There is no such thing as rehabilitation of a family." She also talked about Children's

Jessie Danz (JFS photo collection.)

Orthopedic Hospital (today's Seattle Children's). "Without a moment's hesitation, it receives our children in need of hospital care as do the city and county hospitals."

During the Depression, the JWS was helped with funds from the Seattle Community Fund, membership dues, bequests, and fundraising functions, which included luncheons, card parties, charity balls, and intensive annual drives for new members. Even the Jewish high school sorority Sigma Theta Pi helped by raising a donation of more than $300. The society also was able to meet the qualifications that enabled it to receive federal relief funds while simply striving to survive.

There was a successful party for the Health and Welfare Fund at the home of Mr. and Mrs. Max Silver, which raised $800 with 140 guests present. The hostesses and hosts assisting Mrs. Silver were Mr. and Mrs. Ben Tipp, Mr. and Mrs. Addis Guttman, Mr. and Mrs. Max Block, and Mr. and Mrs. Leo Weisfield.

Additional help was welcomed when Mrs. A. M. Robbins came on as a part-time worker.

In May of 1933, the Jewish Social Service Bureau of Baltimore released a study of the effect of the Depression on family life. They studied the family from two points. One was the economic effect and how they dealt with the change. How were families adjusting to the new standards of living and to living on budgets established by the Jewish Social Service? Adolescent children did not want to go to entertainments and socialize unless they were properly dressed. Girls in their teens were willing to go to work in cotton stockings but felt they could not go to Jewish entertainments unless they had silk stockings. Adolescent boys who were very conscious of their appearance thought it impossible to go anywhere in worn shoes.

The report continued:

> It is impossible to have these changes occur in any family without having an effect on the relationship of the different members. The fundamental cause for the strained relationship is the fear and insecurity under which both the husband and wife are laboring. In most cases, the difficulty between husband and wife is caused by the wife's fear that she and the children will starve. The manifestation of this appears in nagging and scolding and her belief that her husband is not trying hard enough to find work … Also that he is unaggressive. Then there is her tenacious hold to old standards and her struggle not to see or accept the situation as it is. Thus the husband who is also laboring under feelings of fear and insecurity is faced with two situations: his inability to find work and his strained relationship with his wife and children. Some men are finding the escape in withdrawal.

> Children, no matter how young, cannot help be affected when mother or father or both are worried and harassed. One mother said, "I cannot laugh at the funny

things the children do or say, I am too worried about money." The growing boy or girl cannot understand this lack of money. They have to give up social activities where money is concerned or on account of not having the right kind of clothes. Remember this, if they are working, they have to contribute most of their salaries to the support of the family.

The caseworker has tried to encourage the man out of work and to interpret his difficulties to his wife. She has taught the family how to live on limited incomes, to encourage recreational outlets, sometimes provided or made work for them which has averted family disruption. In fact, she has done and is continuing to do whatever is possible to lighten the reality which the unemployed person has to accept at the present. But one is forced to admit that security for the future of any of these families has to be based on something stronger and more tangible than encouragement, interpretation or hope.

Aims stressed to overcome these problems:

1. Strong affection between all members of the family.
2. A sense of security.
3. Sharing pleasures and successes.
4. Unselfish attitude.
5. Hopeful in unified aims.
6. Fortitude.
7. Utilization of opportunities.

Life under such surroundings seems almost certain to turn out children with habits and principles which will ensure the foundation of wholesome enjoyment of their home.

In her annual report to the membership on October 18, 1933, Jessie Danz reported the JWS had been advised the previous winter by the Seattle Community Fund that emergency relief would soon be available from the King County Welfare Board, which at that time was under the jurisdiction of the Reconstruction Finance Corporation. The Seattle Community Fund would provide funds only for maintenance.

In July, the society had been asked by the Seattle Community Fund to consider becoming a part of the King County Welfare Board so JWS could receive money directly from the welfare board. Consequently, the Jewish Welfare Society became a branch of the King County Welfare Board.

Danz continued:

> Instead of giving money to our families as in the past, relief is given in the form of vouchers for food, fuel and clothing. Rents are not included and this is the hardest problem we have to cope with today. It is regrettable that the amount allowed each individual is only $1.20 per person per week for food. This is a small amount as we have always fought tooth and nail to maintain a high standard for our families. Still we are fortunate that we are able to subsidize in many instances from our Health and Recreation fund.

The following February, a new membership drive began and continued until the goal of 2,000 members was reached. Membership dues, formerly four dollars, were then reset at one dollar annually.

Also during 1934, the Educational Center provided medical and dental work for women and children, and Harborview Hospital provided X-ray and special medical treatments. The Red Cross, Gimel T. Fraternity, and the Junior Council of Jewish Women contributed to the Passover Matzos fund. The Temple de Hirsch graduate school, Pi Tau Pi, and Sigma Theta Pi provided holiday baskets, and the Sephardic ladies in all groups belonging to the

Conference of Jewish Women's Organization were organized to sew. The federal government provided for transient men, and Bikur Cholim cooked meals which were made available for a nominal cost.

In her report for 1934, Danz told the assembled members that Mae Goldsmith had been pledged to the Honorary Sociology Fraternity at the University of Washington in recognition of her outstanding service. Danz then continued telling the group that social work had changed again as the federal, state, and county entered the picture and that the organization was operating as both the Jewish Welfare Society and as District 4 of the King County Emergency Relief program. As such, all Jewish transients were being handled by the Federal Transients Men's Bureau. She also reported that as various projects of the Civil Works Administration and WERA materialized, clients of the agency were given a share in those projects.

One positive event during the year was a bequest from the Neufelder estate for $15,000. The bequest directed that the fund be kept intact, but the interest of approximately $600 a year could be placed in the general fund. Melville Monheimer was acknowledged for having donated the legal help needed to complete the gift.

At the time, the Seattle Community Chest allowed bequests of $500 or more to go into an endowment. The interest from the endowment was figured as part of the income of the JWS and deducted from the allocation of the Chest to the agency. This gift became the first identifiable contribution to the JWS Endowment Fund, but legal proceedings took a long time to be settled, and the agency was not able to finally establish its endowment fund until 1947. Once again, Melville Monheimer had handled all the legal work free of charge, and he was honored with a special presentation for his continuing commitment.

Danz was also able to report that all employable men and women were given work by the federal Works Progress Administration (WPA). The blind were assisted through the Blind Pension, and aged citizens by the Old Age Pension. By using all the federal and state relief facilities that were available, the JWS was able

to continue providing the best service possible to the families under
its supervision and care.

During this time, the Council of Jewish Women worked with
the JWS on immigration issues and the Bikur Cholim Hachnosas
Orchim (welcoming guests) Society helped provide meals and
lodging for transients.

In her report for October of 1935, the new president, Viola
Silver, told the gathering:

> For about two years, our society was officially known
> as Zone 24 of the Washington Emergency Relief
> Administration, since changed to the State Department
> of Public Welfare. You are all familiar with the history
> of depressed conditions that brought about the change
> from a small group that functioned as the social service
> agency to a specialized class, to a part of the federal
> system giving emergency relief—conditions that in
> a very short time changed the character and status of
> work offered by this organization that had been giving
> service in our community for 42 years. In an incredibly
> short time we were involved in the federal program,
> and upon our office there devolved the responsibility
> of handling about 200 families each month in place of
> the accustomed 50 or 60. It meant reorganization of
> staff and office. It meant discarding old and established
> methods and standards, and readjustment to a new and
> difficult situation.

Now we are again in the process of change. New laws have
been enacted covering the expenditure of public funds for relief,
and limitations set as to monies from this source that could be
expended by private agencies. Therefore, since July 1st, all families
that had been assisted by the JWS in which there was an employable
man, woman or child, have been turned over [to] the State Dept.
of Public Welfare. This was compulsory, because without federal

funds we had no means of financing these families. Also, through the Department of Public Welfare, the workers were in line for jobs under the newly set up Works Progress Administration. After October 1st, no federal funds whatever were allotted to private agencies. When the Federal Transient Bureau was established, all Jewish transients were referred to them. In this city supplementary service is given transient men by the Hachnosas Orchim.

Once again, JWS was an agency dependent on the Seattle Community Fund and membership dues, donations, and fundraising activities within its own group for its income.

A social service survey of the community recommended that the JWS take over the work of the Ladies Montefiore Aid Society. Accordingly, the Budget Committee of the Seattle Community Fund notified JWS that the agency would be receiving an addition $1,800 a year to handle those cases.

This was also the year that JWS eliminated the open election of board members in favor of the board vetting and agreeing on new board members internally in an effort to keep a person willing to work but vulnerable to being lost because of the popularity of another candidate.

The list of cooperating agencies was getting larger, now including Anti-Tuberculosis League, Bikur Cholim Synagogue, Camp Fire Girls, Child Study Laboratory, Child Welfare Department, City Clinic, City Health Department, City Hospital, Emma Lazarus Society, Educational Center Clinic, Hebrew Ladies Free Loan Society, Ladies Montefiore Aid Society, Medina Bayview Home, Mental Hygiene Society, Orthopedic Hospital, Red Cross, Seattle Chesed Shelemes, Seattle Children's Home, Seattle Day Nursery, Seattle Progressive Society, Seattle Junior Red Cross Clinic, Seattle Lodge – B'nai B'rith, Social Welfare League, St. Luke's Hospital, The Jewish Transcript, Travelers Aid Society, Young Women's Christian Association, Young Men's & Young Women's Hebrew Association, and Washington Women's Protective Department – Seattle Police.

A newspaper article reported, "In 1937 Mrs. John Danz was unanimously elected President of the Jewish Welfare Society beginning her seventh year as its leader. Mrs. A. M. Goldstein was selected to serve as First Vice President."

In recounting the admirable accomplishments of the past year, Viola Silver, retiring president, declared, "We have more than fulfilled our purpose as a relief agency—for the first time in the history of the community, we have not only cooperated, but worked in actual contact with all other Jewish groups in the city, especially those administering social services."

In addition to handling the work of the Montefiore Society, the B'nai B'rith Lodge also entered into an agreement with JWS for it to handle their non-member transient men, for which the society was reimbursed for all expenditures. At the same time, the lodge agreed to form a burial committee consisting of representatives from all congregations, so that when an indigent passed away the funeral could be handled in a dignified manner with a minimum amount of effort and without delay.

JWS also worked with the Council of Jewish Women on its Americanization program. The council paid for the citizenship papers while WPA furnished the teachers. In addition, the society worked with the German Émigré Committee and the problems of accepting German Jewish children into our community. At that time, the executive secretary (Mae Goldsmith) of JWS served as secretary for the German Émigré Committee with all the correspondence handled through the JWS office.

The entire country, perhaps even the world, had hoped to come to the end of 1937 in an atmosphere of recovery. That hope proved false as economic indicators showed a new slide downward. The new year began with new fears, insecurity, and the threat of permanent dependency still menacing the existence of thousands of families. Children were growing up on relief not knowing what it meant to have a wage-earning parent. Persecution and discrimination were still driving citizens from countries that had been the homes of generations of their ancestors. In this world of insecurity, JWS, like other private family-welfare agencies, devoted itself more and more to work that the public agencies could not undertake. The staff was increased again with the addition of Maxine Doctor.

During this time, a successful all-city card party netted more than $2,000, and a tea and book review sponsored by five members netted another $182. The organization faced additional challenges because of reduced federal support.

1.   After World War II, Lowen returned to work for Jewish Family & Child Service as a social worker and then continued her association with the agency as a member. In 1964, she accepted a seat on the board of directors.

Chapter 6

Counseling Services

Clinical counseling as a profession began to develop at the end of the 19th century to address some of the negative effects created by the Industrial Revolution. Later during World War II, vocational counseling became a specialization when the US government needed counselors and psychologists to help select and train specialists for the military and industry. The field grew and expanded until today counseling has been defined as "a professional relationship that empowers diverse individuals, families, and groups to accomplish mental health, wellness, education, and career goals."[1]

In 1927, Mae Goldsmith brought casework practice to the Jewish Welfare Society. The focus changed from simply providing relief to helping families function better. Over time, as counseling continued to develop as a profession, the society's counseling program developed as well.

When Ken Weinberg joined Jewish Family & Child Service in 1975 as an intern, the form of counseling practiced at JFS was the very traditional, decades-old, one-on-one, individual sessions between a counselor and a single client. Sometimes the issues were managed in one or two sessions, but often these individual sessions went on for years.

Before he was appointed director of Counseling Services, Weinberg worked in the Older Adult program (the precursor to the current Aging and Adult Services program) as geriatrics was his expertise. He also carried a counseling caseload and attended weekly supervisory meetings with the Counseling program. His training was as a social worker, not as a counselor, so he worked hard taking additional classes.

Several cases stand out in Weinberg's memory. Some of his more difficult cases involved mothers and their young children. When it became clear that a mother was seriously disturbed, or otherwise unable to provide appropriate care for her child or children, Weinberg found it necessary to call Child Protective Services with his concerns about the child's safety. (Every counselor, therapist, social worker, and medical professional is required to report when any kind of abuse is suspected.) Sometimes the child was removed from the home and placed into foster care, and in some cases, if the mother remained unwell, the child was never returned to her care.

Other memorable cases occurred before the agency became involved with and provided support groups and Family Life Education programming for the lesbian, gay, bisexual transgender, and queer or questioning (LGBTQ) community. People would come with gender identity issues of every kind, and for many years, these were treated as problems to be corrected rather than something to be acknowledged, accepted, and worked with. A few of Weinberg's clients were young people struggling with how to come out to their families.

Weinberg is very pleased that the agency took an appropriate and very early stand by reaching out to the LGBTQ community. Today, JFS offers programs for same-sex couples that adopt or arrange for the birth of their own child, indicative of the huge changes in societal and professional norms.

His role as a case manager for older clients was primarily providing nurturance, maintaining contact, and making sure his clients could access the services they needed and were entitled to. He found that usually people who were in need and qualified for various services did not know what they were entitled to and too often did not receive all of those services.

As he assumed the responsibilities of his new role as director of Counseling Services, Weinberg attended national and regional trainings and meetings. He soon realized that the style of counseling JFCS had been practicing for decades was no longer considered best in the field. If a child was having issues, the JFCS counselor would still usually see just the child; the parents and siblings were not included. Best practices for this situation had moved to family counseling, and Weinberg brought these kinds of new techniques to JFCS. He insisted that the counselors adapt their methods to the new practices. Some of the counselors were happy to learn the new methods. Others were traditionalists and liked working one-on-one with a client with little attention paid to the rest of the family. Those counselors soon left the organization, which over time became an agency counseling families, as well as assisting couples and individuals. If a child suffered an issue, the entire family was usually involved in the therapeutic process.

Weinberg was pleased to be able to hire people with expertise and graduate-level education in counseling. Jeff Gold and later Ruth Saks each brought his or her training and skills to move the agency forward.

Weinberg was very ready to move on to a management role, which he felt was more appropriate for his skill set. He became extremely active in the national Association of Jewish Family & Children's Agencies (AJFCA), serving as vice president several times. Over more than 30 years, he participated in in-service trainings and learned from others about what was new. He was just the person to keep up to date about what was happening in the field and push for change when it was needed. There were always people on the staff who loved the idea of moving forward. Other staff members needed some encouragement to engage the new thinking.

Jeff Gold remembers the field changing rapidly in the 1980s when he worked at Jewish Family Service. (The name had changed again in 1978). For example, before the family therapy approach was adopted, the parents might see one counselor, one of the children see another, and some of the children not be involved at all. Gold says that since that time, the fragmented approach has lost favor in the field.

The family therapy clinical model was appropriate, for example, to work with a young boy who was acting out at school and at home, and clearly very unhappy. Previously, the child would have been dropped off at JFS by his parents and picked up an hour later. With the introduction of the family therapy model, the therapist would recommend that the entire family be engaged, including brothers, sisters, and parents, even if the parents were divorced. This model operates on the belief that when a child is having a problem it is a family issue. If there is a nanny, the nanny is also included so that the entire family system is involved. Applying a family practice therapy model and working with a group of people together is difficult, however. Often, not all the individuals agree with each other's point of view. Also, the way a counselor works with the family as a system is different from the more traditional one-on-one psychotherapy.

There is also an emphasis on family of origin work, although not in a psychoanalytic way. Gold explains that within the context of family therapy a therapist looks at the mother and father, or in marital therapy looks at their parents, their families, and what those families look like as a determinant of behavior that they are displaying.

Jeff Gold practiced with a Master of Social Work on the East Coast before he came to the University of Washington in 1978 to earn his PhD. He selected the UW because there was one professor in the department who had an area of interest that overlapped with Gold's and with whom he wanted to study. After he finished his doctoral studies in 1981, Gold developed a part-time private practice while also teaching in the psychology program at the Seattle branch of Antioch University, and he was interested in connecting with others in family practice. He visited JFS to meet with Ken Weinberg, who was then the director of Professional Services. Learning that one of Gold's areas of expertise was in group therapy, Weinberg asked if he would be willing to help counselor Betsy Rubin start a therapy group and perhaps even co-facilitate the group. The group never materialized, but when John Hellman (who had followed Cynthia Himmelfarb as director of Clinical Services) left for private practice in the fall of 1982, Gold replaced Hellman.

As Gold took on his new responsibilities, the JFS's counselors were working with individuals, couples, and children with their families, helping them deal with alcoholism, domestic violence, growing-up issues, marital discord, and a variety of other struggles families experience. They also were able to recommend other resources when they recognized symptoms of mental illness. Some of these counselors saw clients in the Eastside office (established in 1979) one day a week until part-time counselors were hired to staff that office. Gold also served as a consultant to the Jewish Day School.

Adoption services were also part of the counseling program. A rabbi or someone else in the Jewish community would let it be known that there was a Jewish baby about to be born whose parents wanted to offer the child for adoption by a Jewish family, and Gold assumed the responsibility for screening people as to their appropriateness as adoptive parents.

Because JFS is a United Way agency, the clients were not all Jewish, but for Jewish clients, the ability to work with counselors in a Jewish context was important.

There was also some overlap with services to the newest group of immigrants, those from Iran. Soon after the shah was overthrown in 1979, Iranian Jews began feeling a great deal of pressure from the Islamist revolutionary government. This triggered another mass exodus of Jews fleeing oppression. JFS worked not only to resettle the new immigrants but also to provide financial aid and counseling services. Soon after the wave of Iranian Jews, the immense Russian immigration began.

Working with the Iranian immigrants was interesting for Gold because many of the clients he saw were young people in their late teens and early twenties who arrived without their parents. The parents often had businesses and were going to try to hold on under the new regime. Sometimes the young people he was working with were middle-class, Jewish-oriented, well-educated youth who had emigrated but whose parents had stayed behind. Gold says this wave was similar to immigration at the turn of the 20th century when young people from Eastern Europe would be sent ahead to America to see if they could make it in the new country. The parents stayed behind to try to maintain the family income, business, or property.

It was not uncommon for the counseling staff to see young people of college age or slightly older whose family had been split, and the not-quite-adult children were now living on their own. Their problems might be with boyfriends or girlfriends, school, or simply what to do with themselves. It was like providing parental guidance, but these young people were under additional stress. They were in a new culture. While some of them spoke fairly good English, most needed to improve their command of the language. It was stressful for them to establish themselves when the Iranian Jewish community in Seattle was very small, as opposed to the Jewish community they had left behind, which had been there for hundreds, even thousands, of years and was very close-knit. Mental health and emotional problems developed in addition to all the other normal stresses on families.

Chabad-Lubavitch found a following in Seattle, and JFS was the organization of choice for those who were growing up Conservative, part of the Reform movement, or not even Jewish and got very involved with Chabad.[2] The Chabad rabbis referred to JFS families, individuals, and couples who were struggling with issues because there was no other place with an understanding of what it was like to be ultra-Orthodox in Seattle.

Gold recognized that it was important to have in-service training to accommodate differences in clients' backgrounds. Although all the counselors were Jewish and had varying levels of experience, there were some very specific things about the way some Jews performed practices and rituals. For example, Shomer Shabbos is one observant of the *mitzvoth*, or commandments, associated with Judaism's Sabbath from dusk on Friday until sunset on Saturday.

The counseling program became an important connection between JFS and that community.

The board, Weinberg, and staff members were all very interested in the counseling program being visible, being available, and reaching out to both the affiliated and non-affiliated Jewish community. Part of that outreach included a program run every December by Counseling Services and Jewish Family Life Education (JFLE). This offering was for intermarried families about being Jewish at Christmas time and about the pressures felt by families that were raising their children with both Christmas and Chanukah. (JFLE, eventually renamed Family Life Education, provides culturally sensitive educational events designed to strengthen individuals, families, and the community.)

As supervisor, Gold bought the first video camera for the JFS to use in training. Therapy sessions (with client permission) were taped through a one-way mirror in the library at the Boylston office. Gold could then review the sessions with the therapist and discuss reasons for a certain intervention or what was going on with a particular therapy group or family. The follow-up was sometimes, "How are you going to do that differently?"

Gold recalls that while Irv Goldberg was executive director, Ken Weinberg, as director of Professional Services, was in charge of all of the service programs and really ran the show. When Goldberg left, it was clear that there had been pressure, tension, and differences between Irv and the board and staff.

It was a breath of fresh air for the staff when Ken Weinberg took over as executive director in 1984. They greatly appreciated Ken's hands-on, highly invested style. Gold described Ken as:

> Smart, thoughtful, and very committed to JFS. He was very hands on, very involved, very approachable, and because the agency was small, it had a family-like feeling. When Ken's mother was alive and would come to town, Ken would invite staff to his house so they could interact with her, or she would come to the agency and

have lunch with the staff. Ken was very farsighted and aware and tuned-in and highly regarded by the staff and certainly by me.

Gold recalls that executive assistant Julie Olson was one who really had her finger on the pulse of the JFS—the business end of things, the receptionist, the comings and goings, and certainly the work of the board, and the board members, as well as the executive director. She was always very approachable, very helpful, and great to know.

Gold was director of Counseling Services until the end of 1985. He says he "worked to create a top-flight, highly-effective, very well-trained, very in-tune clinical program." He was part of a group of clinical directors that included Catholic Social Services, Lutheran Social Services, and the United Way agency Family Services of King County, and met once a month to present and talk about cutting-edge issues for the entire clinical community. The group represented similar social service agencies with broad services.

Mental health agencies served the chronically mentally ill, and the 1980s saw the closing down of mental institutions that served this population. The family-service agencies had multi-faceted counseling programs, which included clinical, some mental health or mental illness, family violence, drug and alcoholism, and sexual-orientation issues, which were then being talked about much more. Gold was very pleased with the way the clinical program grew and became not just a *hamish* (cozy, homey) little place where certain people would come if they were tuned in to the Jewish community. The program began to be seen in the broader mental health community and in the Jewish world as a place where an individual could receive very good quality counseling services.

Providing specific services to the LGBTQ community was not yet significant in the work, although there were a few programs for staff orienting them to the particular needs of a community that was beginning to coalesce and find a voice. This was during the same time that the Seattle Association for Jews with Disabilities

(SAJD) became part of JFS, and it began to delve into issues that are a common part of life now but were then newly recognized or unrecognized entirely.

During these years, it was still a surprise that Jews were alcoholics, had domestic violence issues, or used drugs. There was a strong belief that those scourges hit everybody else but not "us." One of the things Gold worked on was presenting to the community that JFS was trained in and available to work on those issues.

When Jeff Gold left the JFS, Dr. Ruth Saks became the new director of Counseling Services. Raised in Great Neck, New York, in a Reform Jewish household, Saks's grandparents had come from Russia and Germany. Her father was the executive director of the Anti-Defamation League, and because her mother had been raised in a modern Orthodox family, her family were very observant Reform Jews.

Saks attended the University of Pittsburgh where she received both her master's and doctorate before moving to New Mexico with her husband. The Southwest was a shock for a person who had always lived where it was easy to find a bagel and lox! When the family moved to the Seattle area, they settled first in Puyallup, not realizing that it was not at all like the suburbs around New York. She discovered that the Puyallup schools had back-to-school night on Rosh Hashanah and the following year on Yom Kippur. Their attitude was expressed with the statement, "You Jews and your holidays!" She did find a wonderful congregation in Tacoma where the people understood her when she spoke. Putting up with the 45-minute commute to Seattle until her son was six and started elementary school, Saks would drop him off at the Jewish Community Center on Mercer Island on her way to work at JFS.

Saks first came to JFS in the summer of 1984 after Ken Weinberg became executive director. She had interviewed with Cliff Warner for a position working with seniors but decided not to concentrate on that population. Later, when Jeff Gold called with a clinical counselor opening, Saks was happy to accept the position.

At the time, the small staff of five or six counselors met every Thursday morning for training and to consult with other experts. Saks was impressed with the quality of the casework and the agency commitment to staying current through regular training and continuing education. Saks says she knew they were going to do good work there.

The work included individual, couples, family sessions, and some group work. Counselors used the therapy approach they were most comfortable with. Saks worked primarily with couples but also with some individual clients. A family-systems umbrella influenced the general work perspective. Rather than psychodynamic, which she described as being a more analytic type of work, there was more focus on family of origin, how the individual was influenced by the system he or she lived in or was raised in, and how that was part of everyday experience. For example, with a couple, she might ask each partner, "How was anger handled in your family?" and "Well then, what does that mean in this [your blended] family?"

As Saks began her new counseling role, she was provided with cards from previous intake calls and phoned people to make appointments, finding her caseload of perhaps 20 to be varied with people from their early 20s to those in their 50s and 60s. She found it interesting to work with her older clients and was aware that, even after many years as a couple, they were doing the same kind of "how can I be better in a couple" work as the younger clients.

Saks remarks on how sometimes the smallest, seemingly unimportant issues can create huge problems. She remembers couples who were having horrible fights and threatening to split up over issues like how sandwiches were cut for the children, who should put gas in the car, or more generally, how the chores were distributed. One not infrequent issue concerned how the family budget was being managed.

One of the things Saks found interesting when she saw couples in their sixties was that, although they weren't fighting about the sandwiches because they did not have little children still at home, the issue was always in some way "how do I feel loved and supported by you and how do we negotiate those changes, which really was what the sandwiches was about."

Saks was at JFS for seven and a half years, coming in as the senior clinician, as she had a PhD. When Gold left, he suggested that Saks apply to be the director of Counseling Services, which she did, and worked as the acting director of Counseling Services before being appointed to the permanent position.

Saks says that Gold had laid a wonderful foundation in terms of supplying training for the staff and that she then brought in new people so that the counselors would have consultation with different people, providing different lines of thought. One consultant might have a much more systems perspective, another more psychodynamic. The counseling program was well respected in the community, and the organization that Gold had set in place was able to expand in bringing in more orientations.

Saks recalls that there was always a conversation about what it means to be a Jewish agency. All the counselors were Jewish at the time, although the level of observance and participation in structured religion varied. It didn't matter how observant each was personally. What was important was that they understood Jewish practices and beliefs and were able to work with clients from anywhere on the continuum of observance.

JFS was, and is, a Jewish agency that supports and is supported by the Jewish community, as well as by a variety of other private and public funding sources. If a client were going to any other counseling service as a Jewish person, he or she would probably get wonderful clinical work but the counselor might not fully understand the person's background, influence of religion, ties to the community, etc.—some of what that shared experience encompasses. For example, to a certain extent when you say the words "the Holocaust," most counselors understand historically what happened, but they do not relate to it in the same way that a Jewish person affiliated with a Jewish community does.

Saks thinks having that fuller understanding was always important. A Jewish person might silently consider, "I wonder what the story is?" and then wonder if this child had nobody else because the rest of the family had died. And the counselor would understand in a way that someone without an intimate familiarity with the culture does not really comprehend. "Culturally, what does some of the anti-Semitism that certain Jews hold in mean? And how do we hold it in? It was and is important to have that bigger umbrella so that you can get it in a different kind of way. It's not just 'how do you pray.' It's a much bigger cultural experience."

One client was a young man in his late twenties. He was not Jewish but came to JFS specifically and wanted to work with a woman therapist. When Saks asked him what brought him to JFS, he said, "Jewish moms are the best moms in the world, and I figured I needed mothering." She then proceeded to provide supportive, professional counseling.

While she was director, Saks received a call from the clinical director at Lutheran Social Services, part of the group Gold had regularly met with, inviting Saks to participate. Saks joined the group and developed wonderful collaborative relationships. Those participating found support and useful information in terms of some legal issues and the opportunity to make a wider variety of training accessible to their staffs.

The agency was providing service to both the Jewish and the greater communities, and some of the JFLE programs focused on what it meant to be Jewish in terms of the broader community, specifically around issues of parenting, single parents, Shabbat, and similar topics.

The sliding-fee scale was in effect at this time, but there were not yet any third-party payments, such as medical insurance. Payment for counseling services was the responsibility of the client. Clients looked at the fee scale and selected where they fit and how much they could afford. Counselors did not ask clients to bring in documentation of income, so there had to be a certain level of trust. Saks is sure that there were people who took advantage of that trust but also thinks that "it was better to be taken advantage of at times and then deal with that if it was interfering with the therapeutic relationship."

For the most part, there were no clients who were seen for nothing. The lowest fee was about seven dollars per session. The top fee was perhaps $95 a session. Part of counselors' training is to help the client understand the value of the therapy, to believe "this service is really valuable to me," and realize paying money for it is how we assign its value. There was (and still is) a feeling that this service should not just be given away because that would lessen its perceived value.

Issues involving singles, like moving through a divorce or working with single parents on how they can feel part of the community, sound like simple things but were not. Sometimes these clients felt shame, and the counselors helped them to move on and still be emotionally present with their children. Those issues they encountered, and still encounter, are deeply felt because the community often does not include singles. It is still very much a couples' world.

Saks always felt comfortable being able to walk down the hallway and knock on Weinberg's door and say, "I need to talk." Most of the time, he would stop and listen. He made an effort to make himself available.

Saks relates that the day after her dog, Freila, died of old age, she was very sad and evidently not her "normal sweet self." She had snapped at someone, and Weinberg looked at her and said strongly, "Ruth!" Saks looked at him and said, "Freila died yesterday," and the tears started pouring down her face. Weinberg gave her a hug, and the tears also ran down his face. "Ken let you be human, and Ken was human. That was what made it feel so good to work there. We could be real." Saks says that the staff wanted to be their best, and that was expected. "You had to work hard, but there was really a feeling of being respected and being supported."

Robin Moss took over from Ruth Saks. Originally from New York and having enjoyed volunteering at a crisis counseling center during college, she went on to earn a double master's in Jewish communal service and social work, completing an internship at JFS in Los Angeles at the Freda Mohr* Multipurpose Center (the senior center for JFS LA). She then worked at JFS in Kansas City for a few years and was able to get experience in a variety of work because it was a small agency.

Moss was always interested in examining what was Jewish about Jewish Family Service and had some experiences in that area. For example, one of her clients in Kansas City was a man who was very driven to perfectionism and really wrestled with it. Moss had heard in a class about one-sixtieth (also called "*batel b'shishim*"). Jewish religious law says that a forbidden item becomes acceptable when mixed with 60 times its volume of another item. An example of this would be that if you are keeping a soup that is kosher and something falls in to it that is *traif*, or not kosher, the rabbis have said that it doesn't make the soup *traif* if it's just one-sixtieth (or less). She brought that information to this young man, and it was like giving him permission that he too did not have to be perfect. It spoke to him because he was trying to live an observant life and trying to do everything just right and had now discovered provisions for imperfection. Moss was fascinated with where the Jewish and the clinical come together and studied the literature on the topic.

At one point, Moss had the opportunity to speak as part of an AJFCA panel that included an executive director, Ken Weinberg from Seattle representing mid-management, and herself, a line worker. When she heard Weinberg speak and discovered what a dynamic man he was and how amazing JFS in Seattle was, she decided that was the man and the agency she wanted to work with.

When she learned about a job opening at JFS Seattle for a senior clinical position, she grabbed for it and was hired. Then in 1992, the clinical director position came open when Ruth Saks became ill, and Moss became the director of Counseling Services. She spent what she says was an incredible 14 years in her dream job. The program was relatively small at that time with mostly part-time

---

* Freda Mohr was the younger sister of JCFS President Jessie Danz and the author's great aunt.

staff or contract employees. One of Moss's charges from Weinberg was to help build cohesion and tighten things up.

At the time, Diane Zipperman was, and still is, on the JFS staff as school social worker. She worked in the various Jewish schools with individual children who had learning difficulties or other issues. Some children had trouble getting along with other children or with a teacher. Some had problems at home. The schools would call JFS, which worked on a retainer basis, providing service whenever it was needed. Zipperman spent a fair amount of time at the various schools, including working with parents when their involvement was indicated. She also worked with teachers to help them develop coping skills for challenging classes or children, and there certainly were some very challenging classes.

There was one issue in 1993 when a camp counselor spoke inappropriately to children at camp, and the children were upset. The temple operating the camp called JFS, and Zipperman did triage work with the children.

JFS began the first Hillel counseling program in the country just a few blocks off the University of Washington campus. Previously, Hillel director Rabbi Dan Bridge would get a sense that something was going on with a student who came in to Hillel, and he would call JFS. Unfortunately, the potential client did not always make it to the agency on Capitol Hill, about five miles away.

Then Rabbi Bridge received funding from a generous donor and wanted to launch a counseling program at Hillel. Betsy Rubin, a strong therapist who had worked at JFS at one time, was looking to expand her private practice and was hired to start the JFS program at Hillel, continuing for nine years. (The program continues to this day.)

Rubin was seeing serious, challenging problems, not just separation or anxiety about school or peer relationships. There were clients with serious depression, suicide risks, and eating disorders—the full range of adult issues. She was a seasoned therapist and able to handle the caseload, working with both individuals and groups and providing confidentiality and trust. In addition, she and Bridge worked well together in serving the Jewish student community.

The JFS counseling program initiated a premarital counseling program in 1992 with Rabbi Bridge. A curriculum was developed that integrated the issues related to Jewish observance into sections about communication, how to launch a healthy marriage, and how to create a shared vision. The same program was presented with a number of different rabbis in the community.

The clinical counseling team also provided staffing for many of the Jewish Family Life Education presentations, and JFLE director Natalie Merkur Rose did amazing work in the area of interfaith couples and Jews by Choice. Moss helped lead a support group at the Herzl ner Tamid synagogue on Mercer island with Rabbi David Rose for people who had converted to Judaism, addressing the challenges of dealing with both their Jewish and non-Jewish families, how to maneuver and how to speak for themselves and still be respectful, plus a variety of other challenges people often don't think about.

Ken Weinberg was very supportive of outreach to the gay and lesbian community, and JFS was one of the first mainstream organizations to offer programs for that community. In February of 1991, JFS started doing outreach to the families of gays and lesbians, offering programs about what it is like being in the Jewish community when you have a son or daughter who is gay or lesbian and talking about how to deal with the challenges.

The reaction of family members when somebody was finally talking to them was heartwarming, and having the program housed at JFS provided community acknowledgement and recognition. As parents, significant others, and adult children came together, there was a sense of being welcomed at JFS that felt very significant and important. Moss gives kudos to Weinberg because the agency sees itself as "being there" for everybody.

Sometimes young, college-aged clients came to JFS wrestling with wanting to come out to their families. Perhaps it would be an observant man who wanted to come out as a gay man. It was quite a conundrum. One of the issues these men faced was about being able to reconcile wanting to live a traditional Jewish life and yet be a gay man. Some of the work they did with their therapists was about finding their own voice and their own place in the community. Over time, the counseling program grew as there was more outreach to children and families, leading to more consultation in the Jewish school communities.

Rabbi Beth Singer recalls that when she was teaching a class at Temple de Hirsch Sinai she wanted to talk to teenagers about certain choices teenagers make, so she called JFS. She was connected to counselor Steve Katz, with whom she ran several workshops that were very effective. She also remembers having a great many people who needed counseling but did not have access to some of the private therapists for financial reasons. Rabbi Singer called Robin Moss, who helped congregants find the right therapist at JFS where they would be able to use a sliding-fee scale.

Weinberg and Moss began discussing the idea of developing a domestic violence program in 1998. They called together a task force of six knowledgeable people, and during the formation process, Moss was persuaded that a clinical person was not the best response. She shifted her ideas and was open to people who came from an advocacy background.

Michelle Lifton was hired to start Project DVORA (Domestic Violence Outreach, Response and Advocacy) in 1999. (See chapter 17, "DVORA.") Lifton thought it was important to deal with the shame of a Jewish woman dealing with domestic violence. The model chosen for the program was one in which counseling and domestic violence advocates worked closely together.

Lifton convinced the counseling program that it made sense to meet with couples first separately to assess if there were domestic violence issues.

In terms of addressing addiction, JFS started small. Liza Restifo was hired to start a program to assist clients trying to deal with addictions in 1999. Restifo had strong credentials and was a fine therapist. She started getting the word out by contacting community and religious leaders and giving presentations in the community.

When Restifo left, Steve Morris assumed the addictions program lead. He then added the director of Counseling Services role when Robin Moss was on leave. The addictions program languished a bit until Eve Ruff was hired to direct it in 2008. (See chapter 18, "Alternatives to Addiction.") When Moss returned, Morris left JFS to work at Swedish Medical Center.

It was felt that it was important when hiring new clinical staff that, if not of a Jewish background, they be knowledgeable about the religion and culture—come in with some basic knowledge and be open to learning more. Bill Drummond, for example, is not Jewish but was always mindful as to what the Jewish issues and the considerations were. He was the epitome of how you can be not Jewish and still be Jewishly knowledgeable and tuned in.

For many staff members of JFS, the meaningfulness of people coming to a Jewish agency goes beyond Jewish in the name and its closing on Jewish holidays, to encompass the full understanding of the Jewish experience and not having to explain everything. If an Orthodox woman comes in for counseling, she does not worry about the counselor looking askew if she practices *Niddah* and goes to the *mikveh* (ritual bath).[3] The counselor may not know the level at which the woman observes but does not respond with a clueless remark like, "Huh, what are you talking about?" There is a comfort level if the client says an expression or talks about a holiday that the counselor has some knowledge about. What is important to many is that JFS has staff that have a certain level of knowledge and understanding that enable clients to feel "you get who I am and what I'm dealing with."

Ruz Gulko, a well-known Jewish educator, was asked to present a life-cycle program to the staff over several consecutive sessions. She taught the clinical staff quite a bit about the basic Jewish life cycle, values, and considerations. Those presentations were taped so that new staff were able to receive that basic level of Jewish knowledge and education. It connected some people with parts of themselves, opened new ways of thinking, and fostered wonderful dialogue and personal exploration.

In one case, a father was minimally functional emotionally, and the couple were having many problems. JFS was able to support them as a family intermittently over time with individual, couple, and child work. Staff did not think the children would have fared as well without the counseling. It was a resource-rich offering that JFS was fortunate to be able to provide at the time.

JFS staff members take pride in their willingness to go outside the box. For example, sometimes when the spouse of a community member dies, the surviving parent has a very difficult time telling his or her young children. In this circumstance, a JFS counselor will go to the home and help the surviving spouse break the news.

In 2006, when the shooting occurred at the Jewish Federation of Greater Seattle downtown, the entire counseling staff provided counseling both on site and at the hospital. It may have been outside of the box, but it was clearly what needed to happen.

Moss says that before she left JFS one of the challenges she experienced was seeing some board members become more focused on the ability of clients to pay for services. Although, since the 1950s, there has been a recognition that it is important for clients to contribute financially to their therapies because people are more likely to value services they pay for, the focus on the bottom line now became stronger.

The exponential growth JFS experienced during these years was both wonderful and sad. Moss says, "There was something special about being small enough that all the program heads could meet regularly and collaborate in a way that is only possible when you are small."

In 2004, Moss was awarded an honorary doctorate from Hebrew Union College for over 25 years of working for JFS agencies.

When Moss left JFS on maternity leave, Steve Morris became the director of Counseling Services. Morris originally became involved at JFS in 1998 when he was teaching at Seattle University in the Addiction Studies program and Robin Moss called to discuss what type of chemical dependency program might be appropriate for JFS. Then in 1999, when he was completing an MSW degree, he did his student placement internship with JFS Counseling Services and then continued teaching at Seattle University. He became the director of the JFS Alternatives to Addiction program in 2002 doing community outreach and training, seeing clients, and being part of the counseling program as a social work mental health counselor.

Morris left the agency in 2008, and JFS looked for someone who had both a management and administrative background, as well as therapy experience. When they had difficulty finding the right person, Jane Relin, director of Aging & Adult Programs, who had the necessary experience, agreed to manage the counseling program too. Some of her responsibilities were moved around so she was able to manage the two departments, which she continued to do until her retirement.

At present, there are three counselors in the department, all of whom are part time, and an intake specialist that works half the time with the Aging & Adult Programs. Theresa Epstein was hired as clinical supervisor and works with the counselors on the clinical issues one day a week, helping to increase the expertise and skill of the counselors.

In addition, while some of the counselors have many years of experience, it is always good to share difficult cases, and the department now has clinical group consultation twice a week. The counselors also meet with Epstein on an individual basis depending on what their needs are. During group consultation, all the counselors take turns presenting cases and getting feedback from the group. On occasion, the Alternatives to Addiction or the Project DVORA staff join the counseling staff, depending on what the situation is, as those departments often share clients.

Most months, a speaker or presenter participates with the clinical staff and others who are interested, and continuing education units (CEU) can be earned on site. Shortly, it is expected that staff from other agencies will be able to participate in those presentations and, for a fee, earn CEU. There are also externs needing two years of supervised practice for licensure in the counseling program. Some of the lower income clients benefit from extern involvement because JFS does not have to charge as high a fee for their time.

One of the counselors works with some of the younger clients who are at risk in the community. She helps them apply for housing or for Medicaid, Social Security, or Food Stamps. She may also coach them on how to dress for an interview or a job and may teach other more basic social skills so they are better equipped to succeed in reaching their goals.

Homeless clients are asked to pay perhaps five dollars a session because JFS wants to keep them engaged. Some are in the Aging and Adult Programs and are helped with more concrete needs—food, clothing, household chores, and general cleaning. Other clients are abusing substances but are not willing to go to Alternatives to Addiction (ATA). Their counselors are helping them get ready to confront their addiction problem. One of the goals of their treatment is to move them over to ATA, and eventually some of them do work with the ATA counselor.

There was recently a referral on a child who may have been abused by a teacher. There are two children's specialists at JFS. One is a marriage and family therapist who works with young children, and the other has been at JFS for more than 10 years and is a children's mental health specialist. He works primarily with boys because finding a male therapist for boys is difficult.

When Betsy Rubin left Hillel, an interim counselor filled in until a new counselor who is a specialist in working with young adults took the position, working half time at Hillel and half time at JFS. She facilitates a variety of workshops (premarital, healthy relationships, dealing with substance abuse) and carries a caseload of clients. Two of these clients were an interfaith couple that came to talk about premarital understandings before they got married.

Counseling Services includes a marriage and family specialist who has an interest in working with interfaith and intercultural families. There is also a therapist who has a specialty in running groups and helped train JFS staff on how to do that work. She also did an eight-week training at an assisted living facility for people who have limited vision. She hopes to start a group for divorcees because recently there have been several requests from rabbis who report that they are seeing more divorced people. The administrator at the *vaad*, the council of rabbis that issues *gittin* (divorces granted in accordance with Jewish law), as well as approves conversions, reports that for the first time in its history the number of *gittin* is going over the number of conversions. Therapists who can be culturally sensitive to the Orthodox community and are able to run good groups for divorced people are hard to find.

There continues to be an issue for people who don't want to be seen coming to counseling or attending a group at JFS, which has also been an issue for Alternatives to Addiction. However, now that the counseling program is in the new building with a separate, more private waiting room, people might be less reticent. The new waiting room does provide an environment more suited for therapy clients. Referrals have been on the increase, and there are now enough clients to warrant an externship program. There has even been a waiting list, which is less than ideal since people will find counseling elsewhere or decide they are better and don't need it.

Relin sees that in the immediate future, between offering continuing education programs and supervision for people working on licensure, as well as offering clients the opportunity to see student counselors from the University of Washington at lower hourly rates, the program is providing a learning environment. She would like to see JFS Counseling Services recognized as not only a program of excellence in counseling but also a program of excellence in training and become an established training site. She says that it is sometimes difficult to attract paying clients because people who can afford the fees often go to private therapists, where there is a smaller chance of being recognized and exposed.

1. "20/20: A Vision for the Future of Counseling Group," www. counseling.org (accessed December 8, 2013).

2. Chabad-Lubovitch is a movement within the modern Jewish tradition. In czarist and Communist Russia, the leaders of Chabad led the struggle for the survival of Torah Judaism, often facing imprisonment and relentless persecution for their activities. After the Holocaust, Chabad became a worldwide movement, caring for the spiritual and material needs of all Jews, wherever they could be found.

3. *Niddah* (nee-DAH) is the separation of husband and wife during the woman's menstrual period. It also refers to a woman so separated and is also referred to as *taharat ha-mishpachah*, or family purity.

Chapter 7

Fund Development
and Marketing

For the first 100 years of its existence, Jewish Family Service in all its iterations was a membership organization with the dues collected from members constituting the major fundraising effort. There was no staff for the first 25 years, so all the fundraising, marketing, and public relations were done by the women who served as volunteers on the board and on the various committees. Year after year, a membership drive was held to retain as many members from previous years as possible and to attract new members through mailings, word of mouth, and other broad community efforts. Even after the organization hired staff to manage and carry out its work, the volunteers were responsible for recruiting and retaining members.

In addition to the membership drives, a variety of other activities helped fund basic services to the most needy in the Jewish community. From card parties and businessmen's lunches in the very early days to the gala auction fundraisers in the 1980s and '90s, the board, other volunteers, and staff members strived to meet the need as best they could within the confines of the Jewish Federation of Greater Seattle's guidelines.

The introduction of communal fundraising in Seattle in 1892 by the Bureau of Associated Charities (later called the Community

Chest and now known as United Way of King County) greatly increased the participation of the community. The stable funding from this organization enabled the Jewish Welfare Society to offer reliable, consistent service to its most vulnerable clients through the 1920s and 1930s. Later, starting with funding of WWII refugee resettlement in 1947, annual funding from the Seattle Jewish Fund (now known as the Jewish Federation of Greater Seattle) added to this stability.

By the early 1980s, primary funding resources for JFS were the Jewish Federation of Greater Seattle, United Way, and the Cooper-Levy Trust. Although each of these had been stable for a number of years, staff and board members alike experienced frustration to have every programmatic increase or addition controlled by outside parties. A few board members started asking key questions. Two board members at the time were professional fundraising executives for other private not-for-profit organizations and recognized the opportunity that was emerging. After many discussions with executive director Ken Weinberg and other board members in the late-1980s, the decision was finally made to make the leap and move into the realm of organizational fundraising to support the vital programs of JFS.

Irv Goldberg, executive director from 1975 to 1984, had sensed the coming need in the early 1980s when he hired a professional fundraiser to assess the possibilities within the Jewish community. Unfortunately, Goldberg chose someone who was not readily accepted by the population he was approaching, and the effort was not successful.

JFS tried a variety of other fundraising efforts before Ken Weinberg hired Stacy Lawson as development director in 1991. A column in the spring 1987 edition of *Mishpacha* (meaning "family," the JFS quarterly newsletter) announced the Kauai Raffle and Coupon Packet, which featured "over $400 in savings to many of Seattle's finest restaurants, hotels, and retailers plus the opportunity to win a one-week vacation for two … to beautiful Kauai." Board members also participated in soliciting for and selling the Seattle coupon book for several years. Lawson's task was to create an annual campaign through which members were encouraged to become financial supporters of JFS.

Deb Crespin came to JFS as development director in 1992, the agency's 100th year of service to the community. She describes herself as an "Ashsepharic Jew" because her father's family was from the Sephardic tradition in Turkey and her mother's from the Ashkenazy tradition in Poland. Crespin thinks her love of food (regrettably) and Sephardic music and language comes from her father's side and her socialist, non-religious viewpoints from the Ashkenazy side. She also received a mix of the religious and the intellectual.

Crespin was born in the Bronx and raised in Southern California's San Fernando Valley. She received a bachelor's degree in ethnomusicology from the University of California at Berkeley and a master's in women's studies from Goddard College in Vermont.

After college, she wanted to return to the West Coast, but not to Los Angeles, and was happy to move to Seattle when her partner found a job at Antioch University. Before the move, Crespin had been working as a development officer in a college setting, so soon after settling into her new environment, she began attending meetings of the Northwest Development Officers Association (NDOA) in Seattle in order to make contacts in the field.

Crespin says that she had not grown up in a family that participated in Jewish communal service and had never heard of Jewish Family Service. In fact, she was unaware of any organized Jewish institutions other than synagogues. What she did know was that working in the development field was about people, relationships, and supporting causes you cared about. When she heard about a position opening at JFS, she thought it would be interesting to work in a Jewish agency. The thought was confirmed after she met Ken Weinberg.

Welcoming her to the agency on the lay leadership side were Michele Hasson, who was immediate-past board president and a fundraising executive, and Carolee Danz, also a fundraising professional and the chair of the Development Committee. Their first task together was putting on a fast-approaching JFS Gala and fundraising auction. Crespin thought it was interesting that these two professional fundraisers were such strong advocates for JFS.

As she took over her new post as development director with responsibilities for both fundraising and communications (public relations), Crespin discovered that there was no written development plan. There was little structure for donor stewardship or for identification and cultivation of donors. There was an excellent board and a smart Development Committee. The other positive was that she had an empty canvas on which to work, which she considered a nice opportunity.

Once the work on the gala was completed, Crespin began her communications task by examining the existing newsletter, which she quickly upgraded. The tribute system—which enables people to make contributions in honor or in memory of a friend or relative—needed to be made more accessible. She soon hired an assistant to help with the next auction and a part-time communications assistant. Richard "Dick" Rosenwald was already on contract to work on print communications.

Ken Weinberg had first contracted with Rosenwald in 1985 intending to do something very innovative for a non-profit agency. He wanted to create marketing and public relations plans to develop, educate, and steer public policy to complement the mission of JFS. Charity and casework helped clients, but changes in public policy could prevent a great deal of suffering in the first place. Rosenwald says that he felt very honored when Weinberg asked him to make a proposal to the board. He thought it created a unique connection to his family because his great-grandmother (his mother's grandmother) Leah Mayer was one of the original members of the Ladies' Hebrew Benevolent Society.

Working with Weinberg and executive assistant Julie Olson, Rosenwald created a plan with a wide array of aspects about messaging and perception and looked at what JFS was trying to do going forward to position itself as distinct from the myriad of other non-profits. After his two-hour presentation, the board had no questions and quickly approved the plan and the expense involved. The only comment from the board was that the next time he did a presentation, they would like to have the 40 pages of the plan numbered. (Rosenwald had committed that he would donate back to JFS 50 cents on every dollar the agency paid him.)

As he began his project, Rosenwald found that the overall perception in the community was that people had no idea what JFS did other than counseling and some adoption work. And, oh yes, Russian resettlement. He had his work cut out for him.

Crespin became one of the first, if not the first, JFS grant writer. She helped secure reparations money from the German government for Holocaust survivors and wrote grants for the Seattle Association for Jews with Disabilities. Later, during the capital campaign to purchase the Jessie Danz Building, she succeeded in acquiring funds from the Kresge Foundation, an extraordinary effort that played a significant part in the successful campaign. Her grant-writing efforts ultimately created a new income track for the agency.

Crespin then turned her attention to the cultivation, demonstration of appreciation, and stewardship of donors and created meaningful propositions expressing why donors would want to contribute funds to support JFS.

A major complication was the delicate dance with the Jewish Federation of Greater Seattle (JFGS). JFS needed to establish a case for support that was distinct from the federation's and to pay attention to the blackout periods during which federation agencies were not allowed to fundraise. (United Way also had a blackout period, but not as long, difficult, or stringent.) Although the federation board was strongly opposed to JFS working to raise significant funds in the Jewish community, it was not possible for the federation to support the agency at the level that was required. JFGS was also not going to be able to keep up with the continuing growth of JFS programs, especially the SAJD, the needs of aging Holocaust survivors, and Emergency Services. In general, this inability of the federation to meet the needs of the community's agencies had the effect of keeping agencies constrained—not able to provide services because there wasn't enough funding and not allowed to raise funds of their own.

When JFS started to tell its own narrative—refugee services, the food bank, and other emergency services—the stories were always compelling because people hadn't been aware that there were so many Jews in difficult, often desperate, situations. People responded to the request that they help provide services to those to whom others refused assistance or for whom there was no other help.

Crespin is proud to have facilitated the beginning of a new relationship with the JFGS, helping to set a strong foundation for future fundraising efforts.

One of the efforts Crespin initiated was a formal major donor program that was specifically created to cultivate and show appreciation to higher-level donors. She was careful always to follow donor intent. She also was respectful of people's choice to give philanthropically and understood that, without the appropriate level of respect, a significant gift might be more transactional than sustainable. Crespin has built her career on the premise that it is necessary to start with donor intent and create a dialogue about individual donor's goals.

Crespin soon recognized that, while the gala provided the biggest stream of contributed income during her tenure, it was also "a boatload of work and not necessarily the smartest way to raise money." In addition, the cost of generating those funds could be as much as 40 or 50 percent of the amount raised, and the event tended to be long on glitter and glamour and short on educating the community about the work of the organization. She began considering moving to a different kind of major fundraising event.

Crespin knows that people give to people, and that has not changed through the social-media revolution that has seemingly transformed society. People need to feel excited about an organization. They want to know that their organization is doing right. Hopefully, a newsletter can tell a story, as can a website, Facebook, Tweets, and other electronic outlets. Ultimately, JFS should appear in the estate plans of its supporters because they know and understand the agency, and are proud of how it has continued to evolve over time with their participation.

Her philosophy of fundraising is and has always been that you start with authentic relationships and the articulation of the case for support. Her job is to be an intermediary, providing a supportive environment in which to give, helping smooth over any obstacles in the way.

After almost three years with JFS, Crespin was wooed away to work in development for the Woodland Park Zoo. The agency had been raising less than $100,000 a year in its annual fund when she started. Because JFS was primarily still serving only Jews, there had not been federal, state, county, or city grants, and the only external funding beyond the community was through private foundations. The Kresge grant in support of the capital campaign to purchase the Jessie Danz Building and one other grant in support of the Seattle Association for Jewish Disabled (SAJD) broke that mold.

The only other income at the time was fees for service from counseling and a small amount of public funding for Emergency Services, plus outside assistance for refugee resettlement. The endowment was not yet significant.

Davis Fox took over from Deb Crespin. He is a multi-faceted person born and raised in New York. A professional bassoonist for 15 years, he received his bachelor's and master's degrees from Julliard and a doctorate from the Hart School of Music. He got involved in non-profit fund development work by raising money for concerts.

In 1991, Fox moved to Seattle where, for two years, he was the executive director of the Youth Symphony. In 1994, he had started working as a development consultant and was looking for a position in that field when he heard Ken Weinberg speak at a presentation. He was so impressed with Weinberg's knowledge of the non-profit world, board development, and fundraising that he wanted to meet him. Then Deb Crespin, who was a colleague through NDOA, told him she was leaving her position at JFS. Fox met with Weinberg and was first hired to be the interim director of the Development and

Marketing Departments (an example of *beshert*, inevitable or pre-ordained) and then was asked to fill the permanent position.

Fox says he had no experience or knowledge of JFS organizations until he came to Seattle, although he understood the concept of social service agencies. He did feel very aligned with the mission of JFS. He immediately found that he enjoyed his new position and working with Weinberg, people on the board, and his colleagues.

He knew he was in a very special place, especially for an aspiring development director. He saw an agency that had a great reputation in the community, and an engaged, dynamic, and excellent board of directors. The executive director was respected in the community and really "got it" as far as understanding development was concerned. He also saw a great program, fantastic management, and a solid financial position. On top of all that, JFS was just moving into a new facility.

Because the development program was so new, Weinberg was on a steep learning curve in development and was a great partner for Fox. He found Weinberg to be supportive of almost every suggestion, such as being more assertive in the capital campaign, creating more publicity materials, and expanding staff. Fox was able to see an opportunity with all the elements necessary for JFS to raise much more money than it ever had, and he had all the tools necessary to accomplish the task.

The goal that had been set for the annual fund when Fox took over was $250,000. Between his first and second full years, Fox was able to increase donations significantly by changing the way he organized and coordinated the department and by being a little more assertive in his approach. He knew that if JFS educated the community and its constituents, they would be more willing to provide support. He saw potential in the existing Friends of the Family major donor program that Deb Crespin had initiated and wanted to take the entire development program to the next level. He started a donor cultivation effort that affected every aspect of his development work. Fox's in-laws, who were very well-known throughout the community, were willing to serve as volunteer chairpersons for a new Friends of the Family campaign, which significantly increased both the number and size of major gifts. There had only been a few donors contributing at the $1,000 level when Fox started in 1995. When he left five years later, there were more than 200 gifts at or above that level, and several of the major annual contributions reached the $5,000, $10,000, and even $25,000 level.

One of the reasons for this success had to do with a donor cultivation system Fox implemented in both the Marketing and Development Departments' programs, techniques intended to help people feel closer to JFS. For example, he favored a personalized approach, rather than what had previously been broad bulk-rate mailings. He developed a newsletter that focused on clients of the agency and was sent in an envelope by first-class mail with a personal note from a board member, which thanked the donor for past support. In addition, the note writer, usually a friend or an acquaintance of the donor, would comment on one of the articles that might interest the donor or mention an upcoming social event at which he or she hoped to have an opportunity to visit with that friend.

A major cultivation event was held when Elie Wiesel came to Seattle to give one of the Jessie and John Danz lectures at the University of Washington. JFS was able to reserve seats for major donors and arranged to get complementary books signed by Wiesel for each JFS invitee. A note was also included thanking participants for their presence or regretting that they had been unable to attend. Wiesel's lecture was excellent and very well received. In addition, the JFS donors felt very special and very much a part of the JFS family.

Another area that Fox is proud of was his work on the capital campaign for the purchase of the Jessie Danz Building. He remembers it as a highly organized effort. He was responsible for the structure of the campaign and recalls that the $1.9 million goal seemed astronomical for JFS at the time—and that they raised $2.2 million. When he announced the final results to the staff at an all-staff meeting, people started clapping in their enthusiasm for such an achievement. Fox credits much of that success to Weinberg and to the leadership provided by the campaign chairmen.

Fox worked at JFS for five years. Holly Redell followed Fox, then, when she left JFS after less than a year, Fox was asked to return as a consultant. He then returned again when the agency was searching for another new development director at the same time that Weinberg was going on sabbatical and needed someone he could rely on during his absence.

One of Fox's most important and successful events was a cultivation affair for donors who were contributing at least $5,000 a year and were willing to commit to at least two years at that level. Howard and Sheri Schultz, the founders of Starbucks, had built a grand and impressive house in the community and called Weinberg to offer him the opportunity to have the first major Jewish community event in their new home as a fundraising and cultivation event for JFS. As soon as word got out, people started calling asking if they could make the contribution commitment and participate, and the event was soon filled to capacity. More than $100,000 of additional income can be attributed to that event.

JFS was on a roll. For five years, from 1995 into the early 2000s, JFS was able to create double-digit increases in income each year, not counting the capital campaign. The development office, including major gifts, tributes, and grants, was bringing in close to $1,000,000 a year to support the programs of the agency.

Those closely involved in and with JFS, including each successive board president, looked for ways to increase and broaden community support. At the same time, each recognized that the annual gala event was flat as a fundraising method. The work involved did not produce the concurrent results, either in income or in spreading the message of JFS. In addition, everybody was tired of asking for or being asked for auction items. What was a brilliant idea in the beginning had tired with age. A different type of event, modeled after the YWCA luncheon, was a powerful experience with a format that made sense in the 21st century. People walk in the door, see old friends, meet new friends, enjoy lunch, hear what the organization has to say, and write a check or make a pledge—all in 90 minutes.

Once again, a more diverse board would be required to attract both a broad spectrum of individual attendees and corporate support. The shift to the luncheon model proved successful. The first year's proceeds of $328,000 represented a small increase over the gala—and people loved it. Tipper Gore was the perfect guest speaker. She spoke about mental health, and attendees of all political stripes enjoyed her remarks. The event not only raised much-needed funds, it also gave JFS an unprecedented amount of visibility and credibility. The annual luncheon continued to grow and became an important event for the Jewish community. In terms of logistics, it was more cost effective (and less burdensome) than the auction. By the fourth year, the gross proceeds had reached $580,000, and in its 10th year (2012), participants contributed more than $1,000,000.

The huge transition in 2001/02 from discontinuing the traditional evening gala to introducing the luncheon format was intimidating for many of those responsible for the event, both staff and board members. The new event is one for which there is no ticket, no invitation, and no price to attend, although attendees are asked to consider a minimum donation of $150. The entire event is underwritten by a combination of corporate and private support. Table captains invite their friends and colleagues to join them at the event, and one of the reasons people show up is because they have a commitment to that colleague or friend. Another is that the event has become "the place to be."

Celia Cohen worked with Fox for several years. She was the primary grant writer and participated in creating events and in the annual fund. She was an excellent writer, helping to create marketing materials and doing much of the writing for the *Mishpacha* newsletter.

Mercedes Sanchez managed the database and also worked closely with Fox on the annual fund, report generation, and donor segmentation using the very sophisticated Blackbaud Raiser's Edge software.

Lisa Schultz Golden, the current chief development officer, recently acknowledged the work Fox and others put in place doing the groundwork and creating the foundation on which she has been able to take the organization to even higher levels. All that cultivation paid off. Over the years, JFS has been able to put itself in a very positive place with the community, starting with the early cultivation efforts that finally brought the agency into people's consciousness.

Fox also had a very successful collaboration with Dick Rosenwald and Ken Weinberg, putting together a wonderful booklet called "The Many Faces of JFS." It put forth a concept representing who and what the agency is, based on the many people of the agency itself, both the ones who volunteer and those who benefit from the services. They went on to create a campaign that spoke about JFS being the heart of the community, conveying a message that not only does the agency care about the community and the people it serves but that the community, in turn, has a heart as well.

After Fox left JFS, the Family Matters model was created. This concept centers around the idea that JFS is a family and the community represents an extended family whose responsibility it is to take care of those family members who are in need.

When Fox left in 2002, the Development Department was raising two thirds of the agency's annual budget of approximately $1.5 million. Continued growth of programs in response to the recognized needs in the community brought the 2012 budget to $8.6 million, enabling JFS to carry out its mission helping more people with more services.

Golden took over the Development Department in 2004. Fundraising has changed dramatically and become greatly sophisticated since the days in 1965 when Eleanor Cohon recruited 100 women volunteers to go door-to-door in the Jewish neighborhoods on Capitol Hill and First Hill with baskets on their arms, soliciting funds from Jewish households to support the work of what was then known as Jewish Family & Child Service.

Golden, whose grandparents originally came from Eastern Europe, was raised in the Seattle area in a Jewish family that was not religious. She attended Vassar College and then worked with the Muscular Dystrophy Association where she discovered a love of working in the development field, which she terms "the people job." She then spent nine and a half very enjoyable years at the Jewish Federation of Greater Seattle, first as a development campaign coordinator and then holding almost every position in the Campaign Department.

She says finding her new position at JFS was *beshert*. After her years at the federation, she was very familiar with JFS and knew many of the senior management staff, as well as the members of the Jewish community. Golden was the right person at the right time. She remembers well that one of the great surprises at the beginning was discovering the joy with which people contribute to JFS.

Golden describes her job as continuously getting information out to the community in order to educate people about what JFS does. Once people have that understanding, it is easy for them to connect with the areas in which they have interest and contribute to support those programs specifically, the agency in general, or any combination they choose. An individual might contribute to help support the HomeCare Associates program in general or to pay for HomeCare Associates services specifically for people who cannot afford the expense. Another person might provide general support to JFS. Still a third might want to provide a bus for a special Endless Opportunities outing to visit the tulip fields in the spring or the eagles fishing in the fall.

Golden believes it is ingrained in the Jewish people that they support and help the most needy, the elderly, the disabled, and the disenfranchised. She says it is the most fundamental way that people can express their Jewish culture in a social justice sense. As she continued her work at JFGS and then at JFS, she came to realize that the values she wanted to express in her life were the Jewish ones of repairing the world.

When Golden first assumed responsibility for the Development Department, there were six full-time staff members working to raise the annual fund goal of $1.8 million. There was also an endowment campaign in progress that had already raised approximately half of its 10-million-dollar goal, although it had stalled a bit because of the turnover in the Development Department's leadership. Her first two goals were to manage a successful annual campaign and to put the endowment effort back in gear.

Golden changed the style of the budgeting process associated with the annual campaign targeting a more intentional approach. Starting with the knowledge that JFS was not even close to meeting fully the needs of the community and then adding the enormous goodwill and caring throughout the Jewish community for the work of the agency, she understood that the community would support greater activity. That became the genesis for the Family Matters Campaign.

On the marketing side, Dick Rosenwald, who had been under contract to produce marketing materials for JFS in the 1980s and 1990s, had decided to close his company and contacted Weinberg about the possibility of becoming a regular staff member of the agency. He interviewed with Golden and in 2006 joined JFS as the director of Marketing and Communications.

Richard Rosenwald was born and raised in Seattle. His great-grandfather on the Rosenwald side, who was the first to come to the United States, engaged in trading with Native Americans as far west as Pike's Peak before travelling over the old Santa Fe Trail in 1862 to become one of New Mexico's earliest pioneers. Besides his great-grandmother being one of the early members of the Ladies' Hebrew Benevolent Society, Rosenwald had numerous connections to JFS. His father, Gilbert Rosenwald, had become a member of the board in 1956, and two of his aunts, Marion Grinstein (1957) and Janet Levy (1961), also served on the board.

Rosenwald remembers his father's strong commitment to JFS and how much he believed in it, so when he first received a call from Weinberg in 1986 to create an advertising campaign, he felt very honored and thought it was a unique connection back to his parents—a very good feeling.

As he was preparing to retire from JFS in 2013, Rosenwald said he was most proud of having been able to create a face and a voice for the agency, enhancing its public perception within both the Jewish and the broader community.

As Golden and her team geared up to increase their efforts in 2006, staff and board members were enthusiastic. They knew from discussions with major supporters that the community would support a greater effort. The board initiated a major strategic planning process to determine what the true needs in the community were and then, working very intentionally, committed to a campaign that would raise the money to meet those needs. This was a major shift away from the traditional process of first raising money and then deciding what additional programming could be supported.

The need for a new building that would provide additional office space to house the increasing staff was one of the major needs identified. Having already outgrown the Jessie Danz building, the agency was renting office space in several other buildings in the area. A portion of the new campaign was targeted for the construction of a new office building on the existing JFS Parking lot. The target campaign goal was set at $25 million, with half going to facilities, a quarter to programs, and a quarter to endowment. Once the campaign was launched, all were amazed to discover how quickly they were able to raise the funds. Golden comments:

> Ken Weinberg, of course, is an incredible fundraiser, and there was a terrific campaign cabinet. Dick Rosenwald created beautiful campaign marketing materials, and the community was very responsive. There were very few people who heard the case who didn't believe that there were more people who needed to be served and that JFS was the agency to serve them.

When the 2008 recession began, the campaign had raised nearly $25 million with commitments stretching out to 2017. Most of the pledges were multi-year pledges, spread over five years with a few of the larger pledges going out to 10 years. Many people involved in the campaign effort were very afraid that the recession would cause the campaign to fail, but while some people asked to extend the length of time over which they completed their commitments, only a few donors had to pull their pledges.

The challenge, going forward, will be to increase annual giving to the point where the new programs started during 2007 and 2008 can be sustained, in addition to funding the ongoing traditional services. Golden believes that there is more potential within the Jewish community to support and grow the programs of JFS. She, and most other people closely involved in non-profit social services, know that the unmet need is still immense. She thinks that people understand the need is great, especially during challenging economic times. The community can be very proud, as is JFS, that the agency never had to cut back on staff or services during the 2008 recession.

The agency's website (www.jfsSeattle.org), which was innovative and state-of-the-art when it was launched in 2009, is a tool that continually tells the evolving story of JFS. Examining the statistics every month, Rosenwald was able to track the impressive growth in the number of hits, page views, and time spent on the site over time. By 2012, in some months, there were more than three thousand hits with many people looking at the food bank, general employment information, and/or the history of the organization. The month before the annual luncheon, there are a great many visits to that page as friends plan to attend and to give.

JFS was very busy in 2010. The recession caused service numbers to increase, reflecting increased needs in the community. The Family Matters Campaign was almost complete, and the new building was moving forward. In addition, the number of volunteers had increased dramatically. Client stories were so numerous and varied it was difficult to decide which ones to feature and how.

Throughout his years of working with JFS, Rosenwald came to recognize and appreciate that "the people who are inside the organization are pretty remarkable people. Not only their talents and skills but their passion and compassion, how much they care about people, and how much they are willing to do to help enhance people's lives." He says that obviously nobody is going to get rich being a social worker at JFS, but "the rewards you get personally... [are] pretty special. The people here are pretty special."

Since first working with JFS in the mid-1980s, the biggest difference Rosenwald sees is in the increased breadth and depth of services. The organization took an old-fashioned, tried-and-true model and evolved into a leading provider of social services to the community. He says that Weinberg had not only the vision but also the dedication and commitment to convert "what if" to "what is."

Rosenwald adds, "In '86, I found a wonderful opportunity to continue my family's commitment, and today I still get a lot of pride and pleasure ... this is something my family has been involved with since the beginning. I don't remember ever not knowing about it."

When Lisa Schultz Golden first came to JFS, the annual campaign goal was $1.8 million. For fiscal year 2013, the goal was $3.5 million. These goals include the revenue from the luncheon event but do not include funding from the JFGS or United Way. It is obvious that with almost one-third of the annual fund goal being raised at the luncheon, that event needs to be strong. However, the majority of major gifts will be developed in ongoing conversation and relationships with the potential donors. Golden's goal is to reach an annual fund total of $4 million by 2015, with incremental growth penciled in for the following years.

Golden credits the many terrific volunteers and staff members for the growth and success that was realized during those several years. One of those contributors was former JFS board president Shelly Shapiro. For three and a half years, Shapiro joined the staff as the agency's Major Gifts officer, working very successfully to increase the number of major donors and to provide continuing stewardship and cultivation to that constituency.

Shapiro joined the Development Department's staff in 2008 to work with major donors and help jump-start the endowment through an outreach program to the community, called the Family Tree Legacy Circle. This effort is focused on building the endowment with the goal of insuring the stability of funding for programs in the future in the event that the willingness or ability of outside funding sources to support JFS programs diminishes. In addition, a strong endowment will help insure the ability of the agency to support much-needed programs in times of widespread economic downturns (as experienced in the recession that began in 2007). The endowment is expected to play a continuously bigger role for the agency in the future. During the program's first year, the Family Tree Legacy Circle Committee publicized the fact that more than 50 agency supporters had left gifts in their wills to JFS and more than 50 others had notified JFS that a bequest has been written into their wills.

Golden acknowledges that JFS is not yet able to address all the needs of the community because the needs are so immense. The agency can no longer count on the support of the government nor of the Jewish Federation of Greater Seattle or United Way to provide sufficient funds to meet fully those needs, so the community, both Jewish and non-Jewish, must be convinced to respond directly. At the present time, about half of the funding for JFS comes from the private sector. New ways to diversify the funding stream must be developed to enable JFS to respond more fully to the many calls for assistance.

In 2012, JFS received contributions from almost 2,400 donors, many of whom could help at much higher levels if they could be educated about the agency enough to be moved by its vision and its mission. At the same time, there are more than 40,000 Jewish people in the greater Seattle area. The opportunities for outreach and expansion are enormous.

Chapter 8

1939–1947: War and Transformation

The Depression still loomed large in the late 1930s, but Seattle's hopes for prosperity and stability were on the rise when suddenly the Jewish community found itself faced with another large influx of Jewish immigrants who were fleeing the deteriorating political situation in Europe. The greatest influx was German Jews, most of whom joined the Temple de Hirsch congregation as it was most similar to their style of liberal Judaism. The agency, still named the Jewish Welfare Society (JWS) in the 1930s, handled the problems of German émigrés after the war in Europe started until the Washington Émigré Bureau (WEB) was established in 1939. With a board consisting of one representative from each local Jewish organization, the goal of the WEB was to provide emergency financial support and assistance in securing lodging and work to the new immigrants and to help them become oriented to their new environment.

As the JWS celebrated its 47th anniversary in March 1939, members were interested to hear Isidor Coons, the executive vice-chairman of the United Jewish Appeal for Refugees and Overseas Needs. The Jewish communities of the United States were responding to the desperate plight of refugees fleeing from Nazi oppression in Europe. The East Coast was pretty much closed to immigration from

Europe because of the war raging there and in the Atlantic Ocean, but refugees were arriving on the West Coast by way of the Soviet Union (then at peace with Germany) and Siberia, with Shanghai providing the major point of departure. Seattle became the main, and one of the few, ports of entry for refugees until the United States entered the war.

The Washington Émigré Bureau was established by the state legislature "for the purpose of assisting all persons irrespective of race, nationality or religion, to legally enter the United States and become citizens thereof, and in furtherance of such purpose to render such legal, medical, financial or other aid as may be necessary or desirable in the premises, including the insurance of such bonds or guarantees as the United States Government shall properly require."

Some of the services offered to accomplish this purpose included providing affidavits required by immigrants, helping to locate relatives overseas, and providing information concerning the transfer of funds and parcels.

In response to this old-but-new community responsibility, local émigré work was reorganized. JWS and the National Council of Jewish Women (NCJW) worked closely with the WEB and members drawn from the Ladies Auxiliary of Temple de Hirsch, Bikur Cholim Congregation, the Hebrew Immigrant Aid Society (HIAS), and the Seattle Jewish Fund. The National Refugee Service provided for an office and personnel, and Saul Haas, collector of Customs, permitted people to come on to the docks to meet the émigrés.

HIAS helped the refugees off the boats by providing them with the amount of money required to enter the United States legally, proving that they would not become public charges. Julius Shafer, who was the principal representative of HIAS, was always on the dock with the cash to great the new arrivals.

NCJW and JWS provided temporary shelter, either at the council-operated Education Center (formerly called the Settlement House) at 18th and Main or at the Morrison Hotel on Third Avenue.

JWS also provided emergency funds and helped the émigrés get work and become oriented. Mae Goldsmith served as secretary of the Washington Émigré Bureau, doing all the investigations, making out affidavits, and writing letters trying to find jobs for the newcomers. Goldsmith, usually with either Jessie Danz or Minnie Bernhard, met the boats, although other JWS volunteers also reported for duty. Rabbi Solomon F. Wohlgelernter of Bikur Cholim Congregation and Rabbi Baruch Shapiro of Machzikay Hadath Congregation were on hand consistently to help with lodging, and their command of Yiddish and Hebrew was invaluable.

A typical arrival was that of Elvira Oppenheimer, who reached Seattle in October of 1940 with her two sons, 19-year-old Heinz and 17-year-old Walter. After the November 8, 1938, Kristallnacht— Nazi-organized riots against Jews—the family knew they had to get out of Germany. Elvira had been born in France and, as a French national, was able to get a visa from the US embassy to go to the United States with her two sons. Unfortunately as a German citizen, her husband, Max, was not included. The decision was made that Elvira and the boys would leave as soon as possible and Max would stay behind and find another way out. It took a year and a half to get a German exit visa to go to the United States via Italy, but that route soon became impossible because of U-boats (submarines) in the Atlantic. The family then heard that people were getting out by crossing Russia and decided that Elvira and the boys would to try

Refugees arriving on the Heian Maru. (Courtesy of MOHAI, Seattle P-I Collection.)

that route, leaving on September 29, 1940, while Germany and the Soviet Union were still at peace. They left everything behind except the few items they could carry in their suitcases. Ten train trips across Russia and Mongolia later, the family paused in Harbin, China. They then went on to Korea and finally boarded the steamer *Heian Maru* for the journey to Vancouver, British Columbia, although with no Canadian visas, they were not allowed to land. During the final leg of the four-week journey from Vancouver to Seattle, Heinz told his family that from that day forward he would be known by the much more American sounding name "Henry."

Henry wrote that the Seattle skyline looked beautiful as they approached the city, and he remembers his first sight of the Smith Tower, at the time the tallest building in the West. He also vividly remembers being met at the dock by Ernie Stiefel, a long-time friend from Frankfurt, and a group of ladies from the Washington Émigré Bureau—Jessie Danz, Claire Nieder, and Marianne Katz. He said:

> They welcomed us, and we piled in their cars, and they took us to the Friedman Boarding House on 14th Avenue. The Friedman family had arrived from Hamburg on a previous transport and were set up by the bureau to receive new arrivals.

The next morning, Jessie Danz telephoned Henry and told him to go to the Palomar Theatre Building for a job interview. There he met her husband, John Danz, and their son, Fred. The men offered Henry a position at the Florence and Circle Theatres (which were across the street from each other). His job involved changing movie posters, fastening down seats, and painting walls and floors for a salary of $18 a week.

After Pearl Harbor, Henry joined the US Army and then returned to Danz's Sterling Theatres after the war and continued to work for the company until he was called back to duty during the Korean War. (Henry's father was finally able to join the family in early 1946.)

These efforts continued in this manner from 1939 until 1946 when the Washington Émigré Bureau was absorbed as a program into the Jewish Welfare Society, although much of the immigration work slowed down after Pearl Harbor for the duration of WWII.

A letter received by Claire Neider at the WEB (located in the JWS office in the Smith Tower Annex) from the National Refugee Service of New York told of a refugee family just arrived from Holland. The family included the parents, their teenage son, and daughter. They were arriving in Seattle by train in less than two weeks, and "unfortunately they will be empty-handed." They had stored their belongings in Holland and paid $973. "This amount of money was the charge of the shipment" to Seattle. The family was sending their belongings directly to Seattle because a brother had preceded them to that city.

In the meantime, Germany occupied Holland, the container with the belongings disappeared, and the money was lost. The family asked JWS to assist them in securing a reimbursement from Holland American.

The letter also provided the information that the father was a carpenter and would arrive ready to go to work, and his wife was willing to work at housecleaning jobs. Neider was able to respond to the letter the following June, telling the writer:

> Within a week of their arrival [the father] had a job with a local construction firm. All the family were enrolled in evening classes to learn English and the children began school the first of the year. Their daughter attends Talmud Torah as well. Our Herzl shul took this family under its wing to help them find housing and new friends. One of the members in the shul—Ben Maslan—is acting as [the father's] advocate in the claim against the Royal Mail Line. Our agency has arranged a campership for their daughter and their industrious son has a job for summer. This family has become a part of

our community already. Now we will be helping to bring
the wife's parents here from South America.[1]

Joe Greengard remembers his mother, Bernice Degginger
Greengard, being involved in the resettlement effort long after she
had left her professional position at JWS. Joe recalls his family and
others served as host families to refugees. One family they were
particularly close to, and Greengard remembers the two families
having wonderful times together on vacations and that he felt the
two families were really just one family.

Greengard tells a story of how their friend had a client in
Berlin who was a professional boxer. In the late 1930s, the client
was going to London for a match, and their friend asked his client
if he would take some valuables with him and put them in a safe
deposit box in London. The client said he would be glad to, took the
valuables, and brought back the safe deposit box key. Later, when
the family was able to get out of Germany and went to London, the
safe deposit box was empty.

Sol Esfeld conceived the idea and was a prime force in
establishing a therapeutic workshop for German refugees to orient
them to the American way of life and help equip them for the labor

market. The community established a
store in the Security Market in Pike Place
for what today would be called a thrift
shop, selling secondhand merchandise
from citywide donations. It was thought
that the proceeds from sales would
support the training site. The National
Council of Jewish Women and JWS
primarily worked on the project. The
Federated Jewish Fund lent money while
JWS contributed the technical skills of
their staff for resettlement and family

Sol Esfeld (Courtesy of
Eleanor Cohon.)

services. The émigrés learned job skills by working to clean, repair,
and make donated items salable. The understanding was that, at

the end of need when the war was over and the influx of émigré's lessened and stabilized, the other agencies would withdraw and NCJW would continue operating the shop.

In the spring of 1939, JWS was faced with an emergency because of reduced federal allocations and the wholesale layoff of Public Works workers affecting many of the families JWS assisted. The reduction in relief was so drastic that, in many instances, food allowances were cut in half. JWS regularly supplemented their clients and found their funds were heavily drained by this emergency. Shoes for children were not available from the public sources that had formerly supplied them. In response, a tea and book review held at Glendale Country Club (the golf and country club formed by the Jewish community in the 1920s), plus a few other donations, raised $203, enabling the agency to provide all the children in their service with the needed shoes and stockings.

A young people's group, called the Greater Seattle Service League, became a tremendous asset to JWS as its members not only participated in money raising activities but also lent a hand in a number of other ways. They transported children and adults to hospitals for treatment, provided clerical assistance at the office, formed a group sewing garments for women and children, assumed responsibility for the New Garment Fund, and assisted in the collection of old clothing, as well as providing a number of other services.

The following year, Mae Goldsmith told the membership, "A few years ago if I had given you a report, I would have mentioned how many pairs of shoes and how many quarts of milk we had given and how much unemployment there was and other problems. Now, we count what are the causes that bring the people to our office, what are their social problems, and how can we, as social workers, help them overcome these causes."[2]

She continued, telling the group that the various governmental agencies were now providing relief in the broader sense and private agencies were only giving relief when there were other problems in the family or where they could work intensively with them to help the family adjust.

The 1936 bequest from Goldie Shucklin had been held up for several years in probate but was finally received in 1940. JWS used the $500 ($8,350 in 2013) to establish the Goldie Shucklin Memorial Fund to be used only for the burial of indigents.

The fourth Monday of each month continued to be visiting day for the board at the Caroline Kline Galland Home. Board members also participated in many of the year-round activities of the Seattle Community Fund, and Jessie Danz became a member of that organization's Executive Committee in 1941.

Significant changes in the work of JWS were brought about by the tremendous increase in population caused by the rapidly growing defense industries. This, in turn, brought its share of people who became dependent or ill and who needed temporary relief or who had some other problem requiring social service. More changes were the result of other widespread National Defense Committee activities. One of the main purposes of this committee was to stimulate the creation of a new social agency to meet community needs and to discourage the organization of unnecessary and non-standard groups. As a result, the National Jewish Welfare Board established offices of its Army and Navy Committee, which served the recreational and entertainment needs of Jewish men in government service. According to Eleanor Cohon, her father, Sol Esfeld, was one of the organizers of this service, which was like a USO (United Service Organization) for Jewish service personnel. Efforts were made through the synagogues to make sure Jewish service personnel were welcomed to Shabbat and High Holy Day services, as well as other special holiday observances. Families were encouraged to invite servicemen and servicewomen to Shabbat dinner or Passover Seder, and young Jewish women were invited to special dances and other social activities to help entertain the Jewish servicemen.

Members of JWS participated in many fundraising activities of both the Jewish and the general community with the biggest jobs being solicitation for the Seattle Community Fund, the Seattle Jewish Fund, and the Greater Seattle Defense Chest Campaign.

Because the policy of the Seattle Community Fund precluded its agencies from having large money-raising affairs and JWS still needed to keep in contact with community members who were interested in and supporters of the work of the society, the board received permission to hold a bridge party to celebrate its 49th birthday in March, at which $568 was raised.

During the Depression, like most private organizations, JWS did not have a large enough budget to help all employable persons who were out of work or unable to work. The advent of the Social Security Department enabled JWS to turn over to them those families who needed special services or short-time relief.

Mae Goldsmith was an excellent steward of JWS through the Depression. She managed to maintain services in spite of the daunting challenges, with support from the Community Chest, the board of JWS, and its members. The JWS budget for 1929 had been set at $19,000 and then increased to more than $27,000 in 1930–1931.

Everything changed as the United States became embroiled in the war in Europe and Asia . Across the United States, employment grew rapidly as defense industries burgeoned.

At the outbreak of WWII, a local office was established of the Anti-Defamation League (ADL) by two community leaders, P. Allen Rickels and Sam Holcenberg. Although it initially was a part-time operation, by 1947 the work of fighting the anti-Semitic lies disseminated by the Nazi regime required a full-time operation. Anti-Semitism had never been far beneath the surface of American and European society, and Hitler's persistent and virulent harangue against all Jews found a foothold in many areas and groups. ADL was up against one of the best propaganda machines in world history.

Now all able-bodied men and women were able to find work, but JWS still had the problems of those people who were not citizens and, therefore, could not work in defense plants, as well as those who were unemployable for some reason.

There were not as many transients, but while many coming for defense work found a job, they still needed financial assistance and a place to live as they often did not receive their first paycheck for as long as two weeks. JWS also helped the wives and sweethearts of the men in the service who came to Seattle following their soldiers, sailors, and marines being stationed in the area. The society assisted Jewish men on their way to jobs with the US Army Corps of Engineers in Alaska and other projects and was designated by the Community Chest as the agency to help returning Jewish veterans.

As the only Jewish organization listed in the telephone book, there were many telephone calls and visits from service personnel wanting information (these inquiries were usually referred to the Jewish Welfare Board).

JWS clients were referred to Dr. Edward Hoedemaker, Dr. Nathan Rickles, Dr. William Baker, Dr. Douglas Orr, or Dr. Frederick Lemerr. Many cases were found to be in need of a psychiatrist or of psychiatric social casework, but at the time, there were no psychiatric clinics in Seattle and only one practicing psychiatrist. Also included in the work of JWS was the supervision of foster homes for five émigré children. The Washington Children's Home Society, a member of the Child Welfare League of America, investigated each of the potential foster homes before the children were placed.

One commentator on the subject of family security said:

Family security is essential not only to the morale of the Armed Forces, but the morale of the entire civilian population in the midst of a period of national emergency. Security is more than a condition of material wellbeing. But without some material foundation there can be no family security. Freedom from anxiety about the physical safety of a member of the Armed Forces may be impossible in a nation at war, but freedom from anxiety about how the family is making ends meet when the breadwinner is in the Army or had lost his employment in a non-essential industry is a form of security that any civilized nation must provide for its citizens.

At the 50th-anniversary meeting in October of 1942, president Jessie Danz told the membership:

> We have come a long way since that first small gathering of women founders. For many years it was a close and personal contact, with the ladies serving as visitors, confidential advisors and friends. Relief was carried in baskets and the applicant for aid would appear at any and all hours at the homes of officers. During these 50 years, we served through a war, which was followed by some years of prosperity and then by the Depression. We became part of the Federal and State Departments of Public Welfare, and when that connection was no longer necessary we withdrew and again became a private agency serving the Jewish people.

The war also caused turnover in the staff as women took jobs in the war effort or followed their husbands to other destinations. Maxine Doctor resigned as a Family Visitor and was replaced by Lillian Finegold, who left shortly afterwards to join her husband, and was then replaced by Shirley E. Schlossberg.

The Membership Committee, headed by Mrs. Ralph Schoenfeld, was successful in securing 600 members whose dues helped support the changing work of JWS. Giving relief was no longer the primary service of the agency as increased demands for services concerning social problems were addressed. The agency found it could be useful "in aiding families and individuals to maintain high moral character in these trying times." Their efforts were helping to combat juvenile delinquency and relieve mental strains, and staff remained ready to help clients face the steadily growing problems created by war conditions.

The President's Report of 1943 was the last one given by Jessie Danz, who had served as president off and on for 11 years, longer than any other board member. She had joined the board in 1925, becoming president for the first time in 1929, and remained on the board until at least 1947, although she may have taken a hiatus for a year or so in-between board terms (the records are not clear).

A major issue for the community involved the *White Paper of 1939*, which was issued by the British government and called for abandoning the partitioning of Palestine for Jews. The president of JWS became a member of the Seattle Emergency Committee for the Abrogation of the Palestine White Paper, which later reorganized under the name of the Seattle Council for Palestine. Its work expanded to include the continued fight for the abrogation of the white paper and to support the program advocating the eventual establishment of Palestine as a Free and Democratic Jewish Commonwealth.

Because this was a controversial subject and JWS did not take part in matters of controversy, the board's decision was to not participate in or join the Seattle Council for Palestine. Zionism, the promotion of Palestine as a home for the world's Jews, met a mixed response in Western nations. Support of Zionism was sometimes perceived as rejecting national political allegiance and the acceptance of Jews into society.

In 1944, the staff of JWS were pleased that the state Health Department finally established a Bureau of Mental Health under the direction of Dr. George C. Stevens, psychiatrist. The Seattle clinic then began to offer services to both adults and children, providing a resource for clients who needed such treatment. Caseworkers had long realized that underlying many of the social problems their clients struggled with was some mental illness that went undiagnosed and unaddressed.

At the September 1944 meeting of the board, the members were saddened to hear Mae Goldsmith read her note of resignation. She had served as the executive secretary of JWS for 17 years and was highly regarded throughout the community. In accepting her resignation, the board noted that the enviable reputation of the agency with the Community Chest and many other social agencies was to a very large extent the result of the work done with them by Goldsmith. Her reputation in the city of Seattle as a practical, understanding, and humanitarian social worker gave JWS a prestige that would have been unattainable without her leadership. She had worked tirelessly throughout the community, had served as a board member of the Social Hygiene Association, and was affiliated with the Family Society, the Educational Center, the Anti-Tuberculosis League, the American Association of Social Workers, and many other Jewish and non-Jewish organizations.

Carolyn Newberger filled in temporarily as executive secretary, followed by Mrs. David Hartstein. Then, on November 1, 1945, Ann Kaufman took over the position. President Danz announced that "Miss Kaufman comes directly to us after heading the Jewish Family Service Association of Minneapolis." She was an alumnus of the Graduate School of Social Science of the University of Chicago and had specialized training in child welfare and psychiatric social work. Maud Shafrin also joined the staff during the year.

The $14,075 budget presented to the board for 1945 anticipated income from the Community Chest of $9,524, $2,447 in operating income, and the rest from contributions and from interest from the trust.

At the next anniversary, the organization was pleased to note that six charter members were still members—Mrs. Jacob Berkman, Mrs. Emanuel Rosenberg, Mrs. Elkan Morgenstern, Mrs. Charles Roth, Mrs. J. R. Holmes, and Mrs. Fred Bories.

In March 1945, JWS received a check for $1,000 from Eugene Levy on behalf of himself and his brothers. The contribution was in memory of the Levys' mother Esther Levy (the founder and first president of JWS), and of her daughter, their sister Lizzie Cooper, who was Isaac Cooper's wife and the second president of JWS. The community had been greatly saddened by the deaths of both Isaac Cooper and Aubrey Levy during the year. Each left very generous bequests to the society.

Nathan Eckstein, a well-loved Seattle citizen and supporter of JWS, who died in October 1945, was remembered at the JWS Annual Meeting of 1945. During his almost 50 years in the city, he had been active and involved in many causes and had been given the city's Most Useful Citizen award. His philosophy was: "To be a useful citizen is more than a duty; it is a high privilege. To be useful citizens, we should ever cheerfully work for the development and welfare of the city we love, for the progress and peace of the country we cherish."

During 1946, JWS concerned itself with the continuing course of change in services, now concentrating on helping clients reach self-sufficiency. Noting that these changes called for expert guidance and service through consultation, investigation, and casework, JWS began the process of affiliating with the Family Service Association of America (FSAA) in order to keep its work at the highest level of social welfare.

The JWS Executive Committee discussed the need to increase the office staff and the difficulty presented in accomplishing this task by the inadequate budget allotment from the Community Chest. The board asked executive secretary Ann Kaufman to request a rehearing with Community Chest, but she pointed out various obstacles, including the fact that it had become increasingly more difficult to find and hire qualified caseworkers. The trend was for workers to prefer the public agencies where the work was viewed as easier and the salaries higher. At the next meeting, the committee agreed to pay the cost of transportation from London, Ontario, to Seattle for Maud Shapiro, a new caseworker who would function as the intake worker. The group also decided that office personnel would be entitled to three weeks of vacation after completing one year's service.

Another issue concerned the need to create firm policies and guidelines for the use of each special JWS fund, such as the Neufelder Fund, that came with certain stipulations for use.

The final topic for the day concerned case-work studies for the Caroline Kline Galland Home, and Kaufman reiterated that under no circumstances would written reports of interviews with clients be given out to persons not directly involved in the decision-making process.

With membership in the Family Service Association of America, the board agreed to follow the FSAA guidelines, suggesting that the board be altered to include men. In response, the members of the Men's Advisory Committee were invited to become board members. It was also noted that the organization should strive to represent a fair cross-section of the community as a whole. The Seattle Council of Jewish Social Agencies made additional changes in response to recommendations from a survey. One of those recommendations was that a trained professional staff member handle the casework required for immigrants by the new Washington Émigré Bureau.

A meeting of the Case Conference Committee of the Washington Émigré Bureau took place on September 16, 1946, with the group discussing the type of cases the bureau would be willing to accept for resettlement in Seattle. One case concerned a couple where the wife had tuberculosis, although the disease seemed to be in arrest. In those days, tubercular patients were quarantined in special institutions with strict bed rest. The committee decided not to accept the case after considering the difficulties that would arise in finding employment for the husband.

A second family was approved for resettlement, and a decision was made to give preference to dependent families, especially elderly people, who had relatives in the city. It was also decided that families resettled elsewhere for five years or more who wished to move to Seattle would not be given consideration for financial support by WEB.

The society's proposed 1947 budget jumped significantly from $14,063 in 1946 to $48,524, due primarily to an additional $30,000 of income from the Isaac Cooper bequest. In submitting the budget to the Community Chest, board president Mary Louise Reiter also noted that an additional $10,500 would be received by JWS from the Washington Émigré Bureau in anticipation of increased immigration from Europe, enough to cover the salaries of one caseworker and one secretary, plus incidental expenses. Approximately half of the funds would be used to provide financial assistance to the new immigrants who would not be eligible for help through regular channels because of residential requirements.

The request for support from the Community Chest remained stable at $11,444, compared to the 1946 allotment of $11,407.

The budget also included a recommendation that $15,000 be set aside in the Building Fund, the earliest indication found of the organization's hope to eventually purchase its own building.

In order to limit duplication of service, in the spring of 1947, the Washington Émigré Bureau was folded into the Jewish Family & Child Service and was then known as the Émigré Committee of JFCS. (The name of JFS had been changed at the annual meeting in March 1947.) There was an expectation that the reopening of the immigration gates would bring immigrants who had been through great suffering and hardship. This group would be much more difficult to deal with and harder to help adjust to their new community. This is another early circumstance of other agencies and services being folded into JFCS and a reflection of its growing stature in the social service community.

Sylvia Weil was still working in the office in 1947, having begun her employment 20 years earlier at the time that Mae Goldsmith became executive secretary. In its discussion of the budget for the coming year, the Finance Committee recommended her doctor report on her ability to work full time. (Although it was not recorded, the report must have been positive as Weil continued her employment.)

By March of 1947, Reiter was able to report that in addition to executive secretary Ann Kaufman, two caseworkers had been added to the staff, doubling the number to four, all holding master's degrees. These four social workers were Bertha Borden, Maria Simon, Lillian Kaplan, and Ellie Gutman. The office staff included Sylvia Weil, Sylvia Pincus, Mrs. Jan Poderson, Mrs. Louis Garfinkle, and Heather Millet.

1. Papers, Jewish Family Service, UW Special Collections, Accession 2003-7, Box 2, Folder: Annual Meetings 1930-1949.
2. May Goldsmith, Executive Secretary's Report, March 1940, Papers, Jewish Family Service.

Chapter 9

1945: Repairing the Wounds of War—A Community Working Together

Seattle historians Molly Cone, Howard Droker, and Jacqueline Williams identify three distinct waves of Jewish immigration to Seattle before 1914: the German Jews from Europe who prospered in Seattle's growth, the Orthodox Jews mostly fleeing the pogroms in Russia, and the Ladino-speaking Sephardic Jews from the Ottoman Empire. The Great War substantially limited Jewish immigration, but Russian Jews in particular managed to make their way across the Pacific to safety in the Pacific Northwest. After Congress clamped down on immigration in the early 1920s, the number of Jews resettling in the United States dropped off dramatically. But still the immigrants came, and a fourth wave arrived from Nazi Germany and what had been Austria.

Ken Weinberg observed, "For 120 years, the organization has never not been engaged in resettlement; it is one of the very few programs that runs through the agency's entire history." Until relatively recently, JFS resettled only Jews. Resettlement was a major program around the end of the 19th century, before and during World War I. A large number of the survivors of World War II wanted to get out of Europe altogether, so after 1945, resettlement was busy through the end of the forties and into the fifties. Then it quieted down again."

A 1943 report from the Washington Émigré Bureau reiterated that since the United States had entered the war, immigration had almost come to a standstill. The work of the bureau included preparation of affidavit forms and applications for change of status, and other matters pertaining to admission of aliens into the United States, although even after 1941 there were a few cases when WEB succeeded in effecting admission of aliens.

US policy fixated on admitting only persons of the "right" ethnic origin and who would be employable and not become public charges. Sponsors had to guarantee to support immigrants financially should they not be able to work. Caseworkers were able to report that, during the war, there was almost no unemployment among those who were employable and high wages and labor shortages meant that most of the immigrant population was able to quickly become self-supporting. The émigré bureau still assisted newcomers with medical expenses, as they were not eligible for free county medical care.

When the United States entered World War II, people of German birth were suddenly classified as "enemy aliens," despite the fact they had every reason to hate Hitler and fled the Nazi regime. Many restrictions fell upon the enemy alien population, including a curfew, a defense zone along the West Coast, and prohibitions against employment in plants having war contracts. (By 1943, these restrictions were removed or minimized.)

After the war, people all over the Unites States, aware of their good fortune at escaping the destruction visited upon Europe, turned their energy and financial support to helping the survivors. Social service organizations across the country were mobilized in the effort, and the Jewish Welfare Society quickly focused the majority of its efforts into its own well-established and long-standing resettlement program. In May, 1946 approximately 500 children were brought to the United States for resettlement. Only half had been properly placed when, within a few months, another 500 teenaged children arrived. The importance of JWS becoming a designated agency licensed to help place these children in foster homes became obvious.

It was also clear that immigration of Holocaust survivors and other refugees from Europe was going to become the primary work of JWS. Sol Esfeld, the chairman of the Washington Émigré Bureau, wrote to Seattle Jewish Fund president Jules Glant requesting $6,000 from the fund to pay for costs of direct relief to refugees. Later in 1946, when NCJW sponsored a survey of the social services of the Jewish community, the results showed that many were duplicated between WEB and JWS, with the exception of helping people procure affidavits. In order to avoid that duplication, centralize administration, reduce costs, and make available to recent émigrés the same services JWS made available to pre-Hitler émigrés, the survey strongly recommended the merger of the bureau into JWS, which was soon accomplished.

The first meeting of the Case Conference Committee of the Washington Émigré Bureau decided to focus on resettling dependent families, especially older people. The first family considered was rejected for medical issues, but the Muenzer family was accepted for resettlement at this meeting. It was also decided that families who had been in the United States for five or more years and families who were citizens of the United States would not be considered by WEB but would be referred to the Jewish Club of Washington or to the Jewish Welfare Society.

Settlement cases were to be accepted from the national office by JWS only with approval of the Case Conference Committee of WEB. The bureau reserved the right to return to New York people who could not adjust to Seattle, at the expense of the New York office. The émigré bureau had control of the number of resettlement cases accepted, the number of children to be resettled, and the number and size of loans to émigrés.

The absorption of the Washington Émigré Bureau into the agency meant that JWS was assuming responsibility for the displaced persons of Europe and other regions who were coming to Washington State. JWS's new Émigré Committee retained the responsibility of deciding which immigrant families would be accepted as part of the Seattle JWS quota. The JWS Refugee Committee—distinct from the Émigré Committee—did the resettlement work meeting families at the boat or train and making sure housing was available for the new families, including basic furnishings. The JWS social workers helped the newcomers with the myriad details of adjusting to life in their new surroundings. Grocery stores, banks, bus systems, school registrations, and housekeeping often presented new and confusing experiences. In general, the social service needs of the newcomers were no different from the needs of other clients, and an agreement had been made between JWS, Hebrew Immigrant Aid Society (HIAS), and the Seattle Jewish Fund that the costs of accomplishing those significant resettlement efforts would be supported by grants from the Seattle Jewish Fund and the Hebrew Immigrant Aid Society. (This marks the first recorded instance that JWS received funding from the Seattle Jewish Fund.) One of the benefits of the merger was that Cooper-Levy funds could then be used to provide services to émigrés.

Irene Ginzburg Epstein was one of the émigré clients of JWS. Irene was born in Warsaw, Poland, in 1924, one of approximately 337,000 Jewish residents of that city, which had a total population of about 1.2 million. Irene's paternal family traced its roots in Poland to 1625, and Irene was an 11th-generation resident of that country. She was 15 years old when Germany invaded Poland in 1939.

In 1940, Irene's family was forced to move into the Warsaw Ghetto as the next step in the Final Solution. From 400,000 to 500,000 people were massed together in a tiny district where death by starvation, disease, and summary execution were daily occurrences. Stealing or smuggling food was punishable by death. The Ginzburg family survived successive deportations to the Treblinka death camp where more than a quarter of one million Warsaw Jews perished. They had finally decided they must escape the ghetto when Irene's 15-year-old brother Jurek was seized by the Germans. Her father, Leon, refused to leave without Jurek.

In March of 1943, 18-year-old Irene bleached her brown hair blond and slipped out of the ghetto by herself. She took on the persona of a Polish Catholic seamstress named Anna Borowska. One month later, the Germans entered the ghetto intending to remove the remaining population and igniting the Warsaw Ghetto Uprising that resulted in the extermination or deportation of the remaining Jews. Karola, Irene's mother, had separately escaped from the ghetto, but the two women lived apart to reduce the chance of being recognized. Leon and Jurek did not escape.

Irene/Anna volunteered to work in Germany to reduce the likelihood of being identified as Jewish and was sent to Berlin in August 1943 to assemble light bulbs for the German war effort. Irene lived in constant fear of being unmasked by the other women with whom she was housed. A year later, she transferred to Dresden where she and the other female workers lived inside a mountain where the factory was located. When British and American aircraft firebombed Dresden in 1945, Irene/Anna and her co-workers remained safe inside the mountain.

On May 8, 1945, Irene/Anna was liberated by the Soviets, and she became Irene again. She went to work for the United Nations Relief and Rehabilitation Administration at the Weinsberg Displaced Persons Camp and for the US Army as an interpreter. (Irene was fluent in Polish, German, French, and English.) In August, she applied to go to the United States and on September 7, 1946, departed for Seattle from Bremen aboard the SS *Marine Marlin*.

Irene soon met and married Irv Epstein, and then in 1947, she was able to travel to Palestine to be reunited with her mother.

Irene's and Irv Epstein's wedding,
October 7, 1947.
(Courtesy of Irene Epstein.)

Of the entire family, only Karola, one of Karola's brothers, and Irene had survived the Holocaust.[1]

Another émigré client in late 1946 was Klaus Stern, who arrived with his very pregnant wife, Paula.

Paula and Klaus met and married when they were working on a farm in Germany growing food for German soldiers. On April 19, 1943, they were deported together to Auschwitz. Klaus's family had been "evacuated" from Berlin to the east a year earlier, and he never saw them again. At Auschwitz, the young couple was immediately separated. Klaus went to Auschwitz III and the Buna Monowit factory where his forearm was permanently tattooed with the number #117033.

Paula and Klaus Stern in 1946. (Courtesy of Holocaust Center for Humanity.)

A typical day started at 5:30 in the morning with a piece of bread, some burnt corn water they called coffee, and, once a week, a spoonful of jam. Then came roll call followed by up to 10 hours of work in the winter, 10 to 12 during summer, with a little watery soup in the middle of the workday. Klaus's first job was digging trenches 50 feet long, five to six feet deep, then placing cables in the ditch, covering them up with rocks and dirt.

Fortunately, Paula and Klaus were young, healthy, and strong from the work they had done on the farm. They survived the starvation, endless work, freezing cold, and forced marches to emerge alive when the Soviets liberated Auschwitz in January of 1945. Although neither had any idea if the other was alive or where the other was, they each made their way to Paula's home town of Arnstadt in Germany where they were joyfully reunited after 28 months of separation.

Klaus's uncle had settled in Seattle and urged the young couple to join him, which they did, despite the warnings given because of Paula's then obvious pregnancy. In the fall of 1946, they became the first Holocaust survivor couple to arrive in Seattle. They enjoyed the nice room that had been arranged for them in a Jewish boarding house, and they fondly remember that one of their first purchases was an outfit, blanket, and diapers for the baby (at a cost of $19.75). They named their daughter Marion because Paula had made a friend in Auschwitz, and the two women had agreed that when they got out

Paula and Klaus Stern in 2007. (Courtesy of Holocaust Center for Humanity.)

alive they would each name their first daughter Marion. Klaus and Paula later learned that Paula's friend had given birth to a daughter just days after their own daughter's arrival .

Through Rabbi Franklin Cohn of Herzl congregation, Klaus found work at the Langendorf Bakeries, where he stayed for almost 36 years. He and Paula joyously celebrated their 65th wedding anniversary in August of 2007 with their daughter Marion, son Marvin, and their families, and the many friends they made over the years. (Klaus passed away on May 12, 2013 at the age of 92.)[2]

The Washington Émigré Bureau had been working to establish policies and procedures to inform the process of resettlement of the expected flood of European immigrants. By the end of 1946, many of those policies were in place. One of the early understandings was that JWS was not responsible to provide transportation. The United Services for New Americans (USNA), the Joint Distribution Committee, or HIAS would take care of that.

In 1946, agency staff geared up to manage the increased workload. A new social worker was hired to start on January 1, 1947. By March, two more professional caseworkers joined the staff of JFCS, bringing the number of social workers with master's degrees to four: Bertha Borden, Maria Simon, Lillian Kaplan, and Ellie Gutman. Executive director Ann Kaufman led the team with the assistance of the office staff, which included Sylvia Weil, Sylvia Pincus, Mrs. Jan Poderson, Mrs. Louis Garfinkle, and Heather Millet.

To help meet the increasing need to find jobs for the émigrés, executive secretary Kaufman interviewed 30 potential employees and 28 potential employers, and placed seven individuals in jobs during a single month. Her next report told of 21 people being placed in jobs in a 10-week period, and Kaufman soon decided to hire an employment specialist.

WEB struggled with whether priority should be given to families resettled through the New York office, as opposed to those resettled in Seattle on their own initiative or with the assistance of relatives. The bureau finally went on record favoring a policy that every case be given consideration on its own merits and that each application be considered in accordance with what was in the best interest of the family.

In addition, a loan fund of $5,000 was set aside for the year May 1947 to May 1948 to be used for small business loans to émigrés. A limit of $500 was set, each loan to be granted on a promissory note without interest. A subcommittee reviewed and appraised each prospective business venture. Later, the Hebrew Ladies Free Loan Society agreed to set aside $3,000 to be used for loans of up to $100 to new immigrants. These loans would be approved without the usual endorsers guaranteeing the loans.

Providing expanded services to children and families had been a longstanding goal of JWS, and the agency quickly completed the process that enabled it to be licensed by the Washington State Department of Social Welfare to provide foster care for orphaned immigrant children, as well as for children removed from their home or for children who had no home at all. A city-wide effort was launched to recruit foster families.

JWS planned to add family casework options by becoming an adoption agency with the ability to place children in permanent situations (this effort was not successful until 1967). Other significant work around children's issues involved the opening of the Bonham Galland Fund for homeless, orphaned, or needy Jewish children under the supervision of a joint committee of Temple de Hirsch and JWS. In order to better reflect this increased range of agency activities, at the annual meeting in March of 1947, the membership approved changing the name of the organization from the Jewish Welfare Society to Jewish Family & Child Service (JFCS).

By 1947, the work of resettling refugees from Europe was well under way as JFCS and the émigré bureau worked to involve as much of the Seattle Jewish community as possible. In July, three families received help, one arriving from Germany and two from Shanghai. In August, there were six families: three from Shanghai and one each from Germany, France, and Palestine. One additional family arrived from Germany in September, bringing the total number of families being served by the agency to 222, with 20 cases having been closed. Between May 1 and October 15, 14 new families arrived, comprised of 27 adults and four children.

Due to the increased immigration through Shanghai, the United Services for New Americans was spending $100,000 a month for resettlement, and the various communities on the West Coast were finding it difficult to absorb the large number of newcomers.[3] Returning servicemen consumed all available housing, which was already in short supply during the war. Similar issues were documented in New York, and the need was recognized for all Jewish communities across the country to participate in resettlement. Kaufman reported that our Washington cities of Walla Walla, Aberdeen, Bellingham, Tacoma, Bremerton, Spokane, and Wenatchee were all willing to consider participating in the resettlement effort.

The total quota for West Coast communities was set at 60 families (called units) a month with the Seattle community responsible for 50 units for the 1947–1948 year. One report calculated that in the first 10 months of 1947, 4,000 individuals arrived in San Francisco from Shanghai, with 8,500 families still waiting. By the end of 1949, those families had been resettled in the United States. Many in this final group were older and required more medical care than previous émigrés. These individuals were also more difficult to place in employment. Émigré families often arrived with a multitude of untreated medical issues, and all Jewish doctors and dentists were asked to help address the problem.

With the reopening of the immigration gates, the resettlement community expected the new, incoming type of immigrants would be much harder to deal with and would have more difficulty adjusting to their new community because of the many hardships and sufferings that had to be endured both in displaced-persons camps and in Shanghai. In the first six months of 1947, WEB provided direct services to 236 families and assisted scores of others. During the year, JFCS accepted 19 new families (39 adults and five children) for resettlement while 24 other families were provided with financial and miscellaneous services during the year.

Under US law, émigrés could not become public charges when they were receiving financial support from public sources, so it was the obligation of the Jewish community alone to support the new arrivals until they became self-supporting. JFCS projected that the Community Chest would provide financial support for the social services, while the Seattle Jewish Fund supplied funds for direct relief to émigrés. The total of expenses anticipated for direct support of a minimum of 18 new families during 1947 was $18,500. HIAS continued a monthly contribution of $110.50 per person toward the JCFS émigré social service program.

Attorney Melville Monheimer recommended in September of 1948 that, if JFCS were to create an émigré committee that would tie in with USNA, the Seattle Jewish Fund could properly allocate money for the work of the émigré committee.

In an interview with the WSJHS in 1972, Minnie Bernhard recalled the work those involved performed during these busy years:

> Mrs. Otto Guthman and I met every boat that came in ... I used to take the wheelbarrow to help them take their baggage, put them in my car, and take them to the house that we had ready for them. We knew they were coming in ... and had a place to take them.[4]

Bernhard used to tell her grandchildren about meeting people at the boat or train with furniture strapped to the top of her car. She told about meeting Irene Ginzburg when she arrived and welcoming her into the family home to such an extent that Irene practically became part of the family. When Irene married Irv Epstein, their wedding was held in the Bernhard home.

Bernhard recalled that the organization established a boarding house on 13th Avenue and installed an immigrant couple, Mr. and Mrs. Freedman, to operate it. The JFCS Refugee Committee sent single men there, and Boeing workers often used the boarding house. The committee also lodged families in the boarding house when they did not have another place to put them. One couple were tenants of the boarding house with their nine-year-old son. Special assistance was needed when the wife had medical problems that required multiple surgeries. Later, JFCS was able to help them open a small notions store in the Security Market. By the 1970s, the young boy had become the president of his own company, was married with three wonderful children, and he and his family were quite prominent in the community.

Bernhard told the Jewish Historical Society, "The rehabilitation of a family ... had to be done with personal contact, friendship." Although the resettled newcomers formed friendships with the volunteers and caseworkers who helped them, it was also important to let them form their own relationships. Agency staff and volunteers were cautioned not to let the relationships go too far towards dependence, which could hinder the immigrants' progress as they moved from refugee to resident and eventually to citizen.

The thrift shop planned by the NCJW agreed to give preference for employment in the shop to clients of JFCS, especially those receiving financial assistance who could not be integrated into the general labor market. The thrift shop's board was comprised of 11 people—six representatives of the NCJW, three from JFCS, and two from the Seattle Jewish Fund. Support was provided to initiate the project by the Seattle Jewish Fund and was repaid from the profits. Assistance was given from an advisory committee of businessmen, and Mr. Scott, president of the board of the Goodwill Industries, was asked for guidance. The shop was in operation by August 1, 1949.

In June of 1947, a report from USNA told of 60 families who had arrived from Shanghai to the West Coast and were awaiting resettlement. Beginning July 1, it was expected that 100 additional families would arrive on each immigrant transport ship landing on the West Coast.

The cost of resettlement rose as more and more refugees arrived. Los Angeles went from 23 cases to 46, and the expense grew from $1,700 to over $3,000 each. Seattle was experiencing similar demand. JFCS staff and board members recognized the need to strengthen the public relations aspect of the work in order to enlist as much voluntary aid as possible. The public relations work was coordinated with a number of other organizations, agencies, and committees. The responsibility of HIAS was to help émigrés with all the bureaucratic details required when crossing various borders en route to the United States. United Services for New Americans' main function was to help people resettle in various communities of the United States. At the time, USNA was the second largest private agency in the United States, exceeded only by the American Red Cross.

When a study showed that people could adjust more quickly and live more productively if they were resettled in smaller communities, the agencies began to move people out of the big cities of the ports of arrival, which had been the traditional home to immigrant Jews.

HIAS was, and still is, the only Jewish immigration agency whose program was international in scope. In 1947, it provided services in 54 countries outside the United States and catered to the special needs of Orthodox Jews. In many South American countries, HIAS was the only immigration agency in existence. Its immigrant reception services helped immigrants to cope with the many perplexing adjustments they faced upon arrival. During the first six months of 1947, HIAS sheltered 20,010 people, served almost 100,000 meals, and rendered almost all services required by detainees at Ellis Island. HIAS also transmitted $869,000 to Romania, Palestine, and Switzerland and handled transportation costs amounting to $549,000.

Under the Displaced Persons Act of 1948, immigration by Jews to the United States was reduced from 1945 levels as allocations for farm laborers and non-Jews from the Baltic region and Poland increased. US legislators assumed that Jews would go to Palestine, soon to become the state of Israel. The US government restricted immigration by displaced persons by establishing a cutoff date, which required that refugees had to have entered the camps before December 22, 1945, to be eligible for immigration into the country. Most of the camps were in Germany for slave laborers and concentration camp survivors. More than 100,000 Jews from Poland and the Soviet Union were excluded from immigration entirely because of the date they entered displaced persons camps. (The war in Europe ended with the unconditional surrender of Germany on May 8, 1945.)

In 1947, JFCS was fortunate to have the services of a legal committee consisting of Melville Monheimer, Edward Dobrin, and Albert Franco. Medical care was organized with the assistance of Dr. Harry J. Friedman, who assembled the medical profession to help ailing clients. JFCS also enlisted the services of Dr. Frank Goodman, DDS, who solicited his fellow dental practitioners on behalf of agency clients.

In addition to the immense postwar resettlement efforts, the responsibilities of JFCS still included all the other services it had provided before the war, including emergency services to families in need, counseling for individuals and families, and services to older clients. The expansion in operations compelled the agency to find new quarters in the Court Building at 408 Marion Street. The roomier offices provided an atmosphere with greater privacy in which to discuss confidential problems with clients.

Assisting in oversight of the Caroline Kline Galland Home was a continuing responsibility of the JFCS board. By 1948, the home was filled to capacity, and director Anne Elizabeth Nassauer had the facility running smoothly. The JFCS annual report noted, "It is unfortunate that the Home cannot handle the numerous cases of chronically ill Jewish aged for whom no adequate facilities are available. The Board of the Caroline Kline Galland Home recognizes the vital need for a convalescent wing."

Contributions from the Isaac Cooper Trust represented more than 60 percent of JFCS' s 1948 budget, and trustees Eugene Levy and the Seattle First National Bank had considerable control over allowed uses of the funds. They filed a suit against JFCS claiming that the preventive work of the organization was not "relief." In her annual report of March 1948, agency President Mary Louise Reiter stated that "the court decision" (which allowed a portion of the funds from the Trust to be used for preventative work) "avoided further conflict and made it possible for us to do both preventative work and give relief—the latter going mainly to newcomers since obviously other clients are eligible to all the county sources of referral."

In June of 1948, JFCS found it necessary to suspend taking new resettlement cases due to the heavy relief load. Workers and money were stretched to the limit. However, USNA prevailed in their ongoing pleas upon Director Kaufman to accept five cases for the month of September, seven cases for October, and another seven for November.

At the same time, it is noteworthy that the organization was reaching ever closer towards the milestone of 1,000 members.

The Seattle Section of the National Council of Jewish Women was also involved in the resettlement efforts in many ways. Members met émigrés at the train stations and collected household items for the new households. Council volunteers also secured a warehouse, rent free, to store furniture for émigré families, and they planned a furniture drive and linen shower to be held during January 1949.

The NCJW women helped integrate newcomers into the community through social and educational activities and taught English as well as domestic science classes. The council also contributed $100 to the Jewish Club of Washington to help defray the expenses for Passover dinners for the newcomers. In 1948, 120 people were expected to attend a Seder on the first night of Passover, and 165 the second night. The Hebrew Immigrant Aid Society assisted JFCS with situations involving immigration, as needed.

When it was recognized that an employment and vocational counselor was needed, Harry Grill, who was working in that capacity at USNA in New York, came to JFCS. In addition to making placements, Grill worked with the board to create an Employment Committee, and Sam Tarshis accepted the chairmanship. This Employment Committee not only acted in an advisory capacity but also facilitated contacts with potential employers, counseled the staff on individual placement problems relating to employer attitudes, and acted as a consultant group on fair employment practices. Twelve men met to form the committee, discussing such issues as the problems involved when émigrés who were applying for work stated that they would be willing to take lower-than-standard salaries. It was the feeling of the group that this practice might have grave repercussions in the community.

The entire membership of JFCS was encouraged to participate in the effort to find employment for the large number of émigrés that were expected to land in Seattle, and a significant outreach to the rest of the Jewish community was put in place. Other problems identified that made finding employment difficult for émigrés included their lack of language facility, non-translatable skills, and an unwillingness on the part of many Jewish employers to hire them.

During one of his employer visits, Grill visited Morris Polack's poultry processing plant and was able to place Charles Goldschmidt as a helper there at pay of one dollar an hour and later referred Mrs. Danziger for a job as a chicken-plucker.

Transient men continued to be a problem, and the Case Policy Committee became involved under the leadership of Dr. Joseph Cohen. The committee formulated a policy for transients as follows:

> To consider each applicant on the basis of his individual needs, extending in every instance casework services and assistance.

> To continue cooperation with local, state and national agencies in an effort to minimize aimless transiency by following accepted casework principles in this regard.

> To refer transients to the King County Public Welfare Dept. for clearance and for transportation where indicated.

One of the purposes of JFCS, outlined in its bylaws, was to "promote education and training for social work and to provide ways and means for staff members constantly to improve their own professional competency." To implement this goal, the JFCS board joined with NCJW in establishing a scholarship for the training of a second-year student of social work. In recognition of the agency's high standards, the University of Washington Graduate School of Social Work used JFCS as a fieldwork training center with agency staff supervising three students during 1948. Student interns have continued to participate at the agency almost every year since. (As this program continued, Ken Weinberg, one of those graduate school interns himself, became the agency's executive director.)

During 1948, it became necessary to set up a Medical Care Committee to study the needs of clients unable to pay for medical or dental care. In most cases, refugees were not eligible for public medical care that was restricted to permanent residents and citizens. After many conversations with the Jewish physicians in the community, the committee established a fee system in accordance with prevailing schedules. The practitioners formed a Medical Advisory Group with Drs. Jack Doctor, Harry Friedman, Frank Goodman, and Alexander Grinstein involved in the creation of the new service.

According to the Displaced Persons Act of 1948, the 90 family units (270 people) that the Jewish community of Seattle signed assurances for had to enter Seattle not later than July 1, 1950. The job of integrating these new people into the American scene involved much more than financial assistance. These newcomers had endured unimaginable traumas in their years in concentration camps, as homeless refugees, as fugitives, and as stateless persons in displaced-persons camps. It was very difficult to help them recapture qualities of dignity and self-confidence.

Helping these folks to become self-reliant was the work of the caseworkers of JFCS. For the most part, the newcomers arrived knowing little or no English and unfamiliar with the customs of the country. Irving Anches and Sam Tarshis, members of the committee charged with finding jobs for the newcomers, worked tirelessly enlisting employers' cooperation in finding or creating jobs for the refugees. The Thrift and Therapeutic Workshop established by NCJW and the Seattle Jewish Fund enabled JFCS to place some of the refugees who otherwise were unemployable and would have had to be entirely on relief. In addition, Harvey Frankel joined the staff as a vocational counselor, having come from the national office of United Services for New Americans, to help determine the potentialities and abilities of the immigrants and to help make proper placements for them.

Washington was among the first states to identify and recognize the various problems created for communities receiving displaced persons and to make a concerted effort to assist them. JFCS board member Rabbi Samuel Penner was appointed by governor Arthur Langlie to serve on the Displaced Persons Committee of the state of Washington.

The JFCS Émigré Committee (distinct from the Washington Émigré Bureau) came to the realization that the public didn't know enough about its work and more should be done to inform them. Members first decided the name was a misnomer and the committee should be renamed the Resettlement Committee, and information should be provided focusing on the fact that charity was not being sought for these clients. What was being sought was the right to earn a living.

Between January 1 and April 30, 1949, JFCS served 16 new immigrants, helped to resettle 19 other newly arrived families, and provided financial assistance to 151 continuing families. Thirty-eight employment placements were made, and of 17 active counseling cases, three were attending school under NCJW grants. Sixty-seven firms received visits from staff and volunteers to solicit jobs for immigrants, and dozens of others were contacted by phone. In May, 38 families received financial assistance, and in June, 35 families qualified for assistance, with costs to the agency exceeding $3,000 each month.

In conformance with the newest thinking, JFCS resettled families directly to smaller, outlying communities rather than in Seattle first. The agency extended casework services to those communities, reaching beyond Seattle for the first time.

In August 1949, it was announced that the Displaced Persons camps in Europe would be closed, and Seattle was asked to accept 70 families for the coming year, in addition to the 21 cases already allocated. Only one of the original 21 families had arrived by that time, but the board voted unanimously to accept the additional 70 cases and grant USNA the additional assurances—promises that the newcomers would be supported and not become public charges. This meant that as many as 91 new families were expected in the following 12 months. As a whole, they were expected to be younger than the previous Shanghai group. Also, many had been retrained vocationally overseas, and most of them spoke, read, and wrote at least some English, so there was an expectation that they would integrate much more easily into the community than those from

Shanghai. JFCS received an allowance of $100 for each person in the displaced unit, which was expected to ease the community's financial burden as the families became self-supporting. This quota did not include families brought into the community on private assurances and affidavits. The agency still extended services to those privately sponsored families.

While overall the individuals arriving were younger, one of the employment issues remained the advanced age of many of the immigrants. Sixty-five percent of the placement load in 1949 was over 45-years old, and the average age was 59.

When the Thrift Shop opened, it was similar to a miniature Goodwill store. Salaries ranged from 50 cents to one dollar an hour, and 14 people were employed. There was also some success placing employees in private industry. Some of the work was provided through contracts with various industries. Plans were made to establish an outlet for rummage sales that would be away from the Thrift Shop location.

Priorities for job placement went to heads of families who were on continuous relief. The second priority was children of families that were on relief, and third was persons who were still self-supporting but who risked becoming recipients of relief unless employed. A fourth category included other persons in the community who needed to be considered for placement.

In meetings with prospective employers, the Employment Committee discovered a prejudice against employing displaced persons and decided to try to mobilize the entire community into finding more jobs for the unemployed newcomers. It was hoped that an aggressive Employment Committee would secure a backlog of available steady jobs and help fit the newcomers into those jobs.

Vocational counselor Frankel met with the board to describe the work he did from the time a client came to JFCS until the person was placed in a job, explaining the importance of the follow-up work as well. During his first year with the agency, Frankel had placed 91 clients. All but 15 were émigrés. He also worked with new arrivals in reviewing/screening scholarship applicants and helped outline the course of study.

It was suggested that the vocational counselor should not be responsible for finding jobs and that more avenues of casual employment should be opened. Sewing, mending, housecleaning, domestic work, catering, gardening, making deliveries, babysitting, berry picking, and similar seasonal employment were mentioned as possible casual job categories. In addition, a loan fund was established to help those who could show an aptitude or desire to set up small businesses, such as modest grocery stores, newsstands, or notion stores where the capital investment would be small.

Two cases presented to the Case Policy Committee concerned JFCS's policy on relief and medical care. The first case concerned an émigré disabled by polio. Requests had been made by interested parties in the community that his budget be increased above the set scale. The committee recommended that relief be continued solely as per policy.

The second case involved a 14-year-old dental patient for whom special orthodontia work had been requested. Unless JFCS could take the responsibility for the bill of $300, the child would have a handicap for the rest of his life. The committee approved the expenditure.

In 1951, the new Washington State Welfare Act made it possible for JFCS to transfer certain displaced-person relief cases of people who were in good health to the King County Welfare Department.

The Bonham Galland Nursery School, started by the community in 1951, was created to help children of immigrants make a successful adjustment to their new environment and more quickly adapt to language, skills, and play materials. Three- and four-year-old children of Jewish immigrants played and learned with American children of all races and creeds. The school operated for a few years, but the costs were higher than the Jewish federation (then called the Federated Fund and Council of Seattle), the major supporting entity, was willing to support, and it was closed in 1956.

A news release from HIAS reported that on Thursday, November 18, the army transport USS *General Bundy* docked in Boston carrying 273 Jews. (The surviving copy of the release is undated.) This was the second transport to arrive under the Displaced Persons Act of 1948. Among the refugees was Rabbi Isaak Haut, who had given up his place on the first boat to a pregnant woman. Also on the second boat was her husband, Jonas Feuerwerker, and their nine-month-old son, Abraham. For many of the immigrants, debarkation in the United States marked the end of two or three years of waiting in the displaced persons camps of Europe, during which time HIAS worked ceaselessly in their behalf to facilitate their entry into the United States

The following year, the proposed JFCS budget estimated the amount needed for relief at $24,000 plus $6,000 for medical care, for a total of $30,000, but when the actual costs for the previous year were tallied, it became apparent that the requested amount was grossly inadequate, and the proposed budget had to be revised.

Employment for newcomers remained difficult, and Director Kaufman discussed the cases of some who had been self-supporting but had recently become unemployed. Many families were expected to be on relief for anywhere from one month to a year, and she estimated that at least $46,000 would be needed—$35,000 for émigrés, $5,000 for others, and $6,000 for medical assistance. Kaufman reported:

> It is the policy of JFCS in the disbursement of money received from the Isaac Cooper Trust fund to use said money solely and exclusively for providing direct material assistance in the form of money, food, clothing, housing, medical aid and hospital services, and other living essentials, to people who are without sufficient funds or earnings to supply such needs, and for maintaining the sick and maimed, and supporting and educating orphans and indigent children.

Neediness is defined as the insufficiency of funds or earnings by any person to supply himself or his family living essentials, such as food, clothing, housing, medical aid, and hospital services.

In early 1950, it became apparent that there were significant problems in the management of JFCS, and questions arose as to the performance of some of the professional staff. The board requested that the Family Service Association of America, the Seattle Community Chest, and the Council of Jewish Federations and Welfare Funds create and evaluate a formal survey and analysis of JFCS operations. Board members were asked to participate and to work with the consultants.

The survey started with the question: What does JFCS do? It followed with questions designed to help evaluate the work of the director and the professional staff, their competence, attitudes, and relationships. One objective constantly held by the study team was to determine how effectively the agency was meeting its responsibility for providing essential casework services to clients. In their conclusions, the consultants found that the agency director had been instrumental in helping the agency to successfully transform itself. It had been a somewhat paternalistic and "friendly helping hand" organization and was now one whose principles of casework were such that it could secure admission into the Family Service Association of America. Kaufman was also given credit for helping the agency meet known needs and to explore unknown needs.

However, the team also found that the director had to take the majority of the responsibility for the confusion, discord, and turbulence within the board and staff. They found the casework being done in an unacceptable manner so that often only the peripheral or superficial aspects of the problems were being met. When working with émigrés, staff seemed to give no consideration to countries of origin or the ability of the émigrés to make progress on their own initiative, and there was a tendency to perpetuate dependency on JFCS.

The investigating team also found several instances of "administrative inefficiency," which interfered with the services provided to clients, and concluded that this was also a result of poor executive performance. The executive was admittedly aware of the poor quality of casework being done but did not respond appropriately with regular performance evaluations and appropriate staff training, nor did she keep the board apprised of the difficulties.

The evaluators "reluctantly" recommended that Kaufman be replaced, which was accepted by the Board. Following Kaufman's departure, members of the board became actively involved in the restructuring of the Agency, in securing adequate local professional assistance during the interim, and in the search for a new Executive Director.

In 1951, the Family Service Association of America, one of the central organizing forces working toward the development of skilled professional community services, was generally accepted as the standard-setting body in its field. Having become one of the 236 member agencies of the FSAA, JFCS was required to meet new requirements to insure better services to families.

FSAA historians note that "at the time, family social work recognized that personal and family difficulties were rooted in a combination of factors—social, economic, physical, and emotional. Relief of economic distress had become primarily a government concern, freeing voluntary family service agencies to extend programs and to serve all populations. The focus had moved to prevention of family breakdown through counseling and other services."

The first requirement was to provide family casework in accordance with those practices evidenced to be most helpful to individuals and families. Harriet Parsons, the field director of the FSAA, provided guidance to insure those practices were understood and implemented, and trainings were held to insure that all counseling staff were aware of and developed skills in those practices.

The JFCS board of directors also made a concerted effort to recruit new members from across the Jewish community in terms of professions, community activities, and interests. Labor union officials and civic leaders helped increase the areas of expertise on the board. Board members were expected to develop a broad understanding of social problems, have the ability and be willing to participate in the work of the board and committees, and "have an open mindedness which enables him to cooperate with others on the board and with other social agencies."[5] This was a great deal to ask of someone who would be donating his or her time and talent, but the mission of the organization was important to members of the community. These changes were part of the very significant alteration of the work of the board as it continued to change. Whereas it had been a board whose members were often involved in providing direct service to clients, it now became focused on policy and guidance of a professional staff.

From the beginning in 1892, board members tended to serve continuously for decades, but the new practice across the country was to create room for new people to be brought in, bringing with them fresh ideas, interests, and energies. For the first time in its more than 50-year history, the bylaws were changed so that a board member could serve only two consecutive terms of three years each. After that, one full year had to pass before a person was eligible for re-election.

One example of board engagement and professionalization is provided through a report of the Personnel Practices Committee. Their assessment of JFCS found that employees' salary scales, work hours, vacations, sick leaves, and attendance at conferences and institutes were all in conformity with those of other progressive agencies.

⟨∞⟩

An April 1951 report estimated that five new families would be received each month through October, after which the displaced-persons load was expected to begin to decrease. JFCS had been informed that the International Refugee Organization had been able to obtain the necessary transportation. During the coming 18 months, the agency estimated the increase in caseload would be 45 cases.

During 1951, $1,562 had been spent for local relief, a per capita cost of $33 per month. The cost of financial assistance was much higher for new American families. It amounted to a total of $45,794, a per capita cost of $109 per month. During the first four months of 1952, financial assistance for new Americans was $23,193; the per capita cost, $131. The differences were a result primarily of two factors: an increase in budgetary allowances and a larger number of new American families who were too handicapped to obtain full employment so that allowances for more families were larger.

The proposed budget for 1951 estimated that JFCS disbursements would total $125,058.90 with $66,000 expected to be spent on relief—primarily in support of the newcomers. The Community Chest would be asked for an additional $16, 556 over the allocation for the previous year.

1. Her detailed story is at Holocaust Center for Humanity in Seattle.
2. Klaus Stern, *My Legacy: Blessings, Love and Courage* (Seattle: Washington Holocaust Education Resource Center, 2007).
3. An omnibus social service agency organized in New York in 1946 to meet the needs of Holocaust survivors. USNA grew out of the National Refugee Service organized in 1939 to assist Jews fleeing Europe.
4. JHS interview with Mrs. A. M. Bernhard, December 1972.
5. Jessie Danz, et al., page 107. paragraph that 65 percent are middle-age, in possession of the author.

Chapter 10

1951-1967: Window into the Past, Guide and Inspiration for the Future

The beginning of the 1950s saw Seattle and the Puget Sound region prosper with postwar construction of new homes and communities. At the same time, the release of consumer spending held in check during the war years, and later military spending for the Korean War as well as the lifting of tolls from the first Lake Washington Floating Bridge, also spurred development east of Lake Washington. Servicemen took advantage of the GI Bill, obtaining their college or university degrees and then joining the workforce. They bought homes, and the birth rate skyrocketed in the postwar baby boom. But prosperity did not extend to all. Jewish Family & Child Service worked hard to meet the demands for more services. New thinking and improved practices in social work provided not only new tools for the agency and its caseworkers but also new answers for old problems that continued to tax limited resources.

During the transition period between executive directors in 1951, the work of the agency proceeded with board members stepping in as needed. At various meetings early in that year, president Dorothea Pickard explained the relationship between the new Displaced Persons Act and the Washington State Welfare Act, which had also just been enacted. Originally, the board thought JFCS could turn over certain displaced-person relief cases to the

King County Welfare Department (KCWD), but these clients were required to be in good health. Pickard worked with the JFCS Legal Advisory Committee, the Legislative Committee, and the state attorney general's office to work out the complications.

JFCS received $1,500 from the state labor relations office for the training of rehabilitation cases and anticipated that the state would also be providing between $750 and $800 per case to take care of the institutional hard-core cases that were expected in the near future.

There were a number of questions about the use of public resources on behalf of the newcomers. The King County Welfare Department suggested that JFCS send through two test cases directly to Roderic Olzondom, state director of Social Security. If those cases were accepted by the county, a new interpretation of policy could be handed down to the public agencies permitting non-citizens access to public resources. Eventually, limited public resources were accessed by newcomers, but great care was taken to ensure that their immigration status was not put in jeopardy.

After a national search, Albert S. White was appointed executive director of JFCS. He was born in Lida, Poland, and came to the United States at the age of eight. He graduated from Harvard and held master's degrees from Boston Teachers College and the New York School of Social Work. White was an experienced vocational counselor, had worked with the American Red Cross, served as the assistant director of Migration Services of the United Services for New Americans, and been Director of Jewish Family Service in Dallas, Texas. He had also been a faculty member at the Evening College of the University of Cincinnati.

A November 1951 meeting was called to review the rising relief costs and the present relief practices. During the month of October, $5,000 had been spent on relief costs compared with an average of $3,800 per month during the first nine months of the year. There were 20 families whose employment possibilities were limited or impossible, and providing support was costly. The Employment Committee was reporting that there was hope for jobs for only a

1951 – 1967: Window into the Past,
Guide and Inspiration for the Future
191

few in this group. In reviewing the agency's relief practices, it was found that JFCS differed in some ways from what the King County Welfare Department did:

Employed clients received the maximum food allowances from JFCS. The welfare department used allowances based on occupation. JFCS also provided a 10-percent increase to families that used kosher food.

JFCS issued clothing as needed, whereas the welfare department provided a sliding-scale clothing allowance based on age, occupation, and sex.

JFCS paid fuel and utility bills, and the county gave an allowance based on the size of the family and size of the rooms.

JFCS provided a higher rental allowance than the county. In some instances, JFCS underwrote allowances for books, transportation, and milk for children attending the Seattle Hebrew School.

In light of the present economic position of the agency, the Employment Committee agreed to alter JFCS financial assistance to more closely reflect the King County policies. The rental allowance, special education expenses, and some transportation costs (for work, education, medical needs, or transportation to the agency) were left the same.

HIAS requested that none of its branch offices consider as "final" any decisions by local immigration offices under the McCarran-Walter Act of 1952 (which, among several provisions, retained a quota on some immigrants allowed into the country) that would cause undue hardships. There had been some success in preventing deportations and, in a few instances, of admitting persons who were excluded under the act. This, of course, did not apply to anyone who was guilty of fraud or whose subversive activity was not beyond question. Very few of the other HIAS branch offices had as much difficulty in naturalization cases as did the Seattle office.

Early in 1952, White requested that, in view of the large financial expenditures for unemployable families, JFCS review its commitment to accept four families classified as hard core. United Services for New Americans had credited Seattle with only one hard-core family, and White had submitted a detailed report outlining the difficulties of the other three. He requested that they be credited to the agency's hard-core commitment. USNA denied the request, but White asserted that Seattle had more than its share of these difficult cases citing limitations caused by a lack of low-cost hospital facilities and by its inability to use public assistance resources for a period of five years. The Executive Committee agreed to recommend to the board that JFCS not accept any additional hard-core families since the community was being drained of financial and other resources due to the large number of these families already being served.

Reports given at another 1952 board gathering included information about a meeting of the panel of physicians that had been held in January to discuss the extensive medical care required to meet the needs of the new Americans that JFCS was responsible for helping to rehabilitate. A rotation plan had been put in place, and the physicians were satisfied with the results and did not feel overloaded with agency clients. Emphasis was placed on making clients of the agency feel that their relationship with their physicians was a personal one, regardless of their ability to pay.

At the same time, efforts were being made to secure emergency dental care and other related services on either a non-fee or reduced-fee basis. Dr. Harvard Kaufman was providing psychiatric consultation on children's problems without charge.

Other board reports provided the information that seven new American families had arrived over a two-month period and 10 to 12 more were expected by the end of April. Five new local cases had been referred to JFCS: one by a rabbi, one by another social agency, one as a self-referral, and two by community people.

There had also been six employment placements: five new Americans and one a local resident. The employment situation for unskilled work in Seattle was critical, creating the need to provide financial assistance for families where there had been loss of jobs. The amount of relief reached $6,500 in February. A suggestion was made by the Employment Committee that a special publicity program was required to make its program more effective. Employment reached its lowest point in March, but by the end of April, the situation had improved considerably with 14 placements. An article appeared in the *Jewish Transcript* highlighting the resettlement efforts JFCS was engaged in and requesting assistance from the community to provide work opportunities for the newcomers. The article received positive results, with three jobs obtained. At the same time, consideration was being given to an expansion of NCJW's Thrift and Therapeutic Workshop.

In light of the considerable cost of financial assistance for families, the Executive Committee set the first priority of JFCS to be the reduction of the cost of relief for new Americans. How this was to be accomplished was not specified.

The Case Policy Committee reviewed several cases, one of which concerned an elderly woman who had no resources except partial maintenance from a daughter whose earnings were barely sufficient to support her own child and herself. The three of them lived together in a single room. The relatives who had sponsored this family were no longer able to provide financial support, and $50 a month was being requested to provide food and more adequate housing for the woman. The support was granted with a review of the situation to take place in six months.

The Employment Committee also adopted a firm policy that financial assistance would be denied clients who refused work they might consider menial, such as housework, babysitting, and other casual labor. In the following months, White reported some resentment among clients about the policy, but he felt that it was professionally sound to bring families to the realization that the resource of financial assistance from JFCS could only be used when they had no other means. The agency considered a work opportunity for a client as a primary resource.

Toward the end of the year, the caseload dropped, but counseling cases of local residents remained high. The decrease was entirely in new American cases with almost 50 percent requiring counseling without financial assistance. During this period, staff members were able to circulate through the community making presentations in response to invitations from synagogues and community groups.

Melville Monheimer reported that $3,000 was received in November 1952 from the Victor Rott Estate. The bequest was added to the endowment fund, which had originated with the Neufelder Fund. The following year, a bequest was received from the estate of Alice V. Meyer.

As the resettlement program for new Americans wound down, the Executive and Employment Committees met to discuss the future of the employment service. The question was whether it should be for all Jewish people or only for new Americans. The point was that women over age 35 in general and men over 40 with no special skills found it difficult to obtain jobs. It was even more difficult for the aged and for people with physical handicaps or personality problems. It was recognized that the state employment resources for those groups were limited and inadequate and that in the private social agency the applicant's needs were given primary consideration. Frankel, the employment specialist, emphasized that employment was a basic need for people and that it frequently complemented casework service. The board decided that an employment service for local residents was a need that JFCS should continue to meet.

At the end of 1952, the Caroline Kline Galland Home was filled to capacity, providing for 35 guests. Nine applicants waited for beds, an increase over the usual four or five. Even the infirmary was being used to house two of the guests. All applications for admission to the home were still being processed through JFCS. Since all guests were required to turn over their assets to the home, a monetary allowance of five dollars a month was allowed for personal incidentals. Funds for clothing were provided as needed.

The board recognized a great need for a regular planned program of recreation for the residents, in addition to the card games, television viewing (still pretty thin in those days), and reading material that were already available. There was also a suggestion that the Kline Galland Committee begin having small group discussions about the various problems of the aged, such as housing, recreation, occupations, and health.

At a subsequent meeting, Mrs. Robert M. Jones, chairman of the Health and Welfare Council of Seattle - King County's Care of the Aging Committee, was a guest. She discussed the work and the findings of the various subcommittees of the council's committee: vocation rehabilitation, housing, nursing home, recreation, personal problems, and extended hospital care.

JFCS's Kline Galland Committee then examined trends in care and housing for the aged. White was able to report recommendations made by Flora Fox, director of the Central Bureau of the Aged in New York, whom he had consulted regarding planning for services to the aged in a city the size of Seattle. Her recommendations included:

Development of a program of convalescent care, which would take into account Jewish cultural factors. Fox felt that, if at all feasible, this should be developed as part of an administrative structure of the established home.

Development of a program of recreational services at the home to meet emotional as well as physical needs.

Development of a program, which JFCS might undertake with the Caroline Kline Galland Home, of maintaining old people in independent living arrangements but of having the home take responsibility for providing them with recreational services and occupational therapy.

⁓

In 1952, Congress enacted the McCarran-Walter Act, creating terror among many Jewish and non-Jewish newcomers alike. The act abolished racial restrictions found in earlier immigration statutes yet retained a quota system for nationalities and regions. A number of social service agencies in the community began calling on JFCS for consultation. Eventually, the act established a preference system that determined which ethnic groups were desirable immigrants and also placed great importance on labor qualifications.

The act defined three types of immigrants: immigrants with special skills or relatives of US citizens who were exempt from quotas and who were to be admitted without restrictions, average immigrants whose numbers were not supposed to exceed 270,000 per year, and refugees.

The McCarran-Walter Act modified a considerable amount of immigration legislation. It mandated non-citizens register once a year, regardless of length of residence in the United States. It retained national-origin quotas, which gave preference to people born in Western Europe, and introduced a new method for selection of immigrants through the regulations, which provided that 50 percent of quota numbers be assigned to skilled, educated people. The definitions of the qualifications were not immediately revealed so immigrants and agencies alike expected immigration to drop considerably on the basis of failure to meet those qualifications. Regulations enabled an employer to petition for entrance of individuals with special skills.

The naturalization process became much more difficult. An applicant had to be able to write, and the literacy test usually involved taking dictation from the inspector. In the past, reading alone had been sufficient to demonstrate literacy. One provision of the act seemed to relax requirements. Applicants previously had submitted first papers and second papers in the entry process. These two applications were checked against each other and any discrepancies could be a basis for denial of entry. Under McCarran-Walter, first papers were no longer required. As more people become aware that JFCS was a comprehensive immigration organization representing

HIAS in Seattle and that it was a cooperating agency for United Services for New Americans, additional requests for immigration service came to JFCS. Executive Director White held qualifications in that field and was certified by the Justice Department to appear at hearings on immigration cases.

There was also a mandatory home and neighborhood investigation. This involved immigration investigators questioning of members of the family, including children, as well as people in the neighborhood. Immigration officials could call upon JFCS to obtain background information, and they were empowered to subpoena case records.

In April, a report by Clara Friedman, USNA field consultant, said that USNA had reduced the number of communities for resettlement from approximately 300 to 76. Experience showed the advisability of limiting resettlement to those communities that were able to provide the resources necessary for the adjustment of new Americans. Seattle had demonstrated that ability.

Because of the necessity for every alien to have a good record of integration into the community prior to being naturalized, it became more essential that the community provide good educational and employment resources. The Bonham Galland Nursery School was invaluable for both parents and children. The services of the nursery school were described in a widely distributed manual of USNA, one of only two projects selected for inclusion.

The director of Latin American Operations for HIAS reported that in many Latin American countries it was possible to purchase visas, and regulations by these countries had very little meaning. His greatest concern was Bolivia where every indication was there would be a Russian-style pogrom. All Jews living there were urged to leave as rapidly as possible. Although the families from Bolivia who sought JFCS services confirmed the fear caused by the rumors, no such pogrom ever occurred.

In Mexico, some newspapers expressed anti-Semitic positions, due primarily to high rates of poverty among its citizens and a relatively large number of prosperous Jews. In Brazil, Jewish people fit in well and enjoyed a fine cultural and religious life, particularly in Sao Paulo.

In Argentina, HIAS worked out arrangements with dictator Juan Perón (a Hitler supporter) to procure visas. In some other South American countries, conditions for Jews varied greatly depending on government policies, which could change quite quickly. HIAS suggested that anyone contemplating migrating to a South American country check first with an HIAS office about specific conditions.

Cuba was also an attractive destination for immigrant Jews since it was so close to the United States. Visas could be secured relatively easily, but the unions did not permit anyone to work there for the first five years. However, it was possible to open a business there.

In the 1950s, the West German government began to pay indemnification claims to victims of Nazi persecution. White worked with experts at HIAS and USNA on indemnity payments so JFCS could refer more clients to public agencies without jeopardizing immigration status.

JFCS's Public Relations Committee recommended that a year-round program of publicity and information be established using the *Jewish Transcript*, occasional informative news letters to the membership, and talks to organized groups. The executive director was assigned this effort, although board members participated from time to time. The committee also noted that the executive director should continue to maintain and develop working relationships with other organizations and agencies.

In 1953, JFCS moved its offices to 1620 Jackson Street. The same year, White attended the National Conference of Jewish Communal Service in Atlantic City. He reported that the yearly conference provided the best possible source for securing, in one place, current information on immigration and services to the aged. He had been able to meet with top experts in these fields and to discuss specific situations of interest to the agency.

Regarding immigration, he reported that, when Clara Friedman of USNA was in Seattle, she had analyzed the McCarran-Walter Act and its implications. With the new law, some program managers pondered how best to provide immigration services, if at all.

At that time, a number of questions were raised, which White took with him to the Atlantic City Conference. First was whether a private family service agency (as opposed to a public agency run by the state or the county), even one as well-equipped as JFCS in the field of immigration, should continue to carry on immigration services in view of the complexities of the McCarran-Walter Act. And if so, would the agency require a paid legal consultant?

Immigration attorneys at the conference and representatives of the national immigration agencies affirmed that there was a great deal of value in having a family-agency continue to provide an immigration service. Situations would arise requiring consultation or referral to attorneys. However, they felt that most cases could be handled by professional workers who had some immigration knowledge.

Conference attendees and presenters emphasized the need for a professional staff in immigration work, especially in the area of naturalization. The naturalization process required a careful review of each applicant's background, and under certain circumstances, it might not have been advisable for some people to apply for citizenship. This presented a difficult decision for the applicant, and it needed to be worked through with a trained professional.

A second question was whether aliens who used public assistance or public hospitals would face any risk of deportation or denial of citizenship under the McCarran-Walter Act.

The McCarran-Walter Act did not affect a person who was eligible to use public hospitals or public assistance, provided that the same safeguards were applied as had been used by the agency previously. That is, public assistance should not be used by the following:

aliens who arrived under a corporate affidavit for whom the government still required an adjustment report;

aliens who arrived on a bond that had not yet been cancelled;

aliens whose physical or emotional handicaps did not permit their employment within the first five years after arrival in the United States.

With the exception of mental illness, active tuberculosis, and venereal disease, even the groups of aliens listed above could use public hospitals, providing payment was made. It was not necessary to pay public hospitals bills for eligible aliens who were not in the groups listed.

A third concern White raised was what would happen to the flow of immigration under the McCarran-Walter Act.

There had not been enough experience under the act to speculate on this. Most authorities felt the provision in the act that assigned 50 percent of the quotas to persons with special qualifications and skills could be so construed that very few people would qualify. The retention of the national-origins quota would continue to make many quota numbers unmet, while larger numbers of people from countries of oversubscribed quotas would still be unable to come to the United States. Although it was felt that, in general, the act would tend to limit immigration, close relatives of US citizens would find it easier to be admitted under the law.

A fourth issue was what techniques were being used by communities to inform aliens and naturalized citizens of their responsibilities under the immigration law. Volunteer groups, such as NCJW, put on campaigns to point out the responsibilities of non-citizens to register annually and to carry with them at all times their alien registration cards. Non-citizens who were concerned about their immigration status, as well as those who desired citizenship, were being urged to discuss their status with professional immigration agencies or with attorneys.

A final question was what was being done to revise the act.

Nearly every national agency concerned with humanitarian services had taken some step to have the act revised. There was a general feeling that it placed unreasonable restrictions upon non-citizens, tending to segregate them from Americans, and that it was too punishing in the many penalties it imposed for what seemed to be petty situations. The point was made that there were many people afraid to discuss the act for fear of being tagged as subversive. The feeling of some of the national leaders was that parts of the act, particularly those concerned with registration of aliens, were here to stay for many years. In the meantime, immigration agencies were urged to meet their obligations to help every non-citizen and naturalized citizen to conform with every provision of the act.

White noted that the increasing requests for services for older people at JFCS was reflected on a national scale. No other single area of service received as much attention at the conference, and it seemed that almost every Jewish community was either expanding existing facilities or setting up new ones. Homes for the aged had become the established resource in most Jewish communities for the aged chronically ill.

Following the convention, discussion was held by the board about facilities for older people in Seattle. While there was general agreement that the Seattle Jewish community must provide facilities for the aged chronically ill, there remained a question as to the best method for making it possible. It was hoped that a committee of the Seattle Jewish Fund and NCJW on planning for the aged would be activated in the near future.

White reported that Jewish family agencies had accepted as their responsibility the job of helping older people who were not chronically ill maintain independent living arrangements through programs of homemaker services, casework help, the establishment of employment opportunities, and the setting up of housing facilities suitable for older people.

In the institutional field, most homes for the aged gave preference to the chronically ill and handicapped. They were equipped to provide comprehensive medical services, including physical and occupational therapy and programs to meet the recreational, religious, and cultural needs of older people. Many made their recreational programs available to other older people in the community, providing a central place for recreation and culture to both residents and non-residents.

Discussions included the variety of ways in which to finance services for the aged. Those sources most frequently used included payment by relatives, old age assistance, endowments and contributions, Jewish welfare funds, and Community Chest.

Many of the programs for the aged at Jewish family agencies around the country were supported by Jewish welfare funds. In the non-sectarian field, programs for seniors had been much slower to develop. It was difficult to secure funds from Community Chest for these services.

White described his visit to the Montefiore Home for the Aged in Cleveland and the Drexel Home in Chicago. In both homes, emphasis was on the admission of the chronically ill. In Chicago, there was an extensive daycare program that made it possible for people who were not residents of the home to participate in its program and to dine together with the residents.

While no immediate action was taken, the board was alerted to the need to begin planning for the future when additional programs would be required to support the increasing aging population.

∽∞∾

Regulations under the Refugee Relief Act of 1953 were considered so unworkable even by the officials in the State Department that the immigrant agencies, including HIAS, were asked to recommend changes. One particularly serious aspect was that no agency was permitted to provide assurances of support. Individuals who could provide assurances had to have a job and housing available for an immigrant for a length of time that seemed unrealistic. There was a general feeling among immigrant agencies that it might take a year before the first visa would be issued. The local immigration officers had not seen the proposed regulations until White loaned his own copy to them.

By 1953, the world situation for Jewish immigrates had changed. Some European countries formerly offering refuge to Jews now felt that, since Israel was available, refuge in their country was no longer necessary. This meant considerable difficulty for Jews who did not wish to go to Israel. In Belgium and The Netherlands, some of the poison of the Nazi philosophy remained. Jews were permitted to work in Germany, which had renounced its anti-Semitic attitudes. Still, Germany remained devastated, and many Germans blindly blamed the Jews.

In the Scandinavian countries, Jews were made to feel welcome, but there was practically no Jewish culture or religious life in those countries, and immigrants hesitated to go there. The Scandinavian countries had recently accepted, with the help of a Ford Foundation grant, a large number of physically and emotionally handicapped Jewish people who could have been excluded from the United States.

⚜

Tragically, Albert White had been executive director of Seattle JFCS for only five years when he died at the age of 43 on April 18, 1956. In his memory, the board of directors established the Albert S. White Memorial Fund to benefit a segment of the Jewish population (to be determined at a later date) whose needs were not filled. A memorial service was held on April 28.

During White's brief administration, JFCS had marked an unprecedented growth in the services it rendered.

⚜

Bernard Rackow assumed the office of director in July of 1956. He had earned his bachelor's degree in social science and his master's in education from City College in New York. He then obtained a master's degree in social work from Carnegie Technical and studied for four years in the Seminary College for Jewish Studies at the Jewish Theological Seminary.

His career included work in the Department of Welfare of New York City, psychiatric services in the US Army, work as consultant for USNA, and a directorship of the Hebrew Home for the Aged.

The Israeli War for Independence in 1948 generated great acrimony against Jews in the Arab nations of the Middle East, despite their living in harmony in their communities for hundreds and even thousands of years. Jews were made to feel unwelcome, and the young nation of Israel could only take so many new immigrants from the Arab nations. By 1958, an estimated 2,500 families were expected to emigrate from Egypt and North Africa to the United States. JFCS was asked to accept six families for settlement in Seattle.

The agency had become more involved in foster care, and Mrs. Rotenberg described a program to the board called the Joint Agency Committee for Kiddies Program (the Jackie Program).

One local Jewish family and their foster daughter were pleased to share their story of involvement in the JFS foster care program for use in this book. The family was happily raising their two sons and wanted more children, but that didn't seem to be happening for them. They decided to adopt a third child and approached JFCS for assistance. A little girl was soon brought to them. She was in need of a foster home as her grandmother, who was her guardian, was no longer able to care adequately for her. An understanding was reached that when the grandmother was satisfied that the new family would be a good one for the child she would relinquish custody and allow the family to adopt her.

The transition was extremely difficult. Living with her grandmother, the child had experienced little structure or rules, and she didn't take readily to an imposed bedtime or simple requirements that she brush her teeth, bathe regularly, do her homework, and eat regular meals with the family.

She was also impulsive and was constantly being injured. Soon after her arrival, the family was pleased to provide her with a new bicycle, which she soon learned to ride. However, one evening she decided to go for a ride but took her older brother's bicycle, which she was unable to control. She crashed into a parked car and broke her jaw.

The grandmother continued to refuse to allow the child to be adopted by her new family and insisted on frequent weekend visits and then, after about five years, ended the foster placement altogether. The girl returned to her grandmother for a time but kept in touch with her foster family. She is now a grown woman with four children of her own and calls her former foster mother Mom.

⚭

In February of 1958, JFCS moved to new quarters at 2017 South Jackson Street. At the time, discussions were taking place in Jewish family service agencies across the country about the advisability of charging fees for counseling services. A 1958 survey conducted by the Family Service Association of America reported that between 5 and 10 percent of agency income was being brought in by fees and, when fees were charged, there seemed to be a greater utilization of counseling services by middle-class groups, which otherwise would not be coming in. The greater income was strongly favored by Community Chests, and in certain cases, the agencies were able to use the fees to expand services. In some instances, the total amount of money invested in social services was greater as a result of fees. The difficulties social workers had in developing comfort in charging fees were soon largely overcome. In summation, aside from the remarks by two agencies that their services for hard-to-reach families had been lessened through services in a fee-paying group, fee charging had become an accepted and valuable mode of agency operation. After thorough review and discussion, Jewish Family & Child Service developed a sliding-fee scale and, on July 1, 1958, began charging for counseling services.

In September of the same year, an evaluation of the costs of children's care in the foster children's program and of the anticipated developments was made. The board reaffirmed JFCS's policy of making realistic payments for adequate care. The higher rates being paid by the agency were based on the proposition that neither the foster parents nor the foster child should be penalized. If there was an expectation that a foster child was to receive equal treatment to that of the natural children in the predominantly middle-class foster homes, the payments should be adequate.

The tripling of the amount used for camperships and the distribution among both day and overnight camps was reported.

A $2,000 grant was made by the Bonham Galland Trust Fund to JFCS for its work with children, and a discussion was held about the absence of intensive treatment centers. The Children's Committee of JFCS was asked to make a study of the mental health needs of the children in the Jewish community and explore the concept of a Jewish regional treatment center, as well as other possible alternatives.

Two significant changes occurred as the decade of the '50s came to an end. First, in November of 1959, the board adopted the Group Health medical insurance plan for members of the staff. The second change occurred in January of 1960 when the Executive Committee decided that the caseworker at the Caroline Kline Galland Home would no longer be the financial responsibility of the agency.

By October of 1960, Sam Hanan was able to present a report on an opportunity to purchase the building at 2017 Jackson Street, where JFCS had moved in 1958. The board approved his recommendations, including the establishment of a savings account at the Washington Mutual Savings Bank and implemented its resolution of the previous month to authorize the securing of the mortgage. The purchase was finalized on November 21.

Turnover continued in the position of JFCS's executive director position as Rackow tendered his letter of resignation, indicating he would continue to work until the end of April 1961. In March, the application of Arthur Farber was presented and accepted. Farber held a degree from the School of Social Work in Buffalo, New York, and a graduate certificate in fieldwork from the International Institute in Buffalo. He had completed 125 hours in casework and community organization with the Jewish Welfare Society of Buffalo and 475 hours in the Child Placement Department of the New York School of Social Work at Columbia University, receiving his master's degree in 1941. Farber had an impressive work résumé, which included supervisory positions with three different Jewish family service organizations in New York State.

Betsy DeBeer Smith was in charge of the office from the time of Rackow's departure until Farber's assumption of executive responsibilities on June 16, 1961.

Arthur Farber (JFS photo collection.)

One year later, Mr. Lobe gave a report of the work of the Special Committee on Aging. The board agreed "that we accept any foster home for aged, either Jewish or non-Jewish, that meets with the approval of the client and the Agency." It was further passed that JFCS "recommend that the resident in a foster home who has assets should have a limited policy with the King County Medical Service Bureau for minimal 30-day care."

The work-study fellowship of $2,500 for a second-year graduate student from the University of Washington School of Social Work to do fieldwork in the agency continued. The plan provided for the student to spend three days a week of fieldwork in the agency, provided the school would consent to this arrangement. The money for this fellowship came out of JFCS's trust or reserve funds. It was noted that income from these fund accounts the previous year amounted to a little over $1,500. Jerry Kelley, assistant dean of the University of Washington Graduate School of Social Work, made a presentation noting the significance of the JFCS fellowship award of $2,500 to an outstanding second-year student. Mrs. Gray announced that the 1964 recipient would be Myron Fishman.

Finally, in May 1963, a letter was received from the State Department of Public Assistance indicating that JFCS continued to meet approval for payment standards of that department for placing children in foster homes. The same year, the agency requested funds from United Good Neighbors to help plan services to the aged. A special committee had been charged with this responsibility, chaired by Morton L. Schwabacher. Dr. Lawrence Schwartz joined JFCS as psychiatric consultant.

Very soon, and much to the board's surprise, Farber submitted his letter of resignation as executive director, to be effective October 1, 1963. He had accepted a teaching appointment at the Graduate School of Social Work at the University of Washington.

Betsy DeBeer Smith, who had been casework supervisor under Farber, acted as director of JFCS until Jerry Grossfeld was hired and assumed the duties on April 1, 1965.

Grossfeld attained his BA from Brooklyn College and his master of social work from the University of Pennsylvania. He had worked as a caseworker for JFCS in Philadelphia and Baltimore, had worked with the Marriage Council in Philadelphia, and was director of JFCS in Dayton, Ohio.

At a meeting of the membership, Grossfeld outlined services the agency provided to the community as they mostly concerned the lower economic strata and confirmed that these programs should be maintained and strengthened, taking cognizance of the changing patterns within the Jewish community. However, because of the growing number of middle-class and upper-middle-class families within the Jewish community, he suggested that the casework and counseling programs should be geared increasingly towards serving the needs of these groups, as well as providing services to the traditional clients. For this reason, he presented an experimental plan for Counseling Services, adding Martin Falsberg, a social worker in private practice, to work for JFCS for the equivalent of one-half day a week. It was expected that his service on the staff would stimulate and strengthen services to families that ordinarily availed themselves of private counselors.

The first agency publication to be distributed to the community was part of a plan created by the Public Relations Committee to improve the image in the community, as well as to provide membership with an ongoing education on JFCS's programs and progress. Board members Laura Weinstein and Joseph deLeon worked with Grossfeld in the creation of what was simply called the Newsletter, and the earliest issues were sent to the entire Jewish community. The 75th anniversary publication, which appeared in March 1967, was the last issue to go to the entire community. After that date, it was sent only to the membership.

Chapter 11

1965-1975: Keeping the Lights On

Jewish Family & Child Service experienced a lag in progress and services after Arthur Farber left in 1964. A full year and a half passed before Jerry Grossfeld was hired and able to take responsibility for the agency. Caseworkers kept serving clients, but there were no new programs or expansion of services. For two years, heavy staff turnover even precluded accepting social work students as interns. Grossfeld then needed several months to reorganize the agency before advancement could begin again.

In early 1965, JFCS reported on the 10 most significant welfare needs in the state of Washington. Number one was adequate assistance grants to maintain at least minimum levels of health and decency for the poorest clients. Other needs listed included changes in the eligibility requirements in order for federal funds to be accessed, mandatory medical services, vocational and on-the-job training, and employment counseling for adult welfare recipients. The article noted that at least the Department of Public Assistance was looking at the issues.

In 1965, a specialist in child therapy was added to the counseling staff, which, as Grossfeld and the board had hoped, attracted families who might not customarily have used JFCS's services. In addition to JFCS serving the needy and destitute, this specialist brought in more Jewish families who could afford to pay for therapy, as well as non-Jewish families who were referred from other social service agencies.

Grossfeld was also interested in directly offering adoption services for the Jewish community. This started with connecting Jewish children with Jewish families seeking to adopt. He hoped that JFCS would put the program into effect within a few months, but the complicated licensing process meant that it took until January 1967 for the agency to begin to accept and process the applications of prospective adoptive parents.

A report of the agency's operations for 1966 compared JFCS to a medical general practitioner who treats a wide range of physical ailments. In the coming year, Jewish Family & Child Service was prepared to continue providing its broad multi-function programs to the community, including foster care, counseling for children and for personal and family problems, employment services (which provided employment counseling and placement), refugee resettlement, emergency relief services (including assistance to transients), and services to the elderly. A plan was also in place to offer casework to a wider segment of the Jewish community with more outreach to the Eastside communities.

As management and staffing stabilized, the student intern program was resumed with at least one master's student from the University of Washington School of Social Work participating every year. Each intern had the opportunity to develop and practice counseling skills under the supervision of JFCS professionals during the second year of MSW study. This program would prove to be a boon to the agency well beyond the extra casework help.

Grossfeld and the board heard increasing requests for additional services from the community, and now considered developing new programs. Although refugee resettlement had been suspended for two years due to budgetary constraints, the board was aware that it was contrary to JFCS tradition to leave that responsibility for others to handle. With new immigration legislation in place since the Castro government's relaxation of Cuban emigration restrictions on

September 29, 1965, plus pressure from HIAS, JFCS committed to accepting a limited number of families from Europe. Four families were resettled during 1966, including one from Romania. They also agreed to accept Cuban refugee families as the need arose.

In December 1966, the leadership of the Soviet Union indicated its willingness to permit Jewish families to leave for reunion with their families in Western countries. JFCS waited to hear from HIAS about the number of families it would be expected to resettle during 1967. JFCS's request to the Jewish Federation and Council of Greater Seattle would be based on that number of families, plus a general request of $12,000 to support ongoing resettlement expenses. (See Chapter 12, "1967-1992: Resettlement of Russian Immigrants.")

One of the highlights of Grossfeld's first two years with JFCS was the launching and full implementation of a Jewish Family Life Education (JFLE) program. The first offering in early 1967 was a six-workshop series aimed at preventing the onset of family problems. During each session, group discussions were held in an educational workshop approach. Such favorable responses from the participants were received that a second session was planned for the spring.

Elizabeth Bannister, executive director of Children's Home Society of Washington, shared information with the board about adoptions of Jewish children through her agency and Medina Children's Service over a three-year period. She reported that the increase in births to unwed mothers, as well as a diminishing number of adoptive parents, required expanding adoption services over the coming decade. The JFCS Case Policy Committee examined the issue, and before the end of 1967, the agency was finally licensed as an adoption agency.

In his annual report for 1968, Director Grossfeld told the assembled group that membership dues had been set at one dollar a year in 1893 and had remained at that level until 1960, 67 years later, when dues were increased to two dollars. He then announced another increase: dues for individuals would be raised to three dollars and from four dollars to five dollars a year for family memberships. Since it had only been nine years since the previous increase in dues, Grossfeld commented that inflation seemed to have finally caught up with JFCS.

During 1968, more than 100 Jewish individuals received financial help, about half of them elderly clients accepting a monthly kosher food allowance. However, there had been a significant number of individuals and families where loss of a job, general unemployment, illness, or other circumstances required JFCS's financial help.

The two-year-old adoption program regularly provided many of the lighter, brighter moments in the operations of the agency. Six children found permanent homes during the year, about the same as during the first year of the program. The responsibility of having to accept or reject adoptive families was very difficult, but engaging a family in a process aimed at enabling them to become adoptive parents was a very meaningful program for the Jewish families. In working with JFCS, they avoided what Grossfeld called independent or "gray market" adoption placements, often not preferable, safe, or reliable.

JFCS's board and staff observed the persistent and growing needs of the oldest members of the community. After careful examination of the issue, several projects were developed. In 1971, the *Jewish Transcript* reported on Federation House, an apartment project operated by JFCS, which opened in 1969. Located in one of the buildings in the Lakeshore Apartment complex at 9014-16 53rd Avenue South, it was an independent living facility for elderly men and women who were able to maintain their own apartments but required a little support. Josh Gortler, director of the Caroline Kline Galland Home, explained that the project was a joint effort of the Jewish Federation of Greater Seattle, Kline Galland, and JFCS. One of the units was used as a day room where residents could visit, play cards, or participate in other friendly activities. JFCS wanted to provide more social contact and activities for some of their elderly clients, and Gortler had an idea for a day center that would serve both residents and non-residents of Kline Galland.

Sophie Glickman, the resident day manager of Federation House, checked in with each tenant twice a day. The night manager, Alice Spahi, was on call evenings and nights for emergencies. Twice a week, the day center would bus the residents of Federation House to the Caroline Kline Galland Home for lunch and to join in whatever activities were being offered. After the National Council of Jewish Women (NCJW) developed Council House in 1972, to provide independent living apartments for senior members of the community with limited income, the Federation House project was no longer needed, and the project was discontinued.

In November 1970, in response to a growing waiting list at the Caroline Kline Galland Home, JFCS launched a new program called Home Care for the Elderly. This program served about 70 clients who had recently suffered an illness or been hospitalized. A licensed practical nurse visited an average of 25 patients each week, providing personal services, including bathing, shampooing hair, grooming fingernails and toenails, helping with grocery shopping, and meal preparation. The JFCS homecare coordinator assisted clients and their families with whatever other issues arose.

An experimental Housekeepers Service was also added to assist seniors in their own homes who could no longer handle heavy household chores. Keeping homes clean and safe helped the residents stay in their homes longer by preventing minor hygiene issues that could develop into serious health issues. Grossfeld recognized that these efforts still left significant gaps in services to independent elderly clients. Those who needed assistance but didn't require a nursing home were in a no-man's land between independent and institutional living. They couldn't manage the former but did not yet require the latter.

In 1969, cutbacks at the Boeing Company launched a five-year recession in the Puget Sound region, dubbed the Boeing Bust. The company slashed about 60,000 jobs. In 1970, the unemployment rate in Seattle hit 10 percent against a national rate of 4.5 percent. The jobless rate peaked at 13.5 percent in 1971 and 1972. It didn't help that inflation ran at more than 5 percent a year. The bust did not end until 1974 when construction of the Trans-Alaska Pipeline brought prosperity back to Seattle.

When the Department of Social and Health Services reduced financial assistance grants in April of 1971, JFCS set in motion a temporary rent subsidy so that elderly clients would not have to move into substandard housing. The JFCS Jewish Neighbors in Need program already provided groceries on a regular basis.

Eleanor Cohon (Courtesy of the Eleanor Cohon.)

Eleanor Cohon became board president in 1965. As a young woman in the 1940s and 1950s, Cohon had accompanied her father, Sol Esfeld, to various meetings and events, including those of JFCS. (Sol Esfeld joined the board in 1948.)

Since Cohon had first joined the board in 1961, she had seen the quick succession of directors. Bernhard Rackow had just left when she came on, and Betsy DeBeer Smith temporarily filled in. Then Arthur Farber came and went, and Smith filled in again. Cohon says that it was very difficult to get someone with the proper credentials to move to Seattle, which at that time didn't have much of a reputation for cultural, artistic, or even Jewish stimulation. Also, the financial incentives were less attractive because JFCS was required to conform to the United Good Neighbor formula that determined what various professionals could be paid. Eastern agencies paid much higher salaries. Finally, Jerry Grossfeld was hired in 1965.

During Cohon's presidency, JFCS helped resettle a number of Egyptian refugees, finding them housing and furniture, in addition to offering acculturation information and assistance. She recalls that Neighborhood House was still giving English lessons to refugees. (Neighborhood House was first operated by NCJW as the Settlement House in 1900, renamed the Education Center in 1916, and renamed again in 1947.)

(Left to right) Gloria Harris, Ernie Golosman and Thelma Coney, colleagues at JFS. (Courtesy of Thelma Coney.)

When Thelma Coney started working as a social worker at JFCS in 1966, the office was still on Jackson Street. The staff included Ernie Golosman, Gloria Harris, Esther Silver, and Martha Becker. Although Martha was not Jewish, the clients thought she was because of her last name.

One of the most gratifying cases Thelma Coney recalls handling was as the social worker for the Blumenzweig family who came from Egypt. They arrived with no money and only the clothes on their backs. Mr. Blumenzweig had been imprisoned in Cairo for quite a long time, and it took a great amount of effort from various Jewish agencies to get him out of prison and out of the country. Coney remembers them as a delightful family to work with. Mr. Blumenzweig and the children learned English quickly, but it was

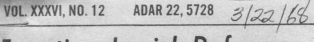

VOL. XXXVI, NO. 12   ADAR 22, 5728   3/22/68

Egyptian Jewish Refugee Family Arrive In Seattle

Extreme Left and Right Mr. Jerry Grossfeld, executive director, and Thelma Coney, of the Seattle Jewish Family and Child Service shown with the Blumenzweig family; Jaque, Sara and children — Cecile 14, Claude 10, Sonia 7, and Joseph 6.

by Barbra Barker

Saturday, March 9th was a big day for the Jaque Blumenzweig family from Cairo, Egypt. That was the day they finally arrived ready and eager to start their "new life" in Seattle.

Jaque Blumenzweig was born and raised in Cairo, knowing through bitter personal experiences, the hardships and cruelty that had befallen Egyptian Jews during this past year. He is a trained technician in natural gas equipment and the appliance field, having worked in this trade until the expropriation of his company by the Egyptian government, forced him to open small shop of his own in Cairo.

It was through the efforts of The Jewish Family & Child Service, in co-operation with United HIAS, that the Blumenzweig family were able to achieve their dream . . . come to America. With deep humility, Mr. Blumenzweig recounted the sequence of events for this Transcript reporter that ultimately led to our interview in Mr. Jerry Grossfeld's office, executive director of the Seattle Jewish Family and Child Service. Jaque Blumenzweig looked at his wife and children, and recalled some of the happy moments they had in the Cairo Jewish Community,

Continued on Page 6

Blumenzweig Family arrive in Seattle - 3.22.68
(Courtesy of the *Jewish Transcript*.)

very difficult for Mrs. Blumenzweig to shift from the French they spoke in Cairo. Their daughter, Cecile, became very active in the Jewish community. The family had a piece of wonderful good luck when, just about the time the children were in their teens, Mr. Blumenzweig bought a lottery ticket and won $2.9 million, which enabled all the children to go to college .

⚬∞⚬

In the 1960s, abortions were illegal and often dangerous. Single women having babies did not receive the social acceptance they would in later years, and most did not feel they could raise their babies alone. Many girls "went to visit" a relative for a few months until their babies arrived. Five or six times a year, JFCS had the opportunity to help a local Jewish family adopt a Jewish baby born to a single mother. Medina Children's Service approached JFCS because they had babies and needed Jewish couples looking for Jewish babies.

Coney helped a very young Jewish couple who chose to offer their baby for adoption, but the mother had one condition: she didn't like the Seattle climate and wanted her baby to grow up in someplace like California or Arizona. When the baby girl was about 10 days old and the doctors said she was healthy and could travel, Coney flew first class with her to an adoptive home in Tucson. She fondly recalls that she and the baby were treated as celebrities by the crew and the other first-class passengers.

One of the counseling cases that stands out for Coney concerned a couple who came for help for their drug addiction. By this time, more unmarried young couples were living together. This particular couple was not Jewish, but JFCS's policy was to serve all who came to the agency for help.

Coney told this couple that they would need to go to drug counseling. The woman agreed, but the boyfriend would not. One day, there was a commotion at the front desk with the man demanding to see Coney. He was screaming that it was her fault the woman would not stay with him after she had gone through treatment. Coney still remembers feeling quite threatened by him.

Eleanor Cohon recalls sitting in a board meeting on Jackson Street one night when a rock sailed through the window. At the time, board meetings were always in the evenings, but after that incident, nobody wanted to go to the neighborhood in the evenings. The board switched meetings to afternoons until 1969 when JFCS moved from the 1200-square-foot Jackson Street office to a quieter location at 2009 Minor Avenue East, just off Fairview Avenue. This space was somewhat small for the agency's operations, and it took some time for the office staff to adjust. They gave up private offices and had to double up, but one significant improvement was a wonderful view of Lake Union and the ships moving in and out. There was room for a very modest food pantry, managed by Estelle Broder.

Early in the 1970s, Grossfeld was able to report a significant increase in the number of counseling sessions. He attributed a great part of this to the larger number of non-Jewish families who were using the service. Grossfeld had approached the overloaded Family Counseling Service (FCS) and made an agreement for JFCS to work with some of the families FCS was not able to absorb, helping to prevent long waiting periods for families facing critical problems and requiring early attention. A steady number of such families were being seen, referred not only from FCS but also from the King County Family Court and other agencies. Of the 3,200 client consultations held during 1969, about two-thirds were counseling cases. The staff noted that the issues Jewish and non-Jewish families faced were essentially the same.

In January 1970, the board established a Public Issues Committee, suggested by the Family Service Association of America during the accreditation process for JFCS. Board positions on public issues, such as civil rights and immigration policy, had previously been handled by a variety of board committees. During its first year, the Public Issues Committee recommended support of the liberalization of Washington State abortion laws, but the board did not go on record with this support because they first wanted to see if it would be consistent with Orthodox teachings. (Washington voters decided to make abortion legal in November 1970.) The committee did publicly oppose the one-third cutback of federal matching monies for skilled nursing care and urged the passage of the Family Assistance Act of 1970. During 1972, the Public Issues Committee expressed concern about budget cuts in the Department of Social and Health Services. Then, in 1975, the committee was merged with several other committees to form the Community Education Committee.

Dr. Abby Franklin (Courtesy of the Franklin family.)

Articles appeared in the *Jewish Transcript* in May of 1971, during the JFCS presidency of Abby Franklin, describing a financial crisis pending at the agency. This was due to a significant cutback in the United Good Neighbors (UGN) contribution, which had been dropping for several years. The UGN contribution had been as much as almost 72 percent of the operating budget at $65,000 and had dropped to less than 40 percent at $44,000. A plea was made to the community for help, and increases were asked for from the Seattle Jewish Fund and from the National Council of Jewish Women. Jerry Grossfeld commented, "It would be ironic indeed if our program had to be curtailed and our staff depleted at a time when the needs of the community are the greatest."

The crisis was weathered with a little more assistance from UGN than had originally been announced. Additional help came from the Seattle Jewish Fund and the National Council of Jewish

Women, plus a supportive, positive response to the crisis from the community.

This era still felt the reverberations of the previous decade of the '60s, with its rejection of nearly every social convention and tradition, young people experimenting and succumbing to drug use, and an increase, or at least a growing awareness, of mental health issues. More Jewish youth sought out the counseling service. The kids reported that they were not specifically looking for a Jewish agency but had heard from their peers that JFCS was an "okay" place to go for personal help. With these young people, the caseworkers focused on helping them to participate fully in their world and hopefully to help create a better tomorrow for everyone.

JFCS continued expanding its presence in the community. One new program in the early 1970s was a partnership with the Central Area Mental Health Center in which a JFCS social worker spent half a day per week as a consultant with the Central Area schools.

The King County Family Court and Juvenile Court, as well as most of the other family and mental health agencies, were now consistently referring clients to JFCS. This harkened back to the days when Mae Goldsmith sat in on juvenile hearings in the late 1920s and 1930s.

Among the hundreds of cases seen each year were families with marriages on the verge of breaking up, youngsters and parents unable to resolve their differing points of view, and depressed or even suicidal individuals seeking relief from their anguish. The goal of JFCS staff was to help these families and individuals reach a point where they could function and relate to one and other and to the world with more ease and confidence.

The 80th year since the agency's original formation in 1892 found the nation and the community suffering through another recession, along with record inflation. In 1971, the Department of Social and Health Services reduced financial assistance grants, including those to elderly clients, at the same time as the costs of food and rent were increasing. JFCS responded with a temporary program of rent subsidy for clients who were in danger of having to move into sub-standard housing. Hundreds of individuals and many local organizations donated to JFCS's Jewish Neighbors in Need program, helping to provide groceries to many struggling clients.

In response to the lengthy recession, JFCS initiated the Jewish Unemployed Manpower Project (JUMP), enlisting Jewish business firms to provide employment opportunities. More than 170 clients used the program in the first 18 months, but in spite of this success, there remained dozens of jobless agency clients seeking employment.

The Boeing Bust was the major reason JFCS did not accept any new refugee families for resettlement during 1972. Because those who had been resettled in 1970 had continued to receive financial assistance from JFCS well into 1971, it was thought that new resettled families might not be able to find jobs and the agency would have to continue providing support.

At this time, approximately half of JFCS's professional program involved counseling for personal, marital, and family issues. While these clients represented a wide range of economic levels, the majority were between the low to low-middle income levels. Some people seeking services were self-referred while others came through referral from Family Court, Planned Parenthood, Family Counseling Service, attorneys, physicians, friends, or clergy. Helping people with problems they could not solve on their own remained the primary service of JFCS. Young people came requesting help with a conflict with their parents, school, or friends. Couples torn apart by problems in their marriages came seeking assistance. Individuals suffering from depression or experiencing a sense of malaise in general came looking for relief, and a large number of older people came for help dealing with a world that seemed to have left them behind. Staff also spent time helping the work of other organizations, like the Seattle Hebrew Academy and the Central Area Mental Health Center.

The budget for 1971 was $117,011 with the UGN providing $47,156, the Isaac Cooper Bequest Fund providing $29,500, and the Jewish Federation $22,789. Financial assistance to clients amounted to $12,265. The average monthly number of client consultations was 401 with 2,591 active cases during the year.

By 1972, JFCS had gathered enough funds to relocate to a larger facility in Suite 201 at 110 Harvard Avenue.

⤬

Olga Butler served as board president from 1972 to 1974. She recalls that in 1972 there were four social workers and a secretary, plus the executive director. The primary services included

counseling, assistance for elderly clients, and help for local and immigrant families trying establish themselves. In addition, JFCS administered the Hebrew free Loan Society loans.

After Jerry Grossfeld left JFCS in 1974, Butler was involved in the interviews to fill his position. The Search Committee consulted with Caroline Kline Galland Home's director Josh Gortler, and Butler

Olga Butler (Courtesy of Olga Butler.)

remembers one candidate asking Gortler, "How many basket cases do you have?" That applicant was not hired. Butler knows that today the board is very different from the one on which she served. Those earlier board members were more involved in the caseloads of social workers.

It was early in Butler's presidency that Uganda's dictator summarily expelled persons of East Indian heritage. The board decided to sponsor a non-Jewish refugee family, and there was a huge outcry. Some people said they would not give any more to JFCS because "we should take care of our own." The board tried to make the point that JFCS was part of a wider community. Regardless of the reaction, the family was settled, and the agency continued with its work.

The green light for Jews to leave the Soviet Union in the mid-1960s was short lived. After the 1967 Arab-Israeli War, the

USSR severed diplomatic relations with Israel, and Soviet policy towards Jews seeking to emigrate changed. For the most part, Arab governments were aligned with the Soviets while Israel was a US ally. The Soviets viewed the act of applying for emigration to Israel as unpatriotic and even treasonous, and applicants deemed to have any information critical to national security were barred, along with their families, from leaving the country. These "refuseniks" were routinely dismissed from their positions in science and academia, or their advancements blocked. They couldn't work, and they couldn't leave. Still, Jews managed to exit the USSR, and the Russian resettlement program brought another wave of immigration into Seattle's Jewish community. The effort remained a significant part of the JFCS budget. (See Chapter 12, "1967-1992: Resettlement of Russian Immigrants.")

Annual JFCS meetings were held at Temple de Hirsch where the board served apple juice and homemade cookies. Butler says that if the board had "even charged one dollar, they would have run us out of town. Twenty or thirty people would be a big meeting."

❦

The spring of 1975 marked the end of the Vietnam War. Tens of thousands of refugees from Communist oppression in Vietnam, Cambodia, and Laos crowded into camps hoping for resettlement in the United States. In April, the US State Department called on the United Hebrew Immigrant Aid Society (HIAS) "to participate, without regard to faith, in helping to resettle Cambodian refugees." One thousand Cambodians still in their native land, along with approximately 1,200 in other countries, needed help in their resettlement. These first 2,200 Cambodians were described as persons who would assimilate easily since they had worked for the US government in various capacities. It was also expected that the government would provide approximately $300 per person to the resettlement agencies.

In May, a similar letter from the State Department was received regarding Vietnamese refugees. A meeting of executives from the

16 largest Jewish federation organizations across the country, plus a number of representatives from the middle-sized communities, produced a consensus that the Jewish communities should mobilize to assist in the resettlement of at least 10,000 Buddhist and Catholic Vietnamese refugees. Each Jewish community was asked to help resettle a portion of the 10,000 Vietnamese out of a total of 130,000 to 150,000 that had either already arrived or were en route to the United States. (In addition to the efforts of the Jewish community, many other resettlement organizations assisted in this massive resettlement effort.)

Congress enacted the Vietnam Humanitarian Assistance and Evacuation Act of 1975, providing special reimbursement to the states for financial and medical assistance, social services, and a requirement to follow the established resettlement and assistance procedures. The Social and Rehabilitation Service (a program of the Federal Department of Health, Education and Welfare) promised 100 percent federal reimbursement for financial assistance and medical and social services to these refugees, including reimbursement for certain administrative costs. The policy was limited to refugees from South Vietnam and did not apply to Cambodian refugees.

Chapter 12

1967-1992: Resettlement of Russian Immigrants

*"You got to understand what they
had to do to survive over decades."*

A Russian immigration program seems to have first been discussed in 1970. After the 1966 announcement by the USSR that Jews would be allowed to leave, many Soviet Jews filed the papers to receive exit visas, but the process took months, or even years. Just the act of applying was deemed treasonous or, at the very least, disloyal. Most of the applicants lost their jobs or were demoted. With all apartments being owned by the state, decent housing was always in short supply in the Soviet Union. A Jewish family whose loyalty came into question could quickly find themselves having to share with other families, or even losing a precious apartment. Applicants needed to rely on friends and family to survive the waiting period, but families often found themselves friendless as fearful citizens ostracized them in many ways.

After a great deal of pressure from the American Jewish community and the US government, the Soviet Union finally allowed Jews to leave. Most of the first wave of emigrants, many of whom were more religious, went to Israel. The first to be resettled in America arrived in 1968, but Seattle didn't receive its first Russian immigrants until 1972. The government allowed them to enter the country as refugees, and after two years, they were eligible to apply for permanent residence.

In July 1972, the Soviets insisted that Russian families must have a letter of invitation from relatives in the United States before any action could be initiated for them to leave. Some of these families had not had contact for 20 or more years, but the call went out for American families to help their Russian relatives. The host families had to certify that the invitations would not create a binding financial commitment for them.

In addition to an Israeli or US letter of invitation, each émigré was forced to pay an exorbitant exit tax to the Soviet government and was not allowed to take money out of the USSR. Shipments of personal effects were crated in unreasonably large containers at exorbitant shipping costs. Once the émigrés left, they feared for the safety of the loved ones they left behind.

Jeanette and Norman Lozovsky (who were pleased to share their history for this project) applied for an exit visa soon after their youngest son was born in September 1972. The massacre of Israeli athletes had just taken place at the Munich Olympics, and Jeanette overheard a Ukrainian woman in the hospital bed next to her comment to her husband that she would consider it a holiday if all Jews were killed.

Lozovsky was convinced that she and her family had to leave the USSR, not only because of the blatant anti-Semitism, which they encountered all the time, but also because she now had two sons and knew, if they stayed, the boys would be conscripted into the Red Army, a horrible fate for Jewish boys.

Just a few people had applied for visas, including Jeanette's father, when she and Norman made the decision to leave. It took them three years to collect the money, complete the paperwork, and be ready. This was a difficult time because they felt they had to hide from everyone, never knowing who was their friend or their enemy or working with the KGB, the Soviet security force.

Immediately after they applied, Norman was demoted from his position at work. Although he was not fired, his salary was reduced. They lived in fear because it was not uncommon for people in the Soviet Union simply to disappear. This was during the time that Richard Nixon was US president and was negotiating with the USSR to allow the Jews to leave, in return for commodities.

In September 1973, Isaak Asnin, an electrical engineer, was the first immigrant of this wave to arrive in Seattle. In announcing his arrival, JFCS asked the community for assistance in finding him employment. Two more Russian families were scheduled to arrive in Seattle during the fall.

The following year, JFCS resettled two Russian families at a cost of $3,071 without reimbursement from other programs. In March 1975, the agency requested that the Jewish Federation of Greater Seattle support the new Russian resettlement program with a grant of $12,000, noting that three more families were expected soon with more to come.

The budget for resettlement of the first three families (a total of 12 people) was set at $10,000. In the meantime, JFCS was asked to resettle 20 Vietnamese refugees expected to arrive during the last half of 1975.

The official JFCS Russian Resettlement program was instituted on June 19, 1975, when the Jewish Federation authorized $71,341 to resettle 17 families from the Soviet Union. The goal was to resettle the families as effectively as possible with help from the entire Jewish community.

The next wave of immigrants from the USSR included a great many Jews who knew nothing or next to nothing about Judaism. Under the Communist regime, teaching Judaism was heavily suppressed. People were not able to attend a synagogue, have a *bris* (circumcision) performed, hold a *bar mitzvah* (Jewish coming-of-age ritual) or a Jewish wedding, or openly celebrate Jewish holidays. A Jewish underground tried to retain some of the traditions, but the vast majority of Jews were not part of that underground or any Jewish community or tradition. However, once the doors opened, hundreds of thousands, and eventually millions, of would-be Jews left the Soviet Union. In the beginning, most went to Israel. Then the situation changed dramatically. Jews who were not particularly attached to their Jewish identity did not care about going to Israel, the Promised Land of Jewish tradition and teaching. They liked the idea of going to the other Promised Land, the United States. They came in large numbers, and JCFS was very busy for a number of years resettling Jews from the former Soviet Union.

JFCS staff understood from long experience that the refugee families were in crisis and would react by becoming overly dependent on the people trying to help them. At the same time, the immigrants would resent their dependency and express this by making excessive demands. When demands could not be met, people often became angry and resentful. Piled on top of these normal resettlement issues was the need to learn a new language, adjust to a totally new way of life, overcome fear of government officials, and adapt to changes in vocation, status, and prestige. Each family had to be helped to understand the realities of their situation and to understand the limits of what the Jewish community could provide.

In addition to resettling the immigrant families, JFCS was the one resource they could turn to for help when making important decisions about employment, housing, education, and such.

As the Russian resettlement program was launched, specific responsibilities were clarified for the agency, for volunteers, and for the community. Irene Steinberg chaired the Russian Resettlement Committee of JFCS, Sylvia Saperstein and Dorothy Wittenberg led the Furnishing Committee, Olga Butler chaired the Housing Committee, Nate Ross took on the Employment Committee, and Sylvia Stern led the Socialization and Religious Committee. Michelle Ancioux headed up the training in English language. Added support came from volunteer case-aides, volunteer tutors, cooperating physicians and dentists, members of the business community, synagogue groups, and other Jewish organizations.

JFCS, the Jewish Federation, and NCJW each took responsibility for specific functions. One of the first efforts was the collection of usable furniture and household items. Harvey Poll stepped up to donate the use of a warehouse in today's SoDo neighborhood.

One family (a couple with a young child) arrived in August 1975. Another family followed with the parents and two children being received on October 30 and another brother and his fiancé arriving on November 26. Both of the husbands had jobs by early December. JFCS also assisted in the resettlement of two other families related to a family resettled the previous year.

The total cost for living expenses and agency salaries, including benefits and overhead was $6,250, of which $379 was reimbursed by Temple Beth Am, the sponsoring organization for the English language teaching effort.

Patsy Policar took over as program coordinator of Russian resettlement in January 1977. Born and raised in Vancouver, British Columbia, Policar was new to Seattle and newly married. She had a background in psychiatric social work with experience in family counseling, marital therapy, and child protective services.

Policar says it was a revelation for her as she started resettling the Russian Jews to see how many things she had thought were her father's quirks were actually cultural. Her father, who came from the Ukraine as a child, was very nice, intelligent, and religious but could be very difficult to deal with. When she resettled Soviets, she realized that many of his characteristics were, in fact, survival behaviors. If the survivors had not watched out for themselves in the USSR, they would have been swallowed up. She commented, "A lot of people who came into contact with these immigrants thought they were pushy, even obnoxious. You could use those words, but when you came to know them, you began to understand what they had to do to survive over decades." Because she understood the dynamics, it was very difficult for these immigrant families to manipulate Policar.

As Policar began her work, across the US, organizations working to help resettle immigrants from the Soviet Union expected that it would take from three to six months for the average family to become self-sufficient. The experience in Seattle was that jobs could usually be secured for the newcomers within about three months.

Initially, the program grew through the generosity of the community. Donations of furniture and house wares were taken to the warehouse where Sylvia Saperstein and Dorothy Wittenberg and members of their Furnishing Committee sorted the contributions. Barrett's Moving and Storage provided vans periodically to move furniture, just one of the companies and individuals who responded to the outreach for assistance in which board members were engaged. JFCS published articles in the *Jewish Transcript*, the synagogues reached out to their members, and many people responded to help.

Estelle Broder, who was the JFCS bookkeeper and jack-of-all-trades, managed the food bank, which by now had actually grown to be an entire closet. Some of the outreach publicized the need for food. When a new family arrived, Policar was able to stock their kitchen with food mostly from the food bank. She then filled in the canned and prepared foods with fresh produce. JFCS received an allotment per family from HIAS that was used to pay rent, to purchase necessary furnishings, and to provide cash for the family during their first three months of residency.

Policar made connections with three landlords who accepted immigrant families that did not speak English. One building was across from the QFC on Broadway, and another was near 23rd Avenue and Madison Street. She usually had a couple of weeks' notice before a new family arrived and found an apartment, arranged for phone and electrical service, and then called Saperstein and Wittenberg who selected furniture and furnishings out of Harcey Poll's warehouse. Over time, a list was developed of what furnishings and house ware items a family would absolutely have to have:

Blankets	Salt and pepper shakers
Tablecloth	Pillows
Shower curtain	Pot holders
Cookie sheet	Teapot
Melmac dish set	Iron
Silverware set	Juice glasses
Serving fork	Rolling pin
Scissors	Wire hangers
11-quart bucket	Wooden spoons
Colander	Drain board mat
Alarm clock	Pitcher
Sheets	Three Pyrex mixing bowls
Kitchen towels	Bath rug
Cookware set	Biscuit pan
Square cake pan	Sandwich knife
Water glasses	Soap dish
Can opener	Spatula
Soup ladle	Three-way grater
Peeler	Sponge mop
Small dish drainer	Vanity wastebasket
Cutlery tray	Laundry basket

A similar list was created for groceries.

JCFS paid the damage deposit (as a loan), signed a guarantor agreement for the telephone, and paid the $10 installation fee for the electricity. In her report to the Resettlement Committee in September 1976, Policar stated that 10 families had been resettled during the year. All but one were self-supporting, and the most recently arrived had several job possibilities. Three more families—

all related—were scheduled to arrive in late October. Each new arrival in need of dental care received a grant of $50 with the remainder of the expense being provided as a loan.

A furniture drive in June 1975 filled the donated warehouse space. Volunteers helped move the items. One item the program tried to include in every apartment was a television set. This proved one of the best tools to help the newcomers learn English, and families reported success in their English as a Second Language classes at Seattle Central Community College.

The next year, executive director Irv Goldberg doubled the JFCS commitment to resettlement, and Policar worked hard serving 24 more families. By the time she left on August 1, 1979, she had brought in 56 families. She remembers that even for a 27-year-old, it was exhausting and overwhelming. First, she found the apartment, and then she set it up with basic items and food. She always tried to include a few toiletries and towels using her mother's shopper training to go to the month-end sales at The Bon Marché (today's Macy's), arriving just as the doors opened. There she found washcloths on clearance for 37 cents and towels at equally low prices.

Most families experienced complete culture shock. The majority did not speak any English, especially the older adults, and that became a serious problem. Policar was fortunate to be able to recruit two Russian-speaking women, Clara and Raisa, to serve as interpreters. Those women proved to be two of the greatest assets to the program. Either Clara or Raisa would accompany Policar to the airport and then join her again when she did her initial interviews with the family. They made it possible to exchange information without misunderstandings as slang and parochialisms had previously made miscommunication a frequent issue.

Part of the resettlement process involved helping the new immigrants to understand that the staff was trying to look out for their best interests, even if JFCS could not do everything for them. The new arrivals usually had unreasonable expectations and anticipated that things would just be given to them, so they were critical when it was not all they wanted. They had gone from standing in line for two hours for bread to being critical that there was not better mayonnaise. They were also accustomed to a society where the only way to get anything was by bullying, intimidation, and coercion, and the men could be quite abusive to young Policar.

Chabad House, a Jewish Orthodox organization serving university students and newcomers, became involved fairly early on. Their goals included making sure all the men and boys were circumcised, and bringing them all in to Judaism. The organization was strong and forceful. Policar saw it as a tradeoff because the members were available to her program. Some involved with the program joked about how Chabad offered the young men a stereo boom box if they would be circumcised. The young men jumped at the chance to own a portable stereo and then learned the real price.

The first wave of people who arrived sought religious freedom theoretically, but they did not really seem to realize what that meant. They did know that they wanted something better; they just didn't know what it was. The Jewish community expected that the immigrants were ready to embrace Judaism when in reality most just wanted to get out of the Soviet Union. There was a process of approaching the newcomers gently and allowing them to see what opportunities were possible as members of the Jewish community and Judaism. Chabad ran an outreach program enabling many, particularly the younger people, to become involved and discover their Judaism. Many local residents were almost offended at the immigrants' lack of interest in the faith, and the abrasiveness of some of the Soviet families caused many volunteers to stop participating.

However, this wave of immigrants was able to survive the loss of their status in the old country, as well as the loss of almost everything of value there. They were survivors, they were resourceful, and they were intelligent. Most were highly educated engineers, physicians, and other professionals who lacked the requisite US certifications and licenses. For the most part, they also did not have English and could not get a job they thought was of value. Doctors did not want to be janitors, and engineers did not want to be gardeners.

Policar helped them to be realistic. To begin with, they needed to take whatever job they could get. JFCS's commitment was support for three months, and then the immigrants were expected to support themselves. Next, they had to learn some English. Seattle Central Community College offered an English as a Second Language (ESL) program, and Policar helped enroll the newcomers immediately. Some of these clients were very motivated, and some were just upset. The support provided for three months was not a great deal of money, but it met their needs. It was enough that they could eat, be clothed, and pay their rent. Many seemed to want more for nothing. They thought they were immediately going to have a better standard of living, only to realize they were starting on the bottom rung of the economic ladder.

Policar took the newcomers to the Social Security office in the first 48 hours to enroll them in a medical assistance program for refugees. Employment Security was to help them find jobs, but the work was usually entry level. However, as the immigrants learned English, more opportunities opened. Policar and many volunteers reached out to the business community to help provide jobs.

The route navigated by one young man stands out. He was a teenager who had begun to study engineering in the Soviet Union. JFCS helped him get into school, and after he graduated, he became very successful. For perhaps 15 years, he phoned Policar on the anniversary of his arrival to say thank you and tell her how well he was doing.

Another young man, in his late teens or early twenties when he arrived, sold shoes at Nordstrom in Bellevue for a number of years until he was able to open an automotive mechanics shop.

Families sometimes invited Policar and her husband to dinner, wanting to give something back. This was particularly true for the elderly women past working age. They found everything foreign and felt lost. Having American visitors helped the women connect with the new country.

The local police offered a class for the newcomers about how to stay safe and not become a victim. They discussed the need to know where they were going before they went out the door and to know their route because, if they looked insecure, they became a target. The newcomers were warned not to ask directions from strangers on the street but to go into a store to ask an employee.

Policar used her own small car and recruited volunteers to help transport arriving families and their luggage until someone donated a station wagon to the program enabling more people to be transported in one vehicle.

At times, immigrants arrived in clusters with relatives of local families coming in as well. The local families were asked to take more responsibility for their relatives so that if, for example, they did not like the towels that were provided they could buy what they liked. If the local family wanted their immigrant relatives to live in a better apartment, they needed to provide that. One of the first two or three families to arrive were bitter and angry that more was not done for them, but when JFCS brought some of their relatives in to assist, those relatives were able to see what was involved in the process. As more supports were built in, it was interesting to watch these newcomers starting to help each other.

Those involved with this huge resettlement effort noticed a significant cultural difference between people arriving from more sophisticated, larger metropolitan cities, like Leningrad, and those from more outlying areas. The Leningrad immigrants included more highly educated professionals. Those from outlying areas included more blue-collar workers, by today's standards (such as mechanics and general working-force people) who found employment if they could get the English. Most professionals could not get licensed to work in their professions, and these misplaced workers did not find it as easy to adjust to their new circumstances. The blue-collar families settled in better, demonstrating that employment was the key to smooth assimilation.

In April of 1977, JFCS launched a major drive to recruit volunteers for the resettlement program. People were needed to find apartments and to coordinate the donations drive. One person coordinated donation pickups and assessed the appropriateness of the donations. People with vehicles were needed to move furniture, and volunteers were needed to furnish the apartments. Other volunteers served as case aides and interpreters and coordinated socialization efforts and the participation of the synagogues. People were asked to invite Russian families for Shabbat dinner and to join their hosts at services. The B'nai B'rith women volunteered to tutor young people, provide driving lessons, and coach newcomers in various daily living tasks. More volunteers were needed to find employment, repair TVs, lend clerical support, and participate in the furniture drive. Over time, more and more members of the Seattle Jewish community stepped in to help at various levels.

By the end of 1977, certain issues and inequities were being recognized in Russian resettlement programs across the country, particularly the disparity in the numbers of families communities agreed to accept. In January 1978, the Jewish Federation of Greater Seattle (JFGS) passed a resolution that recognized the issue was too big for individual communities to manage on their own, and called on the Council of Jewish Federations, United Jewish Appeal, and HIAS to develop a nationally funded program to resettle Soviet Jewish families in local Jewish communities. The following year, Congress appropriated $27.3 million to resettle the 27,300 Soviet Jewish refugees who were expected to arrive during the 1979 fiscal year.

By May 1979, JFCS had resettled 50 families (134 individuals). As the program matured and the dynamics were better understood, the agency's staff made changes. Instead of continuing to rely only on donations to furnish apartments, Neiso Moscatel, owner of Continental Furniture, agreed to provide new furniture on a rent-to-own basis with very low payments for the first six months. At that point, the family could return the furniture and purchase whatever they wanted, or keep it and sign a new contract, continuing to pay for the furniture. Having control of these kinds of decisions helped the newcomers feel they were empowered again. They had a commitment to what they were doing and were motivated to succeed.

By August, at least two families a month were arriving and settling in. Immigrant families were accepted for placement only if the relatives or friends were willing to donate a portion of the money needed and to assist actively in some of the resettlement tasks. The requested contribution by a family ranged from $800 to $1,000, depending on the size of the incoming family. Seattle always accepted first-degree relatives (parent, sibling, or child) so it was necessary that room be left in the quota in case first-degree relatives came up at the end of the quota period.

JFCS provided other services to some of the newly resettled immigrants. One young Russian immigrant came to JFCS because he was very insecure, shy, and introverted and needed help and encouragement to live independently. He got a job and began to participate in Jewish singles events but found life difficult, particularly after resigning from his job. This young man was not sleeping, was unable to function, and needed ongoing support. JFCS was able to provide him with that continuing support.

One Russian client was a widow in need of help with the grieving process. Ken Weinberg met with her when she was suffering deeply from her sense of displacement and isolation. This was common for the elderly Russian Jewish immigrants who left their entire lives and sense of community in the old country. She spoke only Russian and Yiddish. Weinberg helped her to move to Council House where she endeared herself to all who came to know her and settled more comfortably into her new surroundings.

When her need for care became more acute, Weinberg again took action. In a letter pleading her case for entry into the Caroline Kline Galland Home, he remarked, "The Seattle Jewish Federation has joined with the American Jewish community in an attempt to save the last great European Jewish stronghold through the emigration of Russian Jewry to the United States and Israel." He went on to acknowledge that resettlement was one of the highest priorities of the agency and was financially costly to the community, just as it was emotionally costly for the émigrés. He then requested that this woman be given highest priority for placement, which was granted, and she was enabled to live out her life at the home.

As had become the established practice, when a new family arrived, the coordinator would meet them at the airport, usually with the chairperson of the Russian Resettlement Committee and the case aide—the volunteer assigned to help them in their first weeks in Seattle—and take them to their new apartment. Most of the families had been sitting in Italy for months waiting for paperwork and then endured a journey from Rome to New York to Seattle. They were glad finally to be somewhere.

A brief *kiddush* (sanctification or blessing) was held over wine and challah with an accompanying explanation of the ritual and a translation of the prayers. Then the case aide gave the family a short explanation of the appliances and items in the apartment and written material in English and Russian welcoming them to Seattle and providing basic information about the city. The family also received their first financial assistance check at that time.

During the first few days, the case aide helped the family open a bank account, took them to the grocery store, and helped them get state identification cards (drivers licenses came later) and Social Security numbers. On another day, the family came to the JFCS office for an extensive orientation.

One of the issues that was carefully explained was the difference in the norms for personal hygiene. This was a difficult subject to broach but was made much easier when the *Resettlement Survival Handbook* was published. The caseworker reviewed the hygiene section with the family after they had been in the program for at least three weeks. The section covered issues like showering and use of deodorant to avoid body odor, brushing teeth, using mouth wash to avoid halitosis, the after-effects of certain foods, and the necessity of washing or dry cleaning clothing regularly. The staff hoped that providing a greater awareness of American personal hygiene standards facilitated better opportunities for employment, as well as quicker assimilation into the Seattle Jewish community.

An article in the *World Jewish Digest* of November 1979 stated that between 1948 and 1953 only 18 Jews were allowed to leave the USSR. In the decade after Stalin under Khrushchev, 2,000 Jews were allowed to leave. In 1978, 28,000 Jews left, and in 1979, 50,000.

Eighty-nine people in 36 families had been resettled in the Seattle area by the beginning of 1978 at a cost of $12,533. The majority of these families (81 percent) received support for three months. During the period from February 1978 to October 1979, JFCS resettled an additional 64 families.

Towards the end of this vast Soviet migration, Jews were arriving from the far-flung Soviet republics of Azerbaijan, Kazakhstan and the Bukhara region of Uzbekistan. These folks were difficult for new reasons. In addition to the language issues, job placement difficulties and other complications that had to be addressed with the majority of the Russian newcomers, these immigrants often had no experience with modern conveniences like toilets, lights, or electricity. Many came from small villages where they lived at a basic subsistence level and posed the same challenges as some of those from Southeast Asia.

While funding was available to resettle Jews from the Soviet Union, there has never been funding available to sustain the group. JFCS strived to establish services like social clubs and counseling programs specifically in Russian but was never able to obtain funding from the Jewish community to do so. Ken Weinberg thinks that the American Jewish community, including Seattle, flunked that particular challenge. While the United States readily provided close to two billion dollars to bring them all over, the immigrants' needs did not stop when they arrived, but just began.

Jewish Family Service (the board of JFCS changed the agency's name for the final time in 1978) has been able to do a little more in recent years. JFS now has a Russian- speaking counselor on staff, and a Passover Seder in Russian is held annually with almost 300 Russian Jews participating. In addition, volunteer ESL teachers work with groups of some of the more elderly Russian population.

Cliff Warner took over the Russian resettlement program in 1979 when Patsy Policar left. Born and raised in the Bronx in a family that was predominantly of Russian and Polish descent, he was 19 when his father moved his fur business to Seattle to establish the fur concessions for Nordstrom. To Warner, it sounded like too good an adventure to pass up. He had been a freshman at City College of New York but chose to move with his parents and transferred to the University of Washington where he earned a master's degree in clinical social work. (He would return to the UW years later for certificated graduate training in the School of Business.) Cliff worked in child welfare in various group homes and then as a medical social worker at the Northwest Kidney Center before he was enticed to join Jewish Family Service to lead the Russian resettlement program.

When Warner arrived, he found JFS to be a very small operation, located in a building on Harvard Avenue on Capitol Hill, although very shortly afterward, they moved to new space on Boylston. Irv Goldberg was the executive director with a staff of eight or nine, including Ken Weinberg. Weinberg worked with Senior Services, and one of Warner's earliest memories of the agency is that every Friday Weinberg telephoned his clients to wish them "Good Shabbos." They were typically hard of hearing, so Weinberg screamed, "I WANT TO WISH YOU A GOOD SHABBOS! GOOD SHABBOS!"

By May 1979, the United States had welcomed more than 16,000 Soviet Jews, the majority having arrived after 1975. Twelve hundred left the USSR every month, and more than 50 percent chose to settle in the United States. Warner found it quite exciting that the JFS resettlement program was in full swing, growing significantly and increasing case management staff as it took in 100 to 150 people a year through HIAS. Cultural integration programs were being developed, and JFS was recruiting volunteers to host families, find apartments, donate furniture and furnishings, and try to pull together a variety of things to welcome people.

Warner ran the program for six years before being promoted to assistant director of JFS in 1985. He found resettlement to be a very emotional and exciting endeavor, helping so many people get out of the Soviet Union. (His grandparents had fled the czar's pogroms in Russia.) He also found that helping fellow Jews escape from an awful situation and welcoming them to Seattle had a clear *hamish* Jewish component to it. Later in his career when Warner worked at the Caroline Kline Galland Home, he saw many of the people that he had helped welcome into Seattle. One person that he had not seen for 10 or 15 years remembered first arriving in Seattle, being met by Warner at the airport, and being taken to a wonderful apartment. Warner's whole family was there, and everyone enjoyed challah and wine and lit the candles. The man felt that it was a superb Jewish welcome. Warner commented years later, "You don't know what kind of an impact you have, and you don't know what people are going to remember." For him, having such a positive influence in people's lives was a wonderful part of the job.

Warner still sees other people he helped to settle in Seattle. Interestingly enough, his daughter recently married a young man from the Soviet Union (unrelated to anyone Warner helped resettle), who now works for a high-tech company where the young man's mother is a manager. His father works with another high-tech company. The young man's family had gone to Israel and then settled here in Washington. They have helped bring over many other brilliant Jews that they knew in the Ukraine. Some of those friends work for NASA managing projects all over the country. The United States has gained tremendously from the immigration of this population.

Welcoming new arrivals - Russian Immigrants
(JFS photo collection.)

The Russian resettlement program had matured by 1985 and had a staff with a full complement of resources. Some were doing the nuts and bolts of *schlepping* (hauling or carrying) furniture and setting up apartments. Others found employment for the immigrants, worked with DSHS, or organized financial arrangements, while some handled cultural endeavors, such as recruiting families to invite newcomers to Shabbat or Jewish holiday dinners and to accompany them to services.

The first clients Warner welcomed at the airport were Sophia and Leonid Freylekman and their young daughter. Warner resettled them on Capitol Hill in an apartment that was convenient to public transportation. By that time, there were little enclaves of Russian newcomers on First Hill, on Capitol Hill, and in the University District.

Warner recalled a trip he took to Russia: "The first Jews I met in Moscow on my 1973 visit were Vladimir and Masha Slepak, who three years earlier had applied for permission to leave Russia for Israel. At the time, their three-year wait seemed intolerable. I returned to the United States, kept in touch with them for a while, and continued to read about their case, which was frequently cited in the news. Finally, in 1987, 14 years after we had met and 17 years after they had first applied, the Slepaks were allowed to leave for Israel."

Slepak, who was a leading Jewish activist, became the most famous of the refuseniks—Jews whom the Soviet Union refused to allow to leave. The Soviets often gave no explanation for the denial of an emigration visa, though they frequently attributed it to state security. Slepak was told that because he had worked as an engineer years earlier, it was feared that he would divulge Russian secrets to the West. The explanation was absurd since any technological knowledge Slepak and the several thousand other refuseniks had, had long been superseded by the West's. One refusenik, Benjamin Bogomolny, actually entered the *Guinness Book of World Records* as most patient—he waited 20½ years to get permission to leave Russia, 1966-1986, from the time he was 20 till he was 40.[1]

Warner explained that people had a choice. Some designated they wanted to go to Israel; others said they wanted to go to the United States. "There was a controversy at the time with some thinking we shouldn't be offering the United States as an option and that if they were Jews they should be going to Israel." There was a great deal of backlash in Seattle and around the country from the Jewish community. There was pressure from Israel to say, "We need people coming to Israel," and to influence the United States to limit entry to the United States. One reason for offering an American option was that the immigrants had family here. Many also felt the people should have a choice because life is very different in the United States and Israel. The question was, do you give people a choice, or do you force them to go to Israel?

Warner remembers one Russian immigrant who became the lead project manager and engineer for a huge public project in Seattle. He was a lovely, charming human being and very humble.

When Warner was talking to him about bringing other family members to Seattle, Warner commented that this man had 3,000 employees working on this project. The man, not impressed with the status or responsibility his project represented, replied, "You just have to remember one thing. No matter what you are doing in life, where is the bow, where is the stern. Everything falls into place."

People of extraordinary brilliance and ability were arriving, most in a panic from having turned their lives upside down. They would typically say, "It doesn't matter what happens to me. I am doing this for my kids." And they meant it. So whatever it took, however many jobs they would take, they wanted their children to be in good schools and to have all the opportunities that the United States offered.

After families were settled in the United States, there was some secondary migration. A family might have settled in Chicago and later moved on their own to Seattle. The main reason for the location of the initial resettlement was family reunification. If they had a family member in a certain city, that's where they usually went. Then after the initial resettlement period, they were free to go wherever they wanted. However, JFS did not resettle secondary migrants. If they wanted to move, they had to be prepared to support themselves and find their own apartments and jobs. Warner commented that it must have been quite refreshing for the immigrants to be in a country where you are free to move wherever you want. Seattle had a reputation for being a good place to live and experienced a significant amount of secondary migration of people who came from cities they didn't like.

⁕

When Warner started at JFS, the Russian resettlement program was comparatively small. With the tremendous influx of Russians, it became clear that a Russian speaker should be in the program coordinator role. The Jewish Federation provided sufficient funding to accomplish the task, so Warner, who didn't speak Russian, moved to become assistant director for JFS and hired Jeanette Lozovsky as coordinator of the Russian resettlement program in 1989.

Lozovsky's family was one who experienced that secondary migration. They originally settled in Dallas. Her husband, Norman, had 17 years' experience as a brilliant bridge designer and engineer. When they arrived in Dallas, he was told that he had to forget about being an engineer, so he started to work as a draftsman. He spoke fluent English and was soon teaching some of the younger people. When he found out those he was training were earning much more than he was, he decided to look for another job. Norman found an opening with a bridge design company in Bellevue, Washington, went for an interview, and was hired.

The family moved to Seattle in September 1979 and immediately knew it was their place. Norman was later assigned a project in Penang, Malaysia, and the family moved there for three years before returning to Seattle.

When Lozovsky's mother, sister, and sister's family immigrated from Russia in 1980, Lozovsky went to JFS to meet with Cliff Warner about sponsoring them. Then, in 1988 after their return from Malaysia, Warner called saying the Russian resettlement program needed someone to work an hourly job to liaison between the Russian community and Americans and help new refugee families. Lozovsky said she did not know anything about what the work might entail, but remembering what was done for her, she said if they would train her she would be happy to help. She quickly became Warner's right-hand woman and a refugee resettlement caseworker.

Between October and December of 1988, they resettled 43 people. Carol Benedict was a part-time caseworker who worked with Lozovsky. Together, they resettled 226 individuals the first year. As the program grew to a staff of 10, plus numerous volunteers, with a budget of one million dollars, Lozovsky's title was changed to director.

The contract with HIAS required that people be resettled under a matching grant program. The agency received $450 per refugee from HIAS to cover the first four months. During this period, JFS was required to provide financial assistance and help the newcomers find employment. Each state had a different program. In Washington, newcomers could not apply to DSHS for welfare but were eligible for food stamps and medical assistance.

Because clients would reject jobs that were offered and, after four months, apply for financial assistance, the program's performance outcomes (the quantifiable indicators that gauge productivity or effectiveness) began to drop on the requirement of job attainment within the first three months.

It was a complex situation for the agency. As with many refugee populations, finding jobs clients could qualify for and also feel were satisfying and meaningful was extremely difficult. What could they do if the clients wouldn't take an offered job? JFS did its best to find employment for them and encouraged them to take the jobs. They were told this was an opportunity; they should accept the job offered and then go to college and be better prepared for the future. Some people took the advice and accepted the job; for others, it didn't work. Washington State was very liberal. If the Russian immigrants applied for public assistance and were accepted, they could stay on it until their children reached 18. They could get free education and daycare, as well as apply for subsidized housing. Many were content to live that way and were not embarrassed.

Lozovsky experienced both success and failure. There was a quite a bit of education she and her staff were supposed to do to help the newcomers adjust to their new lives. They taught a little about Jewish history and acculturation, most of which was new information for these Jewish immigrants who for the most part had never been exposed to Judaism. Lozovsky and her staff, as well as much of the community, hoped the newcomers would assimilate into the Jewish community. All the synagogues participated with JFS in providing Jewish acculturation, but a great many of the immigrants never affiliated with a congregation.

Everything was unfamiliar from the language to public transportation to the banking and postal systems. The immigrants needed to learn how to work the appliances in their new homes, how to get to and from the grocery store, and how to shop once they got there. They needed to know how to pay their rent, utilities, and other bills. Lozovsky's adult clients needed to be enrolled in English classes, and the children into the appropriate Jewish or public schools. The adults needed to learn how to fill out the forms required to apply for the public assistance they were entitled to and how to complete a job application, conduct an employment interview, use the food bank, everything. (They could qualify for food stamps and medical coverage, but not for financial assistance.)

They all came to America because they were persecuted as Jews and because Jews were fighting for their freedom. Today, Lozovsky feels that many still do not appreciate enough the opportunity that was given to them. In Russia, some people were afraid to go out, even to take a walk. She thinks that she and her fellow immigrants are here because someone was fighting for their freedom.

Larry Broder was the assistant head of the Hebrew Academy in the late 1980s and recalls that the large number of children who arrived from Soviet countries during this time mostly spoke either no or very poor English. He remembers one little girl sitting in the playground crying and crying because she felt totally lost. By the time she graduated from the Hebrew Academy, she had no accent and was a tall, gorgeous young woman who didn't look at all like the little sad Russian child who had been sitting in the middle of the playground crying.

Broder also remembers that many of these children had head lice. When their stocking caps came off and the lice went up into the sky, Larry Broder was the person who confirmed the problem and then made the phone call telling the parents their child could not come to school until all the lice were gone. The language barrier often made it difficult to convey all this because the parents usually didn't speak much English and Broder didn't speak Russian.

Families had options of where to send their children to school, and the Hebrew Academy was one of those options. The immigrant children could attend at no cost to the family. However, the school, being an Orthodox institution, required both boys who wanted to attend and their fathers to be circumcised, and most of the Russian immigrants were not. It's a particularly difficult procedure for adult men to experience, but the fathers were willing to go through the process in order to enable their sons to attend the academy.

The school didn't have Russian-speaking teachers, so the children came in with whatever abilities they had, and they left with whatever they were able to acquire. They had the burden of learning both English and Hebrew. Like that little girl that was crying in the playground, they just picked it up as they went along. Staff were often amazed at how the younger they were the faster they acquired the language skill and the faster they lost their accent.

Then the resettlement program grew and changed, and Lozovsky found herself resettling people from Bosnia, Farsi-speaking Baha'i from Iran, and others from Burma. She worked with Turks who had migrated to Russia generations before and then were deported to Siberia during the Second World War by Stalin. The US government gave them status and asylum. During the 18 years Lozovsky worked at JFS, she helped to resettle many Jews, which was the program's major focus, but she is proud to have assisted many other nationalities as well. She felt it was JFS's mission to educate people, and by doing good things and planting good seeds with families and their children, she would be able to help diminish misunderstandings between Jews and the rest of the world.

Each new family was told about JFS and a little about Jewish history. There was always an interpreter present, whether the client was Russian or, in later years, Bosnian, Burmese, or a Farsi speaker from Iran. It was very important to talk, Lozovsky said, "not about how we are described by a different religion and culture but about how we are people who want to make connections with the entire world and we are for peace. Shalom has many different meanings."

The current resettlement program through the Refugee & Immigrant Service Centers (RISC), still provides ESL classes, guidance for employment, social services, access to the food bank, furniture, and household items. They help children enter elementary school, and Jewish children can receive scholarships to attend the

Jewish schools. Lozovsky worked hard to involve the entire Jewish community. She feels it was important that they were all united and working together.

Under Lozovsky's leadership, the program started receiving federal, state, county, and even city funding to support various parts of the program. ESL classes, attended by all nationalities, were held in the Kirkland Public Library. The cities of Bellevue, Kent, Renton, and Seattle all started to participate, and Lozovsky received a New Citizens Initiative grant (for about seven years) to help newcomers learn how to apply for citizenship. These efforts helped to open doors for JFS to become the major resettlement organization in the state, having developed expertise in resettling a very wide spectrum of ethnicities.

1. Joseph Telushkin, *Jewish Literacy* (New York: William Morrow and Co., 1991).

Chapter 13

1974–1984: Evolution and Expansion

Jerry Anches stepped into the presidency of Jewish Family & Child Service in 1974. His father, Irving Anches, had begun serving on the same board in 1952.

The biggest issue being addressed at the time was Russian immigration. Anches well remembers problems and issues that arose when those who came to this country with advanced degrees were not able to work in their fields. Many of these once-respected and highly educated people were quite resentful and hurt by the process.

JFCS caseworkers and volunteers continued to work hard at finding employment and helping get the newcomers settled. There was some financial assistance for the first few months, and clients received regular visits from someone from JFCS with help for any problems with their immigration status and the other challenges to getting settled and absorbed into the community.

After 10 years leading Jewish Family & Child Service through a recession and then through a period of growth and development, in 1974, executive director Jerry Grossfeld moved on to become the executive director of JFS in Denver, and a search for his replacement began. Both in Seattle and then in Denver, Grossfeld was highly regarded and much appreciated. Thelma Coney was appointed interim director and served in that capacity for 18 months until Irv

Goldberg arrived to lead the organization. Goldberg had attended Case Western University and served as executive director of a small JFS in Massachusetts before coming to Seattle. (Unfortunately, no biography of Goldberg has been found.)

Anches and the board worked through issues concerning the income from the Republic Building and the Cooper-Levy Trust, of which JFCS was beneficiary. Part of the income from the building, located at Third and Pine, had been bequeathed to JFCS through the Cooper-Levy Trust in the 1940s and had provided a significant part of the agency's income since that time. The building was not performing very well, and the board struggled with ways to encourage the trustees to increase the yields from it. As time went by, the building was not well maintained and the income stream slowed down considerably. The Boeing Bust of the early 1970s did not help its occupancy rates.

In the fall of 1975, a young student from the University of Washington School of Social Work named Ken Weinberg arrived at JFCS to work as a counseling intern as part of his training. He spent most of his time working with senior clients, perfecting his chosen specialty as a geriatric counselor.

During the last three months of 1976, JFCS fielded 54 telephone inquiries requesting help that included a wide range of issues. One was a former client looking for a job who was referred to the Washington State Employment Service and to other private employment agencies. Another individual was offering a job opening and was referred to staff. A staff person from the Northwest Kidney Center was asking about help for an elderly patient who needed housing and was provided with a list of resources, and another man was in a crisis situation after his wife left him. He wanted counseling and was referred to a counselor.

The next board president was Harold "Buzz" Coe, who had known about JFCS all his adult life. Active in the Jewish Federation of Greater Seattle, he knew of JFCS as a major recipient of financial support, but his personal interaction with the Jewish agency started because he had a three-year-old son who one Sunday decided to run away. Coe and his wife watched the lad as he packed his bag. When he got to the door, they asked him where he was going to stay. Where he was going to eat? He thought about those things, and he decided he had better stay home. As a result of that experience, Coe contacted the Jewish Family & Child Service and asked for help. It turned out to be just a blip. The child was overtired and grumpy

Buzz Coe, right, with brother Ronald. (Courtesy of the Coe family.)

and needed a little extra support from his parents, and everything turned out to be fine, but because of the good work that JFCS did in educating Coe, for which he was very grateful, he became actively involved with the agency's mission.

Coe was asked to join the board in 1974 and served as president from 1977 to 1979. He says it was a different organization than it is today, obviously much smaller, but it was much larger than it had been in its earlier years. As always, funding remained an issue, and a successful membership drive helped add to the available funds.

One of the issues the board was struggling with was, from a philosophical point of view, what made the organization different from other family service organizations? Was it different because it was Jewish, as opposed to Catholic or nonsectarian? They tussled with the concept, trying to find some meaning in the roots of the community.

The board was a wonderful cross-section of the Seattle Jewish community, and as is typical of the Jewish community, if there are two people, they can generate three opinions. The board had its share of diverse views about what made JFCS different. As they tried to answer the questions, they realized one thing all religious service organizations had in common was a strong belief that their culture, tradition, and religion had important positive aspects and they needed to use them to make their community better. There was also recognition that the non-sectarian organizations also had a strong commitments both to helping the immigrants they were assisting and to improving the community. Every time this discussion is held (which seems to be every decade or so), maintaining the Jewish component of the agency is reaffirmed. The concept of *tikkun olam* (repairing the world) is one of the most basic Jewish values. The idea is expressed by helping those in need and supported by thousands of years of tradition and practice.

Coe thought Irv Goldberg ran the organization very well and remarked that the growth of JFS was constant. The board recognized there were services not being provided to the community that were needed, but having a finite amount of money meant it had to be apportioned in what was considered the best interest of the community. As the agency grew, the board explored many different areas of service, including services for single parents and providing classes and seminars for the agency's constituency, as well as adding service to the Eastside.

Services to the elderly were an important consideration that the board could not resolve because JFS simply did not have enough money. Coe felt there were significant gaps in help for seniors. The Caroline Kline Galland Home was a fabulous institution for those who could gain admittance, but he had to ask, what happens when your elderly parents want to be at home on their own and yet not feel isolated. The Home Care for the Elderly and Homemakers Service programs that had been provided in previous years had to be discontinued during the Boeing Bust recession. This important issue was at least partially, if temporarily, resolved at the end of Coe's term as president by raising close to $15,000 at a gala event, sufficient funding to create a program to help elderly clients. JFS sought to sustain these older clients' lives on their terms by providing food, physical care, and other services in their homes, but one goal that remained to be addressed was to reduce isolation with a program of activities for lonely seniors.

During these years, JFS had a list of lawyers and physicians who were willing to volunteer their services. Unfortunately, neither the lawyers nor medical practitioners participated at the level they once had, perhaps primarily because of the requirements of their insurance companies and the threat of lawsuits. Private attorneys traditionally provided the equivalent of a few days of pro bono legal work every year. In addition, the growth of not-for-profit legal aid services was critical in providing assistance to the poor.

There had been other programs for seniors in place long before Coe came on the board, which were dropped for lack of funding. He recalls:

> It was a constant battle to bring to the Federation programs they would be interested in funding. We all knew that money was finite. For whatever reason, JFS did not feel itself in a position to ask for funds for those kinds of programs. Many people in the community said, "Look, we've got the KG Home. That should be sufficient."

> The reality was that the Caroline Kline Galland Home could serve only a limited number of elderly clients and, over time, focused more and more on elderly clients needing more nursing care. At that time in the late 1970s, there were no intermediate care facilities, and healthy seniors more in need of daily living support than nursing care were usually not able to gain admittance to the Home.

cᐤ∞ᐤ

The Republic Building, which had become old and tired, was purchased by Australian developer Martin Baral, a Jewish man who came from a Holocaust survivor family. He was very interested in maintaining the income for the beneficiary agencies. Baral rehabilitated the 1927 building and reopened it in April 1977 as Melbourne House. Funding sources seemed to think JFS was still receiving a significant income from the property, but that stream kept dwindling, although it never completely dried up. These were some of the pressures behind a push to increase visibility and membership.

The primary focus of Jewish Family & Child Service continued to be the strengthening of the Jewish family, which, like all families, was becoming more vulnerable to the pressures of everyday living. A 1977 report by the executive director on the status of JFCS programs attributed this vulnerability, at least in part, "to the high mobility rate which results in the nuclear family being cut off from their extended family." As families made repeated moves, they left behind not only family but also neighbors, friends, and other affiliations. These losses frequently resulted in depression, acute anxiety, panic, and immobilization. Any chronic conflicts were exacerbated during such periods of upheaval making the break-up of the family more likely.

Counselors noticed an increase in the divorce rate with single parent and reconstituted or blended families becoming almost the norm. These families had inherent problems requiring a variety of services and support from the community.

The report suggested that JFCS make a number of changes, including expanding its educational and growth enhancement services, developing a program to link newly arrived families with a local "buddy" family, and hiring a public relations professional to increase the visibility of the resources available at JFCS. The agency responded with increased assistance for crisis intervention. It also worked on prevention through education employing group sessions focusing on specific issues and series of programs addressing more complicated issues. A Family Life Education series for single parents was implemented, and additional efforts were made to sensitize the community to the needs of those families. (See Chapter 14, "Family Life Education.")

JFCS was providing service to many elderly Jewish men and women and initiated a campaign to increase the support to and visibility of these senior clients. The high rate of mobility of families was noted as cutting off the elderly from their adult children and grandchildren, depriving them of important emotional support. Social isolation was a significant problem for this group, especially when transportation was not readily available so they could access the existing resources. This isolation and disconnection contributed to physical and mental health complications.

In the past, JFCS had been able to provide extra help with kosher food allowances, Passover assistance, and a Jewish Neighbors in Need program for poor Jewish individuals and families. Unfortunately, those funds dried up, and United Way started working to convince the Department of Social and Health Services to reimburse the voluntary agencies for emergency financial assistance to clients. Applying directly to the Department of Social and Health Services (DSHS) took too long for people in true emergencies, so the clients turned to the private agencies.

JFCS also provided services to institutions in the Jewish community, including the schools, Sunday schools, and the Jewish Community Center. A Jewish education social worker was required to improve capabilities in this area. In addition, the Russian resettlement program was continuing to serve an average of one new family a month.

A report estimated that $18,000 would be needed in 1978 to provide these new services. The Jewish Federation of Greater Seattle was asked to help with at least $10,000. The synagogues were asked to continue providing some of the direct material assistance expense, and hopefully, DSHS would respond positively regarding the pressure from United Way. The board tasked itself to figure out other ways to support the rest of the needed program expansions.

Another discussion for the board concerned the balance of services within the organization. It became apparent that during the difficult years of the Boeing Bust, the focus of the agency had shifted away from children's services, especially in foster care and adoption services. The board decided in 1978 to once again change the name of the organization, this time from Jewish Family & Child Service to Jewish Family Service (JFS).

In the spring of 1979, JFS contracted with the University of Washington School of Social Work to study the agency's goal alignment with the needs of the service population and intended service community. The major findings were that education, counseling, and support, in that order, were the priorities of the community.

The study confirmed that there was a need to have a presence on the east side of Lake Washington, as more families from the Jewish community were moving there. JFS was concerned that the lack of social service to that population would create a fracture in the Jewish community that was generations removed from the immigrants of the late 19th and early 20th centuries. In addition, the study confirmed that the elderly and single-parent families were particularly isolated. Based on the study, the board determined to expand the social services network to those sectors of the community and opened the Bellevue office, staffed part-time, to provide a physical presence and better access to services.

JFS also made an effort to increase its visibility throughout the Jewish community and to increase membership. It was interesting and surprising how many people were not familiar with the programs of JFS (a circumstance that would recur over and over again through the following decades). In response, the board and people who were friends of JFS were asked to help increase the agency's visibility by talking to other people about its work. In addition, advertisements and articles about programs were placed in the *Jewish Transcript*. Every year, membership in JFS grew as the community became first more knowledgeable and then more interested in what the agency was doing.

Coe's focus towards the end of his presidency in 1979 came from a strong belief that JFS was under-servicing the elderly. Improving service was imperative. He was determined to reinstate the Home Care for the Elderly program, along with a telephone reassurance program. "Honor thy father and thy mother" was one of the pitches he made to the community to raise funds as he told listeners, "We have to learn how to support our elderly."

A report on the programs of JFS for 1978 and 1979 described the services that were being offered, most of which were traditional and/or continuing programs.

The counseling program employed highly trained social workers who counseled individuals and families through periods of crisis. The problems included the entire range of personal and inter-personal conflicts, e.g., depression, anxiety, and conflicts involving parents and children, marriage, and family. With treatment goals always to prevent further deterioration of the clients' ability to cope and to enable them to function more effectively, the clinical social workers utilized a variety of therapeutic approaches, including individual or conjoint psychotherapy, gestalt, transactional analysis, and family therapy.

Supportive services to the elderly included information and referral, planning and evaluation with the clients and their families, advocacy, friendly visiting, continuing assessment, outreach services, and kosher food allowances.

There was also a full range of programs—what today is called Emergency Services, a Family Life Education program, the Russian resettlement program, and Inter-Agency Services through which JFS supported other Jewish organizations in the community. In 1978, the small group of four professionals and two or three clerical support staff provided service to 252 cases (involving 532 people).

Today Coe knows "JFS is an organization that touches people in the entire breadth of our community, from our poorest to our most prominent members, because of the wide variety of programs they have created. Problems [of] the elderly also cut across economic lines. This organization has much to be proud of."

⤫

Irene Steinberg served on the agency's board from 1967 through 1981 and followed Coe into the president's role in 1979. Jerry Grossfeld was executive director when she first joined the board, and Irv Goldberg had been executive director for four years when she became president. The agency was still small but provided much-needed services to the community.

When Steinberg assumed her new role as a board member, the Russian resettlement program became her primary focus. She recalls that at first the board was not enthusiastic about taking on such an expensive and staff-intensive program but was convinced that helping this group of Jewish refugees was one of the reasons the organization was created and was the agency's responsibility. HIAS could accomplish its enormous task only if every community participated.

Irv Goldberg (JFS photo collection.)

Board president Jerry Anches asked Steinberg to take the chairmanship of the Russian Resettlement Committee, which she accepted. Her tasks included requesting funding in person from the Jewish Federation of Greater Seattle. One individual objected, stating the organization didn't have enough money to support the program and saying, "Let them go to Israel; that's where they belong." Steinberg's reply was that his family could have gone to Israel, but they chose to come to the United States. These new people had also chosen to come here, and she thought it was the community's obligation to help them. She was successful in getting the necessary support (both moral and financial) from JFGS.

Steinberg worked to get as many people from the community involved in the program as possible and believes she was successful in getting this support, starting with the members of the resettlement committee, most of whom were also JFCS members. Still there was criticism. Some people said the agency was doing too much; some said it was not doing enough.

A critical resource at the time was the Hadassah Nearly New Store, for which JFCS caseworkers provided letters of request on behalf of their clients in need. One of those clients had lost most of his belongings when his luggage had been stolen. He needed clothing but had no money. Caseworker Ken Weinberg, now on staff as a professional counselor, wrote to the store requesting that he be provided with, "a jacket, suit, shirt, a pair of shoes, two pair of pants, a blanket and a cooking pot."

Early in her term as board president in 1979, Steinberg needed to learn quickly a great deal of detailed information about each program as she prepared to join Goldberg in presenting JFS's annual

Irene Steinberg
(Courtesy of the
Steinberg family.)

funding request to United Way. In his cover letter, which preceded the in-person presentation to United Way, Goldberg discussed the commitment of the board to the elderly and single-parent families in the Jewish community. JFS had committed itself to increase outreach and preventive services to isolated elderly Jews and to reestablish programs that had been cut during the recession, including services to Council House and the Golden Age Club at the Jewish Community Center.

Goldberg also asked Ken Weinberg to coordinate the program for the elderly and increased program staff with the generous support of the Althea and Sam Stroum Fund. The result was expanded outreach to elderly individuals throughout the Jewish community. Then, turning to programming for single parents, JFS proposed to expand outreach through workshops and support groups.

The board had longed to have a permanent space owned by the organization so they would then not have to worry about rent and rent increases, and a number of different proposals were floated over the years. Coe recalls one in which local philanthropist Sam Stroum was involved. Stroum and a group were going to buy a building and lease it back to JFS, and then gift it in pieces as time went by. The plan never got beyond the talking stage, but having their own building was constantly in the minds of Irv Goldberg and board members. Irene Steinberg, remembers that the rent for the Harvard Avenue office space was about to increase dramatically. For the previous five years, the lease had held the rent stable, but it was about to expire at the end of 1979, and the expense for rent would more than double.

Finally, to gain control over its expenses and with the help of an interest-free loan from JFGS, JFS purchased a building located just two blocks away at 1214 Boylston.

Of the $304,074 in the 1979 budget, the Jewish Federation contributed about one-fifth for general programs plus approximately another quarter to specifically support Soviet resettlement, for a total of almost half the budget. The United Way contribution was 28.3 percent, and the Federal Block Grant to cover costs of resettlement was 12.4 percent. Memberships and other gifts made up the balance.

The proposed 1980 budget was $433,771, an increase of 42 percent. Close to $20,000 was to cover the anticipated increase in occupancy cost as JFS moved to its new building. An additional $35,300 was needed for specific assistance to individuals, and almost $53,000 was needed for increases in salaries and benefits. During the year, the agency would open 608 different cases, serving 1,640 individuals.

In May of 1980, at the request of the Jewish federation, JFS assumed responsibility for the administration and implementation of the Resettlement program for Southeast Asians. It was soon discovered that what had been a rather loosely structured program for a small number of refugees was now receiving people at the rate of 130 each month with demand rising. The number of cases handled through JFS made it the second largest resettlement agency in Washington, accepting approximately 25 percent of the entire

HIAS Indochinese caseload. At that rate, 1,500 people would have to be resettled per year, too much for the agency to handle effectively.

In June, Irv Goldberg informed HIAS that JFS would accept only new applications for first-degree relatives of former HIAS cases. This decision reduced the caseload by almost 80 percent. Goldberg implemented structure and procedures providing greater accountability to HIAS sponsors of resettlement grants, as well as closer monitoring of the families' sponsors and what services they provided.

It quickly became clear there were significant issues that needed study to determine the future of the Southeast Asian Resettlement program. By late August, the assessment made clear that the program was doing little more than processing people; newcomers arrived in Seattle and received start-up monies. There was no screening, no social services, no training, and no backup for the families' sponsors. There was no accountability to insure that sponsors were appropriate, that monies were used effectively, or that clients were receiving any basic services.

After careful study, JFS made a decision that rather than try to create a new program for the resettlement of the Southeast Asian refugees, it would enter into a partnership with the Washington Association of Churches. The goal was to help each refugee family successfully attain economic self-sufficiency, minimizing dependency on state and local assistance and enabling the refugees to become more fully integrated into the local community. Five hundred Southeast Asian refugees were expected during 1981.

Because of the new ownership structure and rehab costs, the net profits of the Republic Building were down, and the diminishing income from the Cooper-Levy Trust became a problem for JFS. The treasurer's report at the May 1981 board meeting projected that the expected income from that source would be $20,000, a significant decrease from the $30,000 contributions of the 1950s. Income from the Cooper-Levy Trust remained in the low $20,000 range throughout the 1980s.

Carolyn Kessler served as JFS board president from August of 1981 until May 1983. Irv Goldberg was executive director. JFS has always been part of Kessler's consciousness. In 1967, her husband had worked with an excellent JFCS vocational counselor who helped him sort out his priorities and values. As a result of his work with the JFCS counseling program, the next fall he entered a training program in a different field of work and was happily and successfully employed in that arena for 45 years.

The Kesslers needed help again in 1972 after their infant daughter died. Some close friends had talked about the excellent support they received from the counseling program at JFCS and encouraged Carolyn to use those services. Carolyn thought she would never smile again or be able to embrace life as she had, but the professional counseling helped her return to living fully, and she has been very invested in the agency ever since.

In 1974, after adopting a baby daughter, Carolyn Kessler wanted to give something back to the community, so she volunteered at the Seattle Crisis Center doing telephone crisis intervention counseling. There she met Esther Quint who, in 1976, recruited her to join the board of JFCS. Kessler participated in the discussions in May 1981

Carolyn Kessler (Courtesy of the Kessler family.)

as the board addressed the issue of whether the agency should begin a fundraising campaign to finance the purchase of the Boylston building. They obtained an interim loan through Seattle-First National Bank, formed a Building Campaign Committee, and the capital campaign was approved and commenced.

At the same meeting of the board, Goldberg reported that because JFS had waiting lists in both the Seattle and Eastside offices, a full-time staff person had been hired for the Eastside office. He also announced that, as had been the practice in previous years, several graduate interns from the University of Washington School of Social Work would be participating in JFS programs during the coming year.

Throughout her presidency, Kessler led the board in an effort to include representatives from all parts of the community. They not only wanted to have the Orthodox, Conservative, and Reform communities represented but also were trying to broaden the socio-economic representation. In addition, the Sephardic community was still underrepresented. By the time she left office, Kessler was content that the board better reflected the demographics of the wider Jewish community.

Kessler also worked with the board to continue and strengthen funding for the Jewish Family Life Education program (JFLE). She felt it was important to work from a philosophy of education, training, and prevention, rather than just waiting for crises. At her urging, board members attended JFLE programs, discovering the breadth and depth of the programming, as well as the positive effect the work was having on participants throughout the community. One program for recent converts, called Jews by Choice, demonstrated how visiting another country enhances one's understanding. Participants and other attendees heard about both the joys and pain that the Jews by Choice had experienced along their path. They learned that rabbis do not always accept a convert the first time, at least partially depending upon what tradition they represent—Reform, Conservative, Orthodox, or ultra-Orthodox. Many of the board members at that training felt the sensitivity they gained helped them to broaden their perspective and understanding to more fully appreciate that journey.

Another ongoing project of the board was strengthening the image of JFS in the community. Graphic artist and illustrator Irwin Caplan created promotional materials, which had a more professional appearance and more flair than what JFS had used in the past. Over the years, Kessler has been touched to see the beautiful invitations and marketing materials JFS has created to represent the agency in the community.

Kessler was president of the board during the 90th anniversary celebration in 1982, which Janet Lackman chaired. The goal for attendance was to attract 250 to 300 people, and board members were tapped $20 each to cover the cost of four people. Three hundred people attended—a huge departure from the usual annual meeting held in a small room at the Jewish Community Center or Hillel. The board became more progressive, charging people to attend (for the first time ever) and elevating it to a gala event with crystal and tablecloths. Past board presidents were honored as part of the program. It was a time for JFS to elevate its image in the community while still showing its humble roots and the legacy of decades of providing for the human needs of our community. It was a profound and proud moment for Kessler personally, and she has a sense that it was a leap for JFS in its growth to where it is today.

The Asian resettlement effort continued with the agency helping to resettle 175 immigrants from Southeast Asia during 1982.

Russian resettlement, however, was still the major program focus. Cliff Warner was the director of the program and doing an excellent job, setting up and creating relationships throughout the community for a jobs program. Two years later, when Kessler was on staff as an employment counselor and advisor, that networking formed the foundation for her program. An atmosphere of Jews helping Jews had been created, with Jewish companies willing to post positions and offer opportunities for the people who were resettled.

Goldberg notified the board in January of 1983 that JFS had outgrown the ability of its two major funding sources, United Way and the Jewish Federation, to "keep pace with our increasing operating costs." The deficit for 1983 was expected to be more than $40,000. With the situation remaining stable, JFS would experience an annual operating deficit of $44,585 by 1985. Over a 10-year period, the cumulative deficit would reach more than one-half million dollars. Of course, it would get worse, even without adding new services, by simply trying to keep pace with the growth of the community.

One solution would be to begin planning to cut programs, a solution he suggested might lead to the ultimate phasing out of JFS altogether. His preferred alternative was to create a Development Committee to face the issue head-on and begin strategizing ways to "(1) improve our annual giving program, (2) carry out successful special fundraising events, (3) look at profit-making ventures, and (4) establish a planned giving program."

Janet Lackman agreed to serve as chairperson of the new Development Committee, which quickly began working on an annual-gift and donor-recognition program. A President's Club was inaugurated to cultivate and involve former board presidents, and former board members were engaged and solicited. There was also a focus on recruiting new members into the JFS family, concentrating on 4,600 identified non-member households in the community, starting with a mailing and following up with a phone-a-thon. It was during this planning process that the annual membership was first raised to $25.

JFS was able to increase income from program fees from 5 percent to 11 percent of its 1983 income, still far below the level required to balance the budget. The board committed itself to raising an additional $65,000 to supplement the decline in its United Way and Federation allocations. Membership income increased by $40,000, a 50 percent enhancement for the year. Benefiting from those and other successful efforts, the Development Committee was able to reach its goal.

When Kessler passed the gavel to Peter Shapiro in 1983, the staff of JFS totaled 15—11 professionals and four office personnel. Several new programs were being considered, and by November, executive director Goldberg was able to report that the agency had reestablished a volunteer service, called Friendly Visitors, to improve outreach to isolated Jewish elderly.

Leah was one of those visitors. Every Wednesday at two p.m., she knocked on Rachel's door. It took some time for Rachel to answer because she suffered from severe arthritis, but she always greeted Leah with a big smile. Leah enhanced Rachel's life in small but important ways. Not only did the visits give her something to look forward to, but they also gave her a reason to bake for the visits, and baking provided useful exercise for her arthritic hands. Leah also took short walks with Rachel, which Rachel was unable to manage by herself.

Leah could not replace the family and friends Rachel had lost over the years, but Leah's visits showed Rachel that someone cared and was looking out for her, reminded her that she was still part of a community, and helped her pass some of the long days more quickly and pleasantly.

⌒∞⌒

During six months in 1983, the employment program placed 129 people in jobs, and the caseworkers interviewed and counseled more than 500 members of the community about their job-related needs.

Sixty volunteers participating in the Mitzvah Corps through Temple de Hirsch and Herzl- Ner Tamid received training from JFS and made over a thousand visits to homebound or hospitalized members of the community.

⌒∞⌒

Peter Shapiro joined the JFS board in 1978 and served as president from 1983 to 1985 . (He returned to JFS several years later to lead the Long-Range Planning Committee.) Like many others, Shapiro has served on other boards and says he has not enjoyed any of them as much as his time at JFS, where he felt he truly made a difference.

Soon after Shapiro became the president of the board in 1983, he began to hear concerns about management of JFS, relationships with various segments of the community, and other troubling issues. After careful consideration, under Shapiro's

Dr. Peter Shapiro (JFS photo collection.)

leadership, the board of directors resolved to release Goldberg from his contract and search for a new executive director. Shapiro, who was chairman of the Department of Orthodontics at the University of Washington School of Dentistry, thought that, as he knew was done at the university, JFS should conduct a national search for this critical position in an agency that was important for the community. He approached Ken Weinberg, then director of Professional Services, about being the interim director. This would prove to be a significant turning point in JFS history.

Ken Weinberg was born in the Bronx, New York, in 1947. He lived in a very Jewish neighborhood in the same little brownstone tenement where his mother's parents, Becky and Isadore (Izzy) Brown, were the building superintendents (the supers). In the old country, Grandfather was a farrier, shoeing horses. When he fled the Ukraine during a pogrom and arrived in New York in 1905, Izzy was able to find work in stables. After the city motorized, he became an ironworker in a factory.

Becky and Izzy had a great influence on Weinberg. Grandfather Izzy was a very pious, religious man, but he didn't shove his faith at anyone. He went to synagogue several times a day, and when he prayed in his home in the mornings, wrapping his *tallis* (prayer shawl) around himself, Weinberg remembers that he felt a great sense of serenity.

Grandfather Izzy learned English in order to find work, but Grandmother Becky stayed home and kept to her Yiddish. Weinberg had some difficulty understanding her, but because most of the neighborhood spoke Yiddish, he picked up some of the language. Weinberg's memories are of a lovely woman who struggled daily with a significant limp. As a child, her father, a hideously cruel man, had beat her, dislocating her hip, and because it never healed properly, she walked with a limp for the rest of her life.

Weinberg's paternal grandparents emigrated from Hungary. Grandfather was an alcoholic who physically and emotionally abused his children. When the grandmother died giving birth to her seventh child, the children were placed in a Jewish orphanage. For a time during the depression, Weinberg's dad even had to spend some of his younger years stealing food to live. The paternal grandfather remarried a woman as abusive as he was, and the children returned to live with their father and step-mother.

Weinberg's father, Sam, was also verbally abusive, particularly to Weinberg's mother, and several of Sam's brothers and sisters displayed signs of poor mental health.

When Weinberg was 10, his parents bought a tiny house in Queens in a mostly Jewish and Italian neighborhood. The two immigrant groups enjoyed similarities in family structure with momma, food, and home being very important. The only drawback was that Weinberg had to pass a Catholic school on his way to school, and several times, the Catholic kids chased him and beat him for having killed Christ.

There were many Holocaust survivors in this neighborhood, and most of his friends were the children of these survivors. Weinberg says that he was very aware of the impact the Holocaust had on his friends' families, which had a profound influence on him.

Weinberg attended Queens College, a branch of the City University of New York, where he discovered a love for the arts, museums, and foreign films. He also developed close friendships with three or four other young men with similar interests, and in many ways, these chums were his saviors. Weinberg hung out with their families and saw that home life could be different from what he knew. "I wanted one of those," he said 45 years later, "but you get what you get." Weinberg was a history major with a minor in education and considered pursuing one of two goals: graduate school in history in order to teach, or acting. The war in Vietnam fairly dominated his consciousness, as it did that of most men and women his age, and he became active in the anti-war movement. He wanted desperately to avoid the draft.

One morning after graduation, while still asleep, his mother woke him with a rolled up newspaper. She showed him a want-ad for social worker positions with the New York City Welfare

Department paying $6,800 a year, and she said, "Get out and get one of those jobs." So he did.

Weinberg was assigned to the Bowery on the lower east side of Manhattan working with a mixed population of elderly Jews, Puerto Ricans, and African Americans. It was a very tough part of the city to work in during the late 1960s when heroin and street crime made lower Manhattan a combat zone, but Weinberg liked feeling useful and felt good about helping people.

A year later, he was notified by Selective Service to report for induction into the United States Armed Forces. His social work did not exempt him from military service, but one of the members of the draft board, a Jewish businessman, saw that he had a minor in education, and teachers were draft exempt. He took Weinberg aside and urged him to get a teaching job. As sometimes happens in life, a woman in his mother's Hadassah group had a daughter who worked for the school system in the Bronx. She did a telephone interview with Weinberg, and a week later, he found himself at Wade Junior High School in the Bronx in front of two dozen incorrigible inner-city teens. But his students grew to like Weinberg. One day, rioting gangs stormed the school and were pulling teachers out of classrooms, but Weinberg's kids stood guard at the door saying, "Don't worry, Mr. Weinberg. Nobody's going to get in here and touch you!"

About two years later, Weinberg was invited to visit a friend attending graduate school at the University of California, Santa Barbara over Christmas break. Weinberg had never been outside New York City, and he was stunned at what he found. There were palm trees. It was warm. It was beautiful. It was like a dream. He returned to New York, finished out the school year, and moved to Santa Barbara. It was 1969, and Weinberg was 22 years old.

After an $80-a-month studio apartment on the beach and a stretch in a commune in the mountains (with flowers in his hair), Weinberg ran out of money. He took a job teaching in nearby Goleta, and it was there that he met Alberta, who would eventually become his wife. Weinberg found that he enjoyed working with the kids after school and helping them with their problems and issues, and was more interested in who they were and what challenges they were facing than in teaching them about the Civil War and Reconstruction. He especially felt drawn back to geriatric social work. He loved older people, and he knew he wanted to do something for the Jewish community he came from.

The University of Washington School of Social Work offered him a full scholarship plus a stipend to work as a teaching assistant. The UW also had an excellent geriatric social work program headed by Art Farber, a former executive director of JFS. Weinberg accepted the package, and he and Alberta moved to Seattle, arriving on August 1, 1975. Weinberg remembers a typical August day, cold and rainy, and the first time they saw Mt. Rainier they didn't know what it was. The young couple hated the weather in Seattle and yearned for a good cup of coffee and the California sunshine and beaches. Alberta made him swear that the moment he finished graduate school they would go back to California. More than thirty-eight years later, Seattle remains their home, and although they still don't like the weather, a good cup of coffee is much easier to come by.

Ken Weinberg came to Jewish Family & Child Service at 1110 Harvard Avenue in 1975 as a graduate student intern. Thelma Coney was his staff supervisor, and Martha Becker was his clinical supervisor. Thelma remembers him as a very conscientious student, very organized, and totally committed to the idea of working in the Jewish community. She says he was a student who always did his reports extremely well, was always prepared to discuss his cases, and was open to any suggestions he was given. He focused on geriatric social work, finding it exciting and fulfilling. He had always been interested in history, and working with a geriatric clientele, he was actually speaking to people who had experienced a significant piece of Jewish history. Many of his clients, while he was an intern and, later, a professional social worker, had come from Germany before the war. Others were Holocaust survivors or had escaped pogroms. It was a wonderfully rich and fascinating job, and he loved it.

Patsy Policar, who also worked with Weinberg during his internship, remembers him as an extremely intelligent, capable individual. When Weinberg completed graduate school in 1977, he was immediately hired at JFCS as a staff counselor working primarily with senior clients, and he and Alberta were soon able to buy a house. "I got to be in a place that allowed me to be me," he recalled 38 years later, "and I was able to work with my community. I could just be who I was. At times I felt that I got to do God's work to make the world a better place, make the community better, and alleviate pain."

Weinberg is frustrated with people who don't seem at all interested in doing even a little bit to help build better lives and a better community. He feels that is everyone's obligation. He thinks his personality and background growing up in New York causes him to focus on the negative: the people who don't help, the people who don't give, the people who don't see, the people who can walk past all the suffering and just keep on walking. Then he adds, "But I've also seen the most wonderful, the most generous, the most giving, the most caring people that one can possibly experience."

One of Weinberg's clients in 1979 was another young man who was insecure, excessively shy, and introverted. Although he appeared to make good progress during the months he worked with Weinberg, two years later when the young man had a series of angry, almost violent episodes, Weinberg referred him to the Community Psychiatric Clinic for an evaluation and follow-up treatment.

Another client was an elderly woman struggling through the grief process with the loss of her husband and very depressed. Weinberg wrote to her daughter about her mother's progress, pleased to report that she was now attending the kosher lunch program on Tuesdays at the Caroline Kline Galland Home where she was able to see many friends, have a wonderful time, and bring enjoyment to others as well as to herself. He also recommended that she participate in an older Jewish widows support group that met bi-weekly at the agency.

Weinberg eventually became the director of Geriatric Services for JFS. In addition, since he had a background in teaching, he was asked to revitalize the Jewish Family Life Education program, which had been dropped several years earlier due to lack of funding. He took on the task of creating educational programs for the community that had a mental health component: communication skills, parenting teens, interfaith marriage, etc.

Weinberg was appointed director of Professional Services in 1981. Then, in 1984, after working at JFS for about eight years and not seeing any possibility of further promotion within the agency, Weinberg started to look for another position. He found a job opening with Jewish Child and Family Service in New Haven, Connecticut, applied, and they flew him out twice for interviews, the second time with Alberta. The couple was wined and dined, and Weinberg was offered the position of executive director. Still, Weinberg asked for time to consider and promised an answer in the morning. He and Alberta stayed up all night long writing down and discussing the plusses and the minuses, and he could not make up his mind. The sensible thing to do was to take the New Haven job.

At eight a.m., when the phone call came, he could hear happiness in expectation of his answer. "I'm terribly sorry," he told them. "It's a wonderful job, and it's a wonderful community, and you did everything right. But I really came to grips with wanting to stay in Seattle." During the entire flight home, Weinberg kept asking Alberta if he had made a mistake.

Then Peter Shapiro offered Weinberg the position as interim executive director in Seattle. Weinberg asked Shapiro if he was a candidate for the permanent position. Peter said, "Ken, I think you are going to be the best candidate, but I feel this obligation to do a search, rather than just trying to hire you." Weinberg was less than excited about that prospect.

Shapiro recalls Weinberg responding, "I've been offered jobs, and I'm in demand, and I don't want to sit and wait for a search committee because I have another opportunity right now. And if you're going to do a search committee, I don't think I want to be a candidate." Shapiro reconsidered and then worked hard to convince the board that they should cancel the search telling them, "I think this is the right person, and I don't really want to risk losing him."

Weinberg was scheduled to leave for Europe on his first sabbatical before the executive director issue had been resolved, and he asked Shapiro if he should stay. Shapiro said, "Go. It won't influence our decision." When the board decided to offer him the job, Shapiro called Weinberg in Italy and said, "Mazel tov! You are the new executive director." He told Weinberg to finish his sabbatical and "enjoy it while you can."

Carolyn Kessler, who was immediate past president when Weinberg became executive director, said, "Ken had already established his presence as being a wise and thoughtful leader but had never had a chance to fully lead because Irv Goldberg had quite a strong personality. But the board believed in our heart of hearts that he was the right person for it." When Weinberg accepted the offer, the board members in the room were jubilant.

Weinberg had little experience looking at, working with, or understanding the financial aspect of an organization, but on his first day on the job, he spread all the financial reports on the floor and tried to comprehend the numbers. What he concluded was that JFS had no money.

"I called the finance person—a bookkeeper. I said, 'I'm looking at these, and if I am not mistaken, we are broke.' And the bookkeeper said, 'Yeah, I'm not sure how we are going to make payroll.'" Weinberg had just turned down a job at an agency in Connecticut that paid more and was in good financial shape. But he knew he wanted to stay in Seattle, he liked this agency, and now he got to be the boss. He was 37 years old.

That first day, he went home and told Alberta, "It's a disaster! There's no money."

With the help of Peter Shapiro, Weinberg gradually put things in order. They made payroll and then slowly and steadily helped get JFS back on sound financial footing. Weinberg simultaneously started working to build morale. The staff of 13 or 14 people was terribly dispirited after some difficult years.

Weinberg was also able to cultivate continuing relationships with most of those donors who had lost faith in JFS, although there was one that took several years to come around. That donor eventually became one of the agency's strongest supporters again, helped to create and support new programs, and left a generous bequest to the JFS endowment fund.

When Weinberg took over, JFS primarily provided counseling to individuals, families, and children; emergency services to the needy; and case management and other services to the elderly. The staff also processed loans for the Hebrew Ladies Free Loan Society. There was a vocational program, resettlement work, and a small amount of adoption and foster care services. There were 12 or 14 staff members, and the kosher food bank was a 10-foot shelf in a closet with cans of food for those few who came for help. The annual budget in 1984 was under $400,000. Funding came primarily from the Jewish Federation of Greater Seattle, United Way, the Cooper-Levy Trust, and membership dues and individual gifts. During the three years it took to get JFS back on sound financial ground, the board and JFGS were kept informed.

Chapter 14

Family Life Education

"Before, I didn't know where we would be welcome or accepted."
—Newly divorced single parent

The FLE program has grown and changed over the past several years. As a result of the 2006 strategic planning process its name was changed from Jewish Family Life Education to Family Life Education because it seemed redundant that Jewish Family Service had a Jewish Family Life Education program. The change was also important to reflect more accurately a program, and in fact an agency, that consistently reached out beyond the Jewish community to the general community.

The program provides educational opportunities covering the entire life cycle from birth—even before—to end of life, concentrating on those issues families typically experience, as well as special programs that families in crises need but that could also hit other families. Clients are referred from all the other JFS programs and participate with many others who take part on a pro-active basis, getting ahead of issues instead of reacting to them later, as is often the case in conventional social work. Participants are intent on enhancing their families' lives, learning some new tools, and making sure they know what they are getting into before or as they enter a new part of life. One offering has been Positive Discipline, a parent education program teaching parenting and emotion coaching. This program presents a method of communication and guidance that is respectful of the child and takes parents step-by-step through validating feelings, problem-solving with their children, and setting consequences when they are needed. The program was developed by the Gottman Relationship Institute and Drs. John and Julie Schwartz Gottman of Seattle, and provides a self-contained tool that people can blend into other parenting skills. It works well proactively and helps rebuild a parenting toolbox.

JFS director of Professional Services Ken Weinberg re-established the Jewish Family Life Education program (JFLE) in 1982 after executive director Irv Goldberg attended a conference where he learned about the program being offered at other agencies. Goldberg thought it was an excellent idea to offer educational programming to the public. He approached Sam and Althea Stroum to help restart the endeavor, and they generously provided a contribution of $15,000 a year for two years, after which JFLE was incorporated into the agency budget. Weinberg became the program director.

Weinberg remembers launching the effort with a program called "New to Seattle" about not only the Pike Place Market and the best place for bagels but also information about how and why moving and adjusting to a new city is a trauma, even when it's something you really want. It was not uncommon for a family to locate to this area because the main breadwinner, usually the husband, had to move for his work.

The women's movement had already begun to change family relationships dramatically and affected what JFS provided. Weinberg remembers programs he presented on topics like "What is it like when your wife is the main breadwinner?" and "What happens when your wife makes more money than you do?" These were topics very much part of the era of change in the world of women and their families. Issues rose about what it meant to be a husband or wife during that time. For many couples, life was no longer just about two kids and taking care of them. Things became more complicated when both husband and wife worked full-time. Too often, the husband's job was his full-time work while the wife's job was her full-time work, plus she had full responsibility for the entire home and the kids, the shopping, the cleaning, the laundry. Obviously, that caused stress, anger, and resentment. Those early programs dealt with those kinds of issues, which were very prevalent in the early 1980s.

Those issues were nothing like what FLE currently addresses. Thinking about the gay-lesbian-bisexual-transsexual programs offered today, Weinberg ponders if anyone in 1975 would have dreamt that JFS would be offering programs for two men or two women who are having a baby, using a surrogate, or adopting. He greatly appreciates what he recognizes as amazing openness and diversity in our community.

Others joined Weinberg in presenting programs of JFLE. The agency instituted a requirement that each professional staff member had to lead at least one program per quarter. This proved contentious. The clinicians, accustomed to closing the office door with one client in the room complained, "Hey, I'm a clinician." But Weinberg and Goldberg felt that in order to build the clinical program it was important for the clinicians to get out of the interview rooms and into the community. There were sometimes conflicts between Weinberg and the counselors over fulfilling this requirement that required change on their part. Weinberg had to keep track of who did how many programs and follow through with "You didn't do any programs in the past three months, and you need to do one." To this day, Weinberg still thinks it was an important move for JFS.

When Weinberg became executive director in 1984, Vivien Benjamin, who had taken over from Weinberg and managed the JFLE program for many years, had retired. Weinberg hired Beth Cordova as coordinator and worked with her to create a more robust JFLE program.

Cordova's background was in gerontology and in Jewish education. One of her early innovations was single-parent programming, deemed very progressive at the time. Single parents needed help, but their issues were not being considered in the Jewish community or in the greater society. It was not uncommon for a single parent to have terrible disagreements with an ex-spouse over finances (usually the ex-husband did far better financially than the ex-wife), visitation, education, health care, or even summer camp. Passions flared regularly.

Salie Rossen took over from Cordova in 1989, working part-time. Rossen recalls that JFS felt like a tight little family at the time. One of her tasks was to involve the synagogues and more of the community and to connect JFS to all those different entities, although she was not as involved with the schools as JFS counselor Diane Zipperman.

Rossen found it difficult to connect with the synagogues and also tough to get people to attend programs. One of the offerings she presented with Rabbi David Rose was a seminar on interfaith marriage. At the time, the topics of interfaith dating and marriage, as well as those concerning the Chanukah-Christmas dilemma, were the most successful offerings.

Rossen's consulting practice in program and organizational development continued to grow. When she was awarded a contract with the state of Washington to train top management executives in management ethics and was also working with Bonneville Power and other government agencies, she had to leave JFS to focus on her private practice. She finds the FLE program of today phenomenal.

Natalie Merkur Rose followed Salie Rossen as director of JFLE. Rose grew up on Long Island in a typically Conservative Jewish family involved in congregational life. Her grandparents, originally from Austria and Poland, had also been strong role models of giving service to and being part of the community. Wanting to work with the elderly, Rose attended college in Albany and then earned master's degrees in social work and Jewish communal services from Columbia School of Social Work and the Jewish Theological Seminary, respectively. Married to a rabbi who became the assistant rabbi at Herzl-ner Talmid, she moved with her husband to Seattle with a plan to return to the Northeast after two years.

Rose was unable to find a position with a Jewish agency so she worked in Chore Services for Catholic Community Services until she was able to create a proposal to work for JFS as a contract worker teaching nursing home staffs how to work with Jewish residents. Cliff Warner, assistant director in 1984, agreed. A year later, Rose and her husband left Seattle for three years, during which time she worked in Senior Services for JFS Tampa.

When her husband was offered the post of senior rabbi at Herzl-ner Tamid, the family returned to Seattle. Rose was able to come back to JFS and worked with Sarah Barash in Senior Services. Then, when Salie Rossen left in 1992, Rose's education made her a great match for the JFLE director's position, combining her expertise in social work and Jewish communal services.

Two ongoing programs were already established as Rose took on her new role. One was an annual retreat for single parents and their children; the other, a monthly group for interfaith couples, a new area for Rose. She was very taken with people who wanted to be part of the Jewish community and were struggling on how to do that, and she soon enlarged and enhanced that piece of the program. It became apparent that the community needed to pay more attention to and embrace interfaith couples. Working with Amy Wasser at the Jewish Federation of Greater Seattle, the two organizations brought Egan Mayer, director of the Jewish Outreach Institute, for a workshop.[1]

Another meeting for the community included representatives from 40 synagogues and community organizations. Rachel Cowan, one of the authors of *Mixed Blessings*, a book about interfaith relationships, was brought in to speak at one of the workshops. On the back of the printed program were listed all the partner congregations and organizations. At the end of the presentations, a woman clutching the program said, "Thank you for doing this. Now with this list of organizations and congregations, I know what to do. Before, I didn't know where we would be welcomed or accepted."

Bridging between welcoming organizations and congregations, and couples who were searching was a valuable role for JFS.

The agency went on to offer as many as four to six programs a year for interfaith couples because there was so much interest in the community.

Both the interfaith program and the single-parent families program served people in the Jewish community who were having difficulty finding their place. Soon programs were also being offered for gay and lesbian Jews and for parents and families of gay and lesbian Jews, which at that time was unheard of and very controversial. Rose remembers that only three people actually signed up for the first session, which was then almost cancelled. Thirty-three people showed up. Rose was moved that those people who had been searching for help thought JFS was a safe place.

One advantage JFS has is that it does not belong to any particular denomination or part of the Jewish community. JFS is also a place where nobody is making judgments. People can be Jewish (or not), and whatever else they are is accepted. All are made to feel welcome, heard, and valued.

Rose is proud of helping to alter and grow the single-parent camp, which was then being held at Camp Solomon Schechter. Recognizing that many single parents have challenging lives, Rose wanted them to find their strengths and discover how they could be resources for each other, as well as ways in which the community could be available for them. She wanted to help them address their challenges through their strengths.

She started by asking people to write one of their strengths as a parent on their nametags as a way to introduce themselves. People wrote, "I'm loving" or "I'm resourceful." One woman said, "I can't do it. Can't think of a single positive way I'm a good parent." Those assembled supported her, and by the time the group left on Sunday, the members had formed strong relationships.

Rose's idea of putting family names on the cabins led one participant to say, "You have no idea how powerful that is because I didn't think we had any kind of family any more. I thought we had a broken family, and just seeing us identified as a family like that was so powerful to me."

At one event, Ruz Gulko, a Jewish educator with a powerful, affirming manner, was brought in to participate. As she led the group in musical offerings and informal religious services, Gulko created an experience for the participants that was transforming so that they were able to go home feeling differently about themselves, their family, and their place in the community.

Throughout her work with the program from 1992 to 2001, Rose had a sense that JFS really mattered in the community and in people's lives. In addition to helping the folks that were underrepresented in the community, Rose co-staffed a year-long task force with Amy Wasser on participation and affiliation in the Jewish community and then continued with implementation of the task force's findings.

Rose worked to increase life cycle offerings and other programming, including topics on interfaith grand parenting, the creation of a Passover Seder for Jewish women living with abusive partners, programs about being childless in the Jewish community, being Jewish during the Christmas season, and several other unique offerings. When she was approached by people in the community who felt underserved in some way, she would, when appropriate, strive to create a program in response.

In 2003, Margie Schnyder followed Natalie Merkur Rose as the director of Family Life Education. She grew up in the Detroit area, moving to Seattle in 1988 after graduating from the University of Michigan in Ann Arbor. She holds a master's degree in social work and has a background in child and family therapy as well as consultation with early childhood and parent-education programs.

Schnyder worked in the community mental health system for eight years and in community college parent-education programs for five years before finding the opening at JFS. In 2003, her position at the community college was winding down, and she wanted to continue in parent education. She saw the ad for a position that was not just parent education but also worked across the whole lifespan. Schnyder says it was *beshert*.

Schnyder's skill set was quite different from that of Natalie Rose. Schnyder came in with a background in child and family therapy but not in Jewish education or older-adult programming, so while she could teach a variety of parent education programs, she was not qualified to teach programs about older adults. She needed the assistance of the Senior Services program in this area, which changed the demographics of who could be served immediately using only internal resources. The result was that when presenting programs with a direct Jewish content piece, outside experts were brought in. Schnyder learned about the Jewish community very quickly spending time getting to know people and learning who were potential partners to co-teach programs, a model that is still used frequently.

A Jewish Community Center (JCC) program called Mom-To-Mom was one of those partnerships. Mom-To-Mom began in response to surveys about what new Jewish parents needed. One of the findings was that many new moms felt isolated, particularly because Seattle had so many transplants who did not have local family ties and support systems. It was essentially a mentoring plan where an experienced mom would be matched one-on-one with a first-time mom. It provided parenting and general support, in addition to helping new moms learn about the local Jewish community. About 10 very committed, sharp, interesting women volunteered as mentors. The Mom-To-Mom effort closed after two and a half years when the original mentors moved on to other activities, and at the same time, the JCC was developing more of its parenting project. By then, FLE offered a class called Bringing Baby Home, and several other agencies were offering classes for new moms.

Bringing Baby Home is for couples who are pregnant or who have a new baby or very young child. It was developed locally by the Gottman Institute and helps strengthens relationships with skills tested and proven by research—a unique occurrence in FLE. There is quite a bit of research behind programming, but for an individual class or series to have curriculum and results tested by research is unusual. Instructors for the Bringing Baby Home classes must be certified by the Gottman Institute.

When JFS started offering Bringing Home Baby, Swedish Hospital was doing it as well, but on Saturday and Sunday afternoons. Because Saturday is the Sabbath, this made the classes unavailable to observant Jews. JFS offers all courses on days other than the Sabbath.

Bringing Baby Home overlaps classes on couple relationships and parenting and is a good example of content that is completely secular but can be designed in a way that makes it more appropriate in the Jewish community. For example, a hospital presentation might not discuss the traditions around a bris or naming of a child.

As FLE expanded, it addressed topics across the entire range of ages, a practice that was reaffirmed during the strategic planning process. The 2006 Strategic Plan also stressed that FLE should offer programs in a consistent, predictable way enabling people to plan in advance to attend a series for new parents, for someone caring for an aging parent, for talking to teens about drugs, for building a strong marriage, or for practicing positive discipline with children of all ages.

⁓∞⁓

In 2008, almost 30 percent of US households were headed by a single parent.[2] FLE offers Single Parent Family programming, which includes lectures and activities targeting single parents, sometimes for the adults only, sometimes incorporating the children as well. There had been an overnight stay for single-parent families at Camp Solomon Schechter for many years, but it was held only once a year, and scheduling was always difficult. During the summer, the camp was in use, and in the spring, the weather is too unpredictable. Finally, the overnight was switched to an all-day event, and several smaller events were added throughout the year, providing more continuity for the families.

One of the single-parent family retreats was held at the Cedar River Watershed Educational Center in North Bend, a facility on a lake with an auditorium and a big fire circle. The group spends the day, has lunch together—some years, breakfast too—and enjoys activities for parents and children. One year, the children participated in an activity about "what my family does together." They wrote on a strip of paper something they like to do with their family and then linked them all together into a giant decorative chain.

A keystone of the retreat is a family project with a Jewish theme presented at the end of the day. It might be an art project, or making a *tzedakah* (charity) box together. A popular activity has been led by Ruz Gulko, the Jewish educator and musician, where she has parents and children write blessings for each other.

There is always a cultural piece, songs around the fire pit, and s'mores. Usually, some of the parents have attended Jewish camps and know the songs, and some of their children attended Jewish camps (although many do not have the resources, have been in transition, or are encountering too many difficulties). The single-parent program typically serves 10 to 15 families at any one event.

From time to time, a parent will attend with a child that has special needs. The parent has usually informed the staff in advance of the child's needs, enabling the well-trained, experienced team to make available appropriate help for these children. Sometimes, what is required is to assign a staff person to provide one-on-one attention for a particular activity or for the entire day. There have been several heartwarming experiences with special-needs children who have attended with their parent year after year and grown confident and comfortable with the experience. Over time, the parent and child mix easily with the group, have a wonderful time, and meet other single parents, including other parents with special-needs children.

The FLE team knows that some families who participate may have mental health needs or learning disabilities, have just come out of a traumatic situation, or are experiencing an economic crisis, so they prepare for all those situations. Sometimes two families meet each other, keep in touch, and become friends away from camp. They might then attend Shaarei Tikvah (Gates of Hope) events together and participate together in parent-education programs. (These special holiday services and celebrations are open to everyone in the community. They are designed to be meaningful for individuals with developmental disabilities or persistent mental illness, as well as their families and friends.) Single moms sometimes request a Big Pal for their sons, and occasionally a single dad will request a Big Pal woman for his daughter. These Big Pals will often attend the camp and Shaarei Tikvah events with their Little Pal and his or her family.

FLE has offered Parenting Mindfully: Drawing on Jewish Values through Mussar, a class that Schnyder teaches with Rabbi Yohanna Kinberg of Temple B'nai Torah. The class looks at Mussar, the set of Jewish ethics and texts for reflecting on and changing your own behavior to be more ethical. The rabbi helps participants examine the texts and traditions, Schnyder examines the social-work/child-development side, and together with a group of parents, they focus on one particular ethical trait through the lens of parenting. They might look at a range of different issues, including honesty, anger, silence, patience, moderation, and presence. For instance, for anger, one of the most popular, Schnyder will discuss the research around how parents can manage their anger. What kinds of things make parents angry? What does she hear parents talking about as being triggers for anger? What kinds of things help parents calm down when they are angry? Rabbi Kinberg will present information from various texts about anger, including texts about God and anger or about various biblical figures and anger, and then will discuss what they tell us in contemporary times about this emotion. A different class would focus on children and anger.

In the area of aging, there are offerings about long-distance care giving, about the balance between independence and safety and security and how to allow people their dignity, respect, and independence while insuring they are not in situations that are dangerous. There have also been workshops on the more difficult behaviors of aging parents, like mental health issues or substance abuse, that people might not realize are happening to their parent. Another offering concerns death and dying, which often includes a cultural piece. This workshop provides emotional support and helps people feel comfortable about Jewish rituals for mourning and funerals by explaining their history and purpose.

For baby boomers, FLE presents workshops on topics like Medicare and Social Security, including helping people find one-on-one resources that can advise them, for instance, about which Medicare supplemental-insurance offering or retirement-planning method works best for them. Many of the second-half-of-life classes are done in partnership with rabbis or other outside experts to bring in the Jewish education and/or clergy piece, particularly with the more serious topics.

⬦

Aging & Adult Programs decided they wanted to do more for Russian Jewish elders the agency helped resettle in the Seattle area in the 1970s and 1980s. Jane Relin, director of Aging & Adult Programs, organized a committee and helped create a Russian language Seder. It was held at Temple Beth Am using a Haggadah (the text that presents the order of the Passover Seder) written in Russian. Cantor Marina Belenky, who is a Russian-speaking cantor, led the service along with Wendy Marcus at Temple Beth Am.

In a Russian community, dancing is so important that the end of this now annual Seder is followed by wonderful, enthusiastic ballroom dancing. A large group of volunteers from Beth Am and JFS are involved with 250 participants who love the event and find it meaningful.

Because the Russian community on the Eastside is one of the biggest groups JFS reaches, a Russian language information-and-support specialist is included on the staff, and Jane Relin has worked with a group of Russian elders to include them in the Holocaust memorial service held at the JCC.

FLE tries to offer couples at least three or four classes a year to provide tools and ways to think about and enhance their relationships. Perhaps they have had extra stress because of the recession or have gone through a transitional point like retirement or empty nest as a couple. One class is about commitment and what that means in a relationship. How are thinking and talking about commitment, good communication, and problem solving with your partner tools to enhance your relationship? Just the act of saying "we are a committed couple" can be an opportunity. This workshop, called "First Comes Love, Then Comes Commitment: Cultivating Relational Strength for All Times," was developed by Max Livshetz, a JFS intern who was writing his PhD dissertation on the topic and said, "This is really interesting stuff. Maybe it could become a workshop."

In 1991, in response to requests from the LGBTQ (lesbian, gay, bisexual, transsexual, and queer or questioning) community for ongoing support, FLE began a series of workshops for them and their families. With this portion of the community, JFS is trying to reframe the conversation away from the pejorative and not use fixed labels and identity. For younger generations, identity has become more fluid, and by saying you are queer, you do not have to be saying specifically you are one way and always going to be that way.

FLE is often an entry point for people to become clients or donors as it may be the first opportunity people have to become familiar with the classes and workshops offered to the community. FLE has reached out to interfaith families for 20 years, and as needs for those families have changed, that programming has evolved. The goal is always to help people get support so they can enjoy healthy, harmonious family lives.

Recognizing that someone who does not know much about JFS may not understand that it is very welcoming, the agency started using more explicit language in its marketing and in conversations with people about who was welcome at their programs. Gradually, FLE offered more programming for couples, individuals, and parents who are gay or lesbian or transgender, etc. This program has become a consistent part of FLE.

The future question will be how can JFS reach people in a much larger multicultural, multi-racial population? One new opportunity is a pilot project on Jewish healing that provides support in a cultural context for people with an acute, life-threatening, or serious long-term illness. Future goals also include reaching out to other people who traditionally have been underserved, including aging immigrant residents (like Russian Jewish elders), interfaith, mixed racial, blended, and other non-traditional families.

Endless Opportunities

The Endless Opportunities program, which was started as part of the JFS Aging & Adult Programs in December 2005, moved to FLE so that FLE would be able to address the entire life span. Endless Opportunities, coordinated by Ellen Hendin, serves adults aged 60 and older with lifeline programming within a community and cultural context. The majority of participants are active seniors who enjoy interesting speakers, outings, and meeting with peers. The program, which meets two or three times a month, is operated in partnership with Temple B'nai Torah and Temple de Hirsch Sinai, both of which provide space and financial support.

Larry Broder, the director of Temple de Hirsch Sinai, had been talking about the fact that the temple had a large population of older people who were disconnected from the congregation because the initial involvement had usually been in connection with their children who had now grown up and were gone. The temple was looking for activities to engage that population. He discussed the issue with JFS and discovered the agency had also been looking at the topic. The problem for JFS was the stigma of coming to JFS for a program or service because people are often self-conscious about being seen by friends or colleagues who might think they are coming to JFS as a client for counseling, addiction assistance, domestic violence, or some other issue. Also, JFS did not have the space required. However, JFS had the staff. Temple de Hirsch had the space and many of the attendees. A meeting with Rabbi Jim Mirel from Temple B'nai Torah in Bellevue, Broder, and JFS resulted in the creation of Endless Opportunities (EO). The Herzl congregation was also a partner in the early years.

Over the years, other congregations began to participate, although Temple de Hirsch and B'nai Torah remain the most significant participants. The Sephardic community has very robust adult education programs of their own while the smaller synagogues feel they are too small to become partners, but everyone is welcome to attend.

The response has been extremely positive with the creation of a program the seniors value and feel very good about. Once the core group of people came together and began to manage the program, they had to decide on a name. Nothing that included the words "senior" or "golden" or similar terms was found acceptable, but eventually Endless Opportunities won approval. Temple de Hirsch can seat more than 1,200 people, and many of the largest events are held in that facility. Temple B'nai Torah can also accommodate a large crowd with many of the programs being held in that Eastside facility.

Broder says that Ellen Hendin has the background, skills, training, and personality that make her the perfect person to manage the program.

There is a volunteer advisory group of very committed community members who direct the program, with event information available online. Anyone can attend Endless Opportunities, Jewish or non-Jewish, and participation has increased every year with an average of perhaps 50 people at each event. Of course, food is served at every occasion.

One goal of the program is to keep people from becoming isolated after they have left their work life when children, grandchildren, and other family are often busy or have moved away. As the program grows and becomes more established, questions are being asked about its direction going forward. Will people still be able to bond with each other at larger events, or might it become too big? If it gets bigger, will people become lost in the crowd and will the staff be able to tell if people's needs are changing? The committee and JFS are aware that bigger is not always better, and the Endless Opportunities staff is mindful that larger events might not allow the close connections and bonding they have been able to encourage in the past.

Staff members also do not want the program to be exclusive or to stagnate; it must evolve. They want people who move to the area from another part of the country to feel comfortable attending, and they hope the people who have been coming for years will continue to welcome to those who come for the first time.

EO started by offering a wide variety of programming to hundreds of senior participants. The first event was a luncheon featuring Seattle City councilwoman Jean Godden. Included in the variety of offerings that followed were some wonderful outings, including, for two or three years, taking groups of 40 or 50 people by bus to view the eagles on the Skagit River. Broder had falconer friends who were capturing and banding birds, and the falconers met the buses, allowing people to see and sometimes hold the eagles. In the spring, similar groups would be bused to the tulip fields in the Skagit Valley. Unfortunately, out-of-town adventures ended when the costs became too high for the program, which is built on the principle that it should be provided at no or low cost for participants. Trips to see the eagle-feeding grounds or the tulip fields will have to wait for other arrangements.

JFS has recently completed a survey asking participants if and how much they would be willing to pay for transportation on out-of-town trips. About 170 EO participants completed the survey: 80 percent of the respondents were interested in local outings, and 20 percent would not want to pay for private bus transportation for out-of-town outings. However, 80 percent would pay $25 to $40. (The survey was not random and likely has a bias that skews the results; it was done mostly by email, and it's likely there were not as many responses from a large number of people with limited incomes or who are older and less technologically savvy.) Schnyder estimates that transportation for 50 guests might cost $600 with the price much higher for an all-day trip, for instance, about $1,500 for a trip to see the eagles.

EO was designed as a no-cost-to-participants program to prevent economic barriers, but some expenses have to be passed along to the users. This has created an issue, particularly during difficult economic times, when there is a docent fee at a museum or another necessary expense. When some trips and guest speakers have to be declined because of the cost to individual participants, outing information is provided so individuals can make their own arrangements.

Expenses for advertising and food (usually a simple bagel brunch) are kept low, and very few speakers charge fees. Ellen Hendin is quite gifted in her ability to convince people they should participate as a speaker for EO with no charge, so perhaps only three or four times a year a speaker will receive an honorarium and sometimes, then, at a special nonprofit rate.

The program originally served a full lunch, which was preferable because the meal allows more time for socializing. EO is gradually building that back in, with one or two luncheons during the past year.

Programming has included a presentation called "What's Washing Up on Our Shores?" about the global problem of marine debris, focusing on the devastating Japanese tsunami in March of 2011, the marine debris it created, and the response activities conducted by the National Oceanic and Atmospheric Administration and its partners. Other presentations included a two-part talk on the Hindu culture, another about the experience of local adults who served in the Peace Corps and VISTA programs, and one by Dr. James AuBuchon, director of the Puget Sound Blood Center about the importance of new stem-cell and platelet research.

1. The Jewish Outreach Institute is an independent, national, trans-denominational organization reaching out to unaffiliated and intermarried families and helping the organized Jewish community better welcome them in.

2. Single Parent Households: 1980 to 2009, Table 1337. US Census Bureau, Statistical Abstract of the United States, 2012, 840.

Chapter 15

1984–1994: New Directions

"Hey, God, is this You working with me here?"
—Ken Weinberg

As Ken Weinberg took on his new role as executive director of JFS, he confronted several issues that needed to be addressed quickly. Besides the low morale of the agency staff and relationships with donors being far from optimal, funding sources and various other constituencies needed attending.

Weinberg reminisces about how, soon after his return from Connecticut but before he knew about the pending changes at the agency, Irv Goldberg called him into his office and said, "I've decided to leave JFS. I thought I ought to let you know." Weinberg remembers thinking, Hey, God, is this you working with me here?

Ken Weinberg
(JFS photo collection.)

When Weinberg was hired to serve as executive director, one of his concerns was that some of the older staff members would resent such a young, comparatively inexperienced person as the new exec. He quickly discovered that people really celebrated his taking the responsibility.

He participated in many meetings with staff in which he solicited input. He wanted to know what was on their minds, what they were looking for, what they wanted to see. Weinberg was not necessarily going to implement everything 12 staff members wanted, but he stayed open to hearing what they were saying and wanted to know the range of their issues.

This communication style remained one of the themes of Weinberg's career as executive director. He periodically received notes and, later, e-mails from staff people who were leaving telling him that one of the things they really liked was his openness. He understood the importance of creating an atmosphere in which people feel they have been heard and understood.

JFS has always been about serving people, and Weinberg describes his job as director as similar to an orchestra conductor who is also a member of the orchestra. He may help various instruments play their piece, but they are all a unit together. Someone has to be conductor, or chaos reigns, but Weinberg's style is to be a subtle conductor as opposed to knocking his team over the head with his baton.

Many things needed to be changed. The first one he addressed was the rule that forbade any staff person from speaking to any board member. Previously, if a staff member spoke to a member of the board, that person could be fired. Weinberg thought it was obvious that the finance director should be speaking to the treasurer and that a staff person working on a committee with a layperson needed to be able to communicate directly.

He had the full support of board president Peter Shapiro, as well as of the rest of the board. He also had the support and expert assistance of Julie Olson who was the office manager and had been Irv Goldberg's assistant. She was loyal to Goldberg, and Shapiro was concerned that she might want to leave when Goldberg left, but when Shapiro approached her, she confirmed that she would stay and was helpful in soothing things during the transition from Goldberg to Weinberg.

Julie Olson was born and raised in Seattle in the Ballard area in an intermarried family. Her father was a secular Jew; her mother, a secular Protestant. Olson grew up very close to her father's family.

In 1980, married with two small children, Olson found it necessary to go back to work and saw an ad for an office manager at JFS. She interviewed and was hired, even though another applicant had already been offered the position. Olson has always called it *beshert*.

JFS had 12 employees, a $400,000 budget, and a smaller board than would exist in later years. Programs included Senior Services, JFLE, a single-parent program, counseling, and resettlement. Resettlement was one of the major programs because Jews from the Soviet Union were arriving in ever-increasing numbers. There was an acculturation program for the Russian immigrants, and the agency was still providing adoption and foster care services, plus a small employment services component. There was also a committee working to help find employment opportunities for the Russian refugees.

In the early 1980s, contributions by board members averaged about $36, which was all they were asked to give, double the membership of $18 per year. Olson remembers that it was a revelation when the fundraising consultant from Tacoma told Goldberg that all he had to do was ask for more and donors would give it. She also recalls that the Jewish Federation of Greater Seattle was not happy that JFS was using a fundraising consultant.

In addition to her work as the assistant to the executive, Olson was also in charge of membership and fundraising and, for 20 years, organized the annual meetings, which were always the biggest event of the year.

Olson continued to be loyal and supportive of Goldberg, helping him to pack his boxes and driving him home his last day. From that day forward, she gave her loyalty to and supported Weinberg in all his endeavors on behalf of JFS.

One of Weinberg's changes was to move Cliff Warner from the resettlement program into the newly created role of associate director, and the director of Professional Services position disappeared. Warner's primary function was to supervise the programs.

Julie Olson's experience with Weinberg has been that he is very inclusive of staff and has never micromanaged. She continued to work as Weinberg's executive assistant throughout his entire term of almost 30 years as executive director.

Olson has great respect for the members of the board who, over the years, have taken responsibility for JFS, its services, and its budget, which by 2013 was approaching nine million dollars. Board members, who are all volunteers, accept fiduciary responsibility for the organization.

From time to time, Olson has found a board member to be problematic when, coming from the corporate culture, he or she has a different idea about running a non-profit organization. Bottom-line corporate minds also sometimes have a difficult time understanding how non-profit agencies like JFS supplement their need to provide a somewhat lower wage and benefit package with more generous holiday and sick leave.

Those on the board who made the decision to offer Weinberg the executive director's position felt very comfortable that they had engaged in an appropriate due diligence process. They were familiar with his work and knew what staff and the community thought of him, and although he was young, he was clearly somebody with great potential. It was a non-controversial decision to hire Weinberg.

One of the topics the board of director discussed at the time was the establishment of a more significant endowment fund in order to be less dependent on JFGS and United Way. Unfortunately, JFS was at first blocked from attempting to establish this safeguard by the rules of the federation, but the conversation became the starting point for eventually creating such a fund. (Bequests intended for use as endowment funds had previously been called "restricted funds.") In the meantime, how the agency was to raise money to support programs remained a priority. Resettlement continued to be the major function of JFS, and JFLE was a newly revived program.

In addition to his pivotal role in changing executive officers, one of the other major accomplishments of Shapiro's term as president was completing the sale of the building on Boylston. By July 1984, it became obvious that selling the building to JFGS for $460,000 was the most reasonable option still available to JFS. The sale was approved and finalized on December 19, 1984, and the federation leased back the space to JFS at $8.50 per square foot.

Janet Lackman followed Peter Shapiro as board president in 1985. She had joined the board in 1980 and felt the work fit with her previous experience working in the Model City program and with disadvantaged populations. She says Weinberg was a breath of fresh air and a pleasure to work with and he had so much support that the transition went well. She was pleased when JFS started to increase public awareness and began doing more outreach.

Janet Lackman
(JFS photo collection.)

The Public Relations Committee was just getting started, and Lackman participated, interviewing some of the oldest members for the 92nd anniversary celebration in 1984. JFS's first Outstanding Service award was presented to Herb Rosen at the 93rd JFS Annual Meeting the following year. Then, on May 8, 1986, the recipients of the first Humanitarian of the Year award were beloved Morris Polack, his brother Jack, and their families. (See "Annual Meeting Awards" in the appendix.) The Southeast Asian resettlement effort was still in progress, and the keynote speaker, state senator Jim McDermott spoke on the issue.

Lackman remembers the 1984 event as one of the first times the annual meeting became more than just a little open house with a few members participating and how thrilled those involved were a few years later in 1987 when 200 participated in the 95th anniversary celebration at the Bellevue Red Lion. During that event, Dr. George Winston was recognized as the Volunteer of the Year (an annual award initiated in 1985; see the appendix), Sam and Althea Stroum received the Humanitarian of the Year award, and all the past board presidents were honored .

In 1985, JFS initiated a more formal solicitation program for both the board and the membership, and during 1986, the first fundraising marketing proposal was presented. In that proposal, a major donor was defined as a contributor at the $250 level or above.

1986 also saw the launching of the Big Pals program through which boys and girls between the ages of six and 16 (Little Pals), whose families want them to have an additional adult role model, are matched with Big Pals adult volunteers. Together, the Big Pals and Little Pals participate in JFS and other community activities, attend cultural and sporting events, and form strong familial relationships. Often the Little Pals are invited to participate in their Big Pals' family events and vice versa.

JFS began to work with the Foundation for Jewish Developmentally Disabled Citizens and the Northwest Association for Independent Living, eventually incorporating those organizations into JFS. (See Chapter 16, "Seattle Association for Jews with Disabilities.") The central issue was whether JFS could take on the responsibility for those programs, both fiscally and administratively. Operating a residential program was an undertaking that no one was quite sure how to fund, what issues it would raise, what liabilities were involved, or what role the agency should play in administering it. When the board decided to accept the responsibility, JFS Seattle was one of perhaps only two JFS agencies in the nation to operate a residential program for persons with mental illness, traumatic brain injury, or developmental disabilities without the benefit of public funding.

Other issues were being attended to as well, including formalizing, codifying, and implementing a personal practices code in order to assure there would be no question about professional behavior. The 1985 budget increased to more than $639,000, at the time considered a very big number. (Incredibly, as fundraising sophistication increased, JFS would raise more than that amount during a one-and-a-half-hour luncheon.)

In 1986, the JFS endowment totaled $32,000, and $40,000 was raised for the annual budget during the membership drive. There was no annual fund drive or development staff, although Julie Olson provided support to the Development Committee. As new people came on the board, they were asked to accept their role as contributors and champions of the agency. As board members began to recognize the possibilities and Weinberg started to expand the services of JFS, people began to accept a new vision of what was possible. During the following two years, 1987 and 1988, membership income increased to $56,000 and then to $60,000, a slow, steady growth accomplished with the help of a telethon.

The year1986 saw JFS's first jump into technology when membership records were computerized. It was also a time when board members started seeing themselves more as advocates. One of the board members, Dr. Julian Judelman, organized other doctors to assist low-income patients. This was just part of how those on the board saw themselves and were willing to use their connections within the community to solve some of the problems. Emerging needs in the community were being recognized, and board members began to accept their role as part of a fundraising board. In the late 1980s, there was another concentrated effort to increase community outreach and formalize fundraising. Again and again, new efforts were made to keep the work of the agency in front of its supporters and to broaden outreach to the rest of the community. The work JFS was doing was largely unknown or underappreciated. Often people assumed some other entity—federal or state government, JFGS, or some alliance—was paying. Weinberg worked hard to create more support from the federation, inviting individual leaders to the agency and encouraging people who were active in JFGS to serve on the JFS board.

JFS transformed itself. For years the agency had provided services to populations that either were invisible or nobody wanted to believe existed. It was now seen as a resource for the community that more and more people were aware of and were willing to support. Originally, many people had a narrow view that JFS should serve only the Jewish community, but Weinberg was able to bring people along with his vision of support for the broader community without alienating or splitting the board.

One facet of Weinberg that few people knew was disclosed when his wife, Alberta, threw a party for one of his milestone birthdays and had an improvisational comedy troupe participate. Unbeknownst to anybody except a few select people, Weinberg actually was in an improv comedy group in Seattle and seamlessly moved right into it with the performers. Those in attendance were soon in hysterics.

Irv Karl followed Janet Lackman into the lay leadership role at JFS. He had first become aware of JFS when a good friend invited him to an annual meeting in the mid-1970s. He was very taken by what the agency was doing, and when he was asked to join the board in 1983, he was pleased to participate.

JFS was attempting to branch out to provide additional services, and of course, money was always an issue. Karl was instrumental in getting the agency to

Irv Karl
(JFS photo collection.)

raise the bar, and donors were willing to participate at a higher level. As Weinberg and the board concentrated on telling the story—the needs and the effect that individuals could have on people's lives—the community responded. Weinberg says it became a different agency.

Much of the focus during Karl's presidency was on the continuing issue of securing funding for and convincing the community of the need for the Seattle Association for Jews with Disabilities (SAJD). He found that some people were very, very generous, but working with JFGS to support the programs was a frustration. The federation had originally encouraged JFS to take on the issue and incorporate SAJD into the agency, but then balked at providing the funding necessary to maintain the program.

Michele Hasson
(JFS photo collection.)

Michele Hasson continued the effort during her term as president from 1988 to 1991. When she was ready to volunteer some of her time, Hasson knew she wanted to work with an organization that provided direct service, and she became involved with JFS in 1984. There were fewer programs and the budget was smaller, but it was the beginning of a period of real growth for the agency.

As Hasson experienced it, what was creating the growth was "need, absolute need." The Jewish community was growing, and whether they identified themselves as Jewish or not, when people who were even peripherally part of the Jewish community needed help, they tended to come to JFS.

Ken Weinberg was absolutely forthright about the issues the community was trying to deny. Through him, JFS started to say, "In our community, there is alcoholism. In our community, there is child sexual abuse. There are all of these things in our community." Once it was said openly, people started to look for help, and if they identified as Jewish, there was no reason why they would not want that context, and with the sliding-fee scale, it was affordable.

Hasson, a professional development officer for other not-for-profit organizations, was instrumental in the development and successful launch of the SAJD Endowment Drive, the first momentous endowment drive in the more than 100-year history of the organization. Launched in July 2001, by August 2002, more than $2.1 million had been committed.

Lesley Mills was hired to take over as office manager when Julie Olson's expanding executive assistant tasks required more of her attention. Mills was born in Walnut Creek, California, and spent most of her young adult life in the Bay Area. After seven years as risk manager for a large real estate investment company, she joined her parents in Seattle intending to stay for only a year or two. She answered a blind ad for an office manager position in a social service agency at the end of 1989, was hired, and continued at JFS for 13 years.

Mills' job started evolving when Weinberg asked her to work with Olson on JFS's 1992 centennial celebration. Then, when Olson was injured in an automobile accident, Mills filled in on both the centennial project and as staff support for the endowment campaign. On September 20, 1992, the 100 Year Anniversary Gala Celebration presented a concert at Meany Hall featuring Seattle Symphony conductor Gerard Schwarz with select musicians from the symphony. More than $87,000 in proceeds was realized from this momentous and wonderfully received event.

Mills' office manager role grew to include human resources, insurance, and building management. She also provided staff support to the Personnel Committee. She loved the challenges and appreciated being given those opportunities.

Ken Weinberg and Cliff Warner faced many issues around staffing. There was also work to be done to enable JFS to move into new areas of programming for which additional funds would need to be raised. JFGS was still supporting the agency at a significant level, as was United Way. The first Development staff was hired, beginning with Stacy Lawson in 1991 and then followed by Deb Crespin in October 1992. The need was apparent: in order to expand programming, which Weinberg clearly saw as necessary, JFS had to find more money. (See Chapter 7, "Fund Development and Marketing.")

Sam Israel, one of the leading philanthropists in the Jewish community at the time, was absolutely appalled when he learned from Hasson that there were Jews who were hungry in Seattle and who needed housing. He said, "What do you want me to do?" Michele Hasson asked, "Do you want to write a check?" That was the start of major support for JFS from Sam Israel's Samis Foundation. (In 2012, the Samis Foundation contributed $28,000, which it has been doing annually, and provided another $20,000 specifically for the food bank.) No one had wanted to believe that the Jewish community was not as healthy as it should be. Now, throughout the community, there seemed suddenly to be an awakening about the needs of some of its members.

Membership in those days was just habit and meant very little. People did not think in terms of also contributing significant charitable funds to JFS. Hasson believes that JFS has become the most successful organization in the Jewish community in raising contributed income, primarily because the agency provides for the most significant needs of the community and has a compelling story to tell.

When JFS hired Lawson, she tried to work within the system by not doing major fundraising during the United Way campaign or during primacy—the period of time during which JFGS was raising its funds in the community. JFS had always been careful about timing membership mailings and was aware of the wide variety of issues that agencies had to be very careful about in order to comply with United Way and JFGS guidelines. The federation-supported agencies listened to what JFGS had to say because it was the accepted umbrella fundraising organization for the Jewish community and a very significant funder for those agencies. The system was simply the accepted, traditional way, not only in the greater Seattle area, but also in most of the country. Then JFS broke the mold. Today almost all the Jewish organizations in the Seattle area have their own fundraising methods. Neither JFGS nor United Way could have kept up with the need.

Resettling Southeast Asian refugees was a large program during Hasson's term in office. Then the program morphed into resettling Russian refugees. Staffing for resettlement was interesting for Hasson because there were then Southeast Asians on the staff for language and cultural purposes. It broadened the agency's communal vision and its role in the broader community. There was a whole world out there, and JFS was participating in it. There was not much controversy about serving these non-Jewish immigrants because the program was paid for by the US State Department. This, in addition to the 1972 resettlement of the refugees from Uganda, established the practice of JFS agreeing to resettle whoever is coming in and remaining able to keep an active program and staff ready when and if Jews from anywhere in the world needed to come. The 1989–1991 board felt that was part of what we, as Americans and Jews, do when people need to be resettled. Hasson also thinks JFS probably knows better than anybody how to do that. However, the subject of resettling non-Jews would be revisited by subsequent JFS boards.

Hasson also comments that we live in the richest country in the world and yet we have these institutionalized food banks for people to come to once a month to get two bags of food. Most of the JFS food bank clients are people who are just barely subsisting, and they would not be able make it through without those extra couple of bags of groceries at the end of the month. The dollars just do not stretch that far. JFS is here to fill in those gaps. It's the safety net.

Whenever serving non-Jews became an issue, Weinberg would usually counter with how small the number was, that people pay on a sliding-fee scale, and that the Senior Services program was still serving only Jews. He would also tell the questioner that serving the broader community allows JFS to serve Jews better, as well as being the only way a program can qualify to receive United Way money. The same was usually true of state, federal, and other governmental monies. Service providers could not discriminate.

During Hasson's presidency, there was a group of JFS supporters from a generation that felt strongly that they had an absolutely unshakable obligation to take care of each other. That sensibility encouraged people to begin to give in very real ways to the agency and do what was needed. They also asked their friends to participate.

Today donors, especially major donors, look more closely at JFS as a community resource to actively support. They are looking for outcomes, and the agency has to be far more accountable to the donors. JFS has always run a very, very clean shop, and the budgets are always transparent with everything accounted for. People trust Weinberg when he tells them what JFS is raising money for.

Cliff Warner left JFS in 1991 to pursue other goals, and Merrill Ringold came in to fill the position. Ringold was born and raised in Seattle. His father, Judge Solie Ringold, had joined the board in 1963 and served as president from 1968 to 1970. Ringold remembers how intensely involved in the agency his father was for many years.

Merrill Ringold's first direct involvement with JFS was as a participant with his wife in JFLE groups for interfaith couples, especially during the time they were considering having children.

During his 15 years with the American Red Cross, Ringold eventually assumed the position of director of Social Services. After returning to school for a master's degree, he was working at the north-end branch of the Jewish Community Center in 1991 when Ken Weinberg suggested Ringold apply for the soon-to-be-vacant assistant director position at JFS. He did and was offered the job, which he accepted. Ringold recalls that, even then, JFS was an excellent organization and had an outstanding staff. The annual budget of $1.8 million supported eight programs: JFLE, Adoption Services, Senior and Adult Services, Emergency Services, Vocational Services, Refugee Services, Counseling Services, and SAJD.

He also recalls that JFS had been working with some of the church groups in the Capitol Hill area that were supportive of the gay and lesbian community and started a Jewish PFFLAG (Parents, Families and Friends of Lesbians and Gays) group, which was almost unheard of in the United States at that time. The biggest concern was not whether it was a good or bad thing but how the Jewish community—from unaffiliated to Reform to Conservative to Orthodox to ultra-Orthodox—would look at this service. Would any of these communities feel disenfranchised by the agency?

A PFFLAG support group began meeting on a regular basis, and Ringold presented a program on the new effort at the Association of Jewish Family and Children's Agencies (AJFCA) convention. JFS Seattle was at the forefront of the awakening of the national community to the services wanted and needed by this specific group. JFS experienced quite a bit of support from the various communities, and Ringold remembers having discussions with some of the rabbis about the issues involved. The agency was saying not that they should support gay marriage or the lifestyle but that people had issues and needed to know how to deal with them openly and effectively in their families. Judgments were not being made in either direction, but the issue existed and needed to be addressed.

In 1994, budgetary considerations necessitated releasing several employees and the suspension of the office of assistant director. Ringold regretted having to leave JFS and considers Weinberg to be a fantastic individual, extremely competent, charismatic, and truly caring.

Steve Loeb, board president from 1991 to 1993, grew up knowing about JFS, most likely because his parents were active in the Jewish community. He joined the board in 1986 when the Russian resettlement program was in a lull between the refuseniks and the Perestroika group. The majority of the Southeast Asian resettlement was past, but the program was still operating.

Steve Loeb
(JFS photo collection.)

Loeb remembers being concerned about the position JFS was put in when Russian immigrants refused to take the jobs offered. This was frustrating and put the agency in a difficult position to keep its HIAS and State Department clearances. Getting the immigrants jobs as a step towards self-sufficiency was one of the primary responsibilities. If the clients turned down too many jobs, JFS could lose its certification, but understandably, it was often extremely difficult to convince a highly educated doctor or engineer that he or she would have to accept a job as a janitor or warehouse worker.

Under Loeb's leadership, the organization began a strategic planning process during which current services were examined:

what each program did, what it had been doing in the past, what it would like to do in the future, and what the emerging needs were. One outcome was that JFS backed away from non-resettlement vocational services because it was not being done as well as it could have and there were other community services and resources that provided that service.

The planning process also confirmed that JFS was an excellent provider of services that were both effective and efficient.

Weinberg worked hard building relationships with donors at all levels with JFGS, United Way, and as many members of the community as he could reach. People wanted to see JFS do well, and contributions began to come in. Weinberg thinks that people loved the agency and felt JFS belonged to their community. He fondly remembers that Morris Polack came forward and began to give significant sums. Weinberg spent as much time as he could meeting with people, not soliciting them but just getting to know them and letting them know what was going on at the agency.

In addition to providing the best possible service for every client, Weinberg's priorities were the welfare of the staff, building community relations, getting on a solid financial footing, and building the reputation of JFS. After the first year or two, he began to think more strategically. The most serious issue he saw was that the community didn't really know what JFS did—a circumstance that would be confronted over and over again during the next 30 years. He asked the board to allocate $15,000 to hire Richard Rosenwald to complete a marketing study and plan. The resulting study indicated that JFS needed to develop a profile in the Jewish community because people, in fact, did not know JFS unless they had been touched by the agency. After 90-plus years, one would have thought that JFS had a profile, but it did not. People knew only that the agency resettled refugees and helped really poor people. Even today, a great many more people are involved in JFS as clients, supporters, volunteers, and in many other ways, but the broader community, both Jewish and non-Jewish, still does not understand the depth and breadth of the agency.

While helping poor people remained an ongoing passion of Weinberg's, helping anyone in the community with any need is always part of JFS's mission. Towards the end of his tenure as executive director, a very prominent member of the community invited 20 of her best women friends to her home to hear about JFS. Even after 37 years, Weinberg was surprised by how little many of the guests really knew about the agency. Weinberg tells groups, "JFS is an agency that is here for you and belongs to you. If everything is going well in your life, it's a sliver of time that you should really relish because it won't last all that long until there's a health problem, a relationship problem, an issue with kids, partners, spouses, job, money, health, all of those. That's life, and therefore JFS is here for you." He also reminds them that they are not always going to be young and healthy. He continues that while JFS takes care of many people who are economically distressed, JFS does more: "We are here for them. But it's not just about the poor. We are here for everybody, not only the needy but everybody in need."

Weinberg once ran into a very well-to-do community member whose arm was in a sling. She told him she had made a colossal mistake when she broke her shoulder. She had no family in the area and needed help, but she did not know JFS had a homecare division. She was desperate. Later someone asked her why she had not called JFS. She had assumed that JFS was there for the poor, which she was not. Her friend told her JFS was there for everybody and many prominent people in the community have used their care.

Weinberg says JFS will always have to get the word out and work to educate the community. Many members of the community over the generations—grandparents, parents, ourselves, our children—have, at one time or another, used every service of the agency. It's the human part that brings people to JFS.

After working to secure the finances and build staff morale, Weinberg turned his attention to helping JFS become the most cutting-edge agency possible. He strived to build an agency that never fell behind the curve in what was going on in the community and was always responding. He wanted JFS always to be looking ahead so that its programs were always evolving, always changing. Careful to preserve the best during the process, he was also constantly moving forward and striving to improve. Across the country, he had seen a great deal of stagnation within agencies in the American Jewish community, and he didn't want that to happen to JFS in Seattle. Weinberg also saw the diversity in the greater community and believed it was the job of JFS to draw the biggest, most inclusive circle possible.

In order to be continuously moving forward, Weinberg felt there must be an ongoing strategic planning component to JFS and a process to insure the organization always looked ahead at what it needed to do, what the priorities in the community were, and what needed to happen for the agency to be ready to meet emerging needs. Since that time, there have been many strategic planning committees, many targeted strategic plans, and many new programs implemented in response. The new office building is a result of the 2006 Strategic Plan, and JFS continues to do strategic planning on an ongoing basis.

When Weinberg first became executive director, JFS's budget was $378,478. During his final year as executive director, the 2012 budget was approaching nine million dollars. This monumental change in funding has occurred through the cultivation and activation of a long, long list of funding sources. One of his early priorities was to diversify funding sources, and his success, although 100-percent intentional, was the result several factors, including what he sees as a fair amount of luck. Weinberg knew JFS was a good, credible agency but thought it was too insular. He knew it was possible to have a Jewish agency that was committed to the Jewish community and Jewish values and at the same time could reach out and create a much higher profile in the greater community. He still considers that a very high priority. By diversifying the population being served, JFS would become eligible for funding that could also help the Jewish community. If it did not diversify, the funds would not be available at all, and many Jews would not be served, at least not as well and not by JFS. Most government funding, and many other granting organizations will not fund projects that restrict access by race, religion, or any of several other criteria. The JFS food bank is a good example. Food Lifeline and Northwest Harvest provide food to organizations only when it will be made available to all eligible people in the community. That reasoning makes sense to those people who are primarily interested in helping Jews.

Weinberg's major reason for helping all, however, is that it's the right thing to do; it's what we are supposed to do; it's why we are placed on this earth. He says we are supposed to build a strong community, both Jewish and non-Jewish, and we have an obligation to build that community. He believes there is no such thing as a strong Jewish community in which there is not a strong general community. We cannot turn our backs on a needy community, but we do have to set some parameters so JFS does not get swallowed up and is unable to serve the Jewish community.

Weinberg felt this particularly strongly in JFS's resettlement efforts. To him it was obvious that Jews have been persecuted and forced to flee for thousands of years. As a result, no one understands the plight of refugees as well as does the Jewish community. When there are members of the Baha'i faith from Iran who are being persecuted and killed, "they are us." It is clear that JFS and the Jewish community have to help them and anyone in such situations— Pentecostal, Muslim, Christian, Buddhist, Rosicrucian, it does not matter.

The result of this point of view is an excellent resettlement program that is held in very high regard by the community, by the state, and by HIAS. JFS is one of the few agencies in the country that resettles everybody and maintains a very vital and large program. Resettlement is the second largest program at JFS, after HomeCare Associates, and has continued to enrich the agency philosophically. Weinberg thinks United Way appreciated, and still appreciates, JFS's role in the non-Jewish community.

The issue of helping all became very clear when JFGS stopped supporting services to Russian refugees while the program still needed English as a Second Language classes. Grants from the state were available to support the classes as long as JFS would serve all refugees, so the agency opened its classes for Russian Jews to Vietnamese refugees, Latinos, and other immigrant populations, and the funds came in.

Weinberg says that often the rationale given by Jewish agencies, JFS Seattle included, in taking money for serving the non-Jewish community is that it ultimately helps Jews. Although that is true, that has never been Weinberg's sole motivation. He also believes it is a social obligation. He has "never heard the term *tikkun olam* [repair the world] used as 'repair the Jewish world and let the non-Jewish world suffer.'" Nor is it what he feels or believes. "I think that we do all we can in the Jewish community and we do all we can in the general community to build a strong general community." In addition, the nature of the family has undergone a revolutionary change. A combination of these factors led many people involved with JFS to say that it had to redefine who this agency is, what it's about, who it serves, and where it is headed.

Weinberg thinks that by doing so, and doing so relatively early, JFS captured support from communities that felt closed out of other Jewish institutions including synagogue life, but not closed out of JFS. These communities included the LGBTQ community, families with members of differing abilities, mixed religious or racial families, and sometimes divorced individuals, single-parent families, and those who were economically disadvantaged. JFS began to say to those communities that, for us, "You are part of the Jewish community. You are part of the JFS family, and we are here for you." Weinberg thinks, "There is some sense of reciprocity when you say we're here for you. The folks you're saying that to will say, 'Well, we're here for you too.'"

As a result of this extended inclusion, the support given to the agency began to broaden. JFS received more financial support, events became much more successful, and far more people became engaged and wanted to come onto the board of directors. Weinberg adds that during this time many well-known, prominent families played key roles in the expansion of the agency.

⟨∞⟩

In 1990, board members started thinking about the way JFS's fundraising efforts were focused almost entirely on maintaining and increasing membership, as had been the situation from the earliest days of the organization. They asked a critical question. "What does a membership in JFS mean?" Members received the newsletter and were invited to the annual meetings and to other agency events. Two or three of those board members were professional fund-development officers for other not-for-profit organizations, and one had led her organization to change its fundraising so donors would no longer be members. The organization began to concentrate on building and cultivating a donor base. Weinberg and the board were soon convinced to move in that direction. In March 1992, JFS dropped the membership drive and initiated its first annual fund drive. This was also the first JFS/SAJD combined fundraising effort. By December, $6,000 more had been raised than during the previous year's membership drive.

Weinberg began to think in different terms and understood how much more there was to JFS than the community knew. "Just tell the story, and people will help," was the message he heard, very much the same message given by the consultant Goldberg had hired. Weinberg was a quick study and open to new ideas. Those board members with professional experience in the non-profit development world brought their expertise to JFS and encouraged Weinberg and the agency to think bigger. Weinberg credits these board members for his growth as a professional. He began to mature as a director of a professional agency and thought more about marketing, his role as a fundraiser, and JFS's capacity to raise money. He found himself thinking in new, expansive ways. Neither he nor the board universally embraced the new direction, and some of the ideas were even scary in the way they would require Weinberg to "put himself out there" asking directly for significantly larger contributions. Weinberg says the new ideas revolutionized JFS. When Lauren Jassny joined the JFS board in 1986, she says, "I was shocked that the needs were as great as they were," which, of course, made it that much more compelling to be part of the agency. The other impression she remembers was "just how much work there was to do with very little: a small staff, little money, and a lot of good work was getting done."

There was never enough money to do what needed to be done, but at the same time there was also a perception in the community

 that JFS was completely funded by the Jewish Federation of Greater Seattle. When Lauren Jassny became president in 1993, one of her challenges was getting out the message that , while JFS needed and appreciated JFGS funding, that organization did not fund JFS anywhere near totally. Her speech at the annual meeting in 1994 helped clarify the situation when Jassny told the assembled crowd that of every dollar contributed to JFGS only a nickel or so came to JFS. This information was a surprise to many people who had previously assumed that a much larger portion of their JFGS contributions would be directed to support for JFS.

Lauren Jassny
(JFS photo collection.)

Weinberg recalls, when he first came to the agency in 1975, no JFS agency across the country was doing fundraising because each Jewish federation had rules for their beneficiary agencies limiting their fundraising endeavors, especially the larger gifts. In 1975, the agencies were not allowed to do fundraising, but Irv Goldberg was doing it, most likely because he knew JFS was going to need more money than the JFGS would be able to provide. When Weinberg became the executive director, JFS was receiving 34 percent of its annual budget from the federation and approximately 20 percent from United Way. That still left half of the budget to be raised. JFS did not have the other half, so Weinberg and the board began to be more assertive in their fundraising. At the AJFCA (Association of Jewish Family & Children's Agencies) national conference that first year, Weinberg met Anita Friedman, the executive director of

JFS San Francisco, who told him she thought that various Jewish federations would not be able to provide for the needs of the rapidly expanding agencies. When she told him he needed to create a very strong development department and begin to raise his own money, he believed her and took that very seriously.

Weinberg had to help the board feel comfortable spending a few thousand dollars that would not be spent on client services to enable Dick Rosenwald to produce a marketing plan for JFS and graphic artist Irwin Caplan to create JFS's brochures. It was difficult, but Weinberg was successful in convincing them that it would be worth it.

An aggressive approach to marketing was implemented. The goal was once again to become better known in the community. Rosenwald helped the board understand that marketing JFS correctly would greatly increase the likelihood of getting both more clients and more donors.

Ads were placed in the *Jewish Transcript* that said, "JFS provides X service. If you need our help call …" These ads talked about the agency helping the poor and the needy, feeding people, supporting the elderly, and helping those with disabilities and the Russian immigrants.

At the end of the 1980s, Weinberg had hired his first development person, Stacy Lawson, to focus primarily on the endowment drive. The other Jewish organizations have since begun their own fundraising programs. In a very carefully planned way, JFS went from the best unknown agency in Seattle to the best and most well-known Jewish agency in Seattle. In 2012, the *Jewish Transcript's* list of "the best of" named JFS the best agency for the fifth year in a row. JFS was also ranked the best for counseling, best place to volunteer, and the best in fundraising.

As a percentage of JFS's total budget, JFGS contributions have fallen dramatically over the years. By 2012, those contributions were approximately 4 percent of the total nearly nine-million-dollar JFS budget. United Way provided around 2 percent, and the agency raised the rest in a variety of ways.

Because of the success of JFS Seattle, Weinberg was being invited to travel to other JFS agencies around the country training on fundraising and on how to build and strengthen boards of directors. People wanted to know what it was doing and how. He told them JFS Seattle developed a very strong board with a great deal of power behind it. In their professions and the community as a whole, JFS board members have high standing, respect, esteem, and credibility and the ability to support the organization financially. JFS assembled a board that could raise money and a Development Department that publicized the agency and raised significant funds using a variety of professional fundraising strategies.

Chapter 16

Seattle Association for Jews with Disabilities

In the early 1980s, Seattle-area Jewish families from two organizations came together to talk about their struggles to provide care for their disabled adult children. The two organizations were the Foundation for Jewish Developmentally Disabled Citizens, which focused on adults with developmental disabilities, and the Northwest Association for Independent Living (NAIL), which helped family members suffering from mental illness.

Herb and Isabel Stusser joined the discussions amongst the NAIL families because of their concern for the lives of other families struggling to care for children with mental illness. They had a son who suffered from mental illness, but he had moved to California where they found the support he needed. In 1986, NAIL opened a residence called Shalom House in the Wallingford district of Seattle in a seven-bedroom house donated by the Stussers. (Shalom means peace, completeness, prosperity, and welfare and can be used idiomatically to mean both hello and goodbye .)

The Stussers found funding for a year or two of operation, but they knew that the home needed other strong support beyond what they and their small group were able to provide. NAIL hired Joel Neier as the director of Shalom House and nutritionist Alice Chang was selected as the live-in staff person. Even though Chang had

Shalom House (JFS photo collection.)

no previous experience with people with cognitive disabilities, she was a compassionate person, and the NAIL families were confident she would be able to oversee the residents care while keeping them properly fed.

Opening Shalom House had a huge impact on the families whose children were able to become residents. Care of an adult with a mental illness or other cognitive disability often meant the family was never able to take a break of any kind. There were no days off, no evenings out, and no vacations. Aging parents confronted the question of what would happen to their children when the parents were no longer able to care for them. Having their child living in Shalom House freed the families to lead fuller lives and gave comfort that their children would be cared for in the future.

For the residents, all members of the founding families, Shalom House provided social connections. Generally, persons with mental illnesses and other cognitive disabilities have difficulty making and keeping friends since they are often suspicious of other people or they exhibit behaviors that turn people away. Shalom House was a safe environment with regular activities bringing members of the community together in a very accepting environment. Although there was no social program at the beginning, the group connected with the Community Psychiatric Clinic in the Wallingford area, and most of the residents participated in the day programs there. The clinic provided a highly structured and supportive environment to help participants learn ordinary daily tasks, like preparing and serving lunch. They provided work-readiness training and a chance for participants to develop self-esteem, self-worth, confidence, and a sense of purpose while building foundations to achieve other goals, such as employment and education. Planning menus, tracking finances, and other life skills could be practiced in this safe environment, and social activities were offered.

At the time, mental illness was not discussed openly and was not widely understood. There were some group-home facilities in the Seattle area, and a few social service agencies focused on mental health, but in most cases, the patient lived at home where the family handled all the details of their care, often an overwhelming task.

One of the first residents who came to live at Shalom House. was a very bright woman who was married and had a daughter. Then she had a psychotic break and was diagnosed with schizophrenia. She became a very difficult mother, and her daughter went through many traumatic episodes.

At Shalom House she almost seemed to run the home. Her goal seemed to be to keep everyone happy and peaceful. She gave instructions on how the other residents should dress, how they should behave, and how fast they should get to the table when it was time to eat. She was something of a benign despot yet was truly admired and respected by her fellow residents. She ran the house like a family and wanted everyone to play nicely together.

She lived out her life—well in to her eighties—at Shalom House as the *grande dame* of the home. She was well liked and accepted by both staff and residents. One day when she was getting into the van, she fell, and was injured. Her health issues cascaded downward from there, and she lived for only about another six months.

Behaviors for a paranoid schizophrenic may include becoming very fearful and delusional. Patients may see people who mean no harm as very dangerous. Sometimes patients become suspicious and cynical accusing family members of plotting against them or trying to steal things. Sufferers can sometimes become verbally abusive.

People who suffer from schizophrenia can also have delusions of grandeur. When the Seattle Association for the Jewish Disabled took one client to social events in the community, she sometimes refused to come back when she expected a limousine instead of the van that was provided. She would refuse to get into the van and wait for the limousine. The staff would wait her out.

People dealing with these issues may also experience active hallucinations and see things that do not exist in consensual reality. They will converse with a person they imagine standing nearby when no such person exists. They can also be oblivious to their personal appearance and dress poorly or strangely and at times might fail to bathe.

Once Shalom House was up and running, NAIL faced the reality of supporting it. Herb Stusser recalls, "By the time we started raising money, the house was already open, and we had staff and bills to pay and supplies to be purchased." He remembers that Rabbi Jim Mirel was the first person to write a check. Later, prior to the merger with Jewish Family Service, the Jewish Federation of Greater Seattle provided some funding.

Isabel Stusser talked about those early years when they didn't have the umbrella of JFS. They held yard sales at Shalom House and then organized a city-wide rummage sale called Treasure Faire Extraordinaire. Families collected and sorted clothes, house wares, furniture, art pieces, and other items. These were all stored in a warehouse in Pioneer Square donated by Harvey and Mel Poll. Marian Aronson agreed to chair Treasure Faire and worked on it almost full time. The general public was invited, and the group advertised in the *Jewish Transcript* and in the local newspapers. Hundreds attended the event, which was held at the Seattle Center Flag Pavilion for three consecutive days.

Joanie Diskin Saran describes Treasure Faire as a yearlong project. Saran was new to the community, and participating in the process enabled her to meet and connect with many people. She says, when she became aware of JFS, she was in awe there was such an institution.

Dennis Warshal, a remarkable arts and events planner, remembers when Saran called to ask for his help. He asked her what the budget was. She responded, "Zero!" Warshal signed on anyway, and they organized the event by renting chain-link fencing to create separate enclosures with signage, such as sports, kitchen, furniture, jewelry, clothing, toys, etc.

Dennis Warshal
(JFS photo collection.)

The funds gained from Treasure Faire and other events, together with what the residents paid for their care, room, and board, helped to support NAIL. Once the home was operating smoothly, NAIL began to invite board members, donors and other guests for Shabbat dinner to introduce the program. (Shalom House

Treasure Faire (JFS photo collection.)

and later Tikvah House—*tikvah* means hope—were both kosher residences.) The NAIL families knew there were other mentally ill people in the Jewish community who might benefit from some contact with other patients, and Shalom House held several events, including the Shabbat dinners and holiday celebrations, where other people with mental illness were invited to participate.

The original hope was that some of the residents would stabilize to the point where they would not need residential care and could move on to more independent living. Though most of the residents were not severely disabled, there was a great reluctance to move.

NAIL organizers were not surprised to find that many families who have mentally ill adult children cannot handle the stress and cannot (or do not want) to handle the financial responsibilities. More than a few of those families drop them at some point creating a situation where these adults live in marginal conditions or in state-funded situations, and many end up on the street.

During this same time period, families of adult children with developmental disabilities formed an organization called the Foundation for Jewish Developmentally Disabled Citizens (FJDDC). Tony Wartnik became one of the prime movers. His wife, Norma, struggled with cancer, and Tony needed help for their developmentally disabled son, Howie.[1] (Wartnik was pleased to provide information about the creation of FJDDC and of the progress his son, Howie has made over the years.) Several professionals were among the original directors of the foundation, including psychiatrist Dr. Ed Friedman, Larry Halpern, a pharmacology professor at the University of Washington, and Irv Goldberg, executive director of JFS. Goldberg participated in the beginning to provide advice and direction to help the families accomplish what they wanted to do.

However, the two groups had separate but nearly identical discussions with Goldberg. While he seemed to think the projects were worthy ideas, hoped they would be successful, and would have loved to provide more help, he did not see that significant involvement or financial support fit into the plans of JFS. When Ken

Weinberg became executive director in 1984, he saw FJDDC and Nail as perfect fits for the agency. Weinberg provided real direction and concrete assistance. He served as an advisor to the organizations and provided office space and the resources of the agency. Most important, Weinberg and JFS could provide professional logistical support, otherwise supplied by the volunteer board and a few paid staff, without the groups being programs of the agency.

In 1987, Ken Weinberg, working on behalf of NAIL, hired Joel Neier to be the director of that program. Working half-time at first, Neier's job was to hire and supervise the house staff, set in place policies, and participate in the fundraising efforts, and funding was always an issue. Neier knew they were creating something very special, both for the Northwest and nationally. Everyone involved believed it was the Jewish community's obligation to provide services to members with disabilities.

In the meantime, in 1986, a JFGS committee recommended that the FJDDC and NAIL merge their two operations. With JFS's advice and support, the two did merge in 1987 as the Seattle Association for the Jewish Disabled (SAJD) and became a legal subsidiary of Jewish Family Service. Joel Neier became director of the combined program. (The organization later changed its name to the Seattle Association for Jews with Disabilities.) For a few years, Treasure Faire continued to be a major source of funds ($75,000 in 1990) to help support the combined program.

Neier hired Bill Drummond to staff a weekend Havorim (Friends) Club for SAJD. The goal was to provide a social recreational environment for persons with disabilities and to offer fun and educational activities. Drummond says, "The individuals who participated loved, loved, loved the club." They would go to Northwest Trek or the Tulip Festival and various other attractions, and everyone always had a really good time. The parents were pleased that their often adult-aged children were getting out into the community with people who became their friends.

Bill Drummond slowly was drawn into JFS. He enjoyed working with people with disabilities, and when an opportunity presented itself to work a shift or two at Shalom House, he was pleased to accept.

Jeanie and Bill Rosen donated a house in the Fremont neighborhood to be used as a group home for adults with developmental disabilities, and Tikvah House opened in 1990. Funds raised in memory of Norma Wartnik paid the initial operating expenses, and JFGS provided funding, although its support for the group homes proved uneven from year to year.

Residents of the two homes were expected to participate in a day program at the Community Psychiatric Clinic or elsewhere. If they didn't participate, they needed to find another program so they had some structure in their life during the day and were not just hanging out in the house. When they returned home around three o'clock, the expectation was that residents would assist in preparing dinner, take care of their rooms, and help with the rest of the house. There were regular house meetings and social activities, and on Friday evening, they celebrated Shabbat with a special Shabbat dinner, including challah, the braided bread baked specially for Shabbat, and beautiful flowers purchased from Ness Florists. Everyone participated.

Drummond was the Shalom House manager when Tikvah House opened as a home for people with developmental disabilities. He remembers that Jeannie Rosen not only bought the house but also donated her Volvo station wagon, which they used extensively until the car no longer functioned adequately. Tikvah House even had an electric lift, which enabled one of the more disabled residents to get upstairs to the bedrooms.

At both Tikvah House and Shalom House, individual plans were developed for each resident. A plan might include educational, social, and vocational goals for the year. The resident participated with his or her family and the staff in the development of the plan.

The goal for a resident of either house might be to enable him or her to be more independent than was generally allowed in their individual management plan. Some of the residents were very verbal and communicated quite well, but could be easily distracted. When

Tikvah House (JFS photo collection.)

on their own, they might be so busy observing what was going on around them or talking to other people they encountered that they forgot to pay attention to their current task. Residents might want to walk by themselves to the store six blocks away on a busy street to purchase their own snacks without a staff person. To assist the resident in achieving this goal, staff would engage parents or other family members to participate in creating a plan, which broke the process down into many different objectives. One step was intended to teach the client how to cross streets safely. The job for the staff was to help him or her to focus—*we are at a corner; what do you need to do?* A second objective was learning to conduct a cash transaction—*how much money do you want to bring? What are you going to buy?*

Each plan was progressive. For one, first, the person needed to bathe and dress without assistance. Next, learn to do laundry. For some residents, the plan might include going out to get a haircut independently or cooking a meal. The program was outcome based so the goals and the progress of each individual were examined and tracked.

There was a great deal of structure at both Shalom and Tikvah House. Times for meals, chores, house meetings, relaxing, and social interaction were all set and posted, and expectations were clear and reaffirmed often.

Neier and Drummond started talking about helping other people in the community, Jewish and non-Jewish, who needed assistance but were not living at Shalom or Tikvah House. People might be living independently and struggling, or they were with their families, and the families experienced challenges and stress. The two started a tenant support program, the goal of which was to offer to individuals who have a disability, such as a traumatic brain injury, mental illness, and/or a developmental disability, an assessment identifying their needs. Then a plan of support could be created for them.

Neier created a case management program within SAJD that was available to members of the broader community as well as to the residents of the two homes. Staff helped people with issues around managing their money, complying with their medication therapies (med compliant), socialization skills or daily living skills, and maintaining their independent living if they were in an apartment by themselves. The program quickly grew to serve as many as 125 people.

Then, in 1991, Neier was promoted to associate director of JFS, a position he held for the next 10 years, and Bill Drummond became the director of SAJD.

Often two clients would share an apartment and one or both of their families assumed primary responsibility for overseeing their care, although that oversight responsibility could be difficult. Some clients had very poor house-cleaning skills, many had unhealthy eating habits, and were extremely overweight or otherwise unhealthy. Clients often had no concept of what was healthy or what and how much to eat. Drummond and other case managers worked with their clients continuously, sometimes with very limited success, to teach them better eating habits, housekeeping, and other skills and to help those skills become part of their everyday practices.

Many clients need ongoing support. Learning respect for others' personal-space boundaries, as well as better communication skills are often issues. Other clients need help learning to recognize when they are asking or saying things that would be deemed inappropriate by others. Again, success has to be measured in tiny increments.

The SAJD program for non-residents grew large enough that it became necessary to hire a supervisor and case managers. Many people who later started their own counseling practices worked for SAJD as they started out. One new aspect of the program was a daytime vocational service begun at Shalom House with an instructor helping residents learn to do jobs like folding, stuffing, and preparing mailings. An average of six people, working with one instructor and an assistant, learned how to accomplish a variety of tasks, or worked on art projects.

JFS never denied anyone service because he or she was not Jewish. Whoever came to the agency and asked for help was accepted and provided the services and support needed. The tenant support program could provide support at a lower cost than the service provided to residents of the homes, and the agency received reimbursement for that support.

The most challenging individuals were those contacted through an outreach effort to the growing population of homeless, mentally ill Jews in the late 1990s. In some cases, people had gone so long without receiving any services that their mental illness had deteriorated to the point where it was difficult to get them back on medications. It proved to be a challenge reaching out to people and finding those who would be accepting of JFS services. In addition, they would be non-paying clients because they had no money. One of the primary goals in working with those clients was to help them receive the disability payments they were entitled to because many weren't receiving any support at all. With a separate organization serving as the receiver, a plan was set in place for when and how each person would receive his or her money. The plan made sure the individual didn't receive the entire monthly allotment at once, in which case all would likely be spent with nothing left for the rest of the month. The goals were to help the clients receive benefits and get set with a provider, like Seattle Mental Health or Community Psychiatric Clinic, to receive meds and other services. The generosity of people who gave to JFS and SAJD enabled the staff to be professionally trained and these clients to receive services that were far above any they would ever get in any public service agency.

Before Drummond left JFS in 1999, a tragedy occurred at Shalom House. There was a space downstairs where a staff person would live, usually staying in that position for a year or so while going to school. The person was required to be there overnight from when the shift ended for the staff, around eight at night, in case of an emergency. In the morning, the night attendant would make sure all the residents had their medications and got out of the house. One very nice young man that held that position was clean cut, and articulate. His résumé showed he was a veteran and was attending the University of Washington. He worked for Shalom House for about nine months, and the residents loved him. He went out of his way to spend time with them. One day, a resident had on a leather jacket and told Drummond that the live-in staff person had given it to her. Drummond thought that was a little too generous and planned to tell the young man they didn't encourage that kind of thing. The next day another resident had something from him that also was quite expensive. Drummond became concerned because a person giving away expensive personal belongings to people he or she cares about can be a sign of contemplating suicide. Drummond wasn't overly suspicious about this young man because he was so lucid, calm, and articulate and gave no indication that anything was going on with him that should cause concern. Then Drummond got a call from staff that the young man hadn't shown up for work. Arriving at the house, Drummond knocked on the door, and no one answered, but he heard music. He opened the door and found the young man had taken his own life.

Drummond met with the young man's family and learned that he had assumed his brother's identity and that the résumé was his brother's. His family knew where he was, but they didn't know what he was doing.

Staff found a way to use the incident as a positive way of talking to the residents about this tragic experience. They helped the residents express their feelings, with some being more open than others in wanting to talk about it. The discussion centered on how important it is to reach out and seek help when you are feeling very sad and hopeless.

༄

One of the agreements between JFS and SAJD was that SAJD would bring a financing package to merge into the overall JFS budget. By 1991, SAJD decided that it was necessary to raise an endowment of at least $2.5 million to support that agreement. Donna Benaroya stepped forward to co-chair the fundraising effort with Herb Stusser. They hired a development advisor, and under his direction, they compiled a list of community families that might help, many of whom had already supported prior campaigns. A small group of 10 or so volunteers spread out to raise the funds. Stusser recalls that the first time it was very hard to say, "We'd like you to give $100,000." For an intensive year and a half, the group persisted with excellent results. Those funds became the corpus that continues to fund a portion of SAJD services. Combined with assistance from JFGS, support from the general JFS budget, and a small amount in fees for service, JFS provides the staffing for the program and other services needed by SAJD clientele.

The SAJD Supporting Foundation is an endowment managed by community volunteers with the appropriate expertise. They meet twice a year to hear how the program is progressing and to determine how much money can be allocated from the endowment to SAJD operations. The allocation averages about $150,000 a year, and the corpus had grown to $3.2 million in 2012. The SAJD Supporting Foundation provides specifically for support of those who are developmentally disabled, mentally ill, or suffering from traumatic brain injury.

Although SAJD is officially a program of JFS, the endowment and the Endowment board remain separate for the foreseeable future.

Don Armstrong came to JFS as director of SAJD in 1998 when Bill Drummond left. Armstrong was born and raised in downstate Illinois near Rock Island knowing he was Jewish but never went to a synagogue until he was in college. He served in the US Air Force in Vietnam and then attended Chaminade University in Hawaii before settling in Seattle. Trained as a teacher, but finding no positions available, he started working at the Helena Maria Children's Home in Port Townsend. This began a long career in the disabilities field and eventually led to his becoming the executive director of the Alpha Home on Queen Anne Hill.

Armstrong was able to meet many of the people in the field of disability services, including SAJD program director Joel Neier. When SAJD was first considering the purchase of Tikvah House, Neier asked Armstrong to do a walk-through to help evaluate its use as a group home. A few years later, Neier called again looking for recommendations for a director for SAJD. Bill Drummond had recently left the position, and might Armstrong be interested? Armstrong replied, "This is really a very difficult time for me to leave Alpha because …" Then Neier asked a question Armstrong has greatly appreciated ever since: "OK, Don, what would be a good time to leave?" "Yeah," said Armstrong. "There will never be a good time."

Armstrong became director of Disability Services in 1998. In 2002, he took on the additional responsibility of directing Senior Services (which later was renamed Aging & Adult Programs). His responsibilities changed when he was appointed director of Professional Services, assisting JFS chief operating officer Claudia Berman with oversight of the program departments. Then in 2009, his title was changed to director of Homecare and Community Based Services with day-to-day responsibility for HomeCare Associates while also supervising the directors of the SAJD and Aging & Adult Programs.

At the time, Tikvah House was home to seven residents who had intellectual disabilities, and Shalom House had six residents living with mental illness or brain injury. There was an apartment in the basement of Tikvah House called the transitional unit/living unit. The idea was that as people gained more independence and skills they could move into the apartment where they lived on their own with staff to provide some level of support. When they became comfortable cooking their own meals, doing their own laundry, and managing other basic life skills, JFS helped them get apartments in the community, and they transitioned out. There was also a small case-management program for clients who were not residents and needed a lower level of support. Staff paid or helped clients pay their bills, helped them shop and manage money, and supervised their medications.

By 2001, practitioners had developed new approaches for treating the mentally ill and developmentally disabled in the community. This new thinking (best practices) redirected the SAJD program towards a more comprehensive and modern series of services. When Don Armstrong became director, he brought in some of the new thinking. He saw that most of the residents were capable of living more independently with some support, and he understood that dependency grows. Many of the clients could do better on their own at less cost, and lowering costs made it possible to serve more clients.

In 2002, after months of research and discussion, the board agreed the program should work to consolidate and, over time, close the group homes, starting with Tikvah House. Those residents who were able moved into a more independent, supported living program where they occupied their own apartments in the community with appropriate support from SAJD.

This was a difficult decision involving complicated changes to a clearly successful program that had become a big part of people's lives, not just staff and residents but also the families. All involved understood the parents' concerns, but the financial picture made it clear that there just would not be enough money to continue to support clients using the existing residential model. Residents who would be unable to live independently and those whose parents would not allow their children into the new program were moved into Shalom House.

When clients moved from the residential facilities into supportive housing, JFS was able to help them secure Section 8 certificates (federal rent vouchers for low-income persons), a necessary element for these clients who could maintain only low-paying jobs at best. Initially, in both Tikvah and Shalom Houses, everyone was expected to have at least part-time employment, and there would be no staffing during the day. However, in each home, there were one or two clients who were not sufficiently independent to succeed in a normal work environment.

One of the benefits of this change to supportive independent living was that JFS could provide services to a great many more clients because they would be living in apartment settings and receiving only the case-management services they each required instead of 24-hour residential support. The program today consists of more than 50 clients, both Jewish and non-Jewish, living in apartments leased by the individuals or their families with JFS providing various services to each client. Many clients have been referred by the Washington State Department of Social and Health Services. Some require very little attention, perhaps a little help with their bookkeeping or shopping. Others require more assistance in terms of cooking, dressing, medications, and other personal care. Often family members provide some of the needed assistance and clients pay SAJD depending on the menu of services they need from the program. In 2012/13, SAJD served 212 clients in all service categories. A total of 138 different individuals participated in Shaarei Tikvah events.

The staff of the SAJD changed a great deal because their jobs changed. Instead of operating a residential facility, staff was now needed to visit individual apartments to provide services tailored to each client. Clients are permitted to choose the neighborhood in which they want to live, but because many neighborhoods are more expensive, most of them live close to the Central Area of Seattle where landlords are more likely to accept Section 8 housing vouchers and public transportation is good.

Howie Wartnik was one of the original residents of Tikvah House. His father remembered that Howie was almost 27 when he moved from his parents' home. An adult chronologically, although not mentally or intellectually, he grew significantly at Tikvah House because he was in a setting where he had more independence and had to learn how to live with other people that he had not met before. Howie's needs were more profound than many of the other residents, requiring 24-hour supervision. When JFS closed Tikvah House and the most capable residents moved into the independent living program, Howie moved into Shalom House with a few other residents of Tikvah House.

Howie worked for a company for several years putting price tags and labels on books and other merchandise. One of the things that triggered his first mental-health episode occurred when the store started automating. Like almost all companies, it went to bar codes and eventually had to eliminate his job. His employers loved him, but they just didn't have enough work to keep him employed. He was the last one in that department to be let go. Still, Howie needed to be occupied and took work seriously, so when his job fell apart, he got depressed, which his father believes most likely triggered a schizophrenic episode. When Shalom House was closed, Howie and a few of his housemates moved into another group home in North King County.

SAJD is a considerably different program from the one started in the late 1980s, but the original donors and supporters feel very good about SAJD serving a much larger population and providing services that are greatly needed in the community.

Thirty years after they started work on the SAJD in 1981, the Stussers reduced the intensity of their involvement. Herb and Isabel say that, while their son will most likely never be a direct participant in the independent living program, they know there is a need for a place in the community with a supporting system for adults suffering from mental illness.

⌀

One young man came to Tikvah House from out of state. Apparently, at the time, there were no Jewish residential programs available for people with developmental disabilities in the region where he lived. He is fairly functional and independent and did very well at Tikvah House. This young man has fragile X syndrome, which has many similarities to autism but people with fragile X syndrome interact better with other people. They are often high functioning intellectually but may have a high level of anxiety, are not as averse to touch as people with autism, and have a black-and-white view of the world and a strong sense of right and wrong.

Several situations with this client illustrate these tendencies. At one time, he had a job in a grocery store as a box boy. When some money disappeared and a question was raised as to whether he had taken it, he denied it vehemently, was extremely indignant, and never went back to that job. Stealing money would have been anathema to him.

With the help of SAJD staff, he was able to secure part-time jobs in the community, but it took him a while to find a place where he was able to stay because of his an unpredictable and sometimes inappropriate sense of humor. Once when he had a job doing cleanup work on a construction site, he thought it would be funny to turn the hose on and spray some of the workers—but there were live wires in the area. Fortunately, nothing terrible happened.

He moved from Tikvah House into supportive living with JFS continuing to assist him. One day he was looking out his apartment window and saw someone climbing in the window of the house across the alley. He did what was typical behavior for him. He called 911. When the police responded, they found it was a break-in, and they apprehended the person. The young observer received a certificate signed by the chief of police, which was perfectly wonderful for him.

This young man is a great guy who loves to participate in sports, is very active and very social. When the decision was made to close Tikvah House, his parents were extremely concerned about his welfare and his ability to survive well in such an independent situation. However, a year later, Armstrong received a wonderful note from his parents about how happy he was in his apartment and how much they appreciated the growth he had experienced. They were pleased to give permission for their son's story to be shared.

In order to assure family members of options if the transition to independent living did not work, JFS committed to reopening the facility if it was needed, kept Tikvah House, and rented the rooms to students for a few years. The house was not sold until 2013.

JFS and SAJD developed a plan to work intensively with anyone who had moved into supportive living who had difficulty adjusting to the change, but everyone made the adjustment successfully. Through the interview and assessment process, the staff can usually tell if clients are going to make it or not.

Shalom House was home for persons with persistent mental illness or brain injury. Sometimes a clients would come to Seattle from out of the area because in many regions it was very difficult to find a Jewish residential environment for people living with these issues.

Sometimes when a person has suffered a head injury or a severe mental illness, their emotions and mental acuity can be affected in various, sometimes negative ways. They may have been highly intelligent and even brilliant before suffering from such a problem then, while remaining very bright and articulate may have lost their short-term memory or developed other deficits. Clients might be able to remember people and things, but might not be able to remember where they had put their wallet or coat 10 seconds before. Others can become extremely emotionally unstable, moving from laughter to anxiety or anger in an instant.

Armstrong believes that, unfortunately, as the older adult population "exponentially grows" over the next 20 years, funding for any kind of program is going to become extremely difficult for people with special needs. Older adults will absorb every last discretionary dollar that the government at any level has, and society is going to have to balance the needs of older adults against those of people with special needs and mental illness.

Of the 13 residents in the two houses, seven moved into apartments as part of the independent living program. The other six, who would benefit the most from continued supervision, remained at Shalom House. Shalom House was open a few more years before it was also closed in October 2008. The remaining four residents went into other adult family homes and continue to receive case management services from SAJD.

Rachael Byer Kwong is the current director of SAJD. Her ancestors came from Europe, Russia, Germany, and Great Britain. She moved from Vancouver, Washington, to Seattle to attend the University of Washington, where she earned her bachelor's degree in social work.

Kwong started her career at the Veterans Administration Hospital in the Outpatient Clinic and then worked as a "float" covering all of the hospital. When she later had the opportunity to work at the Caroline Kline Galland Home, she especially loved working with the people who grew up in Seattle and whose families had been there for 70 or 80 years or more and hearing their stories.

In 2001, she accepted a position working with Don Armstrong as a geriatric care manager in the Senior Services program at JFS where she did geriatric case management and supervised JFS Friendly Visitors, connecting volunteers one-on-one with clients. Kwong wrote the first training manual for that community of volunteers. She returned to the U W to get her master's in social work while continuing to work as an on-call staffer for both the SAJD and JFS Emergency Services.

Kwong's master's program focused on geriatric mental health. She had realized when working with elderly Holocaust survivors who were dealing with post-traumatic stress disorder, anxiety, depression, grief, and loss just how important the mental health component of geriatric work is. She returned to JFS full time in December of 2004 as the Independent Living Program manager.

In 2008, Kwong became the director of what is now known as the SAJD Supported Living Program. In this position, she supervises a staff of 10, including case managers and in-home caregivers. They focus on helping adults with cognitive disabilities to live as independently as possible. The primary populations served are people with persistent mental illness, like schizophrenia or bi-polar disorder, or who live with developmental disabilities and traumatic brain injuries. The youngest client is 19, and the oldest is 83. In addition, Kwong carries a small caseload of her own, mostly with the older clients since her background is in geriatrics.

One client had a job but needed to be able to take the city bus independently to get to work. However, he needed special training to be able to learn the routes and know which bus to take. Bus training is a free service through METRO. One person goes with the client and, while riding the bus, shows the client the things he or she needs to be aware of. "See the number on the front of the bus? That's number 41. That's your bus … See this street here? You know that you are getting off at the stop after that street." The person points things out to help a client know where the bus stop is, how to walk from their front door to the bus stop, how to wait at the bus stop and pay when getting on. After the METRO representative walks the client through that process, he or she gets an opportunity to practice as much as needed and, at the end, go on alone, but the representative watches from afar to make sure the person can make it through all the steps and do it safely. This continues for as long as is needed. It may be that someone is just not able to learn how to do it alone, in which case the client would be able to take the Access bus instead.

A very special client was Doris Fedrid, a woman in her 80s who was a deaf and blind Holocaust survivor. She needed people to do tactile signing into her hand in order to communicate, and some SAJD staff knew sign language, so Doris became a client of the SAJD program. (A video of Doris posted on YouTube became a highly popular posting.)

In Hitler's Final Solution, anyone with a disability was marked for extermination. Doris was born deaf and was able to survive in slave labor camps in Poland only because, luckily, she stayed with her mother. When the Nazis did daily roll calls, her mother would nudge her so she knew to stick her hand up. (Because she was in a slave labor camp and not an extermination camp, she received a onetime payout after resettlement, but not monthly reparations.)

Doris moved to New York in the 1950s where she met her husband, another survivor, and they had three children. She was in her late forties when she was given eye drops to which she had a reaction and became blind. Afterward, she held a deep fear of the medical system, and when a doctor prescribed medication, she was hesitant to take it, always fearful of serious bodily harm.

She had been living independently on Social Security in her own subsidized apartment with low rent before she came to JFS because of her sensory deficits and because, as she reached her late seventies, she needed help cooking and cleaning. SAJD staff visited her a few times a week, cooked meals, and plated them so she only needed to heat one up.

She was able to survive through special accommodations and by learning how to get around her sensory deficits. The Deaf-Blind Service Center in Seattle worked with her for many years, offering advocacy and Support Service Providers who know tactile sign language and help with grocery shopping and other tasks. She had an incredible ability to worm her way into people's hearts and had friends who used to be staff and then later maintained long-term friendships with her. This core group of friends visited her on a weekly basis providing help and support.

Doris moved to an adult family home in Shoreline because, as she became older and encountered more problems, she was no longer safe on her own. Living in Shoreline was challenging because her friends and most of the deaf-blind community were in the Capitol Hill or Rainier Valley area, which is also where the deaf-blind service has their offices. Being in Shoreline and not able to drive was isolating for her, but at least she was safe and had 24-hour care. Medicaid paid only a fraction of what it cost to provide the level of care she needed, and the homes that accept Medicaid are usually outside the core city because operating expenses are so high.

One friend lived nearby and checked in a couple of times a week. Doris also had someone to help her daily needs, and JFS staff visited her once a week, took her for walks, and helped her read her mail. Kwong provided some case management and, when Doris's savings were gone, helped her receive DSHS benefits. Medicaid covered the cost of her adult family home.

Once on Medicaid, patients contribute what they are able towards the cost, and Medicaid pays the rest. For Doris that arrangement left very little money for essentials like her text telephone phone line. JFS helped out with unusual expenses, like a dental bill and occasional gift cards for clothing or extra items. (Doris passed away several months before this manuscript was completed.)

When Kwong first came into the SAJD as program manager, 22 clients received case management and in-home support. Thirty-three clients received service in 2005, and 76 clients during the 2012 fiscal year. Seventeen of these clients have been with the program since 1999.

Much of the service provided by SAJD is about sustaining people, helping them maintain their quality of life, and making sure someone doesn't decompensate (lose the ability to maintain normal or appropriate psychological defenses).

The program now also provides short-term intervention services, which weren't provided historically. More clients are experiencing crisis and need help accessing benefits and resources from the state or federal government or obtaining information about resources, such as where to go for utility assistance. Staff may work with those clients for six months (or for as long as two years) until they are receiving their benefits and are able to maintain stability and be more independent.

Some of the clients Kwong interviews are referred by family members who call asking for help. A few are military veterans who suffer from post-traumatic stress disorder causing anxiety and major depression, a combination that is fairly debilitating. For some of these clients it is difficult just to get out of bed in the morning, focus, or stay organized. Filling out a simple application can be overwhelming. Often these clients need to get to the Department of Veterans Affairs Hospital from various parts of the community to receive medical and mental health services, but just the idea of the effort required in getting to the hospital overwhelms them. When these clients don't get the care, there can be no improvement. They are caught in a catch-22 cycle.

Sometimes a client's living space becomes cluttered and dirty, and the notion of cleaning and organizing is almost beyond comprehension. JFS staff will help organize the space so it will be more livable. Some clients are eligible for a larger unit but they need help filling out the paperwork for the King County Housing Authority. A case manager can help coordinate the paperwork and help clients learn how to use the bus so they can get to the VA. Of course, using the bus creates much anxiety, and some clients need help with that as well. Even getting a reduced-fare disability pass requires more paperwork.

The only medical insurance some of the veterans have is through the VA, even though they may be eligible through Social Security Disability for Medicare. (Three years after a person is awarded Social Security, he or she can receive Medicare.)

These clients often will be eligible for food stamps, low-income utility assistance, and a discount for their telephones. All these things help lower their cost of living and relieve some of the pressure, as well as help them get the medical and mental health treatment they need to get better.

Some clients successfully work for years, until their worsening disabilities prevent them from getting and keeping a job. They may then receive help from the Washington State Division of Vocational Rehabilitation but must also be able to follow up with appointments.

Sometimes this follow up is not possible because their anxiety and depression are so debilitating. When these clients then need mental health treatment, the Medicare and insurance paperwork can be just too challenging. Many veterans keep getting stuck in these bad cycles, which JFS works to help them break.

When young people have a developmental disability, they can continue in the public school system until they "age out" at 21, at which point they are considered to have entered adulthood. Often clients, going through this transition need something more to build a routine—a reason to get out of bed and a way to contribute to society.

JFS can provide some in-home skills training to help these clients become more independent, and even move out of the family home into more independent supported living situations. The client may have never had to learn how to cook, other than perhaps the basics, and may not have ever had to clean other than the bedroom. They are helped to acquire the types of skills that will be needed to be able to live alone or with a roommate. SAJD staff will provide skills training, helping the client learn how to do laundry, shop, cook, clean, and perform other necessary activities. They will also help clients connect with the vocational system and serve as an advocate to make sure that other agencies are following through. Hopefully, staff will be able to help find at least volunteer roles where the clients can feel active and needed and not just lie around the house playing video games all day.

Kwong is working to help SAJD continue to grow and get the word out that their services are here and available, especially in the mental health community. She is not aware of another non-profit that provides the same type of intense case management and licensed in-home care for people with mental illness that SAJD provides. People with mental illness usually become part of a regional support network, so they are going to large agencies, such as Seattle Mental Health and Community Psychiatric Clinic, which receive most of their funding from the state Medicaid system. Still, those agencies are underfunded, and the staffs are overworked. A case manager within that system has anywhere from 80 to perhaps 120 clients on a caseload. SAJD case managers have 15 to 20 clients, so the difference in the level of individualized support a client receives is immense: SAJD is able to do much more for the individual.

Most in-home care agencies are there for the elderly and are used to doing more of the physical care, like helping someone bathe and dress. Because staff in some of the larger agencies frequently aren't well trained to work with someone with schizophrenia, it is difficult for them to know how best to serve someone who is having hallucinations or how to encourage someone who has paranoia that, yes, he or she needs to take the medication because it will decrease the paranoia. SAJD staff have that specialized training, making their services unique within the mental health community in the Seattle area.

SAJD charges an hourly rate for private-pay clients. More than 60 percent are Jewish as the program is most well-known within the Jewish community. There is also a contract with the Division of Vocational Rehabilitation, and perhaps 90 percent of those clients are not Jewish. The majority (about 70 percent) of the people served receive some kind of financial aid—clients simply can't afford the help otherwise and would be homeless or in a mental institution without the service. SAJD has a wide variety of financial assistance available with 35 to 40 percent of its annual budget spent on that one line item.

Providing services for children with disabilities is a definite need, but SAJD is not yet able to serve this population. The demand is not high, and hiring a children's specialist is extremely costly. In addition, children have completely different care needs from adults. Until recently, children with disabilities were served in the school systems and by larger programs focused on children, unless their parents were able to afford individual support. However, in the last few years, a new program called the Friendship Circle was created by Chabad. The Friendship Circle extends a helping hand to families who have children with special needs and involves them in a full range of social experiences.

Kwong receives five to 10 calls a year inquiring about services for children, which she refers to specialized agencies. For adult services, Kwong gets two to four calls a month. The greatest need seems to be in the transition process of moving clients from children's services to adult programs.

1. In 1876, the Association of Medical Officers of American Institutions for Idiotic and Feebleminded Persons convened its first meeting at the Elwyn Training School in Elwyn, Pennsylvania. The group later became the American Association on Mental Deficiency and then the American Association on Mental Retardation. In June 2006, members changed the name to the American Association on Intellectual and Developmental Disabilities. Terms like "mental retardation" and "developmental disabilities" were considered to be medical terms and were tied to IQ and age. Modern research shows that, even though a person might perform as a two-year-old in one area, he or she could have abilities in other areas at higher age-levels.

Chapter 17

Project DVORA

"I know I'm going to be OK. I know the children will be able to be strong adults and the cycle will be broken."
—DVORA client

The understanding of domestic violence—intimate partner violence—evolved out of both political discussions and action during the Women's Movement of the 1970s, which led to the legislation and policies that exist today. Consciousness-raising groups formed in living rooms where women began to see that their individual personal experiences were political, not isolated, not intrinsic to their psychology, and not due to something wrong with them. Many suffering silently in abusive relationships learned they were not alone, and women started saving each other by opening their basements to shelter other women. Victims of domestic violence showed up at women's centers not knowing where to go, asking only for a bit of safety for the night. Women ran crisis lines out of their homes offering support for victims. It was all very grassroots.

Slowly the field became more organized, and women started working nationally and at the state level to make domestic violence a crime, to make it illegal to strike your partner. They believed that perpetrators should be subject to arrest and prosecution. At the same time, many women of color discussed how their experience of male violence was different from the experience of white, middle-class women. While shelter programs and crisis lines became standard interventions, they did not meet the needs of all women, so in response, women in communities of color created culturally specific services. During the 1990s, the Jewish community followed suit. Domestic violence services in King County reflect this history. The program throughout the county is now comprised of domestic violence crisis lines and shelter programs, community programs, and culturally specific programs that serve the Latina, immigrant, Asian, African-American, Jewish, deaf, and LGBTQ communities. The collaboration and coordination of these agencies is seen in Domestic Violence Directors of King County's vision statement in the 2009 "Toward Safe and Equitable Relationships: Strategic Directions for King County's Domestic Violence Advocacy Programs":

> We envision strong, connected communities that support and sustain equitable, respectful, loving relationships and families; where community members are informed about domestic violence, are working towards solutions, and where survivors and their families receive support and can easily access quality services.

Project DVORA had its origins when Michele Hasson (JFS board president 1988-1991) gave a talk at the Women's Division of the Jewish Federation of Greater Seattle about the abuse she had experienced from her father. Her presentation triggered a process at JFS that began, as was typical, with a community assessment. The Women's Division stepped up to help fund the assessment, which confirmed there was the same prevalence of domestic violence in the Jewish community as in the rest of American society.

With more support from the Women's Division Endowment Fund (WEF) and from JFGS, JFS started a culturally specific Jewish domestic violence program in 1999. As the project began, executive director Ken Weinberg realized for the first time that his own mother was a victim of domestic violence, as was his grandmother. Weinberg commented on how strange it is that long-ignored practices are exposed, and then you realize, "Oh my God. That's how I lived my life." In the 1960s, he would never have spoken of this.

Michelle Lifton was selected to create the program and began by researching Jewish women through history. She discovered D'vorah (Deborah) in the Tenach (Old Testament) in the Book of Judges. D'vorah was a judge, unusual in a patriarchal culture. She heard cases for the community and was regarded as a prophet. The Israelites even went to her for advice on military strategy, and she commanded them in their defeat of the Canaanites. Her wisdom and leadership helped unite the 12 Tribes of Israel. The JFS program was named Project DVORA, linking the acronym for Domestic Violence Outreach, Response, and Advocacy to the Israelite heroine from the Tenach.

Lifton was born in North Hollywood, California. Her grandparents had originally emigrated from Russia, Belarus, Poland, and the Austro-Hungarian region. After graduating from the University of California, Santa Cruz, she worked in social services for nine years and then returned to school for a master's of science in women's studies. While completing her degree, she moved to Seattle in 1994.

Lifton worked in Seattle's High Point neighborhood and then in domestic violence and battered women's programs and advocacy. She always had a strong Jewish identity but had never heard of JFS until a colleague suggested she would be a good candidate for the position being offered to create and direct a new domestic violence program at the agency.

Rather than subsuming domestic violence services within the clinical counseling program of Jewish Family Service, Project DVORA was intentionally created as a separate program that adopted an advocacy-based counseling model, the state standard for domestic violence programs. "Advocacy" means the client is involved with an advocate in individual or group sessions with a primary focus of safety planning, empowerment, and education of the client through reinforcement of the client's autonomy and self-determination. Advocacy also means speaking and acting for change or justice with, or on behalf of, another person or cause. Advocacy is survivor-centered and uses non-victim blaming methods.

Contrary to common beliefs, domestic violence is not a mental health issue. Rather, it is a learned pattern of behavior on the part of the person perpetrating the violence; there is nothing about the person experiencing the abuse or the dynamics of the relationship that creates a domestic violent situation. This pattern of behavior is learned within our culture; domestic violence is a microcosm of larger systemic violence. Therefore, mental health counseling was not an appropriate service model.

Lifton started by examining what culturally specific services would be. She wrote to all the rabbis in Seattle and met with each one gathering information about how the new program could support the community. She also researched culturally specific services. She looked forward to starting the program, something about which she felt passionate. At the same time, she felt she was coming home to her Jewish identity. She discovered, or rediscovered, the wonderful story of D'vorah who, through her wisdom, unified the community against a common threat and helped unite the Israelites. Lifton felt that JFS, likewise, was trying to unify the community against a common problem in creating a Jewish domestic violence program.

Studies had already shown that the prevalence of domestic violence in the Jewish community is equal to any other community. Lifton focused on creating a program that would provide culturally specific services in which the response could come from the Jewish community. "We needed to work within the community to figure out solutions," she says. "The question presented was 'what is intrinsic to Judaism that guides how we move forward within a relationship?' There's so much."

Teshuvah, the steps of repentance, are identical to the steps of state-certified treatment programs for perpetrators of domestic violence. According to *Gates of Repentance*, a standard work on Jewish ethics by Rabbeinu Yonah of Gerona, if someone commits a sin, a forbidden act, he can be forgiven for that sin if he performs *teshuvah*. That is one example of Jewish culture that can inform how to move forward in resolving domestic violence.

"When I am working in an Orthodox community, the solution is not going to look the same as when I am in the Reform community," Lifton says, "And that's appropriate." One illustration would be that in the Reform communities she has been invited to give sermons from the *b'mah* (pulpit), which would not be appropriate in an Orthodox community where they might prefer to host a speaker at a luncheon for the *Rebbetzin* (the wife of the rabbi).

Lifton remembers starting out on the wrong foot when she advertised an event for "survivors." That became a learning opportunity when she realized that, even though "survivor" is the term used in the general domestic violence world, that is not the best word to use in the Jewish community where the word has a specific connotation about the Holocaust. In the general community, the word had originally been "victim." However, "victim" is legal terminology, as in victim of a crime, and domestic violence often does not manifest itself in criminal acts of physical assault. "Survivor" may have been an improvement for the general public, but it did not translate well into the Jewish culture.

Another problem was that just walking into the room for this event would identify a person as "one of those"—a woman living in an abusive relationship.* Instead of creating a support group for survivors of domestic violence, JFS created a support group for Jewish women with controlling partners.

The secular approach to group sessions also contradicted the Jewish experience. Conventionally, one person speaks at a time, which is probably not going to happen in a Jewish group where

---

* JFS serves men who experience domestic violence, but this is extremely uncommon.

people often speak over one another. Lifton enjoyed rethinking her assumptions as she developed four tiers of service. She wanted to be holistic, following the idea that natural cultural, social, mental, and physical systems should be viewed as a whole. Their functioning cannot be fully understood solely in terms of the component parts.

The vision of Project DVORA is to create the conditions in the Jewish community to support loving, safe, and respectful relationships, and to build the capacity in the community to respond to domestic abuse.

Project DVORA's strategy is to amplify and affirm Jewish values intrinsic to loving, safe, and respectful relationships and to employ practices that offer support, healing, and accountability around domestic violence. In doing so, four types or tiers of services are offered.

Tier 1 provides confidential, Jewish culturally specific services to survivors of domestic violence. Tier 2 provides outreach, education, and consultation to the Jewish community to assist in promoting healthy relationships and to facilitate Jewish communal responses to abuse. In Tier 3, Project DVORA partners with other organizations to provide advocacy to individual program participants and systems advocacy. In Tier 4, Project DVORA collaborates with the different programs of Jewish Family Service to address domestic violence within all levels of the agency.

During the first year of the program, Project DVORA reached 236 people through 11 workshops, two of which were for Jewish youth. Organizations that sponsored some of those workshops included Brandeis University Women's Committee, Community High School of Jewish Studies, Hadassah, the Jewish Community Center, Jewish Family Service, the National Council of Jewish Women, and Temple Beth Am.

As DVORA grew from one to two and a half employees, it was continuously refined with more depth and clarity. Some of the clients being served are in extremely dangerous situations, while others may be in less lethal circumstances, but all need support, advocacy, and other assistance to achieve whatever goals they have for their own futures and for their children.

People often call JFS for advice or support for "my mom" or "my daughter," and Lifton acknowledges the program provides service not just to people experiencing abuse from a partner but also to family and friends of all parties.

Every year JFS conducts a survey with its clients and then uses that information to make adjustments. Some of the responses to questions asked in the survey have been:

Without [DVORA], I might still be caught in the emotional confusion and physical danger of an abusive relationship.

If it had not been for the confidentiality of the support program and the genuine staff (well-trained), I would have never been able to leave my abuser ... From my four wonderful children and myself, thank you! Shalom.

It took me over five years from knowing about DVORA to actually begin taking action!

Kids Club was an incredible program for my family ... having an avenue through which to discuss safety issues with my daughter. [Kids Club was created by Project DVORA in 2005 to help children who have witnessed domestic abuse. The class is run for 11 weeks twice a year, once for children ages five through eight and once for children 9-12.]

I feel like my boys have experienced excellent role models and much of the domestic violence they witnessed was "reversed" with the Kids Club.

Several DVORA clients were willing to share their stories in videos specifically produced for and presented during JFS fundraising luncheons. For one survivor, violence began during the honeymoon and, over the course of her nine-year marriage, became more intense and more frequent. After their children were born, the violence got even worse. Her husband once shoved her down three flights of stairs. Another time, he started kicking her while she was holding her baby in her arms. He then started hitting her with a suitcase, which hit the baby's head. That was the final warning sign, telling her she needed to leave. She contacted JFS, which became the first place where she felt completely believed and supported. She expressed concern for her children, knowing that what her two boys had witnessed put them at higher risk for repeating that behavior.

The boys were able to find the support and counseling they needed in the Kids Club. One day after they had been participating in the club for several months, one of her sons came home from school and told his mother about an incident that had occurred during the day. He had witnessed one boy picking on another and reported it because he said he had learned that mean and hurtful behavior is not okay. That was the moment she recognized that there is hope. Her children can be transformed, and the cycle of violence can be broken.

Many of the inquiries are one-time calls, and sometimes a person will not call again for two or three years. Project DVORA is actively engaged with 40 to 50 people at any one time, serving 115 families in 2012. While this is a small percent of the families served by JFS during the year, some of these situations represented serious threats of physical harm with serious long-term consequences.

The best interventions for partners who use power and control in their intimate relationships are state-certified programs for perpetrators of domestic violence, and the JFS counseling service refers people who are abusing to these treatment programs. People have to be both willing and ready to get help. It is also neither safe nor appropriate for JFS to serve both parties in an abusive relationship, so if an abused person steps forward, JFS refers the controlling partner to another agency.

Another survivor who shared her story says that abuse started on day one. Her husband would curse at her and put her down, and when the children were born it seemed to progress. He always wanted arguments to be held in front of the children. Her daughter says she was always trying not to get on his bad side. Once, when she ran into him accidently on a ski slope, he hit her over the head with a ski pole and told her he wished she had never been born.

The last straw was when their son was not listening the way her husband expected him to. He got out of the car and started to choke the boy, telling him he had better listen. Later their son went into his room and beat himself unmercifully, screaming that he wanted to bleed and die.

This woman wasn't sure how to get help until she saw a notice posted in the restroom in the synagogue that included the warning signs of abuse and provided Project DVORA's phone number. When she called, it meant a great deal to her to find someone in the Jewish community who would understand what she was going through and could help and guide her. Her first concern was to find a way to keep the children safe, which she was able to do with the advice and assistance of JFS. Later JFS provided funding for an attorney, and staff accompanied her when she went to court. Her daughter recognizes how difficult it was for her mother to leave her father and knows she was doing what was best for the children. Her son attended Kids Club where he was able to learn about anger management and how to walk away from difficult or escalating situations. This survivor received counseling and acknowledges Michelle Lifton as the most supportive, loving, wonderful woman in her life. She says, "I know I'm going to be okay. I know the children will be able to be strong adults and the cycle will be broken."

Lifton also tries to work within the communities around accountability. She will call a rabbi and say there is a person in your community who is engaging in these behaviors, and she will ask the rabbi to help intervene ... to make sure that the approach will be culturally appropriate. She explains:

> The rabbis are willing and are aware that the problem is in all communities, and of course no Jewish community would say that it is acceptable to abuse your partner. All can agree that the behavior is not okay, and there are no Jewish values that support such behavior.

> When we think of someone who engages in those actions, we might be tempted to think of this evil, terrible person—abuser. It's important to try hard not to use the labels. When you call someone an abuser—say, to the rabbi, there is someone in the community who is hurting [his] partner, and this is who it is—you might get the response that "he's not an abuser; he's this guy I've known his whole life, was at his wedding, at his bar mitzvah, we daven [pray] together. He does this and this for the community ... he has some control issues.

> Using terms like "abuser" is dehumanizing, and it's never okay to dehumanize a person, even when he engages in unacceptable behaviors.

Before Lifton started working to raise the awareness of JFS counseling staff around domestic violence issues, couples were seen together, but as Lifton explained, there can be no accurate assessment of a power/control dynamic if the two people are interviewed at the same time in the same room. If a person is being abused, he or she will not feel safe enough to talk about what is really happening in the home.

In addition, the counselor might not recognize the power and control issue. She might see the partner of a client appearing perfectly reasonable during a one-hour initial interview saying his partner does a particular thing and he's just reacting. The counselor might then not believe the abuse is real or could even collude with the abusing person, blame his partner, and then work to change her behavior that is triggering his reaction.

To guard against that situation, JFS acquired an assessment tool for the counselors, provided by the NW Network of LGBT Survivors, and created the appropriate policies and protocols. If that dynamic of power and control is part of the relationship, couples counseling is not indicated. The partners are then seen separately and by different agencies.

JFS has a policy and a process in which the therapists assess for domestic violence. If domestic violence is found within the relationship, the person abusing is referred to a Washington State certified domestic-violence intervention program. The person being controlled/abused is offered services by JFS Counseling Services or Project DVORA.

One of the first clients served by Project DVORA was referred by her rabbi. The woman was being physically and emotionally abused and decided to leave her partner. She started to work with a therapist at JFS, and Lifton worked with her on how to stay safe, creating a safety plan and providing the financial resources she needed to get out of the house.

Lifton is aware that people often think they know what is best for someone else but is firm that seeking help has to be the individual's choice. The person being abused is already in a relationship with someone who is making all the decisions and all the choices. Project DVORA never makes decisions for its clients.

Another DVORA client is a single mom of four boys and was married for 13 years. She also allowed her story to be featured in a luncheon video. Violence took over during her third pregnancy when her husband choked her to the point where she started to black out and slammed her up against a wall. When she finally told him she was getting a divorce, he became violent and started breaking dishes, scaring the children. She phoned the police, but didn't know he had filed a restraining order against her a few weeks earlier, so she was the one escorted out of the house by the law enforcement officers. Her youngest child was not yet three, and during the nine days the woman was out of the house, he thought his mommy was lost and cried every night for her. When DVORA was recommended and the children began to participate in Kids Club, they felt comfortable and safe. They learned about how someone you love and who loves you can sometimes hurt you. They are also learning how to cope with those kinds of situations when someone is hurting them, and even her son who is autistic has been learning how to express himself, which has helped him tremendously.

When this survivor was welcomed into the JFS family, she learned about other resources too. A panic button was installed in her house in case her husband showed up, and she was pleased and grateful that she was able to use the food bank. JFS staff went to court with her, and while her husband was on the stand lying about her, their presence kept her calm so she was able to get up and tell her story. She was awarded a 30-year order of protection because of the extreme violence. She knows she can count on JFS for anything, and she and her children are on the road to healing and recovery and know they have the possibility for a great future.

There is a perception in the community that people go to DVORA to get help in leaving their partner. In reality, more than half the people Project DVORA works with have already left. They come to DVORA because the ex-partner continues the pattern of power and control, even after the person leaves the relationship. The abuse continues through shared parenting, child support or lack of providing child support, and legal battles. Sometimes the ex-partner continues to threaten physical violence. Program participants who have left their relationships come to Project DVORA to receive support around safety planning, legal advocacy, and co-parenting with an abusive parent. The program will help someone leave only if that is the individual's choice. DVORA staff never talk anybody into leaving but always work with clients to help figure out what is safe and what their choices are. DVORA staff then support those choices. The goal is always to support client autonomy, to help them think about if and how their partner might be keeping them from being autonomous, and to help people develop access to autonomy.

Contemporary American thinking seems to be don't tolerate the abuse, leave, do not preserve your marriage if there is abuse. On the other hand, sometimes outsiders will believe what is occurring isn't really abuse—he's such a great guy—and his partner is contributing to the problem through her own behaviors.

Leaving is the most dangerous time. Most domestic violence murders and serious assaults occur when somebody leaves. When an abused partner leaves, the abuser loses control over that person. A counselor never tells someone to leave because that encouragement can get the client killed or seriously injured. Partners who use abuse often never stop trying to "get her back," and until an assault takes place, there are grey legal areas of threatening conduct.

Children complicate the ability of partners to leave abusers. The abusive partner has the same parental rights as the leaving parent and, absent an enforceable court order, can often reach the children without restriction. Partners who use abuse may manipulate maternal impulses for their own ends.

Lifton says sometimes a person is stuck with her ex remaining in her life, even after she leaves. For example, a mother cannot leave the state with her children to keep them safe, and the abusing parent often legally has the right to visitation/joint custody. Thus, the mother does not have a choice except to allow her children to have visitation/ custodial time with the abusing parent. (There are exceptions to this with different legal outcomes for different situations.)

Abusive partners may say negative things to the children, use the children against their mothers, tell them their mother broke up the home, or undermine her parenting.

Early on, Project DVORA received feedback from the community that prevention was important and, as a result, has made this a focus, as explained earlier in Tier 2. An example of how JFS used a federal grant to formalize and expand on the work it was doing in the community is seen in a six-week program that Project DVORA created during the first year in partnership with a synagogue. The sessions presented information that focused on healthy relationships to sixth grade classes. Working with 48 to 50 students, a female and a male facilitator model a healthy relationship. Designed specifically to be appropriate for this age group, the program focuses on teaching the students about relationships, power, and boundaries asking questions like, "What does a healthy relationship look like?" and "What are boundaries, and how do you negotiate and set boundaries?" The program helps young people think about what they want in a relationship and how they hold to that. They examine what gender stereotypes are and discuss appropriate ways to treat a partner. Sometimes the group separates by gender, and sometimes they work together.

This and other programs have been held within the Jewish day schools as well as in other Jewish supplemental schools. Some are one- or two-day workshops; others are presented over several weeks. Project DVORA has also facilitated a Mother-Daughter workshop talking and thinking about ways to promote and maintain healthy relationships of all kinds.

Lifton explains to parents how DVORA talks to their children when in the schools, explaining the tools they use and helping parents think about how they talk to their children about healthy relationships.

Lifton's dream would be to work systematically within one specific community to look at how we, as a community, talk, act, and think about healthy relationships and what we do as a community when those conversations are not happening. She would like to help develop policies around domestic violence; perhaps they could map out the Torah portions for the entire year and look at each portion as an opportunity to get to that teaching and as a way to talk to parents about healthy parenting, positive parenting, and child abuse. She would like to do it on every single level within one community.

More broadly, Lifton asks, "How do we, as a community, hold someone accountable when we see that someone is not treating another person well?" and "How do we do that without shaming?

Chapter 18

Alternatives to Addiction

"Jewish, in recovery, Chemical Dependency Counselor, this job's for you."

—Online want ad

Not the least of the reasons that clients sought help from the Ladies' Hebrew Benevolent Society in its various iterations over the years to today's JFS were problems with addiction. In the early years, this was usually addiction to alcohol, but by the 1960s, drugs entered the picture to further degrade people's lives. As early as June 1969, the issue was featured in the *JFCS News* saying that people in the community tend to ignore the subject until it hits them directly. The article went on to say that drug use is a symptom of underlying problems from loneliness and alienation to physical or emotional illness.

In February 1998, JFS director of Counseling Services Robin Moss contacted Steve Morris, who was teaching at Seattle University in the Addiction Studies program. Moss wanted Morris's thoughts about creating a chemical dependency program at JFS. Long-time JFS supporter Kenny Alhadeff, inspired by his own journey to recovery, was very interested in the idea and was willing to fund start-up expenses. A study had been done which confirmed that of the 30,000 Jews in the Seattle metropolitan area, at least 10 percent would be affected by the disease of addiction: addiction to drugs or alcohol or both.

Moss described an employee assistance model. Chemical dependency treatment would not be offered, but a counselor who was a specialist would do assessments, refer people to treatment as needed, and then be available to offer individual therapy after treatment. The counselor would also work with individuals for whom treatment was not indicated and with their families. For those coming out of treatment, continuing individual and family therapy would also be offered. In addition, the program director would work in the community providing information and support to families, schools, and other organizations, as well as offering community presentations and education. Starting a regular Alcoholics Anonymous meeting in the JFS building was also a goal.

Laura Kramer, the director of the JFS Alternatives to Addiction (ATA) program, explains the difference between addiction and habituation. Habituated people, when faced with a consequence as serious as losing their children, are able to stop. Addicted persons faced with loss of housing, prison time, and loss of family cannot stop.

The treatment is different. People can become habituated to something, which helps them cope. When people are fully addicted, they will continue using unabated until they die. They will find a way to continue purging or starving or using or drinking or eating or not sleeping so they can be on the computer, no matter what. And if they are enabled enough, they will do it until they die.

If a person who has habituated behavior has a heart attack, he or she may be able to change. Not everything is addiction, but from a Western perspective, human beings are habituated to avoid discomfort.

Kramer believes that, no matter how unsafe we feel, the more loving we can be towards ourselves, the more safe we will be. No matter what is going on in the external world, if a person can say,

"I can notice that in this present moment I'm OK and I get to feel OK," then there is a tremendous amount of healing that is possible.

She recognizes that for Jews it is important to feel safe, even if they are not. Jews hold on to their terror in a way that isolates them from each other. In the world where many others want you dead, it's not personal, and actually everything in this world is outside the individual's control, other than what's beneath his or her skin everything.

In 2001, chemical dependency expert Liza Restifo was hired to establish and coordinate the addiction recovery program with support from the Alhadeff Foundation, Jewish Federation of Greater Seattle, and the Employees Community Fund of Boeing Puget Sound. She held trainings at Yeshiva High School, at some of the other schools, and at a few of the synagogues. She did collaborative work with rabbis in the community and helped the clients they referred. Unfortunately, with experience as a social worker and mental health therapist, Restifo was encouraged to fill the hours not occupied by the chemical dependency program with regular counseling clients. This meant the time commitment to support the chemical dependency program was greatly diluted. The program did not go forward to the extent it might have, and Restifo moved away after a year.

Steve Morris applied for the position and became the coordinator in 2002. Morris had first joined JFS Counseling Services in 1999 under an internship as part of his master's in social work at Seattle University. He continued Restifo's community outreach and training, saw chemical dependency clients, and served as a mental health counselor.

Morris commented that coordinating the addiction recovery program was not the best fit for him or for JFS. He discovered he preferred counseling work and admits he did not make sufficient effort to seek out the speaking engagements his ATA responsibilities required. The program slipped even more with no more than 20 percent of Morris's time devoted to chemical-dependency clients. Community presentations became even less frequent.

Then, when Morris became the director of Counseling Services, the addiction recovery program was left without a dedicated specialist, although Morris continued to see clients who were dealing with addictions.

In 2007, interest in chemical dependency reemerged, spurred on by Kenny Alhadeff, whose family has been involved with and supportive of JFS for five generations. His great-grandmother, Rosa Gottstein had even bequeathed $500 to the agency in the 1920s. In addition, his family had always been very sensitive to social justice. This converged with the strategic-planning effort that was in process. Weinberg and Alhadeff, as well as others involved, wanted a full-time specialist dedicated exclusively to making Alternatives to Addiction grow and fulfill its mission, to kick it off with a lot of energy and a big event, and to restart Alcoholics Anonymous meetings on the premises.

Eve Ruff was the perfect person to make things come together. She had been working at Swedish Hospital in Ballard with a treatment program that included an inpatient detoxification unit and a pregnant women's treatment program. (After she left to start the JFS program, Swedish kept trying to lure her back with wonderful offers until Steve Morris successfully applied for that position at Swedish.)

Ruff had responded to a Craigslist ad that said, "Jewish, in recovery, Chemical Dependency Counselor, this job's for you." She said to herself that this job had her name on it—*beshert*. After first interviewing with Don Armstrong and Steve Morris, Ruff interviewed with Kenny Alhadeff, chief operating officer Claudia Berman, and a few other members of the clinical staff. Ruff was quickly hired as director of the Alternatives to Addiction program in 2008.

From the beginning of their working relationship, Kenny Alhadeff stayed involved and was consistently a passionate champion for the program. He told Ruff that if she needed something special or wanted him to come and speak, just let him know. (Alhadeff remains interested in, supportive of, and closely involved in the JFS ATA program.)

The bulk of Ruff's work was not clinical. Rather, she concentrated on outreach and on building relationships and liaisons throughout the community. The clinical work that she did was primarily conducting assessments, making recommendations for people to go to treatment, and then being available to help people acclimate to the post-treatment community. She worked to streamline the process for people who did go into treatment and arranged kosher meals for those who would need them during their treatment stay. She also worked to educate other treatment providers about what it meant to be Jewish and deal with the 12 steps.

Steve Morris related that Ruff played a critical clinical role with families. Often the hardest part is getting people to agree to go into treatment, and she was instrumental in not just getting the door open for them but also getting them motivated to go through that door. Then she worked to find low-cost resources and other needed services.

Eve Ruff was raised in the Bronx in a row house with her grandparents. Her father was a hippy inventor who created many packaging elements for consumer products, including the aluminum foil box, the first lid for to-go coffee, and the container that made it possible to buy ice cream in the grocery store.

Ruff's family on her mother's side was originally from the Carpathian Mountains in Poland and Russia. A family story tells of having two sets of papers for the approach of either the Polish or Russian Army. Her paternal grandparents were from Poland.

According to Ruff, "the rebellious one" became her identity. After she attended Union College (the union of all denominations) in upstate New York, she had a long career as a research bio-medical librarian working for the National Library of Medicine in Bethesda, Maryland. Then she told her boyfriend she wanted to climb Mount Rainier, which they did. She came, climbed, and never left or looked back. She worked for Fred Hutchinson Cancer

Research Center in Seattle as the director of Libraries and Internet Services, married, and had two children.

She says she enjoys starting things, being at the foundational place, and then when stasis sets in and requires a different skill set to manage the ongoing program, she moves on.

For a variety of reasons, Ruff, who had never been much of drinker, developed a problem with alcohol. Her father told her she couldn't be an alcoholic because she was Jewish. Sadly, it took her five years and the loss of her marriage before she could really come to terms with it. She went into treatment and was fortunate to have a counselor who was Jewish. His influence became pivotal in her life. After treatment, she went back to school to become a chemical dependency counselor. She wanted to work with people suffering from this disease because there was so much stigma attached to it. She felt the challenge to help ameliorate the impact.

One day when she was at work at Fred Hutchinson in Seattle, a colleague said JFS was looking for a Jewish chemical dependency counselor. Ruff knew of JFS because her grandparents were involved in New York, and then, when her mom died of cancer, Ruff contacted JFS to get a recommendation for a therapist. She had worked in the field for several years before becoming the new director of the Alternatives to Addiction program at JFS.

The approach she took focused on four pieces. The first three were community outreach and engagement, providing clinical services, and working with the recovery community. The fourth piece of the program was to engage the chemical dependency treatment community to help educate other professionals about needs specific to the Jewish population. It was up to Ruff to decide how best to approach this four-pronged plan. Throughout the process, she kept in mind Morris's admonition to keep track of each and every contact she made because everyone was going to want the numbers.

The program's advisory committee, which included people from the treatment community, a social worker, and other community volunteers, developed strategic objectives, including a vision and mission statement.

One goal was to get an Alcoholics Anonymous meeting in the building with the expectation that it would be just one of the 1,700 regular AA meetings in the Seattle area every week, although none was located in any Jewish space. The intent was not to have a meeting for Jews but to have a visible indication to the Jewish community that the JFS understands addiction exists, AA is a tool, and the agency is opening its doors. (There is a Jewish AA meeting called L'chaim, which is held only once a year at Temple Bet Aleph on Yom Kippur.) If we think about *teshuva* (repentance, the way of atoning for sin) and the whole concept about turning a problem or issue over to the higher power, Jewish tradition fits really well with AA.

For a time, there was also a JFS-sponsored *chavurah* (a small group of families, couples, or individuals who share a common interest and gather together on a regular basis around that interest) that met at Temple B'nai Torah on a monthly basis. This was a gathering of Jewish men and women in recovery—AA, Narcotics Anonymous, Alanon (for family members), and smoking—who wanted to study together using the Torah or other resources, such as the writings of rabbis on recovery.

Ruff began by getting involved with treatment-oriented programs and accepted a position on the board of Recovery Centers of King County. She affiliated with Lakeside Milam and several other residential treatment programs to which she referred JFS clients. Ruff found scholarships to help with the expense of treatment, and she visited a Jewish recovery center in Los Angeles called Beit T'Shuvah. Her goal for the first year was to reach into the community as deeply as she could to discover what needs existed and to determine the array of available resources and services.

Initiating the program was amazing for Ruff. She put on a conference to provide an educational opportunity about the disease of addiction within a Jewish context. Temple B'nai Torah provided support from the Hermine Pruzan Fund as part of the financing for the conference. The 180 people who participated paid a fee. Exhibitors from treatment centers up and down the West Coast came to share information about their treatment centers and their services. The "Recovery Rabbi" from Beit T'Shuvah in Los Angeles was the keynote speaker. Three other renowned speakers discussed the biology of addiction, the family disease, and what happens when there are both mental health and substance abuse issues. The audience was a mixture of professionals in the field (who acquired continuing education credits) and the Jewish recovery community.

The kickoff was remarkable. Rabbis Jonathan and Beth Singer from Beth Am, Rabbi Mirel from B'nai Torah, and Rabbis Kimber and Weiner from Temple de Hirsch Sinai were her five strongest connections from the beginning. They wanted to know how they could support the program and help get this message out. A card was placed on the inside of bathroom doors in 15 synagogues and community centers, and an ad was placed in the *Jewish Transcript*. The cards read, "If you have a problem this is where to get help," and posed four questions like, "Do you wake up in the morning with a headache?" and "Do you think you have to have one more?"

Then in April 2009, actress Carrie Fisher came to Seattle and performed *Wishful Drinking*, her one-woman show on drinking, at the Seattle Repertory Theatre. The *Seattle Times* reported the offering as "Part E! celebrity bio, part 12-step meeting and part irony-drenched stand-up comedy act." This really got some phone calls coming in to ATA.

Temple Beth Shalom was a wonderful friend to Alternatives to Addiction, as was the synagogue community of Kol HaNeshamah in West Seattle, which was the site of Ruff's first presentation on Shabbat T'Shuvah. She spoke about recovery and repentance and the importance of being incorporated and included within the context of our Jewish life. She also spoke about accepting people in recovery. Anson Laytner was interim rabbi at Kol HaNeshamah at the time.

Many other members of the community were supportive as Ruff continued to work to make the program known. She developed relationships with Rabbi Elie Estrin (part of the Chabad movement at the University of Washington) who helped Ruff connect with Jewish fraternities on the campus. She developed strong ties with Rabbi Jacob Fine and Rabbi Will Berkovitz at Hillel, and Rabbi Potek, the Hillel rabbi at Northwestern, opened his doors.

Ruff talked with parents and students at the Yeshiva High School on Mercer Island. Because she didn't go in like a prohibitionist saying alcohol is bad, she didn't find closed doors. Rather, she took a more open approach where she would, for example, go to the religious practices community at Beth Am when they were debating whether or not to serve wine on Shabbat or go alcohol free, and other related issues: How do we make this determination, and how do we respect our alcoholic and recovering members? How do we respect our religious convictions, and where do they interact? Ruff told them the issue was not about alcohol is bad, but about alcoholism or drug addiction being diseases that afflict members of our community. The question needed to be "how can we create safety for them within the context of our doors?" There was a Jewish publication about "someone in your family is alcoholic or someone in your family is a drug addict," which several of the synagogues secured and placed right alongside brochures on "what to do when a family member is grieving or you are grieving."

One of the things Ruff recognized is that, while alcoholism appears throughout the Jewish community, there is a conflict between drinking until you get drunk on Pesach, Purim, and on Simcha Torah, which is not an unusual occurrence in Jewish families, and the question of what do you do about the alcoholics in the community.

She participated in several luncheon meetings with JFS donors, explaining how she worked with parents to help them learn how to talk to their kids about alcohol and drugs. She led discussions with parents about what to do on Shabbat afternoon when that wine bottle is full, and how to encourage your children to make choices other than drinking wine. She discussed the idea that simply telling kids "don't drink" doesn't work. Discussions then became about education and building rituals and assets within their families that would obviate the need for the children to go and drink. They also discussed what defines a healthy family and offered family-oriented events through the Family Life Education program around the topic of what it means to build a healthy family without substance use in the family.

The more Ruff interacted with people, the more visible the program became; and the more visible the program, the more the phone rang. When the phone rang, she often heard about "my son," "my daughter," "my granddaughter," "my father," and not from the person who was the addict. Ruff worked to help families realize that they too needed recovery because the disease impacts the whole family.

Ruff worked with some families over a period of several years. They usually had already turned to several places for help. Part of the problem has to do with the idea that wine is part of ritual; it's part of what we do and who we are as Jews. The issue is compounded if Mom and Dad are unable to set boundaries.

Finally, when a significant crisis occurred, and parents phoned Ruff asking, "What do we do?" they were told, "You call the police." Ruff would then coach the parents so that when the time was right they could give their child a choice to go to treatment or be kicked out of the house. Often by this point the child had previously been arrested for driving under the influence, perhaps also for stealing, and at that point, had abused the parents so severely that the only way to demonstrate love for their child was to hold firm to a boundary.

Ruff spent a great deal of time with these families when necessary. She sometimes visited them in their homes. She drove their children to treatment and called the police when they broke their parole, telling them she would rather see them alive in jail than dead on the streets. Most eventually went willingly to detox and then to treatment.

After treatment, Ruff helped her clients connect with Alcoholics Anonymous. where they were teamed with a Jewish sponsor and mentor (AA teams each new member with a "sponsor" mentor.) Sometimes there were more individuals in a family who needed help including Mom, Dad, and other younger children.

One young client helped by JFS had a very difficult life, came from an abusive home, and had been addicted to alcohol since the age of 13. This client decided not to go to residential treatment but was very successful using AA, attended the meetings at JFS and engaged in counseling with Ruff and with one of the other counselors at the agency once a week for a significant period. Over time, this client was able to raise self esteem, reset career goals, and enroll in a professional training program.

Another young person who found the way to Counseling Services at JFS was employed at a local company whose supervisor had confirmed that, while they really valued the individual, they needed the staffer to stay sober in order to stay employed.

When the JFS counselor discovered the extent of the client's drinking, the counselor told her client they could not proceed with any kind of insight-oriented therapy because it was too clouded by the drinking. She then referred her client to Ruff and the Alternatives to Addiction program. Ruff was able to build a relationship with this client, and the young person loved recovery; loved what it meant, and loved the freedom from the bondage of alcohol. This client is now very successfully working with the same company.

People come to ATA for a variety of reasons: to maintain a job, to maintain a relationship, to get out of a relationship, to heal their lives.

One of Ruff's saddest experiences involved a Jewish client with late-stage alcoholism. This client had tried therapy, treatment, and just about everything. Ruff worked with the client for about a year, including sending the client to treatment on a scholarship. After treatment, the client was still living alone and very isolated, suffering from several serious ailments. When they didn't hear from the client for more than a week, Ruff called a neighbor who went in and found the client dead in the house. This client died of alcohol poisoning, surrounded by bottles. Because this client had no connections, there had been no one who could check in regularly. The client had a house, but no money at all, and had been receiving assistance from the JFS Emergency Services program. Ruff called the client's only relative, who flew in from out of town, and she helped gather a few friends and neighbors for a memorial service. Ruff wants everyone to understand that the disease of alcoholism is so pernicious that if it can't be arrested the alcoholic dies.

The Alternatives to Addiction program became well-known in the chemical dependency community because Ruff worked hard to engage treatment providers, sat on several boards, and went to a great many meetings. She created working partnerships throughout the community, and many of her referrals came from the rabbis who had the pulse of their communities.

Occasionally, Ruff found it necessary to send young clients to in-patient treatment. One teenager had been given the best of everything, but had started drinking in her early teens, popped pills, and stayed out late at night. It took Ruff several years to convince the family that their child was going down a destructive path. Their teenager wrecked the car, and was allowed to continue driving. The child participated appropriately in various activities at school and at the synagogue, and then went out and drank.

When the parents finally called ATA, they said their child was in college, and binge drinking was presenting a significant problem. Ruff advised them that they needed to follow the advice she had given them several years before. Their child needed to go to residential treatment.   She reminded these parents that addiction affects the entire family so they needed help too.

For the Jewish community, there is a cultural aspect that comes into play when dealing with alcoholism. Jews perform a dance between using alcohol as part of ritual, the celebratory nature of alcohol, and the question of how to provide safety for those people in the community who are addicted. The community is making an effort to teach the next generation about the issue. The high school students from Temple de Hirsch and B'nai Torah visit a recovery program in Los Angeles every year. They see addicts getting well and participate in Shabbat at a synagogue that is run by addicts and alcoholics. One Shabbat, they spend in a recovery community. Ruff got together with the students and their parents, explained what they were going to experience, and helped put things into context. Rabbi Septimus from De Hirsch and Rabbi Kinberg from B'nai Torah accompanied the students.

One of Ruff's clients is an example of harm reduction—a person who does not get better but is not getting worse. When Ruff told this man that she never sees him get anywhere, he said, 'Yeah, but I didn't get worse, so I'm just trying not to get worse.'

At one point, Ruff spoke at a national conference about gaining access to a closed population and providing chemical dependency services in the Orthodox community. There were many things she still wanted to do, including a second symposium, but it was time for her to move on, and after three years, in 2011, she had a desire to return to health care.

Upon Ruff's departure, long-time Seattleite Diane Burnett led the program for a short time prior to Laura Kramer joining JFS in 2012 as the new director of Alternatives to Addiction. Kramer grew up in Chicago and moved to Seattle in 2002, working with a variety of low-income housing organizations before returning to graduate school to earn her master's degree as a mental health therapist and chemical dependency counselor. She maintains a small private practice and works at Gilda's Club helping cancer survivors as well. At JFS, she focuses on clients struggling with addiction.

Kramer had been working in an intensive outpatient treatment center for women with addiction when she saw that JFS was hiring for a clinical position. The job also had opportunities for working in educational outreach collaborating with other community organizations. She says she definitely is more of a maintenance person than the start-up organizer that Ruff was and is grateful that so much groundwork was done to create awareness in the Jewish community. Kramer is ready to be of service to people with addiction and family members of loved ones with addiction.

As she began in her new role, Kramer spent her time meeting people, reaching out into the treatment community, and visiting treatment sites to let them know she was available as a referral source, especially for folks who are leaving treatment. Clients began calling, and she has developed a caseload.

Her role is to extend an offer and make sure people know JFS is a safe place to come, a shame-free, stigma-free, judgment-free place to get help. She also looks for opportunities to increase the visibility of the program and to teach, like working with students before they visit Beit T'Shuvah in Los Angeles and presenting a short training at the Yeshiva.

Kramer believes young people receive information about the physical dangers of alcohol and drugs, but they also need to understand that, while drugs and alcohol are potent and potentially lethal, the dependence on them comes from people using them to cope. If one finds these substances are an effective means of coping, it often becomes the only means of coping, which is when real devastation in one's life starts to take place. Kramer talks to young people about healthy coping, life stresses, and family stress. She discusses how people are best served if they have a community to reach out to and safe places to get support so they don't feel alone and have to deal with their feelings by themselves. Kids feel they have to be happy or they have to be OK. But Kramer stresses the reality is sometimes we are not happy and it is all right to be that way—sad and not OK—and fine to reach out for support around that.

She has clients that have an addiction to being on the Internet, who cope by "turning off"—leaving their own physical experience and going into this non-universe of the Internet. She thinks people will never run out of new ways to leave their experience, to avoid what's difficult, and every type of screen offers a very easy out. There is an endless variety of things to occupy someone if he or she chooses to escape in that way. She thinks this is similar to other addictions. Sometimes our internal experience is uncomfortable, and especially younger folks who are so bombarded by technology turn to this form of addiction to cope with their discomfort.

It is not only OK to be uncomfortable; it is also normal. Discomfort is part of how we grow and how we learn things. But today there is such a low tolerance for discomfort, for disappointment of any kind, and for lack of stimulation that a self-perpetuating cycle of needing to escape, escape, escape becomes established.

One of the tasks Kramer sees for herself is to expand the definition of addiction beyond alcohol and drugs. People also have very destructive relationships with dependencies on many different types of externalities: food, exercise, the Internet, sex, driving, aggression, work, although not all of them necessarily constitute addiction from the diagnostic manual. She thinks food addiction is enormous but underreported and overly stigmatized.

She knows that if people are using something external to fix something internal, they are setting themselves up for a futile battle because the internal isn't fixable in that way. People may be addicted not to any one thing but just to not feeling the discomfort. The avoidance becomes the addiction. What is it like to be bored for an entire hour? It's almost a fate worse than death, especially when we have all these options to escape our boredom.

Kramer reached out to the rabbinate, the synagogues, and the schools and received several positive responses, including a referral from the Hillel. She is considering a variety of programs: perhaps a viewing and discussion of one of the many films about Jews with addictions with people who are in recovery themselves, but having it also open to the community. Another idea was to arrange a performance in Seattle of Beit T'Shuvah's Freedom Song (which was realized in 2014). The performance is about Passover and redemption from addiction and redemption from being cast out by Pharaoh. Kramer has experience helping people struggle with how to be with an addicted friend, family member, or loved one and knows that being able to hear one's own story in someone else's mouth can be very useful. She hopes to start a group for family and loved ones of addicts that would be a process group and would not follow the 12-step program so crosstalk would be permitted.

She already works with people who come to talk about family members and then uncover their own pattern of coping that's not really adaptive to them. Most have been willing to shift their focus from dealing with their family member to looking at their own experience. She has one client who is starting to recognize that her attempts to be sober for other people hasn't worked and is now thinking about maybe wanting to be sober for herself. Another of her clients continues to relapse and has been in and out of addiction for many decades but is at least thinking about treatment.

Sometimes a client is very resistant to mental-health counseling, just wants abstinence and does not want to go deeper than that. Generally, that never works. Perhaps it is a client who cannot figure out how not to use drugs and has never been able to string together more than two months of abstinence. Occasionally, after achieving several months of abstinence, a client will try to leave treatment thinking he/she could be through with treatment and would be able to maintain abstinence. Kramer doesn't agree and lets the client know he/she can come back any time. She is still doubtful this type of client can maintain abstinence without dealing with the deeper issues, but with each client who decides to make this choice, time will tell.

Kramer would like to have a process and psycho-education group for family members and to offer a class about the risk of avoidance. She would also like to have the opportunity to go to synagogues and schools and help both adults and young people know there is a safe place to go. In reality, there are many more options for adults than for kids, who tend to be isolated in that they cannot drive themselves somewhere and think they are the only person in the world going through whatever it is they are dealing with.

Kramer thinks marijuana is a major problem and that people do not think it is addictive, do not take it seriously, and cannot stop smoking it. She sees a baby boomer generation thinking it is the same as when they were young, but it is not. Marijuana is much stronger now. One of the resources she has developed is an informational piece, which asks the question, "Is marijuana addictive?" The piece presents information about the addictive qualities of marijuana, especially for young people, and describes what dependency is, explains that those who start to use marijuana under the age of 18 are three times more likely to develop dependency, and discusses some of the consequences of marijuana dependency.

Chapter 19

1995–2005: Continued Growth

"JFS was suddenly bigger and part of
something larger than it had ever been."

—Ken Weinberg

In the mid-1990s, Jewish Family Service worked to incorporate the Seattle Association for Jews with Disabilities (SAJD) into its programming and to establish a formal structure for the combined organizations. With board president Bob Low leading the process, one of the questions was whether there should be one board of directors or two. Another set of issues revolved around how separate and autonomous SAJD would be and the level of responsibility JFS had to accept in order to sustain the SAJD budget.

Low, a commercial real estate appraiser, joined the board of JFS in 1990 and became president in 1995. He remembers feeling he was working with a very hands-on board, closely and constructively engaged in both board and agency activities. Under Ken

Bob Low
(JFS photo collection.)

Weinberg's leadership, the organization was a smoothly operating, successful organization.

Another concern the board and senior staff addressed was JFS's financial dependency upon other organizations—most of the agency's revenues came from outside sources, primarily the Jewish Federation of Greater Seattle, United Way of King County, and the Cooper-Levy Trust. Some years those sources funded JFS's needs almost fully; other years they did not. The board had no control over these funds as they were donated for specific services, so support was contingent on the decisions of others. At the same time, caseworkers and other staff members saw increases in both the number and the types of services needed, especially for treatment for addictions, domestic violence, and mental health. Staff and board alike recognized that JFS operations should be determined by the needs of the community, not by its income sources. How to put the agency in a stable financial position, prepared to serve the growing number of people in need—economic, emotional, and practical—in the Jewish, and in the broader community was a major problem. Achieving greater financial self-sufficiency became a priority.

The Board Development Committee expanded the range of talents and skills of the board itself, including the ability of individual members to both give and solicit contributions. The committee determined that JFS needed a notably diverse group of people with a variety of strengths that reflected the community being served. In addition to dedicated volunteers with passion for the agency's mission, community members with legal, business, financial, fundraising, and other professional skills were sought out. Effort was made to add not only members of Reform, Conservative, Orthodox, and Sephardic communities but also those affiliated with Reconstructionist, Renewal, and other synagogues. In addition, there were thousands of unaffiliated Jewish men and women living in the Greater Seattle area who could be approached to participate. Over time, changes were made in the bylaws, expanding the number of board members, and the committee worked to formalize and educate the board as to their responsibilities. The changes addressed board-member participation, attendance, volunteer activities in which they were expected to participate, and fiduciary responsibilities. The committee also formalized the review process of the executive director.

At the beginning of Low's term as on the board in 1990, JFS's budget was $1.45 million. The combined contributions of the agency's major funding sources represented approximately 50 percent of the annual budget. By the end of his presidency in 1997, the projected budget for JFS was $2.4 million, an increase of more than 60 percent.

Between 1990 and 2000, the number of Jews living in the Seattle area roughly doubled. At the same time, the JFS's budget quadrupled.

By 1994, a move to larger office space became desirable for two reasons: JFS had outgrown the Boylston building, and the rent kept going up. The uncertainty of future rent requirements increased the difficulty for the agency to control its operations and budget. Discussion began about the agency once again purchasing its own building.

After the board made the decision to do so, a capital campaign was organized and moved quickly. A search committee identified a building that all concerned—board, staff members, and community volunteers—approved. The location on 16th Avenue, just off Madison and only a few blocks from Temple de Hirsch Sinai, was excellent, and the cost was manageable, well within the guidelines that had been set.

At the time, Jewish Federation of Greater Seattle agencies were required to seek permission from JFGS to embark on a capital campaign. Further, the order in which agencies began their campaigns was also determined by the federation. If the campaign was approved, the newest applicant would usually be placed at the back of the line, although from time to time, one agency was bumped by another organization when JFGS leaders decided on a higher or more urgent level of need. Understandably, these changes in priority created hard feelings, as well as untoward politicking, in the organization that had to delay its campaign.

Waiting for permission to start the campaign for a new building posed a problem for JFS. The building on 16th was available and in demand by other potential buyers. JFS needed to move quickly to finalize the purchase or risk losing the opportunity. When JFGS declined permission to begin the two-million-dollar capital campaign immediately, the board determined they could not wait and went forward with both the campaign and the purchase.

There were two lots across the street from the new building that could also have been included in the purchase. One, available for $100,000, was the northeast corner of 16th and Madison, where the Madison Market would be built a few years later. The adjacent lot to the north, available for the same price, could provide an additional parking lot (the building being purchased included an adjacent surface parking lot). JFS purchased the north lot and passed on the market property. The lot and the building were purchased for $2.1 million. Today, Ken Weinberg acknowledges JFS should have purchased both lots, but at the time, the cost seemed a veritable fortune. He recognizes there is sometimes a tendency for a not-for-profit organization to be ultra-conservative, but calculated risk taking should also be an important component of any business.

The Jewish community was very responsive, and JFS raised the funds quickly with no loans required. Paul Jassny, long-time agency supporter and father of the then current JFS board president Lauren Jassny, agreed to co-chair the campaign along with board members Carolee Danz (granddaughter of Jessie Danz) and Ray Benezra. Danz, who had previous experience coordinating capital campaigns, primarily worked with the agency's Development staff to organize and manage the campaign while Jassny and Benezra became very engaged with Weinberg and spent their time directly soliciting members of the community.

Weinberg describes Paul Jassny as "a wonderful guy and an old-time fundraiser." Some of the visits he and Weinberg made were to Jassny's pals, and Jassny would say, "I gave you 50 grand last year; you give me 50 grand this year." And they would give.

Weinberg also describes Joyce and Ray Benezra as two of the nicest human beings there could ever be. Very committed to JFS for years, during the time Ray was on the board, he was always the first person to say "yes we can" for whatever projects were on the drawing board, and his yes was contagious. The agency counted on Benezra during the building campaign as he worked to solicit his many friends and associates.

The decision to purchase its own building again was not without controversy in the Jewish community. The majority of the community was very positive about the advantages of JFS owning and controlling its own space. This camp expressed the idea that it was necessary and appropriate for organizations to own and provide a basic infrastructure, as long as those things are in proportion to the need and the organization's capability. There was also an acknowledgement by this group of the positive benefit of the agency holding this type of asset.

Another point of view heard was that the cash needed to acquire, develop, and maintain a building takes those funds out of the community when they could be better spent on programs and distributed to support the services of several other organizations. This side of the debate also asserted that as needs change it might be better for an organization not to be tied to one location.

Still others asserted that often people who participate in a capital campaign have set a personal budget for multi-year charitable capital pledges and those dollars would be committed to another not-for-profit organization (perhaps a building campaign for a museum, the zoo, or a synagogue) if the commitment was not being made to JFS.

The Danz family contributed a naming gift to the campaign, and the building became the Jessie Danz Building, in honor and memory of the Danz family matriarch who was a member of the Jewish Welfare Society board from 1925 to 1947, serving as president for 11 of those years. The Polack family made a similar contribution in memory of long-time supporter Morris Polack. The Polack Food Bank still bears his name.

Jessie Danz building
(JFS photo collection.)

Before the campaign was completed and in order to expedite the move to the new building, a loan of $75,000 from the JFGS at extraordinarily low interest was used to complete a few necessary capital improvements. Because the capital campaign ultimately raised more funds than the original goal, JFS was able to pay that loan off sooner than the terms required.

The building was in excellent shape, but it had been the home of the Seattle Eye Clinic, so the examination rooms had no windows. A bit of remodel work brought daylight into the new offices. Some of the larger spaces were remodeled into offices, and some of the small examination rooms were combined to make larger spaces.

Director of Facilities Lesley Mills was responsible for getting the staff moved into the new building. It was a time when many things in the world were changing, and the use of computers was one of them. When Mills first came to JFS in 1989, there was only one word processor in the entire agency. As the time came for the move to the Jessie Danz Building, it became apparent the staff needed to become computerized. The shift to technology was a slow evolution until the agency became fully networked. One of the first offices to become computerized was that of Development. The Development staff was using an archaic database, and the shift to a more sophisticated program was arduous, although well worth the effort.

Other very interesting changes occurred with the move to the Jessie Danz Building. JFS suddenly became much more of a focal point for the Jewish community, as well as for the non-Jewish community. The new building had meeting space that could be used by others so the Food Bank Coalition began to meet there. Soon various sub-committees of United Way asked to use the space because of its excellent central location, convenient parking, and open atmosphere. Other institutions and organizations, Jewish and non-Jewish, including JFGS, also began to schedule meetings at the Jessie Danz Building. Frequent visits by members of other social service organizations and coalitions helped connect JFS with the broader community.

At the time of the purchase, the bottom floor was already occupied by Western Optical. This provided a fairly small, but welcome, rental income. Later, Dress for Success—a not-for-profit agency that "promotes the economic independence of disadvantaged women by providing professional attire, a network of support and the career development tools to help women thrive in work and in life" occupied the space. This fit in well with the JFS mission.

During the years that tenants occupied the street-front space, the Polack Food Bank was located in a small area in the back but was able to provide much-improved service to the large number of clients who relied on the bags of groceries being provided. Access to the food bank through a separate entrance on Pine Street allowed for more privacy, keeping food bank clients separate from retail traffic and other JFS clients and visitors. When JFS eventually occupied the entire building, the food bank was enlarged considerably. Food drives then became a bigger part of the Jewish community's calendar and were participatory events that helped to create recognition throughout the community that JFS was a singular focal point for people in need.

The agency became recognized as a more significant piece in the fabric of the community. Weinberg observed at the time that, even though JFS had always played an important role, after the move and as more development work began, the community began to see JFS as the central agency for social services for Jews. It was also the start of the agency playing a more significant role in the Greater Seattle community. Those trends continue today as JFS remains very much central to the health of the Jewish community and continuously becomes more well-known in the Seattle area, both for its services and for its willingness to partner with non-Jewish agencies to accomplish important social-service functions. JFS remains a very strong Jewish agency, very committed to the Jewish community while providing critical services to the general community also.

Weinberg played a significant role in the discussion about the balance of service to the Jewish and non-Jewish communities. It was clear to him the nature of the Jewish community was changing and insularity would not serve the JFS mission well. There were also significant financial advantages to broadening the scope of the organization. As it became increasingly clear, JFGS would not be able to support the growth of JFS to the extent required, Weinberg saw that other Jewish agencies across the country were beginning to seek out non-Jewish funds.

The board worked to redefine JFS's mission, what the agency was about and whom it serves. JFS captured support not only from the broad general community but also from Jews who felt closed out of Jewish institutions, including synagogue and JFGS life. Some of those who felt unwelcome included the LGBTQ community, single parents, divorced, remarried, blended, and intermarried families, and families and individuals of differing abilities.

For example, the programming JFS began to offer to the LGBTQ community in the early 1990s stated to members of that group, "You are a part of our community, and JFS is here for you." In general, when an organization (or an individual) says, "We are here for you," the recipient of that message responds by saying, or at least feeling, he or she is here for that organization or individual too.

Rabbi Beth Singer recalls that Temple Beth Am believed that their years of hard work had resulted in tremendous strides in being seen as a mainstream congregation where any Jewish family or individual, regardless of sexual orientation, would feel and know that he or she was welcome. The Beth Am "family" thought they had reached this goal 10 years earlier until JFS provided seminars in partnership with the temple around LGBTQ issues. Rabbi Singer discovered that LGBTQ people still did not understand they were welcome. She came to realize her temple had to promote the welcome continuously for people to know it. Jews who are part of sexual minorities are so accustomed to feeling unwelcome they stop coming unless they see and feel acceptance. Giving the LGBTQ workshops with JFS not only helped to bring in some of the LGBTQ families who had previously been on the margins of the synagogue but also set Beth Am on a path to carry out other related work with single-parent families, mixed families, and others who often felt they might not be welcomed and included by the organization.

The same types of programming offered in the greater community (secular and non-secular) had similar results in increasing the visibility of JFS in new non-Jewish segments of the community. As a result, special funding organizations and grant-making foundations that focused on specific areas, such as domestic violence, addiction recovery, and other special populations, were successfully approached for support.

As Weinberg experienced the transition from a little agency minimally supported by a small portion of the Jewish community to a quickly growing organization providing much broader and deeper services, support for JFS began to broaden as well. Not only was fundraising enhanced, but also JFS events became much more successful, more people became engaged, and seats on the board of directors became highly prized by professionals and philanthropists.

Several families played a key role in the expansion of JFS, and their generosity and leadership began to change the agency in the 1980s. Weinberg could approach any one of them with a special need, and they would say yes. They were willing to help fund start-up costs for a new program or to fill a gap or cover a new expense in the budget. Amazingly, there were times when an enormous contribution would suddenly appear from one of these families to be used for an emergency JFS was experiencing or just to be used for whatever purpose the agency chose.

Soon, many more and larger gifts came in from more and more people, with many new friends appearing. Throughout, the Jewish Federation of Greater Seattle and most of those who work for or volunteer with the federation remained constant supporters of and advocates for JFS.

Those decades from 1990 to 2010 were revolutionary in many ways. "People's priorities shifted somewhat, as well as attitudes towards the organizations and what was being done," says Weinberg. The nature of the Jewish family, of the Jewish community, and of fundraising all changed dramatically. United Way moved to designated giving, and younger donors became increasingly committed to directing their gifts and supporting the local community.

Donna Benaroya became president of the board in 1997. She had not been involved with JFS until friends invited her to join them in managing the Chanukah Tzedakah gift giving program.

This work led to an invitation to join the board in 1988, where she soon turned her energy to SAJD. Once she became aware of the two group homes and the other SAJD services, she was struck by how much the clients and their families relied on the program. She came to understand more about how living with a family member with special needs affected everyone in the family and that many adult children are by necessity kept at home all of their lives, or at least their parents' lives. In addition,

Donna Benaroya
(JFS photo collection.)

she learned there was almost no respite care—short-term care of a person to allow the family caregivers rest. Once the mother of one of these adult children came to Weinberg begging for JFS to do something. She and her husband "could not die" because there was no one to take care of their daughter. They, like many families of children with disabilities, had never been on a vacation since the child had been born, more than 30 years before.

Benaroya decided that within the Jewish community she could help provide resources for these desperate families. By the time she became board president, she recognized the need for increased financial stability for SAJD and became committed to creating a significant SAJD endowment. As a courtesy, she met with Michael Novick, the executive director of JFGS, to discuss the proposal, then joined forces with Herb Stusser to lead a successful two-million-dollar endowment campaign. The resulting endowment continues to fund a portion of SAJD, adding much-needed stability.

Greater support for the senior management staff at JFS was attained in 1999 when the board approved Ken Weinberg's intent to hire a chief operating officer in place of the previous assistant director role. This person would be responsible for daily management of JFS, enabling Weinberg to focus on the financial health of the agency, on the new building campaign, and on a vision for the long-range future of the agency.

Claudia Berman became that COO. She grew up in Brooklyn, New York. After several years in Boston and California, she and her husband moved to Seattle, which she says for New Yorkers is the end of the world.

Berman's career for many years was in psychiatric nursing, followed by nursing administration. She wrote policies and procedures and quality-improvement plans for accreditation. She then worked with multi-disciplinary teams to develop best practices and clinical pathways. The teams looked at what happened to the ideal patients from the moment they started their treatment to post hospital.

When Berman saw an ad in the *Jewish Transcript* for a position at JFS in 1999, she did not think it would be a match, but she was ready for a change and applied anyway. She was familiar with the agency because she had participated in family therapy at JFS with counselor Jeff Gold. In addition, former JFS assistant director Cliff Warner was a friend who added his recommendation to the decision-making process.

The change in position and function to chief operating officer coincided with the tremendous growth, expansion, and sophistication of JFS, which Berman says felt small at the time with at most, 25 people working in the building. The resettlement program had just taken over the Multi-Ethnic Service Center in Bellevue (which became the Refugee & Immigrant Service Center, or RISC). JFS has since grown from a staff of 45 to approximately 100, not including homecare workers and volunteers. More than 65 people now work at the Capitol Hill campus.

Berman remembers that she had to change her vocabulary. The term "quality improvement," familiar to many veterans of government and corporations, was not well understood in a social service seting. She also had to recognize that the social workers were interested in helping their clients and did not have much interest in grant compliance, charging fees, looking at a sliding scale, and maximizing every revenue source. Implementing the necessary changes required a cultural shift for both Berman and the staff at JFS.

HomeCare Associates (HCA) at $1.8 million and Refugee & Immigrant Service Centers at $1.2 million are the two largest JFS programs. Together they represented almost one-third of the agency's total budget in 2012. RISC had 15 employees with six in Bellevue and nine in Kent. The third largest group of programs, based on numbers served, budget size, and hours, is Emergency Services because of the amount of emergency assistance given to individuals and families and the number of those served in the Polack Food Bank.

Berman believes sustainability requires that JFS continue to grow where possible through grants. As JFS moves forward, this will involve a teamwork approach to development. The program directors are the content experts, and the agency's grant writer is able to translate their needs into language that the grantors can understand.

Berman credits Endless Opportunities, which serves hundreds of adults age 60 and older, with increasing visibility and outreach in the community. She also credits the 2006 Strategic Plan (see chapter 21, "2006: A Plan for the Future") with creating several programs that have provided depth for JFS and enabled it to send a message that the agency is there not just for the needy but also for those with needs. Then, when Dick Rosenwald became marketing director, he focused on reinforcing and strengthening recognition of the JFS brand, which further moved the agency forward. Endless Opportunities and Family Life Education, which serve well over a thousand people each year, are each appreciated as important portals to JFS, creating access points for clients who need assistance from other services.

Every former board president comments on the importance of executive assistant Julie Olson. She has been critical to their work as president, to the executive, and to the board. John Phillips said, "She does a superb job for the board. When you are the president, she keeps you informed all the time and makes sure you are prepared when you have an Executive Committee or board meeting."

Weinberg recalls that the board "thought Julie might not stay on when Irv Goldberg left," and he wasn't sure either. However, her loyalty was to the agency, and she has stayed for more than 30 years. Besides keeping Weinberg's appointments and making sure he was where he needed to be, she monitored all the activities of the board and kept the board's minutes. Aware that some things that may seem unimportant, in fact, show that the CEO and JFS are paying attention to its supporters as well as to its staff, Olson would remind Weinberg he should send a card for a board or staff member's birthday or special occasion. She often edited letters and speeches for Weinberg, helping make sure his efforts achieved their goals as much as possible and reflected the agency in its most positive light.

Shelly Shapiro, an employment law attorney, became involved with JFGS when she heard a JFS presentation during the early 1990s. She immediately knew JFS was where she wanted to become involved, and she pursued an opportunity to serve on the Personnel Committee. She joined the board in 1993 and served as president from 2001 to 2003. As a board member, she participated

Shelly Shapiro with
Tipper Gore
(JFS photo collection.)

in the decision to purchase what became the Jessie Danz Building, in deciding key SAJD issues, and in the decision to absorb the Multi-Ethnic Service Center. Shapiro was board president in 2002 when the SAJD Oversight Committee decided to transition out of managing the group homes into staff-supported independent living. This proved fiscally sound, as well as programmatically right and the best alternative for clients and their families, but it was a very difficult move.

The Shaarei Tikvah program focused on outreach to parents and families of people with disabilities who were not in JFS residential facilities, as well as to those receiving direct services from JFS. The effort grew when SAJD transitioned to supported independent living, becoming broader in scope and more visible. The number of clients and families served by SAJD and by the Shaarei Tikvah program grew significantly. (See chapter 16, "Seattle Association for Jews with Disabilities.")

One of Shapiro's goals was to shift the JFS major fund raising event from the gala to a luncheon concept. There was a recognition that once again, a more diverse board would be needed to bring in both a broad spectrum of individual attendees and corporate support. The shift to the luncheon model proved very successful with the first year's proceeds of $327,000 representing a slight increase over the gala—and people loved it. Tipper Gore (wife of former US vice president Al Gore and an advocate for parents and children) proved the perfect speaker who spoke about mental health, and attendees of all political stripes enjoyed her remarks. The event not only raised additional funds; it also gave JFS a tremendous amount of visibility and credibility. The annual luncheon has become an important event for the Jewish community. In terms of logistics, the luncheon was far more cost effective (and less burdensome) than the auction. In its 10th year in March 2013, the luncheon grossed more than one million dollars.

Board members Judy Neuman and Laura Stusser-McNeil together chaired the first JFS fundraising luncheon in 2002. Neuman feels that, by figuring out how to tell the JFS story more broadly and raising significantly more dollars in order to meet more needs throughout the community, the agency is "fulfilling the promise of the wonderful women who started the organization 120 years ago."

Jeannie Butler was a 10-year board veteran when she followed Shelly Shapiro as president in 2003. Her background in special education led to her interest in the SAJD program. She started volunteering in the Development office and remembers her first task was to procure a puppy for one of the JFS auctions. She continued to help with fundraising events, working with Development director Davis Fox and was proud to be asked to join the board of JFS in 1994.

Jeannie Butler
(JFS photo collection.)

As the agency moved towards the new strategic planning process, Butler recruited key board members so JFS would be ready to move into the actual planning and from there to launching the strategy.

The budget was pretty tight in 2003 because the economy took a hit after the terrorist attacks of September 11, 2001, and the dot-com bust. The world changed, and JFS was no exception. The board decided to build and maintain a reserve fund in case another tragedy interrupted revenues or it just happened to snow on the day set aside every spring for the fundraising luncheon. Butler saw the agency become more sophisticated as it settled into a new era of comprehensive services and financial planning.

⸎

On July 28, 2006, a man walked into the Jewish Federation of Greater Seattle offices in Seattle and started shooting. Everything changed again. JFS responded immediately. Weinberg and Berman

immediately requested that some of the best counselors go to the hospital to start working with the victims—family members, staff, and community members. Weinberg, Berman, JFS board president Judy Neuman, and Robin Boehler, president of JFGS at the time, stayed at the hospital for many hours. It was a tragic time from which a rippling effect continues. Many people were wounded,

Judy Neuman and Pamela Waechter, a well-known and
(JFS photo collection.) much-loved federation employee and former JFS staffer, was murdered. The Jewish community and the greater community were traumatized by the senseless violence and the fact that the shooter targeted Jews. Following the immediate emergency activities, JFS remained in "first responder" mode for many months. All JFS counselors continued to be available to work with JFGS employees, volunteers, and their families for the next six months—with no fees charged.

If ever there was a case to be made as to why JFS is so important, this was it. JFS was there doing the good work.

The shooting at JFGS changed the Jewish community's attitude toward security. Even before the September 11 terrorist attacks, security of Jewish institutions had been strengthened, but American Jews enjoyed relative freedom from the violence visited on Jews elsewhere around the world. Armed guards had become normal at synagogues in Seattle during services and at Jewish schools when children were present. Some Jewish organizations already had hired guards during office hours.

JFS made physical changes to the Jessie Danz Building to increase security, including a controlled entry system.

After the shootings at JFGS, an inter-agency organization, called SAFE Washington (a Jewish Community Coalition to Keep Washington Safe) was formed by and for the Jewish community and funded privately by Mark Bloome. Ed Meyer, JFS director of Human Resources and Facilities, originally represented the agency in this group in which 80 Jewish agencies throughout the state train staff and leaders on issues ranging from dealing with difficult people, reacting to active shooters, surveillance, and detection of threats to developing security and evacuation plans. The professionals from agencies across the state speak and collaborate as a new community, working to protect their members, staff, and facilities. Building relationships with state, federal, and local law enforcement is also an important part of the program. Police and Homeland Security officers coordinate with agencies and are ready to respond to potential threat. Larry Broder, executive director of Temple de Hirsch Sinai and a participant in SAFE Washington, says, "Although everybody wishes it was different, that is the way the world is now." He continues to ask the question about how an organization can prove its security strategies are working. Is the fact that nothing has happened proof there is no threat? Perhaps a visible armed guard is enough to deter somebody bent on creating havoc, "but you never really know about what doesn't occur."

⌒∞⌒

Between 2000 and 2010, the board became much more directly engaged with the executive staff. Members with expertise in the areas of finance and social services participated actively in JFS's operations, although not in casework. The agency was successful in its provision of service to the community, in its collaborations with local, state, and federal government agencies, other social service agencies, and in its fundraising efforts—moving forward and reaching out. Those things spoke to these high-functioning, high-achieving individuals who were accustomed to excellence. By design, the composition of the board changed and evolved. Younger board members began to predominate with more individuals coming from the emerging technology sector. The JFS board also became a place for people who were interested in strategic planning and strategic thinking. Board members were still deeply interested in the agency's operations, sometimes posing a challenge to staff, but it was in the best interest of JFS to have a board of critical thinkers focused on helping the agency function at the level of a successful business. Board members continued to provide a significant number of major gifts.

Consecutive board presidents presided over momentous growth and change throughout the next decade as the agency entered the 21st century. John Phillips, Shelly Shapiro, Jeannie Butler, Judy Neuman, Sandy Melzer, and Laura Stusser-McNeil all led the board to create these changes. In 1998, the JFS budget was $2.4 million. The 2001 budget was almost $2.9 million. By 2006, with the addition of HomeCare Associates, it had increased to over $6.1 million. The 2012 budget (the 120th year of the agency) topped $8.6 million.

Part of the change occurred during 2001 when two new programs developed. One was HomeCare Associates, providing personal care and homemaker services to clients requiring assistance in their own homes. At times, the care is needed for a person who has a sudden emergency or illness. In other cases, the service provides extra household support during times of transition, stress, or other situations in which more help is needed, or simply provides support for an individual or couple who wants to stay in their home but needs assistance to do so.

The second new program was Project DVORA, addressing the issue of domestic violence in the Jewish community. The refugee resettlement program also underwent a considerable change. In 1998, there was a small state-funded refugee program on the Eastside called the Multi-Ethnic Service Center (MESC), which was receiving state funding to serve refugees from all over the world, and the state was about to cancel its contract with MESC because it was being poorly run by those operating the program.

Someone in Olympia knew of the positive reputation of the JFS refugee resettlement program and asked JFS to take over MESC and assume responsibility for its contracts with the state. After a board sub-committee met to examine the program and the issues, the agency agreed to integrate MESC into JFS operations.

There were several positive aspects of this decision. Providing services to non-Jewish immigrants would be an excellent way to remain prepared to help the Jewish community of immigrants, as staff would remain in place during the years when there were few or no Jews being resettled. It would also increase the JFS profile in the wider community, as well as with United Way, and would enable the agency to increase its presence on the Eastside. There didn't seem to be much in the way of a downside.

JFS took over that operation 1998. It became what is now the Refugee & Immigrant Service Centers (RISC) and has developed into a large, well-run program that is considered one of the premier refugee resettlement agencies in the state of Washington. "Boom!" commented Weinberg. "JFS was suddenly bigger and part of something larger than it had ever been."

For some time, the board had discussed starting an entrepreneurial venture that could actually provide a profit: perhaps a Haagen-Dazs stand or a Starbucks. They considered various options, but most were not consistent with the mission of JFS until the idea of a homecare business worked to the forefront. That type of venture would be in line with the mission and might produce an income. This approach was also consistent with the fee-for-service model in counseling and other services.

Weinberg told the board he had been hearing for a number of years from his colleagues across the country about homecare services. Stephanie Spiegel, the executive director of Jewish Family Service in Louisville, Kentucky, had started a program that was quite financially successful and served both Jewish and non-Jewish clients. Research had established that patients, disabled persons, and seniors did better in their own homes at less cost than in institutions. Her agency established a business providing services to clients in their homes for a fee. San Francisco also operated a successful program.

The JFS board decided to move forward with the project. Weinberg contacted his San Francisco counterpart, Anita Friedman, and several people flew to the Bay Area to spend a day with that program. Sandy Melzer (board president from 2006 to 2007), a physician and an administrator with Seattle Children's Hospital, acknowledges that his deepest engagement with JFS was his involvement in the creation of the homecare program. He and Howard Behar, then president of Starbucks Company North America and Starbucks Company International, teamed up, devoting at least five years of involvement to develop the program that became HomeCare Associates (HCA). One of the primary objectives was to make a profit while providing a much-needed service. The for-profit purpose has since changed, and while the agency would still like to realize a positive cash flow from the program, HCA is a very important service that the community needs, regardless of profitability.

HCA is a different kind of program to administer because of the challenges of finding, training, and retaining qualified care providers. In addition, demand varies constantly and instantaneously. Client satisfaction depends almost entirely on how well the patient and his or her family accepts the individual care provider, who might be a long-time employee but could also be a less well-known, very recently hired caregiver. There have been both profitable years and years of negative cash flow, but according to Weinberg, "it has always been a superb service to the Jewish community, as well as to the non-Jewish community."

In 2007, when the Visiting Nurse Service (VNS) of Snohomish County decided to close its Home Care Division, and having heard positive reports about the JFS HomeCare Associates program, VNS asked if HCA would be willing to absorb their program.

Claudia Berman, who had many years of experience in medical administration, worked with a board committee to analyze the opportunity carefully. The decision was made to integrate the Snohomish program into the JFS program. Suddenly, another enormous program serving 120 clients was added to the agency's operations. More than 40 part-time home healthcare aids from the Snohomish program became employees of the JFS HCA program.

HomeCare Associates is the largest of the JFS programs with a 2012 budget of a little over $1.8 million. Although it has yet to fulfill the goal of returning a profit, it is drawing close. JFS subscribes to a national database report that compares a given organization regionally and nationally on a variety of factors. One benchmark report showed that HCA was approaching 90,000 hours of service per year, the level at which it should become profitable.

⌘

By 1999, the issue of domestic violence had finally become recognized as a serious issue in Jewish communities across the country. JFS Seattle responded by creating Project DVORA (see chapter 18, "Project DVORA"). As soon as the new program was in place, the number of women coming to the agency for help with domestic violence almost overwhelmed staff, and the program took off. This program also brought with it related coalitions of service agencies and funding from new sources.

JFS had now grown from what Ken Weinberg called a "Ma and Pa shop" to a significant-sized and prominent social service agency, from a small staff of 45 to a large staff of more than 100 (not including the HCA homecare workers), from one location to multiple locations (the primary campus in Seattle, counseling and RISC in Bellevue, and RISC in Kent), from a small budget to a budget of millions of dollars, from modest fundraising to fundraising that was appreciably bigger, from relying on only a few people to fund the agency with large gifts to many people contributing large gifts and many more contributing smaller amounts. By 2006, the Development

Department had become a very sophisticated, successful entity. (See chapter 7, "Fund Development and Marketing.")

Board participation also became more sophisticated. Kathy Berman, who joined the board in 2001 and worked at Microsoft, brought a background and expertise in human resources and technology. Working with director of Human Resources and Operations Lesley Mills and with the Technology Committee, Berman helped to create policies concerning data servers and computers. The question of whether JFS should have a central server led to developing the content, look, and feel of the website, which came from the Marketing Committee. Keeping computers and the servers secure was also a significant issue that had to be addressed. Berman and Mills also worked together to create the agency's privacy policies, per the Health Information and Patient Privacy Act (HIPPA).

When Mills left JFS in 2002, Berman continued her work to develop written policies and practices working with the new director of Administrative Services, Ed Meyer, eventually creating a new handbook and updating the performance-review process.

Ed Meyer was born and raised in Seattle. He retired in 1990 from a career in the Marine Corps that began when he was 17, having reached the rank of major. He spent several years working in personnel while in the military, including consolidating six personnel departments into the single largest in the Marine Corps.

His master's degree in human resources and his military experience, followed by an additional 11 years as a civilian professional administrator, led Meyer to submitting a résumé for a position with JFS as director of Human Resources and Operations. (His title was later changed to director of Administrative Services.) Before submitting his résumé, he had asked a friend at JFGS about the reputation of JFS and was told it was hard to get in and no one leaves. That was good enough for him.

Meyer assumed Lesley Mills' position in 2003, accepting responsibility for information technology (IT), human resources, and facilities. His goal for JFS was to remove barriers to help the entire team do their jobs effectively.

One of his first projects was helping to select a long-term care package for employees, a goal the staff viewed as particularly important. Almost every staff member deals with people who fall on hard times due to illness or injury, so they all understand the importance of protecting themselves and their families. Another of his projects was to reach out to the neighbors before construction of the new building began to make sure they knew what JFS was planning and how it would or would not impact them.

Kathy Berman and fellow board member Eric Levine worked to make sure everybody had a desktop computer and to bring JFS up to industry standards. There are now more than 90 desktops and laptops and three server systems containing a great amount of information the agency is committed to protecting. In the interest of privacy and security, Project DVORA information is kept off the system and separately coded so clients can feel secure. The IT group and a private security company are constantly looking at the shifting landscape of security issues.

In his role as human resources administrator, Meyer was aware organizations were moving away from performance evaluations and into a constant feedback model and the younger employees were used to instant feedback. It was not as meaningful to them to wait a year or more for a performance evaluation as had been traditional and which usually reflected what that manager felt occurred during the last few months. Meyer worked with JFS managers on how to give continuous feedback until the entire agency had changed its practice. Only SAJD and HomeCare Associates use both continuous feedback and written evaluations because the auditors require the written version.

Meyer also contemplated document storage and wanted to be able to digitize all the old documents. He also worked to upgrade the servers, which is an ongoing process.

⌘

Evolution comes to mind when talking about the people who participate at JFS in many different ways. There is often the passing of a torch from family member to family member, generation to generation, in a community whose members have often known each other. Joe Barer did not share that history with the agency but had what Weinberg says was a "major influence on the board and on me starting in 2002." The agency was changing rapidly as the community grew. Joe Barer was part of a new younger group of the agency's supporters.

Although Barer had been raised in the Seattle area, he didn't become aware of JFS until he and his wife, Karyn, looked through a guide of local charities to figure out to which organization they might be interested in giving a major gift. When they read about JFS, it seemed to be exactly what they were looking for, so they wrote a check and put it in the mail.

They became more directly involved only because of a clerical error. Their contribution was supposed to be anonymous, so when they later found their names listed in the annual report in big, bold letters, they called to question the error. They immediately received a call from Weinberg inviting them to coffee. His first question was, "Who are you guys? We don't normally just get checks like that out of the blue." He then apologized profusely for the error and told them more about JFS. Barer left the discussion having volunteered to work on a committee, and his valuable participation soon led to his joining the board of directors.

Weinberg describes Joe Barer as a very bright man, keyed into changing technologies and new ways of conceptualizing the agency and its mission. His profession involves strategic planning and marketing. He thinks about what's happening now, where it is going to go, and what one needs to do now to be prepared for the future. Weinberg grew very close to Barer as an adviser and relied on his input. Barer was, though much younger than Weinberg, a mentor in this area of expertise. One of Barer's first perceptions was that most of the 300 heads attending the most recent annual meeting were grey. He told Weinberg, "I did not see anyone with my hair color, and that's bad. I'm willing to help you do something about it." Barer followed up with a marketing survey segmenting the various markets of JFS and outlining the messaging that would go to each one of those markets, primarily for fundraising purposes. He asked the question, "How do you fundraise from someone who's 70 years old, as opposed to how you fundraise from someone who's 35?"

His work resulted in a more modern and sophisticated approach to marketing in general. Given the limited marketing budget available, paid messaging (ads in the *JT News* marketing for the luncheon) is still fairly broad. However, Lisa Schultz Golden, the chief development officer, reports that JFS has started implementing some strategies to reach out to different constituencies. A series of cultivation events has been focused primarily on social groups, which are often based on age or generation. Several house parties have been given within the thirty-something crowd, and one board member has arranged gatherings of a young profession group. These events, often organized solely on Facebook, are more social, but a program director is always present to speak about at least one of the JFS services.

Another informational/cultivation effort has been a series of small private lunches with Weinberg. Other cultivation events are tailored to the crowd so, for example, a meeting of past board members who are very familiar with JFS will be focused differently from that with a group who have not previously been involved. The agency now uses social media, mostly Facebook and Twitter, to reach out to the younger generations. There is also a new partnership with Repair the World, a Jewish organization inspiring American Jews and their communities to give their time and effort to serve those in need and aiming to make service a defining part of American Jewish life. The goal of this effort is to reach more young folks through service projects, an exciting endeavor that will unfold throughout 2013 and 2014.

There was a strong feeling on the board that JFS could be doing much more to meet the tremendous need in the community. Those involved also recognized that the financial support was there.

Weinberg was aware that JFS was reaching a tipping point where it "was becoming the premier cause in the Jewish community" because of the work it was doing and the way it was telling its story. Teaming up to work together, Joe Barer and fellow board member Howard Behar, who came from the same background, were interested in developing specific, measurable goals and moving towards outcome-based management. Behar says, "We kept insisting that if the agency didn't know where it was going, no path would get it there, and successfully pushed for the development of a strategic plan." Without a plan, where JFS arrived might not be where it wanted to be.

Eric LeVine
(JFS photo collection.)

Eric LeVine, who joined the board in 2003 (president for 2012–2013), was one of several new board members, like Kathy Berman, who came from the technology world. The JFS board began to attract more people with experience in strategic thinking, many with the capacity to give larger gifts, and more people who had access to larger gifts. Others had influence in Olympia, which the agency needed because some of the programs were highly dependent on state money.

All these changes were seismic in scale and scope. They were far, far above even 10 years before. JFS was identifying and beginning to provide new programs and services in new geographic arenas, had an expanded board actively participating, had become increasingly successful in its fundraising activities, and even engaged in revenue-producing business ventures closely related to its mission.

It was also a time when there was a growing recognition and acknowledgement, locally as well as nationally, that although the Jewish community is distinct, it reflects the same issues as the broader community.

John Phillips, who took over as lay leader in 1999 , is a retired zoning and land-use lawyer who practiced in Seattle for 30-some

John Phillips
(JFS photo collection.)

years. He first became involved with JFS through his interest in the SAJD. Once having become more familiar with the work of the agency, Phillips was pleased to accept an invitation to serve on the board in 1992.*

Long-range planning and, as always, fundraising were issues during his board term. He also represented JFS during its successful effort in 1995 to purchase what is now the Jessie Danz Building.

During his term as president (1999–2001), in response to a JFGS study showing that a great part of the Jewish community was now located east of Lake Washington, JFS opened a new counseling office in Bellevue to better serve Eastside constituents.

One of the highlights of his board presidency was hosting the very successful, well-attended, and well-received Association of Jewish Family & Children's Agencies (AJFCA) national convention in Seattle in May 2000. Between 300 and 400 attendees participated in the various workshops. In addition to board members, dozens of community members volunteered to prepare for and help manage the convention, and Howard Schultz, founder and CEO of Starbucks, agreed to serve as the keynote speaker, sharing his involvement with Judaism with the assembled crowd.

Two endeavors were begun before that convention and continue more than a decade later. One is an ongoing effort to reach the 80 percent of the local area's Jewish population who are unaffiliated. The second is outreach to the large number of disabled individuals, Jewish and non-Jewish, who could benefit from the services of SAJD. More than 200 families and individuals now participate in SAJD programs.

---

* Following his board commitment, Phillips continues to participate as a member of the SAJD Foundation board, remaining interested and comitted to making sure it continues successfully.

Chapter 20

Immigration in the 21st Century

"No one feels safe, and people fled. In general, people have lived in refugee camps throughout Africa for more than 10 years."

—Margaret Hinson

M argaret Hinson was first introduced to JFS in 2007 when she applied to serve as an AmeriCorps VISTA (Volunteers in Service to America) volunteer to work with refugees. She had never heard of JFS and Googled it to find out what it was.

Raised as an "Army brat," stationed mostly at Fort Benning, Georgia, Fort Lewis, Washington, and in Germany, Hinson studied history and Spanish at the University of Washington. She moved to Southern California to work as a teacher for a time before deciding it was not the right direction for her career. She returned to the Northwest to live and work.

Hinson remembers her surprise at discovering during her interview with resettlement director Jeff Wendland that JFS resettles refugees who are not Jewish. (Jeanette Lozovsky had retired in 2006 after 18 years with the resettlement program.) Hinson was quickly hired as the first JFS VISTA volunteer and assigned to be the community resource coordinator for the Refugee & Immigrant Service Centers (RISC). She developed both a donations program and a volunteer program specifically for resettlement. During her VISTA year, the program experienced several staffing changes, and Hinson was called on to fill in. She had gained experience in many aspects of resettlement work by the time she joined the staff full-time as resettlement coordinator in September 2008 working with the then director of Refugee Services, Shane Rock. When Rock resigned in March 2012, Hinson took over his position.

Under Rock's guidance that first year, Hinson learned and grew as a person as she helped resettle 99 refugees. Almost half were either Russian speakers or Farsi-speaking religious minorities from Iraq: Baha'i, Zoroastrian, Jewish, and Christian—groups JFS has had significant experience resettling.

A new group landing that first year were Burmese. Although the numbers were small, Hinson remembers that experience as dramatic case management. Funding for resettlement is very limited, and there are specific services that need to be provided within a finite period, at which time the newly resettled immigrants are referred to other agencies that provide ongoing services. Unfortunately, those agencies were not prepared to serve the Burmese, and because there wasn't a Burmese community in the region, there was no Burmese-specific support agency.

There are dozens of ethnic minorities within what is now called Myanmar. Ethnic Burmese persecuted these groups because they had fought for their independence and maintained very distinct cultural differences, including their own languages. The large groups that came to the United States from Burma/Myanmar were the ethnic Karen, probably the largest Burmese ethnic minority, and the Chin, who were the next biggest group, and again each unique. In the old country, the Chin lived near trade routes exposing them to Westerners, other foreigners, and many missionaries. Burma was a British colony where English was the common language, so when the Chin arrived in the United States, they were usually able to speak some English. Even their alphabet is similar to the Latin alphabet. The Karen are from an area closer to Thailand and, for the most part, lived in the mountains and jungles and were more cut off from Western influences. Later, groups arrived in the United States from Burma (Myanmar) that had been even more isolated than the Karen.

There was a small group of Burmese in the Seattle area who had been political activists and came from Burma in the late 1980s and 1990s. They had 20 years of residence in the area, and helped resettle some of the newcomers. However, so many arrived that the JFS program found it necessary to go above and beyond what is required under the State Department contract for services. The Burmese arriving were from a very agricultural society, were experiencing a totally foreign culture, and needed help and education in every area.

To begin with, there simply were not enough interpreters to handle the influx of Karen, Chin, and others. In addition, some of the more isolated groups had never used transportation like a bus, and never used money. Adults and children had never received any Western medical care so they brought with them many untreated conditions and diseases. Across the country, resettlement agencies confronted these same issues, and there were as yet no best practices to guide caseworkers.

Hinson feels very connected to the first family she helped resettle. It was her third day on the job when she accompanied program director Jeff Wendland to the airport. For days, Hinson had prepared their apartment—gathering furniture and furnishings, carrying them up the stairs, and setting everything up. (Hinson spent quite a bit of her first year doing that kind of work.)

She remembers the family of six as they came out as a group. They were travelling with other families, also Burmese of Karen ethnicity. Families often arrive in groups since the organization that provides the tickets usually buys them in blocks. It was obvious they were refugees. They carried a big white paper bag with IOM (International Organization of Migration) printed on it. The IOM has a contract with the US government to arrange travel for refugees from other countries to the United States, helps the travelers navigate the airports and immigration, and sees them on their way to Seattle or whatever is their final destination. It was September, and Hinson remembers thinking their clothing and sandals seemed really light for Seattle's weather. Everyone was frightened and confused, which showed on their faces. The oldest of the four children was perhaps 14, and the youngest was five.

Rukiya, an interpreter who had been in the Seattle area for 20 years, had accompanied Wendland and Hinson to the airport, and she stepped up and welcomed them in their own language. She was crying.

The family was immediately taken to the affordable two-bedroom apartment in the Rainier Valley, close to Rainier Beach High School, and was helped with settling in. They had been in the refugee camp on the border of Thailand and Burma for five or six years, and once they were approved to emigrate, the process moved quickly. Most of the processing takes place in the camp so when they leave the camp they are en route to their new home with perhaps an overnight in Bangkok.

Rukiya had prepared two days of meals using foods familiar to the new arrivals. The entire group ate together in their apartment. Hinson describes their reaction to everything they were experiencing as being "a bit like deer in the headlights," in cultural shock from confronting so much unfamiliar to them in such a short time. The family was introduced to the apartment and oriented to how things functioned. It was the first time they had had indoor plumbing, and the toilet flushing and turning the shower on and off amazed them. Hinson remembers the youngest playing with the toilet flusher and the entire family being very impressed with this modern convenience. The oven was practically unfathomable, especially after 20 hours of travel. That first day was overwhelming.

Hinson worked with the family every day for the first four or five days. She took them to apply for cards at the Social Security Administration and to apply for benefits at the local welfare office. Refugee families are eligible for federal assistance and are mainstreamed into the federal government's Temporary Assistance to Needy Families (TANF) program. This federal welfare-to-work program offers food stamps, Medicaid, and a family cash allotment for up to 60 months. Single adults with no children have up to eight months of that same assistance.

The parents were assigned to a JFS job developer, and the children were enrolled in school. The parents began English classes and were helped to connect with other community members who had volunteered to help. The family owned just two small bags of lightweight clothing, so getting them clothes was addressed quickly. A little more funding came from a special employment program, along with donated items and gift cards. Hinson took the children to a nearby Payless shoe store for more appropriate shoes.

That first family of Hinson's was Muslim, which was unusual as most of the Karen are Christian. Having practiced Arabic from the Koran, the parents were somewhat literate and were able to find jobs quickly, especially considering that they spoke no English. They had the assistance of Toulue Cha, a JFS resettlement staff member who had come to Seattle as a young Hmong refugee from Southeast Asia and had developed relationships with Eastside hotels. Although he has since left the agency, people still talk about him with reverence because he did so much for those early Burmese refugees. Hinson says she would not have been able to support these clients during those first two years at JFS without him.

That family has done very well. The children went to school and by 2013, the two oldest children were in community college and hoping to transfer to a four-year college. The youngest one is Americanized, talks fast, and has no accent. The family had a great amount of support with everyone rooting for them, but they also worked hard and studied English. The parents rose very early every day and rode two or three buses each way, from Rainier Beach to their work in Redmond. They never missed a day and were exemplary employees and models for their community.

JFS is allocated refugees through Hebrew Immigrant Aid Society—HIAS, one of the nine national resettlement agencies that contracts with the US State Department. In addition to allocating refuges to its affiliates around the country, HIAS provides technical assistance on resettlement populations, services, and best practices. HIAS also advocates at the federal level for refugee resettlement. Another resource for resettlement is provided through the Center for Applied Linguistics (CAL). CAL contracts with the State Department to publish very thorough information pamphlets, called backgrounders, and works overseas and domestically to collect information on new refugee populations. Once there is a body of experience for a new group, the pamphlets are created as resources for anyone working with that ethnic population.

Another group JFS resettled was Iraqi refugees, some of the millions who fled to the neighboring countries of Syria, Jordan, Egypt, and Lebanon during the civil war/power struggle between the Sunni and the Shia. For several years, many had lived in camps or urban ghettos. Eventually, the US government recognized that there was a humanitarian concern and a special obligation to help, particularly those Iraqis who had worked with the United States in Iraq. They were uniquely expedited through the US refugee program, whereas the Burmese, the Bhutanese, and other groups spend anywhere from two to twenty years in the refugee camps. During 2012, the Iraqis were still at the height of their immigration process.

Another group arriving was Lhotshampa immigrants from Bhutan. They are ethnically Nepali, a group that migrated to the southern regions of Bhutan hundreds of years ago. They stayed separate from the Bhutanese population and were treated as second-class citizens, subject to much prejudice. In the early 20th century, there was a program to systematically push them out. It culminated in 1991 when it was declared that those who did not have a certificate of Bhutanese citizenship must leave the country. When the Bhutanese military knocked on doors of minority homes, people had to grab what they could and leave. It was another exodus as the refugees hiked to the Nepali border and built a camp.

The next group expected in Seattle was some of the 30,000 people from the Democratic Republic of the Congo accepted for immigration by the United States. Perhaps 15 Congolese were welcomed by RISC in 2012, and the program then shared its experience with the Washington State refugee coordinator because RISC was one of the only agencies in the area that had worked with this population. These refugees had experienced atrocious acts of war against them from war crimes and genocide.

The program has also assisted a few tribal and religiously oriented refugees from the Sudan.

Hinson found the Iraqis to be a particularly interesting group. Their first requests were often for Internet service and to set up their bank accounts. Most of them wanted to know how to look for jobs and how to maximize the résumés they had already created. They were mostly an educated group, urban, familiar with Western lifestyles, and many spoke some English.

The most difficult part of Hinson's job is to find housing. RISC clients will not receive subsidized or Section 8 housing for many years because the waiting lists are years long. RISC must find housing that is affordable, reasonable, safe, and near support services and bus lines. What a Burmese or Bhutanese family views as acceptable might not be the same for an Iraqi family. Although some people might not think it the best strategy, RISC staff makes every effort to accommodate the unique needs and attitudes of each group and to facilitate integration as soon as possible. If refugees don't feel safe or if they are not comfortable with where they live, their integration into the local community is going to be more difficult.

The initial Iraqi family Hinson helped resettle was a couple in their early fifties. The husband had worked for the US government in Iraq, and when security deteriorated and the United States started pulling troops out, he and his wife had to leave immediately. They fled to Egypt where they waited until they were able to come to the United States.

Hinson was called to the airport because the coordinator that had gone to meet them did not have room in her car for the 10 huge bags they brought. As she helped carry all those bags to the third-floor studio apartment, Hinson was dreading the couple's response to the dwelling. She knew the carpets were worn and there was little room in the small space. Hinson could tell immediately when she met them that they came from an affluent background and were well-educated. However, when they walked in, they were very gracious, understanding, and grateful that they had a bed with sheets on it. They thought the arrangement would be fine for the time being, were exhausted, and just wanted to go to sleep.

After a year or two, when things settled down a bit in Baghdad, the couple was able to sell some property in Iraq and bought a house in South King County. In the interim, they had participated in school programs and found jobs. They invited Hinson for dinner soon after they moved in to their new home, which is when she learned that the wife is an artist. The house is decorated beautifully with art everywhere. The husband, a well-educated man, earned an associate of arts degree in business administration and plans to complete his bachelor's degree as his business degrees from Iraq are not recognized in the United States.

Hinson met many of the young Iraqi men who started arriving about 2010. They were around her age, and she tried to imagine being brought to another country and knowing nobody. Most of them had university degrees, and many were engineers who had worked for the US military. Now they all had to start over. These men soon started sponsoring their friends. One was sponsored by an American soldier he had worked with, and he in turn sponsored his friend, and so on. Hinson describes them as outgoing, well-educated, and Westernized, having spent so much time with the American military. Many were able to get security jobs fairly easily.

Another group of Iraqis had engineering backgrounds and were involved in urban planning and rebuilding. Hinson found this group wanted to volunteer and help their people. These two groups of young men seemed to adapt, integrate, and normalize into the Seattle area quickly.

The next group of refugees to arrive were Somalis who have lived in horrible conditions in refugee camps for 10 years or more. The camps are overcrowded having been built for perhaps 10,000 people but accommodating 30,000 or more. The camps are also dangerous. The refugees fled their country because there has been no government, and it has been dominated and run by tribal warlords since the early 1990s and more recently by Islamist militant groups associated with Al Shabaab. These groups want to install Sharia law for everybody. No one feels safe, and people fled. These populations are often very challenging to work with because of their lack of opportunity to work and lack of experience with modern amenities and customs.

For several years, RISC operated a special program for refugee single moms with minor children. This is what started the wave of Somalis coming to RISC. There was no school system in the camps, and for the most part, these refugees were illiterate. Many had never held a pencil. RISC staff and volunteers found it necessary to offer information with a lot of repetition to help them adjust to the new land.

One positive difference, compared to refugees for whom there is not an existing cultural community when they arrive, was the established Somali community in the Seattle area, so it was easier in some ways to connect them. There are stores that stock the types of foods Somalis eat, and several different mosques and religious centers serve Somalis. Still, it was a struggle to help them get jobs. They usually were able to qualify only for low-paying service jobs, like hotel work in laundry or housekeeping.

Single people with no children are provided with eight months of support and assistance. Single moms are mainstreamed into the TANF program and have up to five years. However, a family of three—single mom with two children—receives only $478 a month, and that is supposed to cover everything, including rent, soap, toilet paper, and diapers, which is almost impossible. (Food Stamps are provided to help with grocery shopping.) RISC staff members encourage house sharing, and several single moms have found other members of their tribes and are living together sharing two-bedroom units. Sometimes other tribal relatives help subsidize what the moms cannot afford within their cash allowance.

Daycare is an additional problem if the moms hope to work and earn money. Staff strives to create a program where one mom can take care of several children, but if there are several different ethnic groups and tribal families involved, staff must be sensitive to historic conflicts. Learning about the Somali culture, as with most new groups, has been a challenge.

In general, the local Somali community is helpful, as long as the family tribe can be identified and local residents located. There seem to be dozens of different tribes, and RISC doesn't have the information about which tribe the family belongs to until the new family arrives. Fortunately, JFS now has Somali staff members who are able to talk to the new arrivals. The misinformation in the camps about what to say and not say to the interviewers makes the process more difficult. Hinson thinks the refugees are cautioned not to say too much and not to share that they know people who are already here, so it has been a common occurrence that clients arrive before it is discovered that they have a husband, brother, sister, or other relative in the area that knew they were arriving from Africa. If RISC had known to contact that person, not only would the family member's introduction period have been made much easier, but also some of the funds expended could have been saved. Sometimes the friend or family member in Seattle knows the new arrival is going to come and wants to find the caseworker but does not know which of the five resettlement agencies to approach.

The local Somali community is strong and takes care of their own, although RISC has had some families close to the brink of serious financial difficulties before someone stepped up to counsel or help them.

During 2012, Congolese families, single mothers, and many single men arrived. Most of them spoke French, and most learned English quickly. They wanted to work right away, and the community here is very small and was eager to integrate the new arrivals into it. They got jobs quickly with the help of a few people from the local community who were very active and helpful.

There was a group of brothers who had been waiting for processing in Togo. One had been on the Togo soccer team but was not allowed to stay there because Togo would not absorb the

Congolese. They had to apply for resettlement. In the meanwhile, they had been allowed to participate in the Togo community. These brothers did well and found jobs quickly.

Since Hinson started working with the RISC program, the numbers have doubled to resettling more than 200 refugees a year. The program is also attracting some innovative grants, like the Single Moms program. Only Seattle and Atlanta were awarded that program, which came through HIAS and was based on past performance.

RISC's newest big project is an effort to complete the requirements to become accredited by the Bureau of Immigration Appeals. As of this writing, the US Citizenship and Immigration Services has recommended that the bureau give RISC recognition and accreditation, which would enable RISC to help refugees complete immigration documents.

After one year, immigrants are eligible to have their status adjusted to permanent residency and receive a green card. This requires filling out a long, tedious document. Later, if they want to apply for entrance for relatives or a fiancé, travel outside the United States, or apply for US citizenship, there are many other documents that need to be completed and filed.

RISC expects to train several employees to do that work in order to have sufficient language capacity to work with the various clients. Once RISC's recognition and accreditation are finalized by the bureau, the program will work to expand the services beyond the refugees they resettle to serve other immigrants. The sliding-scale fees that will be charged will help supplement the RISC budget.

There are two RISC offices: one in the Crossroads area of Bellevue and one in South King County in Kent. The Eastside RISC office also provides space for two JFS counselors who make appointments at that site to serve better Eastside residents.

The RISC office is home to a thriving English as a Second Language (ESL) program. The ESL classes are focused on survival English and employment vocabulary. If a student plans to progress on to college credit courses, JFS's ESL classes are an important stepping stone.

JFS offers three mixed-level classes. In these classes, ESL instructors serve a wide range of students—from those who are preliterate and cannot write their name to advanced students, proficient in reading and writing. Curriculum for all levels is focused on employment, and instructors dedicate much classroom time to vocabulary found in the work place.

Hinson wants always to be in the forefront of innovative projects. The program is already recognized by partners and funders as having excellent case management for clients and for being innovative and creative. It is also known for its willingness to collaborate.

Hinson would like to create an experimental ESL intensive or immersion program that operates for perhaps six hours a day instead of the current two hours. She feels clients need more time to spend on English when they first arrive. The staffing is available, but the funding is an issue. The state ESL coordinator is searching for funding for a program that would be operated in Seattle or on the Eastside. (Volunteers living near or willing to travel to Kent are hard to find.)

Because funding for the Single Mom program is ending, RISC is also searching for support to continue that program.

RISC staff works closely with the city of Kent to build a welcoming community for clients. Kent has had a large wave of immigration in the last five years and has been welcoming and supportive. It is important that long-time residents feel the positive contribution that diversity can bring to their community.

Hinson marvels at how JFS has been able to open so many minds as it has worked to resettle Muslims. She knows there are now many Muslim clients who have an entirely different attitude about the West and about Jews. She knows why, at a time when there are few Jewish refugees, JFS is resettling the diverse non-Jewish populations that are struggling to survive. It can be summed up, quite simply, as she is reminded of Ken Weinberg's conviction that it is part of the Jewish narrative to welcome the stranger. Who, besides the Jews, knows so well the struggles of refugees and what it means to be a stranger in a strange land?

The list of ethnicities and country origins from which Margaret Hinson and the RISC office have resettled is long and includes:

Belarus

Bhutanese (ethnic Nepalese)

Burmese (ethnic groups like Karen, Chin, Karreni, Mon, and Shan)

Congolese from the Democratic Republic of Congo

Eritrean

Ethiopian

Iraqi and Iraqi Kurds (both Shia and Sunni)

Iranian (mostly religious minorities, like Baha'i, Zoroastrian, Christian, and Jews, and some political Muslim refugees)

Moldova

Russia

Rwandan

Somali

Sudanese

Ukraine

Vietnamese

Chapter 21

2006 - 2012: A Plan for the Future

Sandy Melzer arrived in Seattle in 1989 to run the Pediatrics Department at Swedish Hospital. He had never heard of Jewish Family Service but was recruited to the JFS board in 1996 by his friend Janet Boguch. Because he was familiar with distributed models of service and the reimbursement schemes in the health care industry, he was able to help the agency as services were expanding east of Lake Washington. He was also able to provide important information during the discussions about additional mental-health and homecare services.

When he first joined the board, JFS was transitioning from Russian resettlement to assisting other groups. The agency was also increasing both its geographic profile and the scope and range of the services offered. Melzer found himself deeply engaged in the creation of the homecare program where he contributed his expertise, time, and energy for more than five years.

The group developing the homecare program came to understand a great deal about the field. They would be competing with many other homecare services, including eventually the Summit/Kline Galland program. For a while, residents and participants of the Caroline Kline Galland Home and the Summit programs were a very strong source of new clients until the Kline

Galland organization implemented its own new homecare program. Over time, it became apparent HomeCare Associates was not going to become a significant net revenue contributor for JFS for the first several years, primarily because the program was assisting many people who were unable to pay the full cost of care. However, after a few years, the program was providing more than 80,000 hours of care and was important to the community and highly regarded. The breakeven point was considered to be just under 90,000 hours of care, and by the time it reached the provision of 95,000 hours of care, it was expected to be generating positive net revenue.

Sandy Melzer
(JFS photo collection.)

Melzer participated in developing the 2006 Strategic Plan, which resulted in, among other things , the expansion of the senior services program. He says, "There were some really powerful things about that plan that energized people to think about what we could do." He was also very involved in planning for the new building.

Melzer served as board president during 2006 and 2007. He was strongly supportive of the proposed changes to the SAJD program that resulted in the move from providing group homes for clients with developmental disabilities, mental illness, or chronic brain damage to more independent living environments with JFS support.

Laura Stusser-McNeil followed Melzer into the president's chair in 2007. Stusser-McNeil is the fifth generation of her family to be involved in JFS. Her great-great-grandmother, Mrs. Jacob (Mina) Berkman was one of the original members of the Ladies' Hebrew Benevolent Society in 1892. When Stusser-McNeil was invited to serve on the board in 1997, she thought it was an organization she could become deeply involved in, and it felt meaningful. The board was then working on merging NAIL and SAJD into one program, and soon Donna Benaroya was kicking off an endowment campaign.

Laura Stusser-McNeil
(JFS photo collection.)

Stusser-McNeil was very pleased to partner with Judy Neuman to co-chair the first and very successful luncheon fundraiser. She also enjoyed her time working on the board's Development Committee and later the Governance Committee. Making board meetings worthwhile and engaging became one of the themes of her 2007 to 2009 presidency.

Implementation of the strategic plan occurred during Stusser-McNeil's presidency. Funds had been committed for the plan, but pledges would be paid over a period of several years. This delay in receipt of some funds made it clear in hindsight that the planning process always involves a fine balance between resources and resourcefulness and it takes tremendous effort to sustain planned changes and program expansion.

Between 2004 and 2008, JFS experienced significant turnover in the chief financial officer position, with four individuals serving during this period of change, expansion, and planning for a significant capital project. The agency experienced some inconsistencies and inefficiencies in accounting practices over this four-year period. In June of 2008, Marie North was selected from Leora Consulting Group, LLC as interim CFO. Six month later, she was offered and accepted the full-time position of director of finance.

With the assistance of the financial experts from Leora, JFS began to develop multi-year financial projection tools to evaluate the best strategy to obtain financing to fund the new building project. They also examined ways to provide stability and sustainability over the long-term for the agency's operations, which had grown both organically and through the implementation of the programmatic objectives of the strategic planning process. As part of the initial assessment, it was determined that it was not yet the right time for the agency to begin the capital expansion.

Around this same time, the nation's financial markets suffered the largest correction that had been experienced in decades. (The National Bureau of Economic Research, or NBER, dates the beginning of the recession as December 2007.) To weather the catastrophe, JFS made a variety of adjustments, starting with prioritizing spending and reducing costs wherever possible without significantly impacting services to clients. By 2009, out-of-state travel was limited, the agency's retirement contribution had been lowered from 5 percent to 4 percent, and hourly staff members were asked to take one unpaid furlough day a month during each of the last five months of the year. Salaried employees experienced a 5-percent, temporary pay reduction during those five months and were encouraged to take one unpaid day off during each of those months. By putting these changes into operation, JFS came through this Great Recession rather well, compared to other area social-service agencies. No programs were cut, and although some staff vacancies were left unfilled, no staff was laid off.

In addition, many donors asked to revise their original pledge schedules, which impacted the timetable for beginning the capital expansion.

Once the agency was ready to proceed with the new building project, a financing task force of board members, staff, and consultants was formed to competitively bid for the financing. The complicated transaction involved obtaining tax-exempt debt and a nuanced bond issuance with very favorable rates. This was available only because the agency was able to meet specific requirements for which a purely religious non-profit would not be eligible. Under the umbrella of the Washington State Health Care Authority, JFS qualified for financing for health care organizations because of the services provided through its HomeCare Associates and Seattle Association for Jewish Disabled programs. In the end, the agency was able to obtain this financing for a capital project at a time when very few entities, let alone non-profit entities, were able to obtain bank financing. The success of the process can be attributed to the commitment of the board and committee leadership, as well as to thoughtful financial planning and the generous support from the JFS Seattle community. Without the commitment from donors, the agency would not have been able to successfully complete this significant capital project.

In 2012, with reduced program funding from the Jewish Federation of Greater Seattle, JFS was able to compensate because it had built provisions into its budgeting process for just such an eventuality. The funds come from unrestricted annual contributions that are received above the budgeted amount. The Federation allocations, which previously had been a lump sum that the agency could spend in the areas of greatest need, more recently have been program specific.

When United Way stopped funding the Refugee & Immigrant Service Centers in 2011, JFS also had to use unrestricted contributions to make up the difference.

⌒∞⌒

One of the issues Claudia Berman dealt with when the new building was completed was organizing the use of the parking facilities.

The new building was built on the former surface parking lot adjacent to the Jessie Danz Building. Forty-six parking spots had been created between the new garage and the lot across the street, and the city wanted assurance that the number of additional cars trying to park on the street was not going to burden the neighborhood. JFS was required to create a robust codified covenant concerning its transportation plan in order to receive building permits. After allocating eight spaces for guests and a few for the food bank van, loading, handicap permit spaces, and other requirements, there were only 24 spaces available for staff members.

Three stalls were reserved for executive staff, each of whom pays $50 a month for his or her spot. Assignments for the remaining stalls were decided within each program by staff members talking to and negotiating with each other to decide how the spaces allocated to their program would be assigned.

Each of the 66 staff members located at the Capitol Hill office at the time was given a stored-value smart card for public-transport fares in the Puget Sound region, called an ORCA (One Regional Card for All) card. Commuting by bicycle was encouraged by the addition of a second shower and special bike racks.

For Claudia Berman, keeping the building project on budget while maintaining program focus was challenging, as was dealing with the various constituencies, each with strong feelings about what should happen.

The 2003 combined budget for JFS and SAJD was $4,650,000. By 2012, it had expanded to $8,653,000.

⌘

Howard Behar, former president of Starbucks Coffee Company, joined the board in 2000 with a strong personal interest in services to the aged in general. He took it upon himself to lead a strategic planning process with director of Senior Services and Disabilities Don Armstrong for the Senior Services program. The process eventually led to the home health care program, HomeCare Associates, which it was hoped would lead to additional revenue in a way that would both be legitimate for a non-profit and true to the mission of JFS. This limited strategic planning process around aging adults spun off from the agency-wide strategic planning process.

At one of the annual board retreats, the staff presented a new way of talking about the services of JFS, calling the interconnections between services "wrap-around care." The new terminology helped everyone recognize and appreciate that each program supports every other program. A client coming to Project DVORA might also need the food bank, often needs to work with a counselor, might want a Big Pal for her son, and can benefit from the offerings of the Single Parent Family efforts and Family Life Education.

During the recession that began in late 2007, JFS further addressed the needs of the steadily increasing number of working poor and the unemployed. More and more people with jobs came to the food bank, and every program was scrambling under far greater numbers of requests for services. An additional advocate was added to DVORA so phone calls could be responded to quickly, instead of clients in dangerous situations having to wait.

When the Limited English Pathways and the RISC program were in danger of having their Washington State funding reduced, the board led a successful effort to advocate for the program with legislators in Olympia.

One of the highlights of Laura Stusser-McNeil's presidency was the award of federal stimulus funds to remodel the food bank. To lobby effectively for those funds, a group of supporters that included staff, donors, and board members made many trips to Olympia to work with every legislator they could reach. In order to qualify for part of President Obama's stimulus plan money, a shovel-ready project was required, and JFS had a plan in hand to enlarge, enhance, and remodel the food bank so it could more adequately serve its four heavily populated zip codes.

Kathy and Steve Berman also stepped forward to provide funding for the project. The remodeled space allows a new "consumer choice" model of service, allowing clients to shop for what they want with far greater dignity.

Dianne Loeb followed Stusser-McNeil as president of JFS in 2009. She originally became involved with JFS because of her skill in strategic planning. She became part of a strategic planning effort to understand how other agencies defined their target markets. The group confirmed that in many areas JFS was similar to other agencies, but that there were a few ways in which JFS was unique. For example, the decades of work in refugee resettlement and the magnitude of the effort required to resettle Jews, especially from eastern Europe and Russia, was distinctive. Loeb's own connection with immigration services included relatives who were resettled with the help of JFS. In addition, when Loeb

Dianne Loeb
(JFS photo collection.)

and her family had some extra furniture to donate, she was able to contact a newly resettled immigrant family directly. Over time, the then 12-year-old daughter of the Russian family became good friends with Loeb's much-younger daughters. (That young girl is now a practicing physician.)

After she met Ken Weinberg, Loeb realized there were many parts of JFS she and her family could become involved with, including working in the food bank together.

As Loeb became more familiar with the agency, she was impressed that JFS did strategic planning continuously. The board and staff knew it was planning for opportunities—a way of looking into the future and seeing what service was needed, how to provide for it, and where the stumbling blocks might be. Other organizations often move toward strategic planning because of some sort of crisis. With continuous planning, even with the number of programs that have been added over the years, JFS has stayed true to its mission of helping the community in times of need.

The first strategic planning effort Loeb was involved in was examining the question of how JFS could increase fundraising appropriately. Board and staff members knew that government subsidies were not always going to be available, and a large part of the budget was tied to city, county, state, and federal resources. Nor was JFGS going to be able to maintain even its recent percentage of support, which had fallen over the years from 30 percent to 9 percent or less of the agency's annual operations as the JFS budget had doubled and then quadrupled. The question became whether JFS would be able to raise the funds necessary to support its programs from donors and grant resources if the need arose. The answer was yes, provided reserves were built up and preserved, and an appropriate development program was put in place.

Loeb remembers the situation that evolved as "an interesting sea change for the community." When JFS intimated that down the road JFGS's ability to proportionately support programs would diminish, some community members complained. They did not complain about JFS specifically, but in general, the idea was that if the agencies had not created their own development departments, the community could have kept fundraising through JFGS as its principal channel for giving. Loeb thinks it's a tough sell and not the whole issue. Others in the community understood that many donors wanted more control over where their money went. The percent of contributions taken off the top for overhead was also an issue.

JFS was one of the first JFGS agencies in the Seattle area to hire development staff. Irv Goldberg had not only been ahead of the times but also been on the right track when he hired the first development specialist in the early 1980s. Soon after Ken Weinberg was appointed executive director, he hired a development director and established a Development Department at JFS, and other agencies soon followed suit. Nationally, JFS Seattle was a leader as it moved in this direction because, at the time, very few JFS agencies had started creating their own development departments. (See chapter 13, "1974-1984: Evolution and Expansion.")

Loeb (and a great many other people) was astounded by the number of partnerships JFS has developed. This cooperation helps both to limit duplication of services and to enhance the provision of services. Different organizations are able to cooperate to participate in the areas of their greater strengths with more effectiveness and efficiency. (See appendix five, "Partners and Coalitions 2012.")

When Loeb first joined the board, JFS had recently moved into the Jessie Danz Building on 16th and Pine. Very soon, there was a realization the agency had to plan for the future and for the time when the Danz Building would also be too small for the steadily growing organization. As success bred success, it was barely a decade before this prediction became a reality.

Planning for the future now also meant looking at larger geographic areas of responsibility as more and more constituents moved to the Eastside, to the south and north suburbs, and into the South King County cities.

The JFS board continued discussions about programs for older adults who had transitioned away from their previous occupations and avocations, as children grew and left home, and as retirement became a reality. These older adults wanted to keep informed about issues, participate in social and educational activities, and remain vibrantly connected to the community. They began to involve themselves in planning, implementing, and attending Endless Opportunity programs. The constant question for those involved in planning for the future of JFS was, "How do we continue to meet the needs of our senior population in a dignified manner as those needs change over time?"

Loeb says she hit a sweet spot during her presidency. Her predecessor, Laura Stusser-McNeil, had already helped the board to hash out all the pros and cons concerning the building, and a large portion of the money had already been raised, both for the building and for the incremental growth of programs. Loeb's biggest responsibility was creating a committee to work through the nuances of providing funding for construction, finally agreeing that it made the most sense to borrow the money against the pledges that had already been committed. She found it was not difficult for the banks to react favorably to the JFS request for proposal. Loeb gives an enormous amount of credit to Lee Rockoff for shepherding the agency through the process. Gerry Goldman was also part of the Executive Committee and worked diligently with Rockoff and Marie North, then the outside consultant, to figure out the financial package.

Just as Loeb's term as president was ending in 2011, it was discovered the Jessie Danz Building needed some renovations. It is a quality building, which was built so additional floors could be added, but the building was aging, the roof and the south wall around the windows were failing, and part of the front wall's surface needed attention. Repairs and renovations were addressed and completed promptly.

The Jessie Danz Building was ideal for counseling and confidentiality, containing many private rooms and compartmentalized in a way that facilitates privacy. There are separate waiting areas for general visitors and for counseling clients, who are able to feel secure that seeking counseling with their spouse or child will not be revealed to the rest of the community. Conversations in offices remained unheard in the hallway or next door. During the renovation process, privacy was enhanced with insulation even added to electrical sockets between the rooms and buffering placed in the walls. A completely separate entrance from the side street already served the Polack Food Bank. The elevator shaft connecting the two buildings provided accessibility to anyone unable to use stairs.

Board member Will Daniels (a great-grandson of Jessie Danz) was in charge of overseeing both the construction of the new building that would be constructed on the existing parking lot, and the Jessie Danz Building renovations.

Will Daniels
(JFS photo collection.)

Loeb is passionate about the whole concept of working in teams to get things done. She says she has never seen a place where the staff, board, and volunteers work so well together. "There is bound to be tension here and there, but for the most part, because the place is so important to so many people, it's really easy at the end of the day to say we accomplished it and we accomplished it together."

༄

The board of JFS, determining that younger people were needed to help keep the agency current, created a Generation X Committee. Emily Alhadeff first became a member of that committee and then became a member of the board of directors in 2005.

Alhadeff remembered coming to JFS as a child when her family came in for family counseling. Then in 1988, her father, Dennis Warshal, served on the board, and she was aware that JFS was where her parents directed most of their philanthropy.

Alhadeff's first paying job was at JFS in the Senior Services program. After college, at a house party given by Renee Herst,

Alhadeff heard Ken Weinberg speak— just the spark she needed to re-engage. The Gen X Committee explored ways to get that generation involved with JFS, forward thinking that Alhadeff admired. The committee's task was to help get JFS on the radar of their friends and associates by contacting and encouraging people to come to what usually turned out to be very successful events. At one, David Stillman, co-author of *When Generations Collide*, talked about his book, which targeted the Generation X audience.

Emily Alhadeff
(JFS photo collection.)

As Alhadeff first participated as a member in 2005, the board was starting to work on the strategic plan, which in turn led to the Family Matters fundraising campaign and the construction of the new building.

While working on the various issues the agency was dealing with when she accepted the presidency in 2011, Alhadeff came to understand how important it is that JFS sustain delivery of services while retaining sufficient funds to insure the future. She appreciates how skilled, loyal, and passionate the staff are about the mission and recognizes that those qualities are present in everything that is done, from the people who answer the phone or help set up for a meeting to the clinical staff who deliver counseling services. She also recognizes how the influence of Ken Weinberg as a phenomenal leader trickled down to all.

Alhadeff thinks that being able to run a successful capital campaign through an economic downturn signifies the strength of JFS in the community and the community's commitment to the spirit of the ladies of 1892. She and others reflect on how the agency has become more and more an organization that belongs to the community. People say, "This is my organization. I don't use its services, and I hope I never have to, but it is always here for me and for my family."

Alhadeff says JFS fundraising is genuine and the dollars are translated into action in very effective, real ways that speak to everyone. She also says fundraising is heartfelt, not about raising money but about serving people in need. She has had the pleasure of seeing JFS reach higher and higher levels of success in generating support from the community.

The next step, now that the new building is in full operation, is to focus on sustaining the programs. In a different vein, Alhadeff would like to help integrate the large Russian Jewish population more fully into the broader Jewish community. She knows there are many young, talented professionals who are the second and even third generation of the original Russian immigrant families of the 1970s and '80s who are not yet part of the Jewish community. She is also concerned about helping JFS be ready to address the many critical issues of the aging baby boomers in need of senior services.

Chapter 22

Volunteers: The Heart and Soul of JFS

"Wherever there are people in need, you go. You don't go there to help people who are Jewish. You go there to help people because you are Jewish."
—Nancy Pelosi, To the American Jewish
Joint Distribution Committee, December 2013

The history of JFS is a history of volunteerism. Founded by Esther Levy, her daughter Lizzie Cooper, and their friends, the Ladies' Hebrew Benevolent Society relied entirely on volunteers to accomplish every task for the first 25 years of its existence. The women who served on the board and who joined as members devoted uncounted hours walking up and down the hills of Seattle, baskets over their arms visiting the needy. They delivered food and clothing, arranged for medical assistance, and gave a great deal of advice and a little money to immigrants from Eastern Europe, Russia, Greece, the Island of Rhodes, the Ottoman Empire, Turkey, and many other countries. The member volunteers held fundraising events, attended innumerable meetings, kept the minutes, attended to all necessary correspondence, donated, collected or purchased food, clothing, household items, milk, coal, and dozens of other items to provide for the needs of their clients. For many of these volunteers, their work for LHBS became the equivalent of full-time jobs. It wasn't until 1917 that Florine Coblentz became the first paid clerical staff member, working from the home of the board president.

At first, the work was guided by the president. Then, as committees were formed to oversee various functions and activities, the chairperson of each committee directed those volunteers involved in the work of the committee. Later the secretary and then the director of the agency organized the work of the volunteers. Eventually the director of the Emergency Services program added the task of coordinating volunteers to her growing list of responsibiliteis.

In October 2013, more than 120 years after the founding of the organization, Will Berkovitz, the new chief executive officer of Jewish Family Service expressed the idea that all those who work at JFS as either a volunteer or as a staff member are "making a statement about what our community is and what it can be." He commented that, for the men and women who are volunteers or staff members, their work is a calling, "an expression of their highest selves, what they are meant to be doing in the world." Both those who volunteer and those who choose to work for pay in the non-profit world are expressing their values through their efforts on behalf of others.

For several years, Carol Mullin, the director of Emergency Services, was also the volunteer coordinator. Later, Pam Waechter took over, followed by Salie Rossen who generously spent her time volunteering in the same role.

Salie Rossen was born in Indiana and attended Indiana University. Her parents had both immigrated from Lithuania. A strong Zionist (the national movement for the return of the Jewish people to their homeland and the resumption of Jewish sovereignty in the land of Israel), Rossen lived and worked in Israel several times. One of her jobs was to create a Department of Social Work at Shaare Zedek Hospital in Jerusalem, one of the most Orthodox Jewish hospitals in the world.

In those days there were often explosions in the Jerusalem market or elsewhere in town, especially on Friday afternoons while people were getting ready for Shabbat. Because the hospital was close to the market, the victims would be brought to Shaare Zedek, and crowds of people would come calling out, "My mother was in the market ..." or "My daughter ...". It was obvious that a program of psychological first aid was needed not only for the victims but also for community members that thronged to the hospital. Rossen created that program and later led an effort for the American Hospital Association to put the same program into US hospitals. As AHA national director of hospital social work directors, Rossen was pleased to be able to grow the program to include more than 1,000 hospitals.

After 10 years in Chicago, Rossen moved to Seattle where she created a program to provide ethics and values training for the Catholic hospital system. She also developed a consulting practice. Then in 1989, Cliff Warner hired Rossen to fill a part-time position leading the Jewish Family Life Education program for JFS, taking over from Beth Cordova. Rossen had not been familiar with JFS before she saw the advertisement for the JFLE position.

Rossen also continued her consulting practice, and when she accepted a major contract with the state of Washington, she had to give up the JFS position. However, after her marriage in 1992, she returned to JFS as a volunteer, and Ken Weinberg asked her to create a formal volunteer program.

Rossen began by asking each program director what volunteer positions they needed and then matched volunteers to those positions. Each program director created his or her own orientation program to familiarize volunteers with the specific department. Over time, the volunteer program grew to the point where it needed a paid staff director, so Rossen stepped down, and Pam Waechter became the first paid director of volunteers. (Rossen later became a member of the board of directors and continued to volunteer at JFS for many years.)

Jane Deer came to JFS in 1998, first as coordinator and then as director of Volunteer Services. Her father's Hungarian Jewish family came to the United States from Budapest, Hungary. Her mother's family, from Turkey and Russia, settled in Harlem, where many of the

Sephardic Jews lived. Born in the Bronx, Deer remembers growing up with a mix of Ashkenazi and Sephardic foods and traditions.

The family later moved to Connecticut where there was a small community of Jews, which provided Jane an opportunity for a leadership role in the regional B'nai B'rith Girls organization. She attended Antioch College in Ohio, concentrating on education and counseling and later earned a master's degree in clinical counseling in California.

Deer worked in educational research in California for 14 years and then as a parent education coordinator in the Oakland public schools for two years. When in 1998 her husband wanted to return to Seattle where he had lived in the 1960s and where Deer's two daughters were already living, they left California for the Northwest.

After the move, Deer was thinking about working with volunteers, an area she had enjoyed in her own volunteer life and where she had taken leadership roles in both the Jewish community and the broader community, when she saw a JFS advertisement for a half-time volunteer coordinator. Deer says she "felt as though something led me. I didn't interview or apply for or look for any other job." *Beshert* again.

When she took over her new role, she found a set of files labeled according to various volunteer rolls: Friendly Visitor, Telephone Reassurance, refugee resettlement, office, food bank, mailing lists, vocational, Big Pals, special projects, etc. In previous years, Carol Mullin, Salie Rossen, and Pam Waechter had each been involved in coordinating volunteers, and Rossen had written to other JFS agencies to get information and copies of forms they used, including an interest form and a volunteer application form, and she had developed position descriptions.

Deer soon enrolled in a United Way volunteer management training and spent time reading books on the subject to learn more about ways to organize her department and about what she could do as an executive to create success in her volunteer program. She interviewed the JFS management staff and program directors and began attending the JFS directors' meetings. She also became a board member of the local chapter of DOVIA (Directors of Volunteers in

Agencies). As she got to know other volunteer managers, she was able to visit their agencies in order to look at their files, databases, structures, and forms.

She quickly discovered that people in those other organizations did not know anything about JFS, and she had to explain that it was a social service agency, much like Catholic Community Services, and describe some of the services JFS was providing.

As she attended various conferences, Deer found an emerging sense of professionalism among volunteer managers. Over time, she was able to develop and elevate the program at JFS until the position warranted a full-time director, as well as additional staff assistance.

While working to develop the program, Deer was always interested in and aware of risk management—the assessment and planning for safety for clients, staff, and volunteers. Today things are very different than when the agency was founded. Laws and guidelines and a Washington State code regulate what volunteers are allowed to do, including guidelines for teenaged volunteers. Other risk management guidelines concern what kinds of background checks volunteers have to undergo.

Risk management leads to a significant amount of record keeping. All volunteers must be treated the same, with background checks for each category of volunteer task. People who are working in the office would have a different kind of background check than people who are visiting vulnerable clients. This would include Big Pals, who work with vulnerable children, as well as those who want to volunteer with adults with disabilities, immigrants who don't speak English, or seniors.

When she first took over as volunteer coordinator, Deer was working with approximately 200 volunteers. In 2012, the list included more than 1,500 individual volunteers. Deer started entering each volunteer into a computer program called Volunteer Works, organizing folks into categories according to the types of work they wanted to do. For example, she might have a request for a volunteer who can drive in order to make a delivery and, with the database information, is always able to find the appropriate individual. Later the information was added to the current general JFS database (Raisers Edge) so that agency volunteers would get all the same mailings as the donors and other supporters in a timely fashion.

Deer worked to educate program directors about volunteer policies and helped them create meaningful roles for volunteers. She discovered that some of the staff were resistant to using volunteers because they had a feeling that managing volunteers was too much work. Some also felt and that it was hard to rely on volunteers because they sometimes leave on vacation or have a sick child just when there is an important project to accomplish.

Deer was the representative who had to say, "A volunteer is only a difference in pay day." She affirmed that JFS volunteers are just as committed to the agency as the staff people who work there. "They can be just as professional, devoted, smart, reliable, skilled, and creative, and you have to integrate them into your program so when they are working with you they feel valued and recognized."

She spent time with each department to learn how they were using volunteers and to help them determine other tasks volunteers could assist with or take on. She established a set of procedures about who does what and when: who contacts the volunteers and within what time period, how volunteers' hours are tracked, and contact expectations, especially for those volunteers working off-site, like Friendly Visitors. Deer helped the programs' staff understand that volunteers need to be imbedded into the organization and that they care about what is happening within the department in which they are volunteering. The department contact needs to inquire about more than the details of their hours and the clients they are working with. They also need to ask how the volunteer is feeling about the work, what problems they might be encountering, and other issues, including any vacation plans they may be considering—and always asking, "Is there anything else I need to know about?" It works well, when possible, to have one staff person in a department who is in charge of matching the volunteers with specific tasks or clients.

Currently, JFS regularly relies on volunteers, including retired or semi-retired volunteers, college-age service learning students, interns from various social work programs, interns from undergraduate programs and VISTAS, as well as on families with children, community groups, etc. The VISTA volunteers are very helpful in recruiting other volunteers, which is one of their core assignments. One VISTA task for the RISC resettlement program is to go into the various ethnic communities to recruit individuals to help new arrivals from those specific communities.

Deer describes her role as staying in the community eye, being visible, meeting volunteers, and talking to everybody. She helps to decide what the best match might be and then helps find, recruit, and place the volunteer. She tracks each volunteer and makes sure he or she is acknowledged regularly. She notes that the Annual Volunteer Award provides a wonderful opportunity to highlight a particular part of the volunteer program.

The Big Pals program usually works with 14 to 16 volunteers, sometimes reaching as many as 20. Most of the requests come from mothers with sons who need a male role model and companion, but there are also requests from mothers looking for a supportive adult for their daughters or from lesbian couples who want a male role model for their children. None of the agencies, including JFS, match opposite gender.

Deer describes the volunteers as the jewels, many of whom made a commitment and stayed with it for years. She tries to have a creative, flexible mind as she works to find the right opportunity for each volunteer. For example, the children who help create the holiday baskets love the project because it is a task

Holiday gift basket
(JFS photo collection.)

they can relate to. As part of the basket-making events, children also make cards to send to senior clients. Many of those seniors appreciate the cards and write JFS to let them know how they enjoy receiving them and say, "I put those cards up on my refrigerator."

One volunteer is a man who lives in Federal Way and whose family has been involved in the Jewish community for many years. Deer introduced him to Shaarei Tikvah (Gates of Hope), a JFS program for people of all abilities, and he has now volunteered with Shaarei Tikvah for several years and participates in every one of those events. During the year, he keeps JFS in mind and when he spots various Judaica items, perhaps napkins or tablecloths, he purchases those items at his own expense for use during Shaarei Tikvah events.

Deer explains that she provides the key that opens the door, but the volunteers have to step through and actually do the volunteering. Michel Brotman, who had been on the board, is a great example. He decided he wanted to do something more hands-on and started making monthly home deliveries from the JFS food bank. He and his wife, Valerie, continued to do that for several years. Being able to help people personally in that way was something that really spoke to him. However, it's important to keep in mind the whole process—somebody has to do all the background work of sorting the food, boxing it, and shelving it, as well as making the delivery. Each piece is important. While many people want to see the clients that are receiving the food, most of the work and the preparation leading up to the delivery happens behind the scenes.

The largest number of volunteers in any single program during 2012 were the 600 volunteers working with Emergency Services. Second were the 400 who worked with Volunteer Services in other capacities, including doing office work, organizing volunteer events, making baskets, collecting food for those baskets, delivering items to people, or performing various other tasks.

JFS can always use more volunteers in many programs. There have never been enough volunteers who want to visit people with disabilities, so the agency uses interns and college students to make some of those visits. These young people are open-minded, wanting to learn, and often planning to work in human services or social work. Working with adults with disabilities is excellent experience for them. Unfortunately, this type of work makes many people uncomfortable so the opportunities often go unfilled. However, many are willing to participate in the Shaarei Tikvah events. It is also a struggle to find enough volunteers to help with various Family Life Education events, like the Single Parent Summer Retreat. There is competition between agencies for volunteers, and JFS is just one opportunity. High school students can volunteer at their schools to earn the community service hours required for graduation, people can volunteer through their congregation, and many serve on various boards and committees throughout the Jewish and greater communities.

Deer tries to be as flexible as possible and creates many different opportunities for a variety of demographics. For example, at the annual Food Sort (a Jewish Community wide food collection event to stock the food bank) some tasks are appropriate for the older Endless Opportunities participants, and for others who want to be able to sit, such as helping at the registration table or sitting down while folding up all the bags that came in full of food. In the food sorting, work includes more than *schlepping* boxes of food back and forth.

The biggest unmet need is for people to visit seniors. Most of the calls are from people who want to help in the Polack Food Bank or with English as a Second Language (ESL), tutoring. People fear that visiting a senior might be depressing, or they say they have their own parents to care for. When someone calls to volunteer for ESL, Deer might suggest the person choose to visit on an ongoing basis with a senior who might be a Holocaust survivor who is sparkling and happy to have survived. There are many very lovely, if lonely or isolated, seniors.

When a senior dies, it is not unusual for the volunteer visitor to pull back and take a break. These volunteers often become quite close to their senior friend, and the loss reminds them of their own mortality and the loss of their own parents and grandparents. People can experience a deep sadness in these losses. Fortunately, many of these volunteers eventually return for a new assignment.

Friendly Visitors have also wanted to stay with their seniors when they move to the Caroline Kline Galland Home. Unfortunately, sometimes when the senior moves, it's too hard for the Friendly Visitor to get there because of its location in Seward Park.

Another area of volunteer openings that goes unfilled is assisting refugees living in the Kent area, partially because South King County is viewed as too far away from where most of the volunteers live. More family mentors are always needed for many newly arrived refugees.

Each Friendly Visitor sets up his or her own schedule with input from Deer. After a long relationship, some see the connection with the client as friends, but risk and liability issues still remain because JFS facilitated the relationship. It's important that the volunteer realize that while he or she is a friend, he or she is also a person who is not supposed to take on a problem; instead, the Friendly Visitor represents the agency and the volunteer's responsibility is to report to the caseworker. As perhaps the only person that has regular contact with the individual, the volunteer needs to keep Deer and/or the case manager in the loop and report concerns, for instance if the client is not doing well, seems confused or otherwise diminished. This is also true with other volunteer participation that continues over time, whether in a Big Pals program or as an office volunteer who might have regular phone contact with clients. However, for participants of the Big Pal program the relationship between the participants is often closer and more personal.

One Big Pal started meeting with his Little Pal when the child was seven. That child is now almost 18, taller than his Big Pal, and aging out of the program. It is not unusual for Big Pals to stay all the way through until their Little Pal is age 18 and then continue as a family friend. The Big Pals will write to their Little Pals at college, send emails and birthday cards, gifts for birthdays, Chanukah, and other occasions, and share holidays. They attend the weddings of their former Little Pals and their sons' brises and continue over the years with their relationship. In most cases there is a great bond between the Big Pal and the Little Pal.

Many of the Big Pals are married, and some have grown children. Frequently, their wives are involved and supportive of the idea that their husbands have taken this on. One of the JFS board members is the wife of a Big Pal, and she's the one who gave him the idea. Both of their sons are grown and away at college, and Deer was able to find a great match for him.

Another man is a Big Pal to a fabulous, sweet little boy. Deer has watched them together as she always tries to involve the Big and Little Pals in various volunteer events, like the Food Sort and basket making events, so they can volunteer together—a nice activity for a mentor to do with his young friend. Deer says she has seen that Little Pal blossom with all the love and attention his Big Pal pours on him. He's verbally affectionate and makes a lot of jokes. The Little Pal just lights up and really shines under all that positive attention, which is wonderful for his self-esteem. The child is about twelve now and has a younger brother for whom Deer has now found a Big Pal, another very kind, supportive man.

Some of the boys have had more than one Big Pal, and some of the Big Pals have had more than one Little Pal. Big Pal Marty Schnitzer, for example, has had several. When his Little Pal ages out, Schnitzer says, "OK, where's my next Little Pal?"

Schnitzer decided that when he retired he would give three days a week to volunteering, and in 2005, he received the JFS Volunteer of the Year award. He worked in the food bank, was an ESL tutor, did home deliveries, was a Big Pal, and when Deer needed someone to take a senior to a doctor's appointment or take someone to a cancer treatment, he was the one she called. He always said yes. He is now a docent for the parks and provides that service for JFS when the Seattle Association for Jews with Disabilities goes on its summer picnics.

Will Daniels was Volunteer of the Year in 2001, along with Jay Lipman, who volunteered at SAJD for many years, and Jerry

Sussman, who started volunteering in the 1990s teaching an ESL class for JFS. Several volunteer ESL teachers hold their own classes, including Erica Kaplan, Gail Kessler, Laura Stusser-McNeil, Leslie Taub, and Alice Kaderlan. Daniel Heathman, a visually impaired person who decided ESL teaching would be something he could do, taught for several years before he returned to school to earn a master's degree in ESL education. He and Erica Kaplan were recipients of the 2009 Volunteer of the Year award.

Former board member Jeanie Rosen has been a hands-on volunteer and has been delivering produce to JFS every week for years. She also spent time welcoming new immigrants and organized other volunteers to help. In 1990, Donna Benaroya and Paula Rose were the Outstanding Volunteers of the year and in 1991 all the congregations sponsoring Soviet Jewish families were honored.

Steve Simon was the Volunteer of the Year in 2006. He delivers the centerpiece and holiday baskets, does home food deliveries, drives the truck to the warehouse in Kent to pick up food, helps with Food Sort and truck unloading every week, and helps host the bulk packaging work party. Simon is always very particular, wanting to make sure that what he is doing is really helping people. (See "Volunteer of the Year Awards" in the appendix.)

Volunteers are always needed for SAJD clients to take them on a walk, visit at home or in their institution, read aloud, play games, take recorded music, food, or gifts from time to time, and let the agency know what the client's needs are. SAJD volunteers and Friendly Visitors to the elderly are asked to keep notes and keep in touch with the case managers. Some clients enjoy going out for lunch or want someone to accompany them to the opera, the symphony, or a movie. Visitors might take a client out for a manicure or help them shop for clothes, which some SAJD clients and older folks find very difficult to do on their own.

One of the problems confronted continually is that neither JFS nor the Jewish community has a transportation program. A great many people would like to attend Endless Opportunity programs, as well as other community events, but don't have transportation.

There is a need for people who are willing to drive, not only to events but also to medical or other appointments or to religious services.

The dramatic increase in the number of volunteers participating in various ways shows both the growth and popularity of the program and of JFS. It also reflects that the program has done a much better job of identifying and counting who is volunteering.

The agency has also grown in terms of its use of technology. When Deer arrived, JFS was using computers sparsely and did not have a database that she could access. Two or three people did word processing and worked for everyone on the staff. During most of that time, everything was on paper, including flyers that were passed out and mailed to help recruit volunteers and publicize events. The records system is much more dynamic today, and the use of social media has altered volunteer information and access for all non-profits. A short time ago, when Deer was looking for volunteers to help make a wall hanging for Project DVORA, she was able to post the request on Facebook and within a few minutes received a call from a young woman who said, "I'll do this and have my friends help me." That group cut out 1,200 apples, punched the holes in pieces of ribbon, and put the pieces together.

JFS has more than one Facebook page—one for the agency as a whole, one for the Family Life Education program, and one Facebook group for young adults, called "dash at jfs." There is also a Twitter account that JFS friends can follow. Very with-it!

When Deer first started in her role at JFS, she participated in outreach fairs at the University of Washington providing information about the volunteer opportunities, internships, and service learning projects for academic credit. The number of internships offered depends on the agency's need and on how many interns the staff is able to supervise. In 2012, there was one MSW and one BSW student from the University of Washington working with SAJD. Seattle University also sends BSW students to work with SAJD, and there is a new relationship with the online MSW program at the University of Southern California. There have also been MSW interns in the RISC program, and discussions are being held with the Lake Washington Institute of Technology for agency internships.

Seattle Central Community College offers a bachelor's degree in human services through a new four-year program, and some of those students have served their internships at JFS. One graduate became a SAJD staff member.

Some University of Washington students have been very creative, requesting that their departments approve their internships at JFS for credit. One student helped Deer design the following year's internship. Many interns are students from Seattle University or Seattle Central Community College, which are located close to the agency's campus. For the most part, those students are not Jewish. Deer hopes to recruit more Jewish interns through the University of Washington and JConnect (a program which describes itself as Seattle's most vibrant community for Jewish young adults) because sometimes it would be preferable to have young Jewish adults volunteering at events like the Jewish Single Parent Summer Retreat. One of her new resources is the partnership between the national JFS organization and Repair the World, a national service organization dedicated to making service a defining part of American Jewish life. Through this partnership, agencies are helped and encouraged to develop strategies to reach out to young Jewish adults, which has resulted in the Facebook group *dash at jfs*.

One of the most successful collaborations is with Seattle University through the Seattle University Center for Service and Community Engagement. Every quarter, Deer has a new group of college students who sign up to do 10 weeks of service learning. They work mostly with the Polack Food Bank, but some volunteer as Friendly Visitors to walk dogs for elderly clients or to visit clients living in the surrounding area. These young people, working with a case manager through the Aging & Adult Programs, are asked to make a two-quarter commitment so that when the agency introduces them to a client and a relationship is begun, it does not end at the conclusion of the student's 10-week quarter. Many continue the relationships after the two quarters, and three of the students decided they would use their personal vehicles to deliver groceries, which they continued to do every month for two or three years until they graduated. Other young people have returned to volunteer more over the years as well.

The service learning relationship with Seattle University led to a new relationship with a bachelor's program in leadership, which provides undergraduate student interns who stay with the agency for a year. The first year of the program, JFS had six students for the year and, in 2012, had two students who worked on a weekly basis with the department they had chosen. The following year, JFS continued to offer positions in RISC, SAJD, FLE, Emergency Services, and Volunteer Services.

Internships help young people by giving them an opportunity to have supervised practice in a social service agency where they receive guidance. One extremely helpful young woman was a summer intern from Brigham Young University, which has a Family Life Education department. She was planning to become an FLE educator and was a tremendous asset to the program.

Deer is extremely proud of building the available volunteer opportunities, making them more flexible, and creating programs to give volunteers an opportunity to help in new areas. For example, the Holiday Basket program creates 100 baskets for Rosh Hashanah, Chanukah, Purim, and Passover. Thirty to forty volunteers help put those baskets together, and then they are delivered to 100 clients in the Aging & Adult Programs, SAJD Supported Living, and Emergency Services programs. These clients are not necessarily needy, other than for companionship. It gives them pleasure to be remembered with a small gift from JFS at a time when they may not have any other way to celebrate the holidays. This basket might contain a Challah, a honey cake, some Shabbat candles, maybe apples and honey, plus a card made by the children. A low-income single parent client might receive a very large basket that has the same items in it plus other staples. Some of the volunteers collect food and other items for those baskets throughout the year, and some of the food comes from the food drives held by the Jewish day schools, congregations, and community groups.

Deer started the baskets project during her first year at JFS by creating 20 traditional Purim baskets, or *mishloach manot* (gifts of food or drink that are sent on Purim day). Her own family and grandchildren were joined by Karen Treiger and her children to make the baskets and deliver them to senior clients at the Caroline Kline Galland Home, plus a few at the Summit (an apartment community operated by Kline Galland which offers a residential program for seniors able to live more independently or with some assistance). The project then grew every year until approximately 100 clients receive baskets for four holidays during the year. Now several board members attend and support these events, and the project not only engages a broad section of the community; it also provides an opportunity for many bar-mitzvah and bat-mitzvah aged youths to be involved, as well as families with younger children.

Volunteer Services also participates in the United Way Day of Caring every year, working to complete one or two projects with 15 to 20 people, usually corporate groups. Often the project involves doing yard work at clients' homes. One client is a disabled woman with several children she is raising on her own. She needs help with yard cleanup and with building vegetable boxes. One year, volunteers from Microsoft painted her living room and dining room, as well as cleaned up outside. The following year, the same group continued with the yard work. One Microsoft volunteer who was not able to help on the Day of Caring called afterward and went to the house with his family to help her with yard work.

Another yard-work cleanup project has been done for a Holocaust survivor and resistance fighter in her eighties; she was the only one of her siblings who survived.

Wonderful Friendly Visitor volunteers continue for many years, and one Big Pal visitor signed up to take care of three children whose mother had cancer. He did activities all year with all three while the woman was undergoing treatment.

Another boy had lost both parents and lived with his grandmother, but she was not well. His Big Pal recognized the boy's need to work out some of his stress and anxiety and took him to play baseball, ride bikes, and participate in many different kinds of aggressive outdoor activities.

JFS Volunteer Services represents the basic premise of the Ladies' Hebrew Benevolent Society and honors the tradition of *tikkun olam*. The program helps brings the community together to actively gather the shards of light.

Afterword

O ur agency was founded in 1892 by a group of volunteers who saw need in their community and devoted their lives to ending it. Today our agency continues to rely on volunteers to accomplish our mission. The tradition of volunteering is part of our heritage as an agency and a community, and we continue it proudly.

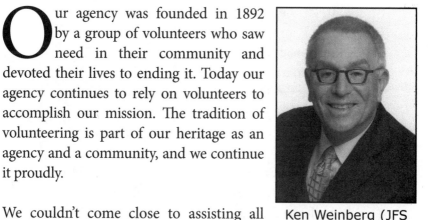

Ken Weinberg (JFS photo collection.)

We couldn't come close to assisting all those in need who come to Jewish Family Service without our volunteers. At all levels of the agency, we are blessed with truly outstanding members of the community who give their time and hard work to JFS. They surely have helped to build this for well over a century. With your help, our agency and our community will continue to grow and thrive.

—Ken Weinberg

Appendix 1

Presidents

Esther (Mrs. A.) Levy	1892–1912
Lizzie (Mrs. I.) Cooper	1912–1915
Mrs. M. Harris	1916–1917
Mrs. A. L. Cohen	1917–1920
Mrs. Marcus Harris	1920–1921
Mrs. A. L. Cohen	1921–1922
Mrs. Henrietta Schneider	1922–1923
Mrs. Henry (Gertrude) Shopera	1923–1925
Mrs. Henrietta Schneider	1925–1926
Mrs. Henry (Gertrude) Shopera	1926–1929
Mrs. John (Jessie) Danz	1929–1932
Mrs. Henry (Gertrude) Shopera	1932–1933
Mrs. John (Jessie) Danz	1933–1935
Mrs. Max (Viola) Silver	1935–1937
Mrs. John (Jessie) Danz	1937–1943
Mrs. Ben (Florence) Levinson	1943–1946
Mrs. Bernard (Mary Louise) Reiter	1946–1949
Mrs. Robert (Ida) Shapiro	1949–1951
Mrs. Paul (Dorthea) Pickard	1951–1954
Mrs. S. Harvard (Leone) Kaufman	1954–1956
Mrs. Sam (Jean) Rotenberg	1956–1959
Mrs. Herbert (Pearl) Karpel	1959–1961
Mrs. A. Bernard (Arva) Gray	1961–1963
Mr. Albert Hanan	1963–1964
Mr. Melville Oseran	1964–1965
Mrs. Julian (Eleanor) Cohon	1965–1967
Mr. Ludwig Lobe	1967–1968
Judge Solie M. Ringold	1968–1970
Dr. Abby Franklin	1970–1971
Mrs. Jerome (Adelyne) Freiberg	1971–1972
Mrs. Henry (Olga) Butler	1972–1974

Jerome Anches	1974–1977
Harold "Buzz" Coe	1977–1979
Irene Steinberg	1979–1981
Carolyn Kessler	1981–1983
Peter Shapiro	1983–1985
Janet Lackman	1985–1987
Irv Karl	1987–1988
Michele Hasson	1988–1991
Stephen Loeb	1991–1993
Lauren Jassny	1993–1995
Robert A. Low	1995–1997
Donna Benaroya	1997–1999
John E. Phillips	1999–2001
Shelly C. Shapiro	2001–2003
Jeannie Butler	2003–2005
Judy Neuman	2005–2006
Sanford Melzer	2006–2007
Laura Stusser-McNeil	2007–2009
Dianne Loeb	2009–2011
Emily Alhadeff	2011–2013

Appendix 2

Executive Directors

1921-1927	Bernice Degginger Greengard, Executive Secretary
1927-1944	May Goldsmith, Executive Secretary
1945-1950	Anne Kaufman, Executive Secretary
1950-1956	Albert S. White (died April 18, 1956)
1956 -1961	Bernard Rackow
1961-1964	Arthur Farber
1965-1974	Jerry Grossfeld
1974-1975	Thelma Coney (Interim)
1975-1984	Irwin Goldberg
1984-2013	Ken Weinberg
2013-Present	Will Berkovitz

Appendix 3

Members of the Board of Directors, 1892–2012

Each person is listed in the format in which the individual was originally listed as a member of the Board of Directors.

Sydney A. Abrams	1971
Edie Adler	1980
Doreen Alhadeff	1992
Emily Alhadeff	2005
Harry Alhadeff	1983
Mrs. M. J. Alhadeff	1953
Rosalie Alhadeff	1972
Mrs. Alexander Allper	1952
Eli Almo	1988
Mrs. Alfred B. Alper	1949
Chaya Amiad	1978
Irving Anches	1952
Jerome Anches	1969
Trudy Angel	1995
Eugene Arfin	1978
Mrs. Herbert Arnstein	1972
Miriam (Mrs. F.) Aronson	1894
Miriam Aronson	1975
Mrs. S.Aronson	1892
Mr. Harry Ash	1949
Michael Austin	1977
Stephanie Axelrod	2006
Joe Barer	2001
Scott Barron	2003
Etan Basseri	2009
Dorothy Becker	1973

Howard Behar	2000
Jack Behar	1966
Salvo Behar	1997
Donna Benaroya	1988
Mrs. Earl P. Benditt	1963
Raymond Benezra	1970
Joel Benoliel	1975
Maureen Benoliel	1999
Mrs. Lester Berg	1944
Dr. Abraham Bergman	1971
Bonnie Berk	2007
Kathy Berman	1996
Mrs. Nicholas (Gizel) Berman	1955
Mr. Sanford Bernbaum	1949
John Bernhard	1985
Mrs. A. M. (Minnie) Bernhard	1934
Dr. Z. W. Birnbaum	1955
Mrs. Alvin Block	1955
Max Block	1947
Dr. Olga Bloom	1969
Mrs. S. Blum	1928
Mr. Irwin Blumenfeld	1958
Beverly Bodansky	1977
Stephen Boehler	1997
Janet Boguch	1995
Mrs. Max Bornstein	1895
Mr. George Brandt	1956
Mr. Gene Brandzel	1968
Harvey Bresler	1976
RADM Herb Bridge	2001
Pam Bridge	1990
Shirley Bridge	2001
Richard D. Brody	1988
D. Michel Brotman	2002
Mrs. F. Brown	1892

Mrs. L. Bukofzer	1917
Mrs. Bud Burnett	1949
Mr. Harry C. Bush	1964
Jeannie Butler	1994
Mrs. Henry (Olga) Butler	1968
Mrs. Harry Buttnick	1942
Harry Caraco	1996
Mr. Jack Caston	1959
Bobbi Ross Chamberlin	1996
Diane Topp Cheifetz	1998
Jerome Chiprut	1979
Harold Coe	1974
Mrs. A. Lou Cohen	1892
Barney Cohen	2010
Mrs. Harry Cohen	1941
Mrs. Hyman Cohen	1956
Dr. Joseph Cohen	1949
Mrs. Ruben S. (Claire) Cohen	1960
Shelly Cohen	1992
Mrs. Julian Cohon	1961
Mrs. I. Cooper	1892
Simon Dadoun	1980
Ted Daniels	1987
Will Daniels	2007
Carolee Danz	1990
Mrs. John (Jessie) Danz	1925
Mrs. Wm. (Carolyn) Danz	1964
Mrs. Ida Davis	1894
Miss Lilly De Jaen	1966
Mr. Joseph DeLeon	1962
Mrs. Edward Dobrin	1946
Dr. Jack Doctor	1949
Susan Eastern	2008
Miss Joanna Eckstein	1943
Mrs. Nathan Eckstein	1927

Sharyn Edelman	1999
Mrs. H. Elster	1892
Mrs. Jesse (Sylvia) Epstein	1942
Sol Esfeld	1948
Jack Faghin	1974
Joseph Feinberg	1978
Mr. Nathan Feinberg	1958
Jeff Feinstein	2008
Jonathan Fine	1992
Mrs. Lawrence B. (Sharon) Finegold	1972
Eddie Fisher	1979
Dorothy Forman	1942
JoAnn Forman	2009
Mrs. A. Fortlouis	1892
Mr. Albert M. Franco	1949
Mr. David A. Frand	1953
Joseph Frankel	1979
Dr. Abby Franklin	1965
Mrs. M. M. Fredericks	1895
Mrs. Jerome Freiberg	1967
Mrs. Nathan Freiberg	1927
Mrs. Edwin J. Friedman	1953
Dr. Harry J. Friedman	1952
Laurie Friedman	1989
Mr. Louis A. Friedman	1968
Susan Friedman	1980
Mrs. C. Friend	1892
Mrs. E. B. Friend	1892
Amy Fulton	2005
Mrs. Morris (Betty) Fuson	1965
Barrie Galanti	2000
Jeannette Galante	1982
Mrs. Isaac Gamel	1972
Mrs. L. Garfinkle	1919
Mr. Ben (Jean) Genauer	1955

Eva Genauer	1983
Mrs. Mendel (Ruth) Genauer	1962
Mrs. M. Gerber	1922
Mrs. Sidney Gerber	1944
Mrs. Jules Glant	1940
Mr. Harry Glickman	1963
Gordon Godfred	2011
Cathy Reiner Godwin	1987
Bernard Goffe	1985
Sheldon Goldberg	1988
Gerry Goldman	2006
Peter Goldman	1995
Mrs. Thornton Goldsby	1924
Mrs. A. M. (Minnie) Goldstein	1934
Mrs. Frank Goodman	1946
Dr. Frank Goodman	1957
Dr. David H. Gordy	1970
Mrs. K. Gottstein	1892
Mrs. Bernard (Arva) Gray	1959
Janet Gray	1987
Yudit Greenberg	1981
Beth Greene	1976
Joe Greengard	1982
Mrs. Samuel Greengard	1942
Mrs. Alexander Grinstein	1957
Mrs. Otto Grunbaum	1941
Shirley Guterson	1983
Mrs. Otto Guthman	1932
Stan Habib	1999
Gerald M. Hahn	1970
Larry Hamlin	1984
Mr. Al Hanan	1956
Mr. Albert Hanan	1964
Mrs. Hardman	1917
Walter Hardman, Jr.	1974

Mrs. Marcus Harris	1920
Mrs. Maurice Harris	1916
Barry J. Hasson	1983
Michele Hasson	1984
Mr. Henry Hayum	1949
Mrs. Edith Heinemann	1968
John Hellman	1986
Michael Hershey	1999
Renee Herst	1999
Mrs. J. R. Hiller	1932
Mrs. Joseph Hirshberg	1967
Mr. Donald Hochberg	1980
Mrs. Donald Hochberg	1960
Mrs. Samuel Holcenberg	1944
Robin Home	1988
Mrs. Michael (Daisy) Israel	1973
Virginia Israel	1979
Louise Irving	2001
Mrs. Jay Jacobs	1955
Robert Jacobs	2003
Mrs. J. L. Jaffe	1892
Stanley Jaffe	1982
Delia Jampel	2009
Larry Jassen	1978
Lauren Jassny	1986
Mrs. Paul (Jo) Jassny	1946
Mrs. Andrew (Rose) Jordan	1933
Julian Judelman	1986
Mr. Max Kaminoff	1955
Mrs. J. S. Kane	1930
Larry Kaner	1974
Mrs. Charles (Lillian) Kaplan	1960
Mrs. Herbert Karpel	1956
Irv Karl	1983
Laura Karl	1995

Dr. Alvin Katsman	1961
Mrs. Archie (Harriet) Katz	1963
Max Katz	1981
Mrs. S. Harvard Kaufman	1946
Ann Kaye	1974
Frances Keller	1983
Carolyn Kessler	1976
Mrs. Kierski	1892
Marc Kittner	2008
Jackie Kotkins	1998
Jane Kowals	1985
Margot Kravette	2011
Janet Lackman	1980
Mrs. Arthur Lagawier	1964
Mrs. J. Lang	1917
Mrs. Richard Lang	1940
Mrs. Harvard J. (Nancy) Leavitt	1970
Mr. Robert Leavitt	1956
Mike Lemberg	1985
Millard Lesch	1979
Mrs. E. E. Lescher	1939
Mrs. J. Lesser	1892
Mr. David Levine	1949
Eric LeVine	2003
Mrs. Irving Levine	1959
Mrs. Raphael Levine	1943
Mrs. Benjamin Levinson	1934
Mrs. Harry (Henrietta) Levinson	1972
Mrs. Samuel Levitt	1941
Esther (Mrs. A.) Levy	1892
Mrs. Leon B. Levy	1961
Mrs. Sigmund Lewis	1941
Mrs. Wm. Lewis	1918
Mrs. Robert Lindenberger	1942
Mrs. D. Lipman	1917

Mrs. Harry (Sema) Lipsett	1973
Mr. Ludwig Lobe	1961
Dianne Loeb	1997
Donald Loeb	1994
Stephen Loeb	1986
Mrs. Hugo Loewy	1931
Bob Low	1990
Mrs. Walter (Jeanette) Lowen	1964
Mrs. Alvin S. Luchs	1956
Miss Elise Lurie	1940
Mrs. Myer Lurie	1953
Mrs. Robert Lurie	1925
Dr. Leslie Mackoff	1973
Esther (Mrs. A.) Maimon	1988
Ed Malakoff	2011
Barry J. Margolese	1982
Mrs. Aaron Maslan	1945
Carol Maslan	1987
Gail Mautner	2004
Lois Mayers	1987
Sally McKenzie	2007
Sidney Meltzer	1976
Sanford Melzer	1996
Mrs. Boris Merport	1955
Mr. Howard Michel	1955
Michael Milder	1980
Jeremy Miller	1999
Laurie Minsk	2011
Mr. Marvin Mohl	1953
Mr. Melville Monheimer	1949
Mrs. E. Morgenstern	1894
Mr. George Mosler	1960
Albert Mossafer	1983
Gretel Motulsky	1975
Judy Neuman	1994

Jon H. Rosen	2010
Michele Rosen	2009
Stan Rosen	2006
William M. Rosen	1982
Mrs. E. B. Rosenberg	1892
Mr. Theodore Rosenblume	1964
Mrs. Roy G. Rosenthal	1940
Gilbert Rosenwald	1956
Judy Ross	1991
Lawrence Ross	1977
Nate Ross	1976
Salie Rossen	1999
Mrs. Samuel Rotenberg	1953
Ellen Rubinfeld	2003
Alvin Rubenstein	1978
Mrs. Sarah Rucker	1895
Mrs. Joseph Russak	1960
Shana Saichek	1981
Joani Diskin Saran	1992
Carol Schapira	1992
Julia Schechter	2008
Gilbert Scherer	2002
Mrs. H. (Henrietta) Schneider	1917
Mrs. Ralph (Florence) Schoenfeld	1942
Julie Schoenfeld	1992
Mrs. L. Schoenfield	1892
Amy Schottenstein	2004
Mr. Gerald Schucklin	1949
Mrs. Edgar Schwabacher	1940
Mrs. Leo Schwabacher	1917
Pepper Schwartz	1985
Mrs. Albert Schreiber	1969
Shainie Schuffler	1979
Joseph A. Schuster	1977
Mrs. Alfons Schwarz	1937

Mrs. Lawrence H. (Jane) Schwartz	1973
Steven J. Schwartz	2009
Miss Gertrude Seelig	1924
Mr. Henry Seidel	1971
Mrs. L. Seitsick	1919
Andrea Selig	1992
Mrs. Julius Shafer	1938
Mrs. Louis A. Shapiro	1917
Mrs. Louis A. Shapiro	1954
Peter Shapiro	1978
Mrs. Robert Shapiro	1945
Shelly C. Shapiro	1993
Mrs. Alfred (Sally) Sheridan	1961
Mrs. Henry Shopera	1922
Eva Shulman	1991
Mr. Alfred Shyman	1974
Amy Sidell	1975
Ann Sidell	1974
Sanford Sidell	1976
Mrs. Henry (Eleanor) Siegl	1962
Mr. Abe Silver	1949
Mrs. Max (Viola G.) Silver	1921
Mrs. E. Silverstone	1922
Mrs. Ray S. Silverstone	1923
Mrs. I. (Bertha) Simon	1917
Mrs. R. Simon	1918
Robert Simon	1988
Judy Soferman	2004
Charlotte Spitzer	1987
Mr. Myron Spring	1962
Mr. Edward Starin	1956
Mrs. Herbert Stein	1949
Mrs. L. Stein	1917
Mrs. Sheldon (Irene) Steinberg	1967
Mrs. Edward F. (Pauline) Stern	1954

Michel P. Stern	1970
Mrs. Samuel Stern	1929
Sylvia Stern	1977
Mr. Ernest Stiefel	1969
Anita Stolov	1976
Mr. Irving Stolzoff	1956
Mrs. Samuel (Althea) Stroum	1971
Herb Stusser	1987
Isabel Stusser	1986
Mr. Max Stusser	1964
Laura Stusser-McNeil	1997
Barbara Sulman	1987
Stuart Sulman	1996
Shelley Swerland	1985
Patricia Tall	1996
Dr. Samuel Tarica	1960
Mr. Sam W. Tarshis	1948
Mrs. Sydney Tarshis	1954
Mrs. Max Tobias	1940
Fred Tobis	2001
Mrs. Sam S. Treiger	1963
Deb Trevino	2005
Remy Trupin	2005
Reva Twersky	1975
Alan Waldbaum	1996
Dennis Warshal	1988
Mrs. Lewis Weiner	1970
Sylvia Weiner	1974
Mrs. Max Weinstein	1943
Ronald Weinstein	1975
Mrs. Sydney Weinstein	1955
Dr. Sydney Weinstein	1956
Mrs. William Weinstein	1964
Alisa Weise	2011
Mrs. Douglas (Elaine) Weisfield	1970

Mr. Richard Weisfield	1952
Stuart Weiss	2001
Mrs. Matt Weissman	1966
Gary Wenet	2008
Eileen Glasser Wesley	2002
Dr. Lawrence Wilets	1970
Julius Willenzik	1978
Mrs. G. Winehill	1892
Barbara Wolf	1988
Beatrice Wolf	1974
Mr. Henry E. Wolf	1965
Mrs. George Wolfe	1935
Mrs. Marvin (Marian) Zak	1973
Nancy Zeitz	1981
Michael Zwell	1984

Appendix 4

Names and Addresses of JFS

Names of JFS

1892	Ladies' Hebrew Benevolent Society (LHBS)
1895	Men's group – Seattle Hebrew Benevolent Society founded
1917	Two groups merged and became Hebrew Benevolent Association (HBA)
1929	Name changed to Jewish Welfare Society (JWS)
1935	JWS known as zone 24 of the WA Emergency Relief Administration
1947	Jewish Family & Child Service.
1978	Jewish Family Service

Addresses

1892	Homes of officers
1917	Smith Tower Annex (the Pacific Block), 4th floor
1940	Smith Tower Annex, moved to 3rd floor
1948	Moved to Court Building, 408 Marion Street
1949	207 Court Bldg, 408 Marion
1953	1620 Jackson Street (17th & Jackson)
1958	Moved to 2017 Jackson Street
1960	Purchased building at 2017 Jackson Street, 11-21-60
1969	Moved to 2009 Minor Avenue East
1972	Moved to 1110 Harvard Avenue, Suite 201
1979	Added Eastside branch, 11101 NE 8th Street in Bellevue
1979	Purchased and moved to1214 Boylston
1992	Purchased and moved to 1601 16th Avenue

Appendix 5

Partners and Coalitions 2012

The following summary outlines the many partnerships and collaborations Jewish Family Service has with other social service organizations. This list is dynamic and subject to change. JFS frequently looks at its programming to determine if there are better, more effective ways to meet clients' needs.

Category I – JFS is a member of an organization or committee and may work collaboratively on projects.

Category II – Contractual relationship; JFS has entered into a formal relationship with another organization, with or without reimbursement.

Category III – Other agencies provide services, donations, or assistance to JFS at no cost.

Category of relationship	JFS Program	Organization	Relationship	Comments
Category I	Project DVORA	King County Coalition Against Domestic Violence	Member and participate regularly	Maintains DV services as a part of a larger movement, updates[J53] on trends and best practices, and lends a Jewish perspective to the movement.
Category I	Project DVORA	WA State Coalition Against Domestic Violence	Member and participate regularly	Same as above.
Category I	Project DVORA	Domestic Violence Directors	Meet monthly to support and collaborate on DV issues	Keep abreast of DV issues/concerns. Lend Jewish voice to group.
Category II	Project DVORA	Wellspring Family Services	Memo of Understanding to partner in providing Kid's Club	Wellspring provides a facilitator at no cost; advertises[J54] and makes referrals to the program.

Category of relationship	JFS Program	Organization	Relationship	Comments
Category III	Food Bank	Eastside Food Bank at the Jewish Day School		Students assist in providing food bank services.
Category III	Food Bank	Neighborhood Farmer's Market Association	Collaboration	Glean donations at the Broadway Farmer's Market.
Category II	Food Bank	Solid Ground - Cooking Matters		No-cost cooking classes for food bank clients.
Category II	Food Bank	Food Lifeline Contract		Weekly donations of food for food bank program.
Category I	Food Bank	Seattle Food Committee	Member of our local food coalition	This coalition provides extensive advocacy through the city of Seattle, educational opportunities, and support from other food banks.

Category of relationship	JFS Program	Organization	Relationship	Comments
Category III	Food Bank	Food Resources	Contract with the Seattle Food Committee	No-cost transportation from Food Lifeline warehouse to the Polack Food Bank.
Category III	Food Bank	NW Harvest		Supplies 15 percent of food bank[J55]
Category II	Emergency Services/ Foster Care	Amara Adoption and Parenting Services	Agreement to provide licensing and monitoring of Jewish foster homes	JFS recruits and supports Jewish foster families. This relationship guarantees that JFS goals are met while not providing direct service.
Category I	Emergency Services	Seattle King County Coalition on Homelessness	Provider's group	Keeps JFS abreast of activities in the community, provides grant opportunities, and shows others JFS is an active partner.

Category of relationship	JFS Program	Organization	Relationship	Comments
Category II	Emergency Services	Tacoma Jewish Community Fund	Memo of Understanding	With funds provided by the Tacoma Jewish community, we offer Emergency Services to the Tacoma Jewish community.
Category I	Emergency Services	King County Committee to End Homelessness	Community-wide response to 10-year plan to end home-lessness	Serve on sub-Employment Committee and participate as an active partner.
Category I	Emergency Services	Federal Emergency Management Agency	Member of the local FEMA board	Jewish seat on this local version of a federal government board.
Category I	Emergency Services	Jewish Prisoner Services International	Collaborative relationship	Work with offenders after release from prison or otherwise as requested by Chaplain Gary Friedman.

Category of relationship	JFS Program	Organization	Relationship	Comments
Category II	Emergency Services	Temple Beth Am H2R Program	Contractual agreement	Beth Am raises money, which JFS distributes to clients needing security deposits.
Category III	Refugee and Immigrant Service Centers (RISC)	Coalition of similar refugee agencies supporting the New Citizen Initiative (NCI) contract		Provide ESL classes and assistance to become US citizens with focus on elderly Russian immigrants.
Category I	RISC	Refugee Forum	Representatives of resettlement agencies	
Category I	RISC	Burmese Round Table	Representatives of agencies and volunteers planning for the Burmese population	
Category II	RISC	Refugee Advisory Committee Statewide[J56]	All service providers/ DSHS/college representatives[J57]	

Category of relationship	JFS Program	Organization	Relationship	Comments
Category II	RISC	Refugee Planning Committee King County Region 4	All service providers/ DSHS/college representatives	
Category I	RISC	Local Planning Allocation Coalition	Coalition of agencies providing services to Limited English Pathway clients	
Category II	School Counseling	Jewish Day School, Seattle Community School		School counseling services to reach the widest possible Jewish community. Enhances JFS visibility and presence in the community.
Category II	Clinical Counseling	Hillel		On-site counseling services.

Category of relationship	JFS Program	Organization	Relationship	Comments
Category II	Clinical Counseling	National Association of Social Workers (NASW)	Contract to authorize continuing education programs	JFS provides continuing professional education CEU credits under the auspices of NASW.
Category II	Aging & Adult Programs (AAP)	National Associations: Professional Geriatric Care Managers, Alliance of Information and Referral Systems, National Academy of Certified Care Managers	Member of national associations	
Category I	AAP	King County Elder Abuse Council	Member	Law enforcement, service providers, and government [J58].
Category I	AAP	Healthy Aging Partnership	Provider group	

Category of relationship	JFS Program	Organization	Relationship	Comments
Category IV	Volunteer Services	Synagogues, schools and colleges, organizations, corporations and businesses, community groups and individuals, etc.		Raise and donate money and goods for clients; provide volunteers; collaborate in supporting volunteer projects.
Category I	SAJD	SAAJ - Directors of Disability Organizations	Member; participate regularly	Policy, advocacy and opportunity to work with other organizations.
Category I	FLE/SAJD	Shaarei Tikvah Holiday Services		Temple B'nai Torah and Temple DeHirsch Sinai are ongoing partners.
Category II	FLE	FLE Programming	Co-sponsor and host events	About half of FLE events are co-hosted or co-sponsored by Jewish and secular organizations.

Category of relationship	JFS Program	Organization	Relationship	Comments
Category II	FLE	Endless Opportunities	Partnership with Temple B'nai Torah and Temple DeHirsch Sinai congregations providing educational, social, and recreational programs for seniors	JFS staff facilitate the advisory planning committee and events. Synagogues provide space and contribute funds.
Category I	Alternatives to Addiction (ATA)	Communities that Care and Prevention WINS	Mercer Island and Seattle coalitions against underage drinking and drug use	
Category I	ATA	Take Back Your Meds	Statewide coalition	
Category I	ATA	King County Adult Chemical Dependency Providers, Washington State Chemical Dependency Professionals, Evergreen Council on Problem Gambling	Professional organizations	

Appendix 6

Annual Meeting Awards

Annual Meeting	Keynote Speaker	Jessie Danz Award Volunteer of the Year	Outstanding Service Award	Special Recognition Award	Number of Attendees/Chair
120th/2012	Ken Weinberg	Jeanne Tackitt, RISC	Michael Hershey, Richard Galanti	RISC	160, Margot Kravette
119th/2011	Ken Weinberg	JFS Big Pals	Zach Carstensen	Program Highlight - Endless Opportunities	200, Susan Eastern
118th/2010		Fran Hasson	Ken Weinberg, 35 years of service to JFS		Emily Alhadeff, Dianne Loeb, Michele Rosen

Annual Meeting	Keynote Speaker	Jessie Danz Award Volunteer of the Year	Outstanding Service Award	Special Recognition Award	Number of Attendees/Chair
117th/2009		Erica Kaplan, Daniel Heathman	**Holocaust Ghetto Workers Reparations Project** Joanna Plichta Boisen, *Pro Bono Counsel, Foster Pepper,* Cozen O'Connor, Davis Wright Tremaine, Foster Pepper, Garvey Schubert Barer, Morris & Morris, Perkins Coie, Stoel Rives, Wilson Sonsini Goodrich & Rosati		250, Dianne Loeb
116th/2008		Rita Segelbaum, Pola Doenyas	**Alternatives to Addiction Program** The Kenneth & Marleen Alhadeff Charitable Foundation, Employees Community Fund of Boeing Puget Sound, Special Initiatives Fund of the Jewish Federation of Greater Seattle		223, Laurie Stusser-McNeil

Annual Meeting	Keynote Speaker	Jessie Danz Award Volunteer of the Year	Outstanding Service Award	Special Recognition Award	Number of Attendees/Chair
115th/2007	MCCAW				250, Stephanie Axelrod
114th/2006	MCCAW, Dr Anita Friedman	Steve Simon		Strategic Plan	175, Suzi and Eric LeVine
113th/2005	MCCAW, David Stillman	Marty Schnitzer	Kathy and Steve Berman	Ken Weinberg 30th anniversary	275, Judy Ross, Bobbi Ross Chamberlin, Alexis Chamberlin
112th/2004	Vignettes	Elaine Weisfield	Isabel and Herb Stusser, Michael Stusser, Vanessa Timmen, Ken Ahroni, Pam Stusser	Remy Trupin	
111th/2003		Elaine and Marshall Hartholz, Doron Weisbarth, Jewish Day School food bank volunteers, Iris Kalach and her students	Carolee Danz		
110th/2002	Pepper Schwartz				
109th/2001	Book-It Rep Theatre	Will Daniels, Jay Lipman, Jerry Sussman	Dennis Warshal		

Annual Meeting	Keynote Speaker	Jessie Danz Award Volunteer of the Year	Outstanding Service Award	Special Recognition Award	Number of Attendees/Chair
108th/2000	Danny Siegel	Merle Sidell, Bob & Melinda Stubbs	Jewish Federation, Samis Foundation, United Way of King County		350
107th/1999	Ron Wolfson	Jeanie Rosen	Carolee Danz, Bob Low		360
106th/1998	Mayor Paul Schell	Ben and Ida Dortch, Fred and Eva Hirschel, Bernie and Shala Perlin	Jeannie Butler		325
105th/1997	Gov. Gary Locke	Salie Rossen, Yekaterina and Alfred Schmidt	Ted Daniels		380

Annual Meeting	Keynote Speaker	Jessie Danz Award Volunteer of the Year	Outstanding Service Award	Special Recognition Award	Number of Attendees/Chair
104th/1996	Sen. Ron Wyden		**JFS Humanitarian Award:** Benaroya Family, Raymond & Joyce Benezra, Danz Family, Fanny Feinberg, Polack Family, Harry & Elizabeth Poll, Bill & Jeanie Rosen, Shulman & Loeb Families, Sam & Althea Stroum, Herb & Isabel Stusser		315
103rd/1995	Helen Jackson	Ronald Leibsohn	Michael Levin, Alpha Omega Fraternity, Ralph Moldauer		
102nd/1994	Bert Goldberg	Rosalind and Melvyn Poll	Jeff Atkin		
101st/1993	Richard Thompson	Patti Newby, Pam Waechter	Larry Hamlin/ Irv Karl, Donna Benaroya/Herb Stusser		
100th/1992	100th Anniversary V				

Annual Meeting	Keynote Speaker	Jessie Danz Award Volunteer of the Year	Outstanding Service Award	Special Recognition Award	Number of Attendees/Chair
99th/1991	Virgil Fassio	Congregations Sponsoring Soviet Jewish Families	**Humanitarian of the Year:** Seattle Jewish Coalition for Homeless People		
98th/1990	Mayor Norm Rice	**Outstanding Volunteers:** Donna Benaroya, Paula Rose	**Outstanding Service:** Peter Shapiro		
97th/1989		**Outstanding Volunteers:** Marian Aronson, Marlene Burns, Michele Rosen, Betty Lou Shulman, Vladimir Silverstone	**Humanitarian of the Year:** Judy Balint		
96th/1988	Pepper Schwartz	**Outstanding Volunteers:** Schick Feinberg, Laura Karl, Rose Klein, Jennifer Malakoff, Lorraine Sidell	**Family Service Award:** The Bridge Family		

Annual Meeting	Keynote Speaker	Jessie Danz Award Volunteer of the Year	Outstanding Service Award	Special Recognition Award	Number of Attendees/Chair
95th/1987	Jule Sugarman	George Winston	**Humanitarian of the Year:** Sam & Althea Stroum		
94th/1986	Jim McDermott	Gerda David	**Humanitarian of the Year:** Morris & Jack Polack Families		
93rd/1985	Michael Rothenberg		Herb Rosen		

Selected Bibliography

Bernice Degginger Greengard Papers. Accession 2403. Special Collections. University of Washington Libraries.

Buttnick, Mrs. Harry, Mrs. John Danz, Mrs. Elias Lescher, and Mrs. Meyer Newberger. "A History of the Jewish Family and Child Service from 1892 to 1967." Undated typescript. In possession of author.

Cone, Molly, Howard Droker, and Jacqueline Williams. *Family of Strangers: Building a Jewish Community in Washington State.* (Seattle: Washington State Jewish Historical Society, 2003).

Cooper and Levy Families Papers, 1890-1959. Accession 2366. Special Collections. University of Washington Libraries.

Florence Flaks Papers, 1920-1975. Accession 2519. Special Collections. University of Washington Libraries.

Hebrew Ladies Free Loan Society Papers. Accession 1568. Special Collections. University of Washington Libraries.

Jeanette Lozovsky oral history. Accession 5655. Special Collections. University of Washington Libraries.

Jewish Family Service Records, 1883-1998. Accession 2003. Special Collections. University of Washington Libraries.

Minnie Bernhard Papers. Accession 2055. Washington State Jewish Historical Society. Special Collections. University of Washington Libraries.

The New York Times.

Olga Butler Papers. Accession 4526. Special Collections. University of Washington Libraries.

Rose Arensberg Papers. Accession 2122. Special Collections. University of Washington Libraries.

Seattle City Directory, 1889 to 1921. R. L. Polk & Co. Special Collections. University of Washington Libraries.

Seattle Post-Intelligencer.

The Seattle Times.

Sollie Ringold Papers. Accession 1891. Special Collections. University of Washington Libraries.

Stern, Klaus. *My Legacy: Blessings, Love and Courage; A Memoir.* Washington State Holocaust Education Resource Center. Pre-publication printing. 2007.

Temple De Hirsch Sinai records, 1883-2001. Accession 2370-018. Special Collections. University of Washington Libraries.

Transcript (Seattle).

Washington Holocaust Resource Education Center, http://www.wsherc.org (accessed October 6, 2014).

Washington State Jewish Historical Society, Landmarks Committee Records, 1948-1982. Accession 3128. Special Collections. University of Washington Libraries.

Index

Adult Protective Services case, 74–75
Aging and Adult Programs, 67–68, 81,
          290, 334. *See also* Claims
          Conference; Jewish Family
          Service; Senior Services
    baby boomers projection, 72–74, 77,
          80
    caseloads, 79, 80
    case management, 69, 71, 72, 79–80
    clinical counselors, 122
    directors (White, Grossfeld, Coney,
          Barash, Gortler, Relin), 68–72, 77
    Endless Opportunities program, 292
    experimental program, 68
    fee scale, 73
    Holiday Basket program, 451
    home-based/in-home care, 72, 74
    HomeCare Associates, 75–76
    managers, 78
    Russian senior assistance, 84, 290
    services provided, 69
    volunteers, 450–451
    "When to Worry" program, 80
AJFCA. *See* Association of Jewish Family &
          Children's Agencies
Alanon, 369
Albert S. White Memorial Fund, 203
Alcoholics Anonymous (AA)/alcoholism,
          366, 369, 371, 373–374
Alexander III, Jewish repression, 6
Alhadeff, Emily, 433–434 (photo)–435
Alhadeff, Kenny, and Alhadeff Foundation,
          363, 365, 366–367
Alley Cat Acres, 32
Alpha Home on Queen Anne Hill, 334
Alpha Omega Dental Fraternity, 41
Alternatives to Addiction (ATA) program,
          122, 123, 124, 363–364
    addiction conference, 369–370
    Alcoholics Anonymous, 364, 369, 373
    community support, 371
    director Kramer's expansion beyond
          alcohol and drugs, 377–378

    director Ruff's approach and clients,
          368–372, 373–375
    employee assistance model, 364
    kickoff, 370
    marijuana concerns, 379
Althea and Sam Stroum Fund, 263
American Association of Social Workers,
          157
Americanization program, 100
American nativist groups against
          immigrants, 5
American Protestant influence, 6–7
Anches, Irving, 179, 253
Anches, Jerry, 253, 254, 262
Ancioux, Michelle, 230
anti-Semitism
    and Anti-Defamation League (ADL),
          153
    in European countries, 203
    in Mexico, 197
    in USSR, 228
Anti-Tuberculosis League, 99, 157
Arab-Israeli War, 224–225
Argentina, Jews in, 198
Armstrong, Don, 76, 334, 335, 340, 366, 428
Aronson, Eva, 10, 13
Aronson, Marian, 324
Ashkenazi immigrants and traditions, 13,
          58, 440
Asian resettlement. *See* Southeast Asia
Asnin, Isaak, 229
Association of Jewish Family & Children's
          Agencies (AJFCA), 105, 116, 309,
          317
    national convention, 407
AuBuchon, Dr. James, 295
Auschwitz, 168. *See also* Holocaust

baby boomers
    aging, and anticipated increase in
          need, 72–74, 77, 80
    marijuana problem, 379
    workshops for, 290

Baha'i, Farsi-speaking from Iran and Iraq, 250, 314, 410

Baker, Dr. William, 154

Bannister, Elizabeth, 213

Baral, Martin, 257

Barash, Sarah (Sarah Gortler), 70–73, 77, 83, 283

Barer, Joe, 404–405, 406

Barer, Karyn, 404

Barrett's Moving and Storage, 232

Baskin, Debby, 70, 71

Becker, Martha, 217, 274

Behar, Howard, 400, 406, 428

Beit T'Shuvah, 369, 376
    Freedom Song performance, 377

Belenky, Marina, 85, 290

Belgium, anti-Semitism, 203

Bellevue office, 260, 392, 401, 419

Benaroya, Donna, 333, 390–391, 424, 448

Benedict, Carol, 247

Benezra, Ray, 384

Benjamin, Vivien, 281

Berkman, Mrs. Jacob (Mina), 157, 424

Berkovitz, Rabbi Will, 371, 438

Berman, caseworker, 57

Berman, Claudia, 334, 366, 391–392, 396, 401, 427, 428

Berman Kathy, board member, 402, 403, 406

Berman, Kathy and Steve, 30, 34, 429

Bernhard, Minnie (Mrs. A.M.), 147, 173–174

Beth Am synagogue/Temple Beth Am, 38–39, 53, 85, 370

Bet Tzedak, 82

Big Pals and Little Pals programs and volunteers, 26, 64, 289, 302, 428, 440, 441, 443, 446–447, 452–453

Bikur Cholim synagogue, 22, 53, 89, 97, 99, 146, 147
    Hachnosas Orchim, 98, 99

Blind Pension, 97

Block, Mr. and Mrs. Max, 93

Bloome, Mark, 397

Blumenzweig family from Egypt, 217, 218 (photo)–219

B'nai B'rith, 6, 99

burial committee for transient men, 100
    volunteer aid, 238

B'nai Torah, 375

Boehler, Robin, 396

Boeing Bust, difficult years, 215–216, 223, 254, 256, 259

Bogomolny, Benjamin, 245

Boguch, Janet, 423

Bolivia, pogrom concern, 197

Bonham Galland
    Fund for homeless, orphaned, or needy children, 171, 206
    Nursery School, 182, 197

Bon Marché/Macy's, 19, 234

Borden, Bertha, 160, 170

Bories, Carrie, 64

Bories, Dr. Emil, 16

Bories, Dr. Henry, 57

Bories, Mrs. Fred, 157

Borowska, Anna, 167

Bosnia refugees, 250

Boylston building, 266, 301, 383

Brandeis University Women's Committee workshop, 354

Brazil, Jewish people in, 197–198

Bridge, Rabbi Dan, 117, 118

Bringing Baby Home class, 286

Broadway Farmers Market, 31

Broder, Estelle, 232

Broder, Larry, 249, 292–293, 397

Brotman, Michel, 444

Brown, Becky and Isadore (Izzy), 271

Bureau of Associated Charities, 15, 60

Bureau of Immigration Appeals, 419

Bureau of Mental Health, 156

Burma/Myanmar refugees, 250, 410–413, 414, 415

Burnett, Diane, 375

Butler, Jeannie, 395 (photo)–396, 398

Butler, Olga, 224 (photo), 225, 230

Buttnick, Mrs. Harry (Meta), 10, 58

Call 211 program, 36

Cambodian refugees, 225

Camp Fire Girls, 99

Camp Solomon Schechter, 284, 287

Caplan, Irwin, 267, 318

Caroline Kline Galland Home, 51–52
(photo), 61, 152, 206, 423, 446. *See also*
Kline Galland Home
basic rules, 54–55
capacity in 1952, 194
case investigations/studies, 88, 159
Federation House visits, 214, 215
Frankel, Sol, executive director, 56
(quote)
Holocaust survivors aid, 84
JFCS oversight, 176
kosher lunch program, 275
Russian Jews entry, 239, 243
services to aged/elderly, 68, 256, 257
volunteers, 452
Castro, Fidel. *See* Cuba
Catholic Community Services, 72, 441
Catholic Social Services, 110
Cedar River Watershed Educational Center,
288
Center for Applied Linguistics (CAL), 414
Central Area Mental Health Center, 222,
223
Century Club, 7
Chabad/Chabad-Lubavitch, 85, 108, 125
Chabad House, 235, 346
Chang, Alice, 321–322
Chanukah Tzedakah program, 40, 44–45,
390
Chanukah volunteers, 43
Child Protective Services, 104
Children's Home Society of Washington,
213
Children's Orthopedic Hospital, 92
Child Study Laboratory, 99
Child Welfare Department, 99
Child Welfare League of America, 154
Chin, ethnic minority, 410–411
Chisholm Hall, 8
City Clinic, 99
City Health Department, 99
City Hospital, 99
Civil Works Administration, 97
Claims Conference for Holocaust victims,
75–76, 81, 82–83
Coblentz, Florine, 57, 61, 438
Coe, Harold "Buzz," 254–255 (photo)–256,
260, 261, 264

Cohen, Dr. Joseph, 178
Cohen, Ida, 57
Cohn, Rabbi Franklin, 169
Cohon, Eleanor, 152, 216 (photo)
Cole, Jacob J., 16
Communists. *See* Soviet Union; USSR
Community Chest, 60, 64, 153, 154, 157,
158, 159, 160, 172, 187, 202, 205
Community Fund office, 89
Community High School of Jewish Studies,
354
Community Psychiatric Clinic, 323, 328,
332
Cone, Molly, 163
Coney, Thelma, 28, 68–69, 74–75, 217
(photo), 219–220, 253, 274
Conference of Jewish Women's
Organization, 97
Conference on Jewish Material Claims
Against Germany. *See* Claims
Conference
Congolese families, 414–415, 418–419
Congregation Ohaveth Shalom, 8
Consolidated Homeless Grant, 38
Cooking Matters, 32
Coons, Isidor, 145
Cooper, Isaac, and Isaac Cooper trust, 18,
157, 159, 176
Cooper and Levy Store/Cooper-Levy Trust,
18 (photo)–19, 21, 166, 254, 265,
278, 382
Cooper, Lizzie, 18, 19, 21 (photo)–22, 47,
157, 437
COPES (Washington State Community
Options Program Entry System),
72, 73
Cordova, Beth, 281–282, 439
Council House, 70, 146, 150–151, 215, 239,
263
Council of Jewish Federations and Welfare
Funds, 184, 238
Council of Jewish Women, and
Americanization program, 98, 100
counseling, definition, 103
Cowan, Rachel, *Mixed Blessings* co-author,
283
Crespin, Deb, 306

Crossroads neighborhood with Russian Jews, 33

Cuba, immigration of Jews, 198, 212–213

Daniels, Will, 433 (photo), 447

Danz, Carolee, 384

Danz, Jessie (Mrs. John), 10, 64, 92, 93 (photo), 96, 97, 99, 147, 148, 152, 155, 156, 157, 385

Danz, John, and son Fred, 148

Danziger, Mrs., 178

Davidson, Dr. A.J., 57

Day School. *See* Jewish Day School

Deaf-Blind Service Center in Seattle, 342

Deer, Jane, 439–440, 449

Degginger (Greengard), Bernice, 57–58
    annual report, 59–60
    interviews, 58–59

deLeon, Joseph, 209

Denny, Arthur A., 3

Department of Public Welfare, 98–99

Department of Social and Health Services (DSHS), 72, 216, 221, 222, 259, 336

Department of Veterans Affairs Hospital, 344

Depression. *See* Great Depression

Displaced Persons Act of 1948, 175, 179, 183, 189

Displaced Persons Committee of the state of Washington, 179

Division of Vocational Rehabilitation, 346

Dobrin, Edward, 175

Doctor, Dr. Jack, 179

Doctor, Maxine, 101, 155

domestic violence, 349–350. *See also* Project DVORA

Dress for Success, 387

Drexel Home in Chicago, 202

Droker, Howard, 163

Drummond, Bill, 120, 327, 328, 330, 334

Dutton Home (Kline Galland Home), 52 (photo)

D'Vorah, Biblical judge, 351, 352

DVORA. *See* Project DVORA

Eastside community and office, 107, 290, 399, 413, 419, 420

Eckstein, Mina, 65

Eckstein, Nathan, 158

Education(al) Center/Educational Center Clinic, 90, 96, 99, 146, 157, 217

Egyptian refugees including Blumenzweig family, 216–217, 218 (photo)–219

Emergency Services (ES), 25–26, 40, 261, 309, 392, 451. *See also* Polack Food Bank; financial assistance
    alcoholic clients, 374
    associated programs, 43
    budget, 39, 41
    collaboration with other programs, 31–32, 40
    early cases, 37
    financial assistance, 36–37
    flexible funding, 40
    food bank, 27–29, 31
    geographic area served, 31
    housing stability, 41
    mission and values, 26–27
    United Way funding, 43
    volunteers, 438, 444

Emma Lazarus Society, 99

Employees Community Fund of Boeing Puget Sound, 365

Endless Opportunities program, 67, 85, 292–295, 392–393, 432, 445, 448

Epstein, Irene Ginzburg, and Ginzburg family, 166, 168

Epstein, Irv and Irene marriage, 167 (photo), 173

Esfeld, Sol, 53, 150 (photo), 152, 165, 216

ESL (English as a Second Language) classes and tutoring, 234, 236, 251, 314–315, 419–420, 445, 448

Estrin, Rabbi Elie, 371

Excellence in Collaboration prize, 34

Exeter Hotel, 8

Falk, Dr. Frederick, 57

Fall Food Drive, and award, 34, 43

Falsberg, Martin, 208–209

Family Assistance Act of 1970, 221

Family Counseling Service (FCS), 220, 223

Family Court, 223

Family Life Education (FLE), 79, 261, 276, 279–280, 285, 288, 393, 428, 451. *See also* Endless Opportunities
for baby boomers, 290
Bringing Baby Home classes, 286–287
Cedar River Watershed Education Center retreat, 288
cultural sensitivity,109
directors, 285–286
Facebook page, 449
future goals, 292
interfaith families, 284, 291
for LGBTQ community, 104, 285, 292
Mom-To-Mom partnership, 286
Parenting Mindfully, 289
Positive Discipline, 280
for single-parent families and camp, 258, 284, 287, 288, 445
Strategic Plan, 287
workshops, 289–290, 291
Family Matters fundraising campaign, 434
Family Service Association of America (FSAA), 158, 159, 184, 185
accreditation process, 220
survey about fees, 205
Family Services of King County, 110
Family Society, 87, 157
family therapy clinical model, 105–106
Farber, Arthur, 206–207 (photo), 208, 211, 216, 274
farmers market project, 31–32
Farsi-speaking immigrants, 250, 410
Federal Transients (Men's) Bureau, 97, 99
Federated Jewish Fund, 150
Federation House, 214–215
Fedrid, Doris, 341–343
Feuerwerker, Jonas, and wife, and son Abraham, 183
financial assistance. *See also* Emergency Services
back-to-school supplies, 40
Beth Am H2R program, 39
Call 211 program, 36
Chanukah Tzedakah program for children, 49
collaboration with Chaplain Gary Freedman and Jewish Prisoner Services, 40

Consolidated Homeless Grant, 38
dental assistance, 41
Emergency Food and Shelter program, 38
flexible funding, 40
King County Community Information, 36
Ladies Hebrew Benevolent Society, 36
State Temporary Assistance for Needy Families, 38
Temple Beth Am Homeless to Renter (H2R) program, 38–39
Fine, Rabbi Jacob, 371
Finegold, Lillian, 155
Fisher, Carrie, *Wishful Drinking* show, 370
Fishman, Myron, 208
Florence Crittendon Home for unwed mothers, 50
Food Bank, 27–28, 71–72, 232, 387. *See also* Emergency Services; Polack Food Bank
agreement to serve three zip codes, 29
coalition with Food Lifeline and Northwest Harvest, 28, 29, 33
Food Lifeline, 34, 314
Ford Foundation grant, 203
Fortlouis, Mrs. 21
Foundation for Jewish Developmentally Disabled Citizens (FJDDC), 302, 321, 326
merger with NAIL, 327
Fox, Davis, 395
Fox, Flora, 195
Franco, Albert, 175
Frankel, Harvey, 179, 181–182, 194
Frankel, Sol, 56 (quote)
Franklin, Dr. Abby, 221 (photo)
Freda Mohr Multipurpose Center, 116
Frederick, Donald E., 17
Frederick and Nelson Department Store, 17
Freedman, Chaplain Gary, 40
Freedman, Jacob, quote from 1903 *Seattle Times*, 1
Freedman, Mr. and Mrs. (immigrant couple), 173
Free Loan Society, 60. *See also* Hebrew Ladies' Free Loan Society
Freidberg, Minnie, 65

Freidman, Mrs. Jacob, 17

Freylekman, Sophia and Leonid, 244

Friedman, Anita, 317–318, 400

Friedman, Clara, 197, 199

Friedman, Dr. Ed, 326

Friedman, Dr. Harry, 57, 175, 179

Friedman, Jennie, 60

Friendly Visitors, 70, 71, 77, 269–270, 340, 440, 446, 448, 450, 452

Friendship Circle, 346

Furth, Jacob, 6, 17

Galland, Bonham, 51

Garfinkle, Mrs. Louis, 160, 170

Gates of Repentance (Rabbeinu Yonah), 353

Gatzert, 18

Genauer, Eva, 80

Generation X (Gen X) Committee, 433–434

German Émigré Committee, 100

Germania Hall, 50

German Jews, 4, 6, 16, 82, 100, 203

    and refugee influx, 145–148

    fleeing Nazi regime, 164

Gimel T. Fraternity, 96

Ginzburg family (Jurek, Leon, Karola) in Treblinka death camp, 166–167. *See also* Epstein, Irene Ginzburg

Ginzburg, Irene/Anna, 167, 173

Glant, Jules, 165

Glickman, Sophie, 215

Gmilith Khesed, 22

Godden, Jean, 294

Gold, Jeff

    family therapy, 106

    Iranian immigrant clients, 107–108

    at JFS, 105–106, 111, 391

    Weinberg, description of, 109–110

Golden Age Club, 263

Goldberg, Irv, 109, 234, 242, 253–254, 256, 261, 262 (photo), 264, 265, 266, 268, 269, 271

    FJDDC director, 326

    fundraising 277, 317

    JFLE program, 280, 281

    and Julie Olson as office manager, 298–299

    and Weinberg association, 263, 297, 316

Golden, Lisa Schultz, 85, 138–144, 405

Goldie Shucklin Memorial Fund, 152

Goldman, Gerry, 432

Gold Rush, 4, 5

Goldsby, Libby, 65, 90

Goldsmith, Mae (Mrs. A.M.), 53, 56, 87–88, 97, 100, 103, 147, 151–152, 153, 156–157, 160, 222

Goldschmidt, Charles, 178

Goldstein, Minnie, 64. *See also* Bernhard, Minnie (Mrs. A.M.)

Golosman, Ernie, 217 (photo)

Goodman, Frank, 179

Goodwill Industries and board president Mr. Scott, 174

Gore, Tipper, 394 (photo)

Goren, Anna, 32

Gortler, Josh, 53, 70, 71, 214, 224

Gottman, Drs. John and Julie Schwartz and Gottman Relationship Institute, 280, 286

Gottstein, Rosa, 366

Grand Army of the Republic, 7

Gray, Mrs., 208

Great Depression, effects of, 91–94, 145

Greater Seattle Service League, 151

Greengard, Bernice Degginger, 57, 87

    difficult cases, 58–59

    interview about Dutton home, 52

    interview about Russian immigrants, 58

    quote in *Mishpacha*, 58

    resettlement efforts and approval, 150, 159

Greengard, Joe, 150

Grill, Harry, 177, 178

Grinstein, Alexander, 179

Grossfeld, Jerry, 68–69, 208, 209, 211–214, 215, 216, 220, 221, 224, 253, 261

Grunebaum, Morris L., 16

Gulko, Ruz, 120, 285, 288

Guthman, Otto, 90

Gutman, Ellie, 160, 170, 173

Guttman, Mr. and Mrs. Addis, 93

Haas, Saul, 146

Hachnosas Orchim, 98, 99

Hadassah

Nearly New Store, 263
Project DVORA workshop sponsor,
    354
Halpern, Larry, 326
Hamlin, Larry, 29–30
Hanan, Sam, 206
Harborview Hospital assistance, 96
Harris, Gloria, 217 (photo)
Harry and Jeanette Weinberg Foundation,
    75
Hartstein, Mrs. David, 157
Harvard Avenue offices, 28
Hasson, Michele, 305 (photo), 306–308, 350
Haut, Rabbi Isaak, 183
Health and Welfare Council of Seattle
        – King County's Care
    of the Aging Committee, 195
Health and Welfare Fund, 93
Health Information and Patient Privacy Act
    (HIPPA), 402
Heathman, Daniel, 448
Hebrew Academy, 249–250
Hebrew Benevolent Association, 2
Hebrew Benevolent Society (HBS), 56, 57,
        60, 87, 88, 90
    Annual Luncheon, 1927, 64
    basic needs provision, 62–63
    board and legal services, 57
    correspondence cases, 63–64
    medical assistance, 57
    membership in 1921 and 1922, 61
    services to migratory or transient men,
        63–64
Hebrew Free Loan Society, 60, 224
Hebrew Immigrant Aid Society (HIAS), 13,
        60, 146, 166, 174, 177, 197, 198,
        202, 213, 310, 413–414
    branch offices, 191–192
    contributions/allotment to JCFS, 172,
        232, 247–248
    Indochinese caseload, 265
    international services, 175
    Russian resettlement program, 262
    Settlement House, 59
    Single Moms program, 419, 420
    South American migration
        arrangements, 198
    Soviet Jewish family resettlement, 238

transportation services, 169
USS *General Bundy* news release of
    docking with Jews, 183
Hebrew Ladies' Free Loan Society, 2, 22, 23,
    42, 99, 170, 278
Heian Maru ship, 147 (photo), 148
Hellman, John, 107
Hendin, Ellen, 292, 293, 295
Hermine Pruzan Fund, 369
Herzl-Ner Tamid Religious School/
    congregation, 45, 53, 169, 270,
    283
HIAS. *See* Hebrew Immigrant Aid Society
Hillel, 377
    annual meetings, 268
    counseling program, 117, 123
    intern recruitment, 450
    rabbis Fine, Berkovitz, and Potek, 371
Himmelfarb, Cynthia, 107
Hinkley Hall, 12
Hinson, Margaret, 409–413, 415–416, 418,
    419, 420, 421
Hitler/Nazis, and anti-Semitism, 153, 164,
    342
Hoedemaker, Dr. Edward, 154
Holcenberg, Sam, 153
Holiday Gift Basket project, 43
Holland, refugees from, 149
Holmes, Mrs. J.R., 157
Holocaust Education Center, 84
Holocaust memorial service, 290
Holocaust Survivors Advisory Committee,
    81–82
Holocaust survivors and assistance, 75–76,
    81, 82, 83, 84, 165, 169, 272, 353
Holocaust Survivors Emergency Assistance
    Program (HSEAP), 75
homecare programs, and transitions, 70,
    72, 423
HomeCare Associates (HCA), 67, 75–76,
    314, 334, 392, 398, 400–401, 403,
    424, 426, 428
Home Care for the Elderly and
    Homemakers Service programs,
    256
H2R program (Temple Beth Am), 38–39
Humanitarian of the Year awards, 302
Hungarian immigrants, 271–272

Idaho Block, 5
immigrants/immigrant waves
    anticipated after 1947, 160
    between 1880 and 1890, 4
    Bhutanese, 414
    Burmese, 410–411, 413, 415
    Congolese, 414–415, 418–419
    and costs of resettlement, 174
    Cuban, 212–213
    employment difficulties, 177
    family reunification, 246
    German Jews in World War II, 164
    from Iraq, 410, 414, 415–416
    Kent area, 420, 446
    Ladino-speaking Sephardic Jews from
        Ottoman Empire, 163
    from Nazi oppression, 145–146
    from Ottoman Empire, 163, 437
    quotas, 172
    from Russian pogroms, 163
    Somalis, 416–417, 418
    by train, 3–4
    volunteerism for\, 437
Industrial Revolution, negative effects, 103
Inter-Agency Services, 261
International Organization of Migration
    (IOM), 411–412
International Refugee Organization, 187
Iranian immigrants, 107–108, 250, 314
Iraqi refugees, 410, 414, 415–416
Isaac Cooper Trust, 159, 176, 183, 223
Islamic militant groups, flight from, 417
Israel, Sam, 306
Israeli athletes massacre at Munich
        Olympics, 228
Israeli War for Independence in 1948, 204

Jassny, Lauren, 316–317 (photo), 384
Jassny, Paul, 384
Jennifer Rosen Meade Preschool, 45
Jessie Danz Building, 29, 385, 386 (photo),
        387, 394, 397, 407, 431, 432–433
Jewish / Jews
    acculturation, 248–249
    backlash, suggesting going to Israel,
        245
    delinquents in juvenile court, 88
    early U.S. population, 4, 6

on east side of Lake Washington, 260
    European denial, in 1953, 203
    immigrants in 1939–1947, 145
    population in Seattle between 1990
        and 2000, 383
    security concerns after shooting at
        JFGS, 396
    servicemen and servicewomen,
        programs for, 152–154
    from Soviet Union, 230
    woman in Seattle, early charity, 12–13
    youth with mental health and drug
        issues, 222
Jewish Club of Washington, 165, 177
Jewish Community Center of Seattle
        (JCCS), 68, 259, 309
    Golden Age Club, 263
    Holocaust memorial service, 290
    integration of new people, 179
    Mom-To-Mom program, 286
    Project DVORA sponsor, 354
    Shoah commemoration, 85
    summer camp, 32
Jewish Daily Forward "Bintel Brief" advice
        column, 19
Jewish Day School, 33–34, 107
Jewish Family & Child Service (JFCS), 2,
        23–24, 26, 55, 68, 69, 70, 160,
        253, 255–256. See also Jewish
        Family Service
    adoption services, 107, 212, 213, 214,
        219
    bylaws, purposes, and mission, 178,
        186, 258
    Case Policy Committee, 178, 182, 193,
        213
    changing field in 1980s, 105–106
    Children's Committee, 206
    counseling/counseling programs, 118,
        176, 194, 223
    Court Building offices, 176
    crisis intervention, 258
    directors, 109–110, 111, 206, 216
    displaced-person relief cases, 189–190
    emergency services, 176, 212
    Émigré Committee, 180
    Employment Committee and services,
        177, 181, 190–191, 194, 212

family counseling/therapy and
casework, 105–106, 185, 208, 258
Federation House joint effort, 214
fees and sliding-fee scale starting in
1958, 205–206
foster care programs, 204–205, 208,
212
furniture drive and warehouse, 234
Home Care for the Elderly program,
215
for homeless clients, 123
Housekeepers Service, 215
integration of newcomers, 179
for Iranian Jews/immigrants, 107–108
Jackson Street and Harvard Avenue
locations, 206, 220, 224
LGBTQ community, 104
medical and dental care, 192
membership dues over time, 213–214
name change from Jewish Welfare
Society, 171
90th anniversary celebration, 268
Older Adult program and elderly
services, 104, 212, 214
proposed budget for 1951, 187
Public Issues Committee, 220, 221
Public Relations Committee, 198, 209
Refugee Committee and boarding
house, 173
resettlement and Resettlement
Committee, 171, 172, 176, 180,
233, 237–238
restrictions on families served, 192
Russian Resettlement program, 229,
230, 259
scholarship, 178
Special Committee on Aging report,
207
survey and analysis of operations, 184
three distinct programs for older
people, 67
traditional, 103
transition period in 1951
vocational counseling, 266
volunteer recruitment, 237–238
Volunteer of the Year Award, 447
welfare needs in 1965, 211
work-study fellowship, 207

Jewish Family Life Education (JFLE), 109,
114, 118, 213, 267, 281, 299, 309,
439. See also Family Life
Education
Jewish Family Service (JFS), 2, 23–24, 26,
68, 81, 85, 97–98, 113, 116,
242, 388. See also Aging &
Adult Programs; Claims
Conference; Emergency Services;
financial assistance; HomeCare
Associates; Jewish Family
& Child Service; Polack Food
Bank; Project DVORA; Refugee
& Immigrant Service Centers;
Seattle Association for Jews with
Disabilities; Senior Services
addictions program, 119–120, 121–122
adoption and foster care services, 299,
309
awards, annual, 302
board and presidents/President's Club,
261–262, 266, 269, 398
budget proposed in 1949, 183
budget in 1990, 383
budgets, 1998, 2001, 2003, 2006, 2009,
and 2012, 398, 430
camps, 45
centennial celebration, 306
charity balls in 1905 and 1906, 50
children's specialists, 123
computer database, 449
Counseling Services/counseling
program, 121, 122, 123, 124, 261,
299, 373
Development Committee and staff,
269, 303, 306, 382, 425
Development Department, 39, 319,
386, 401–402, 431
donors/donor base, 308–309, 316, 426
DVORA survey, 355
emergency shelter, for homeless,
46–47
employment and Employment
Committee in 1951, 191, 193, 248
executive directors, 68, 85
expansion of mission, 388–389
Facebook pages, 449

Family Life Education (FLE) program,
        79
fee scale, 73, 114–115
food bank, 34, 43, 308, 314, 429, 430
fundraising efforts and financial
        support/grants, 50, 303, 315, 316,
        392, 430, 435
gay and lesbian outreach, 118–119
Governance Committee, 425
grant for Holocaust survivors, 75–76
growing membership after 1979, 260
Hillel counseling program, 117
history, 50, 437
HomeCare Associates (HCA), 75, 76
Home Care for the Elderly program,
        260
Independent Living Program, 341
lawyers and physicians, 257
loan program, 42–44
locations/moves, 383–387
luncheon model shift, and Tipper
        Gore as speaker, 394–395
membership drives, 127
mentally ill outreach, 331–332
name change from Jewish Family &
        Child Service, 259
new building, 427–428
Older Adult staff, 76
organizational/board changes between
        2000 and 2010, 397–398
out-of-town transportation survey,
        294–295
Outstanding Service award, 301
Pike Place thrift shop, 150
programs in 1991, 309
Public Relationships committee, 301
Raisers Edge database, 442
recession and financial adjustment,
        425, 426–427
resettlement programs and efforts,
        163, 166, 242, 251, 262, 299, 301,
        314, 398, 429
Russian speakers, Russian-speaking
        counselor, and acculturation
        program, 241, 246–247, 299
SAJD association, 333, 371
Shapiro and Lackman as board
        presidents, 301

single-parent program, 299
social media, 405
Southeast Asian resettlement, 264
staff in 1983 and later, 269, 392
transitioning, 304, 423
volunteers and Volunteer Services
        and Emergency Services joint
        project, 32–33, 43, 437, 441–443,
        453
"wrap-around care," 428
Jewish Federation (and Council) of Greater
        Seattle (JFGS), 2, 223, 231, 259,
        264, 268, 269, 278, 299, 300, 303,
        306, 307, 382, 390, 427, 430–431
addiction recovery, 365
Buzz Coe on board and as president,
        254–255 (photo)
Federation House for elderly, 214
funding/financial issues, 304–305, 317,
        318, 383
funding for Russian speaker, 246–247
JConnect, 450
Russian/Soviet resettlement, 33, 213,
        229, 238, 262, 264
shooting, 121, 396
Women's Division, 350
workshop, 283
Jewish Historical Society, interview from
        Bernice Degginger Greengard, 58
Jewish Neighbors in Need program, 216,
        223, 259
Jewish Outreach Institute, 283
Jewish PFFLAG group, 309
Jewish Prisoner Services International, 40
Jewish religious law, 116
Jewish Single Parent Summer Retreat, 450
Jewish Social Service Bureau of Baltimore,
        94
Jewish Transcript articles and ads, 99, 193,
        198, 214, 221, 232, 260, 318, 324,
        370, 391
Jewish Unemployed Manpower Project
        (JUMP), 223
Jewish Welfare Board, 23
Jewish Welfare Society (JWS), 2, 53, 54–55,
        89, 97, 100–101. *See also*
        Goldsmith, Mae
adoption agency, 171

board, 91, 153
Émigré Committee, 165–166
and émigré services in 1939–1946,
    145–146, 147, 149, 165
Endowment Fund, 97
Executive Committee in 1946, 158
family services, 171
foster care, 154, 170–171
gay-lesbian-bisexual-transsexual
    programs, 281
goal, 90–91
Great Depression effects and study,
    91–92, 93, 94–95, 100
as King County Welfare Board branch,
    96
Medical Care Committee and Medical
    Advisory Group, 178–179
name change to Jewish Family & Child
    Service, 171
1935 report, 98
presidents, 98, 100, 103, 385
resettlement program after World War
    II, 164
WERA, 91–92, 97
World War II aid to servicemen and
    servicewomen, 154
Jewish Women's Congress, 19
Jews by Choice, 267
JFCS. See Jewish Family & Child Service
JFCS News, article on drug use, 363
JFLE. See Jewish Family Life Education
JFS. See Jewish Family Service
Joint Agency Committee for Kiddies
    Program (Jackie Program), 204
Joint Distribution Committee,
    transportation services, 169
Jones, Mrs. Robert M., 195
Judaism, repressed under Communist
    regime, 229, 235
Judelman, Dr. Julian, 303
Junior Council of Jewish Women, 96
JWS. See Jewish Welfare Society

Kaderlan, Alice, 448
Kamuhanda, Hamis, quote from "Rwanda
    Eyewitness to Genocide," 2
Kane, Mrs. J.S. (Dora), 17, 65\
Kaplan, Erica, 448

Kaplan, Lillian, 160, 170
Karen ethnic minority, 410–411, 413
Karl, Irv, 304 (photo)
Karl, Laura, 45
Kashrut, laws, 32
Katz, Marianne, 148
Katz, Steve, 119
Kaufman, Ann, 157, 158–159, 160, 170,
    171, 176, 183–184, 185
Kaufman, Dr. Harvard, 192
Kelley, Jerry, 207–208
Kent area immigrants, 420, 446
Kent, Emma, "A Glimpse of Gleaning at
    Seattle Farmers
    Markets" (author), 31–32
Kessler, Carolyn, 266 (photo)–268, 277
Kessler, Gail, 448
KGB, Soviet security force, 228
Kinberg, Rabbi Yohanna, 289, 375
King County Commission to End
    Homelessness, 40
King County Community Information, 36
King County Domestic Violence Advocacy
    Programs (excerpt), 350
King County Emergency Relief program, 97
King County Family Court and Juvenile
    Court, 220, 222
King County Housing Authority
    paperwork, 344
King County Recovery Centers, 369
King County Welfare Board and King
    County Welfare Department, 96,
    183
King County Welfare Department
    (KCWD), 190, 191
King Solomon's poem "A Woman of Valor,"
    12
Kline, Lazarus "Louis," 51
Kline Galland, Caroline, will 52–53
Kline Galland Home (Caroline Kline
    Galland Home), 51–52 (photo)
    admissions committee, 69
    advisory board, 53
    Committee discussions and
        recommendations about aged,
        195
    Federation House joint effort, 214
    guardianship program, 70

homecare program, 423–424
rules, 54–55
Kline and Rosenberg Building/Kline and
        Rosenberg Clothing, 51
Klineberg, Mrs., 65
Klondike Gold Rush, 18
Knights of Pythias, 7
Koch, Rabbi Samuel, 50–51
Kohn, Leo, 16
Kol HaNeshamah
        "Death and Dying" series, 80
        Alternatives to Addiction friend, 370
Kosher food shelf and Kosher Food Bank,
        26, 31, 71, 259, 278
Kramer, Laura, 364–365, 375–379
Kristallnacht, 83, 147
Kwong, Rachael Byer, 340–341, 343–345,
        347

Lackman, Janet, 268, 269, 301 (photo), 304
Ladies Colored Social Circle, 7
Ladies' Hebrew Benevolent Society (LHBS),
        xviii, 2, 10, 11, 51, 53, 89, 363,
        424
        annual report of 1896, 15–16
        annual report of 1900, 17
        Broadway Hall meetings, 21
        charter members, 10–12
        constitution, 12
        early aid, 13–14, 27
        financial assistance, 36–37
        Hospital Committee, 21
        letters to and from Esther Levy, 19–21
        mission statement and premise, xvii,
        453
        name changes, 56
        Russian Jews as first clients, 14
        volunteers, 437–438
Ladies Montefiore Aid Society, 16, 89, 99
Ladies Relief Society, 7, 87
Ladino-speaking Sephardic Jews, 13, 163
Lakeside Milam, 369
Lang, Julius, 17
Langlie, governor Arthur, 179
Laos refugees, 225
Latin American Operations for HIAS, 197
Lawson, Stacy, 306
Laytner, Anson, 370

Lemerr, Dr. Frederick, 154
Lescher, Mrs. Elias, 10
LeVine, Eric, 403, 406 (photo)
Levy, Aaron, 5
        Cooper and Levy store, 18
        Idaho block construction, 5
        Seattle Times interview about minyan,
        8
Levy, Aubrey, 157
Levy, Esther, 5, 13, 47, 157
        founder of Ladies Hebrew Benevolent
        Society, xvii, 437
        letters to and from, 19–21
        photo, 9
        as president of LHBS, 10, 21
Levy, Eugene, 157, 176
Levy, Lizzie, 18
Levy, Louis, 18
LGBTQ inclusion, counseling and
        workshops, 104, 110, 291, 315,
        388–389
LHBS. See Ladies' Hebrew Benevolent
        Society
Lhotshampa immigrants from Bhutan, 414
Lifton, Michelle, 119, 351–354, 355, 357–
        358, 359, 361, 362
Lipman, Jay, 447
Livshetz, Max, 291
Lobe, Mr., report on Special Committee on
        Aging, 207
Loeb, Dianne, 429 (photo)–431, 429
        (photo)–432
Loeb, Steve, 310 (photo)–311
Lozovsky, Jeanette and Norman, and family,
        228–229, 247–251, 409
Low, Bob, 381 (photo)
Lowen, Jeanette, 88, 101
Lurie, Mrs. Isaac (Rose), 17, 64
Lutheran Social Services, 110, 114

Machzikay Hadath Congregation, 147
Malakoff, Jennifer, 44
Marcus, Wendy, 85, 290
Marianna band, 85
Marine Marlin ship, 167
Mayer, Egan, 283
Maynard, Doc, 3

McCarran-Walter Act, 191, 196, 199–200
McDermott, Senator Jim, 301
Medina Bayview Home, 99
Medina Children's Service, 213, 219
Melbourne House, 257
Melzer, Sandy, 398, 400, 423, 424 (photo)
mental health agencies, 110
Mental Hygiene Society, 99
Meyer, Alice V., estate, 194
Meyer, Ed, 397, 402–403
Millet, Heather, 160, 170
Mills, Lesley, 305–306, 386, 402
Millstein, Jeanette, 88
Minhag America prayer book, 7
Mirel, Rabbi Jim, 293, 324, 370
Mishpacha (newsletter), 58
mitzvah, 22, 108
Mitzvah Corps, 270
Mohr, Freda, 116–117
Mom-To-Mom program, 286
Monheimer, Melville, 57, 97
Monheimer, Melvin, 57, 172, 175, 194
Montefiore, Sir Moses, 6, 16
Montefiore Home for the Aged, 202
Montefiore Society/Montefiore Aid Society, 2, 88–89
    B'nai B'rith involvement, 100
    Board of directors meeting at Bikur Cholim, 89
    first officers, 17
    ladies, 17
    Purim Ball, 17
Morgenstern, Elkan, 16
Morgenstern, Mrs. Elken, 157
Morris, Steve, 120, 121, 363, 365–366, 367, 368
Morrison Hotel, 146
Moscatel, Neiso, Continental Furniture owner, 238
Moss, Robin, 115–117, 119, 121–122, 363
Muenzer family resettlement, 165
Mullin, Carol, 26, 27, 34, 37, 40, 42, 47, 438, 440
Multi-Ethnic Service Center (MESC), 392, 394, 398–399
Munich Olympics, massacre, 228
Muslim resettlement, 420
Mussar, Jewish ethics and texts, 289

Myerson, Miriam, 26

Nader, Robert, quote from 1922 New York Times, 1–2
Nagler, Edna, 64
Narcotics Anonymous, 369
Nassauer, Anne Elizabeth, 176
National Conference of Jewish Communal Service, 68, 198
    naturalization process, 199
    public assistance safeguards, 199–200
    quotas, 200
    responsibilities of non-citizens, 200–201
    suggested revisions to McCarran-Walter Act, 201
National Conference of Social Work in San Francisco, 89, 90
National Council of Jewish Women (NCJW)
    contributions, 221–222
    Council House, 70, 146, 150–151, 215, 239, 263
    DVORA sponsor, 354
    Neighborhood House, 217
    resettlement efforts, 177, 231
    scholarship, 178
    thrift shop/Thrift and Therapeutic Workshop, 174, 179, 181, 193
National Defense Committee activities, 152
National Jewish Welfare Board, Army and Navy Committee, 152
National Refugee service, 146, 149
Nazi persecution victims, 198. See also Hitler
Neier, Joel, 321, 327, 330, 334
Neighborhood House, 217
Neufelder estate/Neufelder Fund, 97, 158, 194
Neuman, Judy, 395, 398
Newberger, Mrs. Meyer (Caroline), 10, 157
New Citizens Initiative grant, 251
Niddah, 125
Nieder, Claire, 148, 149–150
Nixon, US President Richard, 229
No Nothings against immigrants, 5
North, Marie, 425, 432
Northern Pacific Railroad, 3

Northwest Association for Independent
        Living (NAIL), 302, 321, 322
    Havorim (Friends) Club, 327
    mergers, 327, 424
    Treasure Faire, 110–111, 304, 305, 309,
        327
Northwest Harvest, 314
NW Network of LGBT Survivors policies,
    359

Odd Fellows, 7
Ohaveth Shalom (photo), 9
Old Age Pension, 97
Older Adult program, 104
Olson, Julie, 110, 298–300, 303, 305, 306,
    393
Olzondom, Roderic, 190
Oppenheimer, Elvira, sons Heinz (Henry)
        and Walter, and husband Max,
        147–148
ORCA (One Regional Card for All), 428
Orr, Dr. Douglas, 154
Orthodox Congregation Bikur Cholim, 22
Orthodox and ultra-Orthodox Jews, 6–7,
        13, 16, 88, 108, 111, 120, 124, 221,
        235, 267, 309, 382
    and Hebrew Academy, 249
    Jerusalem hospital, 438
Orthopedic Hospital, 99

Pacific Conference for Social Workers, 89
Pale of Settlement, 6
Palestine, to become state of Israel, 175
Parsons, Harriet, 185
Passover
    dinners for newcomers, 177
    Matzos fund, 96
Patterson, Fraser, 17
Pearl, Gertrude, 57
Pelosi, Nancy, 437 (quote)
Penner, Rabbi Samuel, 179
Perón, Juan, 198
Pesach (Passover) volunteers, 43
Phillips, John, 53, 393, 398, 407 (photo),
        406–407
Pickard, Dorothea, 189–190
Pincus, Sylvia, 160, 170
Pi Tau Pi, holiday baskets, 96

Planned Parenthood, 223
Poderson, Mrs. Jan, 160, 170
pogroms, and refugees, 6, 13
Polack, Jack, 301
Polack, Morris, 178, 201, 311
Polack Food Bank, 392
    alliances, 31
    client vegetable seeding project, 32
    Cooking Matters classes, 32
    emergency services, 37, 43
    home-delivery program, 34–35
        (photo)–36
    at Jessie Danz Building, 29–30, 387,
        433
    Resource Access Project (RAP), 34
    visitors in 2012, 30
    volunteers, 445, 450
Poland immigration exclusions, 175
Policar, Patsy, 231–232, 233–234, 235,
        236–237, 275
Poll, Harvey and Mel, warehouse, 231, 233,
        324
Project DVORA (Domestic Violence
        Outreach, Response
        and Advocacy), 119, 122, 398,
        401, 428, 440–441
    advocacy, 352
    computer and security update, 403
    goal, 360–361
    Kids Club, 355, 356, 357, 360
    Mother-Daughter workshop, 362
    origins, 350, 351
    prevention, 361–362
    survey of clients, 355
    tiers, 354
    video cases, 356–357, 359
    vision, 354
    volunteers, 449
Puget Sound Hotel, 60
Puget Sound National Bank, 6
Purim volunteers, 43, 452

Quint, Esther, 266

Rabbeinu Yonah, 353
Rackow, Bernard, 203–204, 206, 216
railroads, early, and Jewish migration, 3, 6
Reconstruction Finance Corporation, 96

Red Cross, 96, 99
Reform Judaism/Jews, 6–7, 13, 26, 51, 85,
    108, 111, 267, 309, 382
Refugee & Immigrant Service Centers
    (RISC), 250, 392, 399, 401, 409,
    414–415, 417–418, 427, 451
    ethnicities and country origins, 421
    offices, 419, 420
    VISTA task, 443
refugee influx. *See also* immigrants
    from Africa, Balkans, Anatolia,
        Ukraine, and Bohemia, 2
    children and teens, 164
    Egyptian, 216–217
    four waves, 163
    from Nazi oppression in Europe,
        145–149
    resettlement and relief, 164–165, 171
Refugee Relief Act of 1953, regulations,
    202–203
Reiter, Mary Louise, 159–160, 176
Relin, Jane, 77–78, 80–81, 84–85, 122, 124,
    290
Repair the World, 405, 450
Republic Building, rehabilitation, 257, 265
Resettlement Survival Handbook, 240
Resource Access Project (RAP), 34, 43–44
Restifo, Liza, 119–120, 365
Rickels, P. Allen, 153
Rickles, Dr. Nathan, 154
Righi, Amelia, 32
Ringold, Judge Solie, 309
Ringold, Merrill, 309, 310
RISC. *See* Refugee & Immigrant Service
    Centers
Robbins, Mrs. A.M., 94
Rock, Shane, 410
Rockoff, Lee, 432
Rose, Natalie Merkur, 118, 282–283,
    284–285
Rose, Paula, 448
Rose, Rabbi David, 282
Rosen, Herb, 301
Rosen, Jeanie, 448
Rosen, Jeanie and Bill, 328
Rosenberg, Caroline, 51
Rosenberg, Emanuel, 16
Rosenberg, Mrs. Emanuel, 157

Rosenwald, Richard (Dick), marketing
    study and plan, 311, 318, 393
Rosh Hashanah volunteers, 43
Roslyn, Washington, mine explosion, 14
Ross, Mrs. Harry, 17
Ross, Nate, 230
Rossen, Salie, 282, 283, 438, 439, 440
Rotenberg, Mrs. 204
Roth, Mrs. Charles, 157
Rubenstein, Louis, 57
Rubin, Betsy, 107, 117–118, 123
Ruff, Eve, 366, 367–369, 371, 372, 373–374,
    375
Rukiya, interpreter, 412
Russian Jews/immigrants, 6, 14, 33, 34, 58,
    84–85, 163, 213, 225, 227–228,
    244 (photo), 253, 299, 307, 318
    from Azerbaijan, Kazakhstan, and
        Uzbekistan, 241
    cultural difference, 237
    dance activity 290
    employment challenges, 236–237
    English language learning, 236
    family requested contribution, 239
    on First Hill, Capitol Hill, and
        University District, 244
    furniture and groceries for, 233–234
    integration into Jewish community,
        435
    interpreters Clara and Raisa, 234
    Leningrad immigrants, 237
    national recognition, 238
    Passover Seder in Russian, 241
    police safety class, 236–237
    Seder, 290
    survival behaviors, 231–232, 235
    volunteer aid, 437
Russian Language Haggadah, 85
Russian Resettlement Committee, 240, 262
Russian resettlement program, 261, 268,
    310

SAFE Washington, 397
SAJD. *See* Seattle Association for Jews with
    Disabilities
Saks, Ruth, 105, 111, 112–114, 115
Samis Foundation, 45, 306–307
Samuels, Maimon, 57

Santa Barbara JFS, 81
Saperstein, Sylvia, 230, 232, 233
Saran, Joanie Diskin, 325
Scandinavian countries, Jews in, 203
Schlossberg, Shirley E., 155
Schneider, Henrietta, 61
Schnitzer, Marty, 447
Schnyder, Margie, 285–286, 289, 295
Schoenfeld, Ralph, and Mrs. Ralph, 18, 155
Schoenwald, Dr. Phillip, 57
Schultz, Howard, 407
Schwabacher, Louis, 17
Schwabacher, Morton, 208
Schwartz, Dr. Lawrence, 208
Schwarz, Gerard, symphony conductor, 306
Seattle
    annexing of Magnolia, Green Lake, Wallingford, Fremont, and Brooklyn, 3
    care of aged, 201–202
    fire of 1892, 3
    Great Fire of 1889, 5
    population boom between 1880 and 1890, 4
    Russian immigrants and assimilation, 228, 240, 241
    women's early relief efforts, 12–13
Seattle Association for the Jewish Disabled/ Seattle Association for Jews with Disabilities (SAJD), 110–111, 304, 305, 309, 324, 327, 335, 336, 337, 343, 403, 407, 426, 447
    agreement with JFS and later combination, 333, 381
    budget in 2003, 428
    case managers, 346
    cases, 341–343
    director Kwong, 340–344
    Donna Benaroya's involvement, 390–391
    Endowment board, 334
    case management program, 330
    expansion, 394
    independent living environments, 424
    in-home skills straining, 345
    for non-residents, 331
    Oversight Committee, 394
Supported Living Program, 341
Supporting Foundation, 333
    volunteers and college internships , 448, 449, 451
Seattle Central Community College, English as a Second Language classes and internships, 234, 236, 450
Seattle Chesed Shelemes, 99
Seattle Children's Home, 7, 87, 99
Seattle Community Chest, 97, 184
Seattle Community College volunteer program, 32–33, 450
Seattle Community Fund (United Way), 51, 60, 87, 92, 93, 99, 152, 153
Seattle Council of Jewish Social Agencies, 159
Seattle Council for Palestine, rejection, 156
Seattle Crisis Center, 266
Seattle Day Nursery, 99
Seattle Defense Chest Campaign, 153
Seattle Emergency Committee for the Abrogation of the Palestine White Paper, 156
Seattle First National Bank, 176
Seattle Food Committee, 33
Seattle Hebrew Academy, 223
Seattle Hebrew Benevolent Society, 16, 56, 88
Seattle Housing Authority, 35
Seattle Jewish Fund, 146, 153, 165, 166, 172, 174, 179, 201, 221
Seattle Junior Red Cross Clinic, 99
Seattle Library Association, 7
Seattle Lodge—B'nai B'rith, 99
Seattle Mental Health, 332
Seattle Mental Health and Community Psychiatric Clinic/Medicaid funding, 345
Seattle Pacific Puget Sound National Bank, 6
Seattle Progressive Society, 99
Seattle's Jewish Family Service (JFS), xvii. See also Jewish Family Service
Seattle University
    Addiction Studies program, 121, 363
    Center for Service and Community Engagement, 450

opening in 1891, 4

volunteer services and internships, 32–33, 449, 451

Senior Services, 67, 76, 242, 283, 283, 286, 299, 308, 428. *See also* Aging & Adult Programs

caseload, 71, 73

directors Coney, Barash, and Relin, 68–72, 77

geriatric case manager Kwong, 340

kosher food shelf, 67

Sephardic Jews/tradition and Sephardic Bikur Holim, 13, 53, 58, 61–62, 88, 96, 163, 267, 293, 440

Septimus, Rabbi, 375

Settlement House, 146, 217

Shaarei Tikvah program and events, 289, 336, 394, 444, 445

Shaare Zedek Hospital in Jerusalem, 438–439

Shabbat T'Shuva, Ruff's recovery presentation, 370

Shafer, Julius, 146

Shalom House, 321, 322 (photo)–323, 328, 330, 335, 339

closing, 340

dinners and holiday celebrations, 326

move from Tivkah House, 336, 337

suicide case, 332

vocational service, 331

Shanghai group of immigrants, 180–181

Shapiro, Maud, 158

Shapiro, Peter, 269, 270 (photo)–270, 276–277, 298, 301

Shapiro, Rabbi Baruch, 147

Shapiro, Shelly, 393–394 (photo), 395, 398

Shomer Shabbos, 108

Shopera, Gertrude , 63

Shucklin, Goldie, 16–17, 89, 152

Sigma Theta Pi

high school sorority donation, 93

holiday baskets, 96

Silver, Esther, 217

Silver, Mr. and Mrs. Max, 93

Silver, Viola, 60–61, 90–91, 98, 99

Silverstone, Rachel, 64

Simon, Maria, 160, 170

Simon, Steve, 448

Singer, Rabbi Beth, 119, 370, 388–389

Singer, Rabbi Jonathan, 85, 370

Singerman, Paul, 16

Single Parent Family and Single Parent Summer Retreat, 428, 445

Single Moms program, 419, 420

Sisters of Providence, 7

Skid Row transients, 88

Slepak, Vladimir and Masha, 244–245

Smith, Betsy DeBeer, 207, 208, 216

Smith Tower Annex, 57, 149

Social and Rehabilitation Service, 226

Social Hygiene Association, 157

Social Welfare League, 87, 99

Solid Ground, 32

Somali refugees, 416, 417, 418

South America migration arrangements, 198

Southeast Asia immigrants and Southeast Asian Resettlement program, 265, 268, 301, 307

Southwick, McDougall, 17

Soviet Jewish families, awards, 448. *See also* Russian Jews

Soviet Union and release of Jews, 213, 224–225, 227–228, 230, 299. *See also* Russian Jews

from Azerbaijan, Kazakhstan and Uzbekistan, 241

funding needs, 241

population in US, 242

US Congress appropriation, 238

Spahi, Alice, 215

Spanish Inquisition, fleeing, 4

Spiegel, Stephanie, 399–400

SS Portland docking, 18

Stalin, 250. *See also* Soviet Union

State Dept. of Public Welfare, 98, 99

Steinberg, Irene, 230, 261–263 (photo), 264

Stern, Klaus and Paula, 168 (photo)

daughter Marion and son Marvin, 169

Stern, Louise, 64

Stern, Sylvia, 230

Stevens, Dr. George C., 156

Stiefel, Ernie, 148

Stillman, David (*When Generations Collide* co-author), 434

St. Luke's Hospital, 99

Stroum, Sam and Althea, 263, 264, 280, 302

Stroum Jewish Community Center, 45

Stusser, Herb and Isabel, 321, 324, 333, 337

Stusser-McNeil, Laura, 395, 398, 424, 425 (photo), 429, 432, 448

Summit/Kline Galland program, 423

Sussman, Jerry, 447–448

Swedish Hospital
    Bringing Home Baby program, 287
    detoxification program, 366

Talmud, 22

Talmudic precept, 8, 10

TANF. *See* Temporary Assistance to Needy Families

Tarshis, Sam, 177, 179

Taub, Leslie, 448

Taylor, Mrs. David, 17

Temple Beth Aleph, L'chaim, 369

Temple Beth Am, 85, 231
    DVORA workshop sponsor 354
    H2R program, 38–39
    LGBTQ inclusion, 388–389
    Russian language Seder, 290

Temple Beth Shalom, 370

Temple B'nai Torah, 289, 292, 293, 369, 370, 370

Temple de Hirsch, 8, 45, 50, 53, 85, 96, 119, 145, 397
    annual JFSC meetings, 225
    Bonham Galland Fund, 171
    Endless Opportunities, 292, 293
    high school visits to recovery program, 375
    Ladies Auxiliary, 146
    rabbis Kimber and Weiner, 370
    volunteers, 270

Temporary Assistance to Needy Families (TANF) program, 412–413, 417

teshuvah, 352–353, 369

Thomson, Reginald Heber, 4

Thrift and Therapeutic Workshop, 179

Tikvah House, 326, 328, 329 (photo), 330, 334, 335, 336, 337
    closing, 339
    fragile X syndrome case (Armstrong), 338–340
    Howie Wartnik, resident, 337

Tipp, Mr. and Mrs. Ben, 93

Toulue Cha, 423

Tovin, Mrs. P., 89

Trans-Alaska Pipeline for jobs and prosperity, 216

Travelers Aid Society, 99

Treiger, Karen, 452

Trudeau, Dr., 57

Turks in Siberia, 250

Uganda
    dictator expelling East Indians, 224
    refugee resettlement, 308

United Good Neighbors (UGN), 208, 216, 221

United Hebrew Immigrant Aid Society (HIAS), 225

United Jewish Appeal for Refugees and overseas Needs, 145, 238

United Nations Relief and Rehabilitation Administration, 167

United Services for New Americans (USNA), 169, 171, 174, 176, 179, 180, 192, 197, 198

United Way, 43, 51, 60, 110, 259, 263, 264, 268, 269, 278, 300, 306, 307, 308, 314, 318, 382, 387, 399, 427, 440
    Day of Caring, 452

University of Washington. *See also* ESL
    geriatric social work program, 274
    Graduate School of Social Work fieldwork training, 178, 207, 212, 267
    internships, 450
    move to campus overlooking Portage Bay, 4
    School of Social Work, 69, 260, 274

USSR. *See also* Soviet Union
    policy toward Jewish emigration, 225, 228–229
    under Stalin and under Khrushchev, 241

US State Department, 308

Vaad (Council of Rabbis), 31

Varon's Kosher Meats, 71

veterans and Veterans Affairs, 344, 345

Victor Rott Estate, 194

Vietnamese refugees, 225–226
Vietnam Humanitarian Assistance and
    Evacuation Act of 1975, 226
Visiting Nurse Service (VNS) of Snohomish
    County, 400–401
VISTA volunteers, 30, 31, 32, 409–410, 443
Volunteer Works computer program,
    441–442
volunteers/volunteerism. See also VISTA
    volunteers
    Annual Volunteer Award, 443
    Big Pals/Little Pals, 440, 441, 443,
        446–447, 452, 453
    B'nai B'rith women, 238
    Chanukah, 43
    ESL, 445, 448
    Facebook requests, 449
    JFS, 437, 442
    Emergency Services, 438, 444
    Food Sort, 445
    Friendly Visitors, 70, 71, 77, 269–270,
        340, 440, 446, 448, 450
    holiday gift basket, 443 (photo)–444,
        451–452
    Ladies Hebrew Benevolent Society,
        437–438
    Pesach (Passover), 43
    Polack Food Bank, 445, 450
    Project DVORA, 449
    Purim, 43, 452
    risk management, 441
    Rosh Hashanah, 43
    for SAIJ clients, 448
    Seattle Community College program,
        32–33
    Seattle University services, 32–33
    Shaarei Tikvah, 444, 445
    transportation, 448–449
    United Way training, 440
    unmet senior needs, 445–446
Volunteer of the Year awards, 302, 447, 448
Volunteer Services, 451, 453
    and Emergency Services joint project,
        32–33, 43
    United Way Day of Caring, 452

Waechter, Pamela, 396, 438, 439, 440
Wagstaff, Jack, 34

Warner, Cliff, 26, 242–243, 244–247, 268,
    283, 306, 309, 391, 439
Warshal, Dennis, 325 (photo)
Wartnik, Tony, Norma, and Howie, 326,
    328, 337
Washington Association of Churches, 265
Warsaw Ghetto/Warsaw Jews, 166, 167
Washington Children's Home Society, 154
Washington Emergency Relief
    Administration (WERA), 91–92,
    98
Washington Émigré Bureau (WEB), 145,
    146, 147, 148, 149, 159–160, 164,
    169, 170, 172
    Case Conference Committee, 165
Washington State abortion laws, 219,
    220–221
Washington State Community Options
    Program Entry System (COPES),
    72
Washington State Department of Social and
    Health Services. See Department
    of Social and Health Services
Washington State Department of Social
    Welfare, 170
Washington State Division of Vocational
    Rehabilitation, 344
Washington State Health Care Authority
    financing, 425
Washington state fires of 1889 and 1892, 3
Washington State Jewish Historical Society,
    84
Washington State Welfare Act, 182, 189
Washington Women's Protective
    Department—Seattle Police, 99
Wasser, Amy, 283, 285
Weichbrodt, Dr. Irvin, 57
Weil, Sylvia, 87, 160, 170
Weinberg, Alberta, 273, 274, 276, 277, 304
Weinberg, Ken, 85, 103–105, 106, 109–110,
    115, 116, 118, 119, 163, 178, 242,
    272–274, 366, 381–382, 396
    budgets, 313
    communication and leadership style,
        298, 434
    domestic violence program support,
        351

funding and fundraising/ donor
relationships, 311, 313–314, 317
Jewish Family Life Education
Program, 280
as JFS counseling intern, then Director
of Geriatric Services, 254, 263,
271, 274–276
help with Russian clients, 239–240,
241
homecare interest, 399–400
in improv comedy group, 304
invitations from other agencies, 319
"Ma and Pa shop," 401
NAIL association, 327
as new executive director, 277, 278,
281
photos, 297, 455
quote re JFS, 381
reflections and philosophy, 312–313,
314, 384, 385, 387–388, 389, 390,
393, 399, 400, 404, 405–406
service expansion, 303, 308, 309
staff changes and issues, 306, 300, 391,
431
strategic planning, 313
transformation and redefining of JFS,
304–305, 315
Weinberg, Sam, 272
Weinsberg Displaced Persons Camp, 167
Weinstein, Laura, 209
Weisfield, Mr. and Mrs., 93
Wellspring Charities, 15
Wendland, Jeff, 409, 411, 412
WERA. See Washington Emergency Relief
Administration
White, Albert S., 68, 190, 192, 193, 195, 197
death, 203
at National Conference of Jewish
Communal Service, 198–201
visit to Montefiore Home and Drexel
Home, 202
White Paper of 1939, 156
Williams, Jacqueline, 163
Winehill, Gustave, 16
Winston, Dr. George, Volunteer of the Year,
302
Witherspoon, Dr., 16
Wittenberg, Dorothy, 230, 232, 233

Wohlgelernter, Rabbi Solomon F., 147
Women's Division Endowment Fund
(WEF), 350
Women's Suffrage Association, 7
World's Fair: Colombian Exposition, 19
World War II
family security, 154–155
Jewish organizations, 153
Stalin's deportation, 250
vocational counseling, 103
Works Progress Administration (WPA), 97,
99, 100
World Jewish Digest, 241
World's Parliament of Religions, 19

Yeshiva High School trainings, 365, 371
Yiddish speaking, 13, 16, 147, 271
Young Men's and Young Women's Hebrew
Association, 99
Young Men's Hebrew Association (YMHA),
57
Young Women's Christian Association/
YWCA's Opportunity Place, 35,
99

Zeeve, Dora, 22, 60
Zionism, 156
Zipperman, Diane, 117, 282
ZRBG (Ghetto Pension Law), 82